LIFT EVERY VOICE AND SWING

Lift Every Voice and Swing

*Black Musicians and Religious Culture
in the Jazz Century*

Vaughn A. Booker

NEW YORK UNIVERSITY PRESS
New York

NEW YORK UNIVERSITY PRESS
New York
www.nyupress.org

References to Internet websites (URLs) were accurate at the time of writing. Neither the author nor New York University Press is responsible for URLs that may have expired or changed since the manuscript was prepared.

Library of Congress Cataloging-in-Publication Data
Names: Booker, Vaughn A., author.
Title: Lift every voice and swing : Black musicians and religious culture in the jazz century / Vaughn A. Booker.
Description: New York : New York University Press, 2020. | Includes bibliographical references and index.
Identifiers: LCCN 2019029138 | ISBN 9781479892327 (cloth) |
ISBN 9781479890804 (paperback) | ISBN 9781479801831 (ebook) |
ISBN 9781479899487 (ebook)
Subjects: LCSH: Jazz—Religious aspects—Christianity. | African Americans—Religion. | African Americans—Music—Religious aspects—Christianity. | Calloway, Cab, 1907–1994. | Ellington, Duke, 1899–1974. | Gillespie, Dizzy, 1917–1993. | Williams, Mary Lou, 1910–1981.
Classification: LCC ML3918.J39 B65 2020 | DDC 781.65089/96073—dc23
LC record available at https://lccn.loc.gov/2019029138

New York University Press books are printed on acid-free paper, and their binding materials are chosen for strength and durability. We strive to use environmentally responsible suppliers and materials to the greatest extent possible in publishing our books.

Manufactured in the United States of America

10 9 8 7 6 5 4 3 2 1

Also available as an ebook

In memory of Clarence Gary, Jr. (1931–1999) and Ida Ruth Newton (1935–2018), the grandparents who sparked my joy for jazz

CONTENTS

Introduction   1

PART I. REPRESENTATIONS OF RELIGION AND RACE

1. "Jazzing Religion"   25

2. "Get Happy, All You Sinners"   47

3. "Tears of Joy"   78

4. "Royal Ancestry"   109

PART II. MISSIONS AND LEGACIES

5. God's Messenger Boy   139

6. "Is God a Three-Letter Word for Love?"   159

7. Jazz Communion   187

8. Accounting for the Vulnerable   205

9. Virtuoso Ancestors   231

Conclusion: Black Artistry and Religious Culture   263

Acknowledgments   271

Music Appendix   277

Notes   281

Bibliography   309

Index   319

About the Author   331

Introduction

Nobody would think of swingin' "Ave Maria" or "Silent
Night," yet I often hear bands rip into our spirituals and turn
them every which way but loose. To me that's sacrilege, and
I'll argue anybody, anytime about it.

  I walked off a Paramount [Pictures] lot once because some
wise guys insisted on burlesquing "Deep River." As I told a
group of young Y[MCA] fellows in Frisco, if we don't work up
our own race pride, who, pray tell me, is going to do it for us?
—Lionel Hampton, "Swing by Lionel Hampton"

Lionel Hampton was an African American multi-instrumentalist and
composer who entered the jazz profession in the late 1920s as a teenager.
By 1940, he had attained his own big band and enough prominence to
speak regularly on the "state" and trajectory of jazz music. Granted a
regular column, "Swing," in the *Baltimore Afro-American* newspaper, the
thirty-two-year-old vibraphonist and percussionist used the December
28, 1940, edition to voice his opposition to a recent trend among big
bands to "swing" spirituals—to arrange up-tempo, syncopated versions
of African American religious songs for popular consumption. Hampton made his artistic integrity clear by forgoing a paying performance
at Paramount Studios, which likely would have been lucrative for him
and the musicians in his employ. Sacred African American music was a
cultural possession of Hampton and other African Americans, and, in
his view, to transform it into a festive or entertaining commodity was
to commit sacrilege and a racial offense. No one should swing it, as no
one would think to vulgarize sacred Euro-American Christian music.
Hampton conveyed his religious opposition to artists and producers of
any race who sought to profit by popularizing African American religious music. In voicing his discontent, he signaled his position as a race
representative: an authoritative role model for younger black men, par-

ticularly black Christian men, whom he charged with taking seriously their responsibility to safeguard African American artistic and entertainment output.

As a jazz artist, black print press columnist, and by 1944 a convert to Christian Science from Roman Catholicism, Hampton represented his religion, his race, and his profession to various audiences.[1] To encourage different communities to take jazz seriously, Hampton and others worked to secure the music's reputation as a constructive, creative art form and to convince a fretful, critical religious leadership and cultural elite among African American middle-class Protestants that its composers and performers had their moral bearings. The sense that African American religion was vulnerable to improper commodification for popular consumption, evident by the 1940s in criticisms of jazz for "swinging" spirituals, arose from existing concerns throughout the early twentieth century that popular culture and urban living had impeded African American pursuits of uplift and damaged the race's unassailable moral standing.

In the twentieth century, the emergence of jazz music propelled black artists into fame on a national scale. Many, like Hampton, took on the roles of race representatives and leveraged their popularity toward social progress for their racial communities. These jazz professionals also played an important part in shaping the religious landscape of twentieth-century African American Protestantism, wielding the power to both define their religious communities and craft novel religious voices and performances. Jazz figures such as Duke Ellington and Mary Lou Williams stood outside of black Protestant churches, but they put forward a religious culture that was shaped by Afro-Protestantism. At the same time, their artistic expressions conveyed personal religious movement beyond, and challenges to, this tradition. These figures, though they did not hold religious positions, were celebrities. By releasing religious recordings and staging religious concerts, they became integral to the artistry of African American religious expression.

From the late 1920s through the 1950s and 1960s, jazz artists worked to change public opinion about their music's appropriateness in society. Meanwhile, nothing was static about their musical genre. Young jazz musicians grew up and matured as artists, and jazz as a competitive profession produced constant innovations in rhythms, instruments, ways of playing instruments, vocal techniques, and sensibilities about the cultural significance of a music that came to constitute an art form and a tradition. They faced claims voiced in religious and nonreligious language that jazz music represented the opposite of proper culture, namely, that not only was it bad-sounding music, but it also encouraged indulgence in the immoral or uncivilized pleasures of the urban nightlife. Over time, several musicians emerged who treated their profession as a tradition to be defined, refined, defended, and challenged. Given the realities of a segregated America and the desire to challenge this segregation, jazz artists strove to claim their profession as an appropriate musical outlet for positive racial representations of African American men and women. Part of their social project was to convince the broader white public in America that what they believed were the musical gifts or talents of African Americans stemmed from both a proud racial history and a providential story of a faithful race.

This book argues that with the emergence of new representatives, religious authority for African Americans found a place and spokespeople in popular culture beyond traditional Afro-Protestant institutions and religious life. It examines jazz musicians' expressions of belief, practice, and unconventional positions of religious authority. It demonstrates that, through their recorded music, public words, private writings, and live performances, these jazz professionals enacted theological beliefs and religious practices that echoed, contested with, and diverged from the predominant African American religious culture. The lives and work of Cab Calloway, Duke Ellington, Ella Fitzgerald, and Mary Lou Williams—prominent jazz artists in this novel culture of religious expression and authority—anchor this book's narrative of racial and religious representations as well as of religious beliefs and practices in the middle decades of the twentieth century.

In the history of civil rights legal activism, race representation is a concept that identifies "those who claimed to speak for, stand in for, and advocate for the interests of the larger group." Since the nineteenth century, for African Americans to call for a "representative colored man" or "representative Negro" has involved a tension between an atypical member of the race in terms of her or his accomplishments and an "authentic" member of the race who was "as much like the masses of black people as possible." The representative colored men, "the lucky few who had attained enough education and training to become doctors, dentists, schoolteachers, ministers, and lawyers," were to serve as the best cases for full and equal African American citizenship.[2] Popular black jazz professionals became de facto race representatives because of their coverage in the black and white press, their travel and publicity nationally and abroad, and the emergence of music criticism as a form of discourse that brought major intellectual attention to African American cultural creativity.

Representation is a concept that spotlights black religious expressions in twentieth-century African American history and popular culture, regardless of the degree to which a jazz professional affiliated with Afro-Protestant denominations or churches. Representation centers the images, scenes, roles, discourses, and music of African American religious practice. Religious representations in popular culture were often presented as authentic reproductions of African American religious thought, expression, and practice. They became content not simply for popular consumption and criticism, but also for religious reflection by the faithful and even for potential religious innovation. As prominent African Americans in an emerging jazz profession, Calloway, Ellington, Fitzgerald, and Williams bore representative racial authority and the ability to represent African American religious belief and practice through live performances, recording sessions, films, prose, press interviews, and private reflections.

This book offers a novel rethinking of African American religious history. Its focus on jazz musicians, and their representations of African American religious life, illuminates the significant Afro-Protestant cultural presence that informed, surrounded, and opposed their professional and personal lives while also contributing significantly to their artistry. As a study of religion that makes African American jazz women and men central actors, this book expands the portrait of Afro-Protestantism as a mode of professional, middle-class black cultural production with distinctive features relative to other emergent African American religions and their popular cultural production in the first half of the twentieth century. This set of jazz artists expands the concept of Afro-Protestantism beyond its traditional understanding as a collective of black religious institutions by bringing into focus its significant artistic religious dimensions that impacted black popular culture in the twentieth century.

The Consumer Challenge to Cultivating Christian
Race Representatives

A "new" African American middle class arose in the early twentieth century. This socioeconomic class maintained the "subjective markers of ancestry, culture, and education" that defined nineteenth-century black elites. However, "occupation, wealth, and skill" also defined this new black middle class. In the 1910s and 1920s, "a new elite composed of entrepreneurs, professionals, and skilled workers, and whose existence was tied to the segregated world of consumer capitalism, vied with the traditional black aristocracy for the economic, political, and moral leadership of the race." In part, the concept of a black middle class was an "ideological self-invention." The older elite black middle-class "positions of journalists, ministers, educators, and entrepreneurs who catered to a white clientele" faced the emergence of new black middle-class professions, which consisted of "social workers, lawyers, doctors, and dentists; small entrepreneurs who increasingly serviced segregated communities, such as grocers, retailers, beauticians, restaurateurs, hoteliers, real estate agents, and undertakers; and individuals engaged in larger financial ventures such as banks, building and loan associations, and insurance companies." Urbanization in the early twentieth century fostered this new and substantial African American middle class. At the same time, urbanization produced a new consumer culture that challenged existing Victorian ideals of stability, thrift, and refinement that had characterized late nineteenth-century black elites' strategies of racial uplift.[3]

This new crop of middle-class race leaders encountered the freewheeling spontaneity of the urban landscape's leisure culture. African Americans enjoying such spontaneity jeopardized race leaders' attempts to depict their people as progressing rapidly toward "civilization." The construction of urban arenas like the dance hall and the nickelodeon "afforded blacks the space and anonymity to experiment with new identities beyond that dictated within the stiff rubric of Victorianism, which remained a central component of race uplift ideology." Black middle-class leaders' principal concerns centered on the behavior of rural black migrants who had come to the cities, a population that they deemed susceptible to gambling parlors and saloons. Along with courting, these illicit private activities took place in new spaces that resulted from "the freedom to mingle in an unregulated environment with men and women of varying classes and ages."[4] For race leaders in positions of religious leadership in the 1920s and 1930s, new forms of leisure continued to present a social dilemma in both the American South and North. They encountered, debated, and at times accommodated an evolving leisure culture beyond their professional regulation, a culture that black working-class migrants and middle-class city inhabitants alike found alluring.

At the turn of the century, W. E. B. Du Bois claimed that the rise of black commercial entertainment would become a chief challenge for urban churches to address in the new century. Historians of African American religions have noted that popular entertainments in the early twentieth century challenged the authority and centrality of African American churches in directing black social, educational, economic, and political activity. Noted historian Judith Weisenfeld has shown that these churches "were in the midst of a cultural shift that involved the separation of many of these activities from their purview, and their leaders felt the potential for churches' cultural influence to decrease." The rise of black popular entertainment culture took the forms of "film, theater, nightclubs, professional sports, and radio as well as consumer items like beauty products, records, literature, newspapers, magazines, and toys marketed specifically to their communities."[5] Historian Clarence Taylor notes that the responses of leading clergy included "offering their own brand of popular entertainment, remaining moral leaders of the community as they attempted to adopt mass forms within the boundaries of Christian principles."[6] Furthermore, as historian Lerone Martin has shown, black ministers of largely rural black Baptist congregations who viewed popular entertainments as a moral problem responded to popular recreation by overhauling these churches' missions for the new black urban reality. In the 1920s, African American leaders advocated and worked toward providing migrant churchgoers with alternative, bourgeois forms of commercial entertainment, such as creating alternative amusement spaces, hosting annual festivals for concert and opera performances, and church sponsorship of musicals, operas, race films, and dances.[7]

These black middle-class Protestants, deeply critical of jazz, dance, and popular entertainment, went beyond theologically conservative moral opposition in their expressions of disdain. Their protestations reflected their middle-class, interracial, ecumenical, and integrationist pursuits of racial progress. Claiming that race progress depended on cultivating and maintaining a professional class of African Americans, they became voices in the press, pulpit, and academy who made no room for jazz as an emerging popular art form to serve as a meaningful alternative for moral representation of African American culture and society. Jazz historians have focused on black religious opposition to blues and jazz music and the ministers who targeted urban migrants with alternative, "wholesome" forms of recreation to keep them from patronizing the dens of urban vice.[8] This book complements this history of working-class black migrants by considering the religious leaders who focused on middle-class black youth and black professionals, instead of black migrants, because they charged these populations with forging the race's progress in the present and future.

Despite concerns about the cultural and moral worth of jazz lingering for black Christian clergy over the next few decades, by the Cold War era jazz music came to represent an idealized set of democratic and expressive possibilities. This evolution in jazz's perceived worth accompanied innovations and developments in music and performance, with jazz enjoying a smaller audience no longer interested in big band dance music and more invested in the music as a listening, intellectual artistic experience that small instrumental combos created. Fans and professional critics exalted jazz musicians as artistic virtuosos, America's international cultural ambassadors, and representatives of an elite African American culture capable of capturing, through music, the sounds, moods, and political desires of a people.[9] Jazz musicians who were religious even consecrated the music for spiritual purposes—Lionel Hampton eventually composed works like the "King David Suite" to express his adoration of the nation of Israel. This jazz music that was eventually deemed appropriate for race representation and religious expression had precursors in the early twentieth century among other forms of African American artistic production.

Popular Black Religious Representation in Entertainment

Before and during the rise of popular jazz musicians like Duke Ellington and Cab Calloway, major African American musical artists, composers, and film impresarios who were intimately familiar with African American Protestant religious expressions were producing representations of African American religiosity in classical compositions, operas, modern spiritual compositions, theatrical productions, race records, short films, radio programs, and major motion pictures. Among these artists, black musicians participated in projects of racial uplift that stemmed from romantic schools of musical composition and performance, inspired in part by European musical nationalist composers like Antonin Dvořák (1841–1904). According to music historian Lawrence Schenbeck, Dvořák's "advocacy of African American and American Indian music as the ideal basis of high art had the effect of pushing these folk sources from the margins toward the broad, safe center of American musical life." Dvořák had two prominent African American students: composer and baritone singer Harry T. Burleigh (1866–1949) and composer and violinist Will Marion Cook (1869–1944). In 1916 Burleigh produced *Jubilee Songs of the United States of America*, and "widespread use of Burleigh's spiritual arrangements in the recitals of ranking American singers of the day contributed further to the acceptance of the spiritual as authentic American music worthy of cultivation by serious musicians."[10]

Following Burleigh in the classical tradition of African American cultural production at the beginning of the twentieth century was R. Nathaniel Dett (1882–1943), a Canadian-born composer, choir director, and writer. Dett presented defensive portraits of African American Protestantism through his music from the 1900s until the end of his life in the 1940s, striving "to create an atmosphere of piety and solemnity in his choral concert performances" of spirituals and other forms of sacred music. Schenbeck notes that Dett found in spirituals "the absolute antithesis of the degrading blackface minstrel ditties that remained a commonplace of American popular theater in the early twentieth century."[11] Dett's central project was "that of battling racism by eliminating the secular—and especially the erotic—in Negro music."[12] Elements of nonreligious African American life permitted modern artists to construct "primitivist" representations of African Americans as essential racial markers, and "one had to avoid, at all costs, association with negative stereotypes that migrated so easily from black popular styles and white imitations of them. Otherwise the degree of distinction (read *class* distinction) inherent in 'the best class of Negro music' would never be recognized, and its efficacy in uplift would be lost."[13]

Many white Americans were eager to consume African American musical culture in the 1920s, but "the relatively widespread adoption of arranged spirituals by white and black classical artists alike, combined with their genteel sentiment, unstintingly earnest tone, and obligatory lack of wit, rendered them less attractive to a white avant-garde seeking cultural work that mirrored its own alienation from mainstream American culture after World War I." For these white consumers, jazz and blues became the preferred African American music, with jazz representing "youthful vitality, rebellion, sophistication, and sensitivity toward the racial Other in a way that radically reinscribed white definitions of blackness and reconfigured white elites' usages of black music."[14] However, the popular rise of jazz and blues did not signal the end of African American musicians' efforts to proffer the spirituals. Beyond African American classical artists and composers, choral singing of the spirituals carried the sounds and images of African American Protestant culture further into mainstream American entertainment with advancements in the industries of film, radio, music, and theater. The works of Will Marion Cook, another Dvořák student who produced popular African American music for Broadway musicals in the early twentieth century, establish an alternative lineage for the "uplifting" promotion of African American Protestant cultural production with his use of African American folk cultural elements. Cook was one of Duke Ellington's songwriting instructors, and according to Harlem Renaissance scholar Paul Anderson, Alain Locke considered Cook "the real father of symphonic jazz," a genre of which many Ellington compositions became exemplary.[15] Ellington showcased one of his earliest symphonic jazz compositions, "Black and Tan Fantasy," in the 1929 short film *Black and Tan*, which also featured the spiritual sights and sounds of the Hall Johnson Choir.

Another African American cultural producer in the alternative lineage of Cook was the prominent spiritual arranger, composer, and choral director Eva Jessye (1895–1992). Jessye first met Cook while she attended Kansas's Quindaro State Normal School, affiliated with the African Methodist Episcopal (AME) Church. Cook provided Jessye with professional and publishing connections in her early career. Jessye's collection of her spiritual arrangements in 1927, titled *My Spirituals*, with its "music-drama" style, became popular with African American concert performers like Paul Robeson. According to Weisenfeld, "Jessye used the arts to assert her authority regardless of gender, to act as an interpreter of scripture and as a Christian evangelist within and outside church institutions and before racially diverse audiences."[16] Jessye's repertoire of spirituals established a performance style of African American religious music that was intentionally dramatic—she crafted performances of "authentic" religious emotionality through her selection of vocal performers and in her arranging and composing instructions for them to act out certain verses, constructing an atmosphere of "spontaneity within an overall unity."[17]

During the mid-1920s to 1930s, Jessye created and directed large choirs, including the Dixie Jubilee Singers, the Eva Jessye Choir, and a male quartet called the Four Dusty Travelers, who performed on radio programs, for phonograph records, in MGM feature films such as King Vidor's *Hallelujah* (1929), in Virgil Thomson and Gertrude Stein's opera *Four Saints in Three Acts*, and in George Gershwin and DuBose Heyward's Broadway play *Porgy and Bess* (1935). King Vidor claimed to the black and white press that the African American actors' performances in *Hallelujah* were "natural" expressions of "the negro race," evidencing for him, in Weisenfeld's assessment, "a racially compromised moral sensibility, sexualized religious expression, and emotional musical display devoid of deeper theological content." However, Jessye "countered Vidor's claim of the set as dominated by the true religious frenzy of the black cast members," asserting that religious scenes resulted from the black cast members' intentional and artistic performances emerging from their "professionalism and preparation."[18] Ultimately, Jessye's presentation of spirituals in nonreligious, commercial arenas inevitably garnered her critical ire, resulting in her decision to stop performing in stage shows and in films.[19]

In addition to Jessye, Francis Hall Johnson (1888–1970) commanded a reputation for representing black Protestantism within Hollywood, arranging music for more than thirty feature films, shorts, and cartoons from the 1920s through the 1940s with a choir that became a fixture on film and for many film soundtracks. Johnson's productions and performances of spirituals served as a counterbalance to white playwrights who depended on their commodification for white audiences. As Weisenfeld illuminates through a study of his Bible reading habits, Johnson went further with his own compositions to engage in religious explorations beyond the conventions of the era's black Protestantism.[20] Beyond directing the Hall Johnson Choir, Johnson also employed vernacular African American religious elements with his music, critiquing "the conservative tendencies and restrictive parochialism of some black church members and leaders and insist[ing] on the ability of the individual religious self to range freely across a variety of spiritual possibilities."[21]

Musical representations of black Protestant culture existed within the "race film" industry of motion pictures directed and produced by African Americans. African American religious life became a frequent subject of representation and criticism through the race film industry. With all-black casts, these films in the interwar period depicted various "uneducated, corrupt, scheming, or ineffectual" fictional black ministers in an era when African Americans increasingly moved beyond sole reliance on black religious institutions by looking to social and political leadership. Oscar Micheaux (1884–1951), the African American filmmaker, writer, director, and producer known for his "scathing criticism of black clergy," produced more than thirty race films between 1919 and 1948. His 1925 silent film *Body and Soul* portrayed a con man preacher (played by Paul Robeson) in addition to an extended church scene showcasing his theatrical sermon and the congregation's emotional responses to it. For Micheaux, according to Weisenfeld, "the overly emotional approach to worship in some black churches makes black congregations more susceptible to manipulation by unscrupulous clergy. He proposes, instead, a sedate, rational religiosity grounded in knowledge of the Bible as a key to the uplift of African American communities." Micheaux's depictions of ministers offered a critical and dramatic portrait without the levity of comedic parody.[22]

On a variety of popular fronts, Dett, Jessye, and Johnson served as cultural guardians of African American spirituals throughout the 1920s and 1930s, refuting assertions that Hollywood productions featuring depictions of African American Protestantism through music or acting represented or captured authentic religious expression. Micheaux's works, starting in the silent film era and produced for black audiences, set a template for African American self-depictions that were of upstanding religious figures or cautionary presentations of nefarious and unlettered preachers and their naïve, unwitting church members.

The world of the arts and entertainment of the 1920s and 1930s saw the commodification of black Protestant sights, sounds, and bodily performances for modern, racially uplifting purposes. Black jazz entertainers were able to participate in this racial and religious project. As we will see, some musicians tilled this fertile religious soil to produce modern forms of intimate humor. This humor was principally for black audiences to enjoy, distinct in performance from the racial and religious representations of white minstrels in blackface, and seemingly lacking the long-standing black religious concerns that such musical comedy was counterproductive to social and political progress. Other musicians viewed jazz as popular music whose cultural ownership African Americans must defend for the sake of their fans and also for their detractors. Part of their defense strategy was to root the new, modern music in a tradition of African American musics, tracing jazz through the blues, ragtime, the spirituals, and ultimately through the sounds of gospel and West African music. Black musicians who were committed to constructing noble narratives of African American history in the lineage of historians such as Carter G. Woodson engaged in the parallel constructions of musical versions of proud racial histories. These stories told through music unavoidably reflected themes of deeply devout black Christian women and men from the antebellum slave period into the twentieth century.

Chapter Structure

Part 1, "Representations of Religion and Race," reveals that black jazz musicians emerged as popular, professional race leaders because of the artistic, intellectual work of African American middle-class Protestants in the first half of the twentieth century, who modeled religious and racial representations of African Americans as professional duties. Accompanying the development of jazz as part of a leisure culture that religious African American middle-class professional men and women decried was the emergence of middle-class youth as professional jazz musicians, aficionados, and advocates in the black press. Together, this new generation shaped the music into an art form that they believed to be an appropriate, alternative vehicle for race representation. In intended and unintended forms, various expressions of early twentieth-century African American religious belief and practices accompanied jazz professionals' race representations, which this book explores through three major themes:

(1) jazz musicians' irreverent performances of African American religious leadership and expressive acts of worship
(2) jazz musicians' commitment to black Protestants' social and political activism against Jim Crow
(3) jazz musicians' sacralization of "Africa" in narratives of African American history

The first chapter introduces one group of "religious race professionals"—educated black middle-class Protestant clergy, academics, and writers in the religious and nonreligious black press in the 1920s and 1930s. It establishes the concept of religious race professionalism to capture the variety of religiously invested black middle-class race leaders beyond only ordained male clergy who led prominent black Protestant denominations and churches. The chapter focuses on these men and women's professional work as cultural critics, who employed strong and dramatic language to criticize "jazz" along with a perceived "jazz culture" and its effects on the morality of youth. Because of their commitment to race representation, these men and women generated and participated in commentary on the religious image and moral standing of black middle-class youth. They maintained that the black middle class's duty was to act as the race's brokers to white America on behalf of working- and middle-class blacks in order to ensure African American economic, social, and political advancement. Importantly, they argued that middle-class black youth must emerge as the next generation of committed, irreproachable leaders. In this capacity as public intellectuals, these professionals extended the complicated racial reformist work of producing both a "counter-discourse to the politics of prejudice" and a "bridge discourse" with white Americans through perceived black social propriety, as Evelyn Brooks Higginbotham established in her foundational study of the "politics of respectability" among turn-of-the-century black Baptist women.[23]

In depicting the professional objectives of the African American Protestant mainline in the 1920s and 1930s, the first chapter relies primarily on the denominational writings that circulated throughout their religious networks. The *Star of Zion*, the weekly paper of the African Methodist Episcopal Zion Church (AMEZ), has been relatively unexamined by historians of African American religions but is a valuable and critical resource.[24] Its position as the print outlet of a black Protestant mainline denomination with a comprehensive primary focus on domestic African American affairs stands in contrast to the more internationalist missionary focuses of the black Baptist and AME print publications. These religious periodicals circulated throughout the nation according to the landscape of each denomination's churches and schools. They reflected middle-class black Protestant efforts to produce a national religious identity for black America and to claim the position as its professional racial and religious representatives. By focusing on religious race professionals, the first chapter highlights black professional figures with religious commitments and critical religious investments as their print discourses generated rhetorical artistry about the modern business of black religious institutions and leaders.

The second chapter centers on the early jazz career of Cab Calloway. In his 1976 autobiography, *Of Minnie the Moocher and Me*, Calloway conveys a tone of irreverence and humor about his black middle-class youth and adulthood. Though he used humor to depict his church life, such irreverence never took the form of full-throated maliciousness. Rather, Calloway attempted to convey through music and prose the humor he found with religiosity without denouncing religious persons or institutions. Nevertheless, the music Calloway performed and recorded reflected his decision to withdraw from regular participation in the institutional life of black Protestantism. His music resonated with many other African Americans who preferred Saturday leisure to Sunday service.

Calloway's autobiography serves as an important resource because the authorship of jazz autobiographies parallels the musical genre. Jazz scholar Christopher Harlos writes that "like jazz itself, where the completely solo performance is atypical, jazz autobiography also easily lends itself to being produced on a collective basis."[25] To compose his autobiography, Calloway collaborated with Bryant Rollins, the African American author, columnist, playwright, and editor for the *New York Sunday Times* and *New York Amsterdam News*.[26] Such collaborative efforts represent jazz musicians' intentions to offer their own historical narratives, collectively forging a "musician-as-historian" ethos in popular culture as a response to what they perceived as the inauthenticity of jazz histories produced by non-musicians.[27] Racial representation is evident in the production of more than forty jazz autobiographies between 1936 and 1996. For instance, Duke Ellington's 1973 autobiography, *Music Is My Mistress*, revealed that the musician was "always on stage" when performing, and "his racial identity forced him to become a representative, linking public perception of African Americans irretrievably to the individual achievement of celebrities and artists such as himself."[28]

The autobiography, as a document, cannot be considered to reliably convey the absolute and authentic truth about every moment in an individual's life. In Calloway's case, however, it can reveal the author's own attempt to arrange the details of his life to make meaning of who he was and what experiences he recalled as formative, instructive, or pivotal.[29] Calloway's autobiography was a humorous and irreverent portrait of himself, a reliable indicator that he sought to identify these qualities in many aspects of his life.

The third chapter situates Ella Fitzgerald, who produced no extensive written discourse about her profession, as nevertheless central to debates over genre, gender, and racial performance within the jazz world and as the producer of racial and religious representations through her vocal performances. To center Fitzgerald's vocal jazz career represents a departure from the standard narrative of jazz virtuosity that centers black male musicians. This chapter analyzes the artistic self-fashioning practices of male and female performers in the big band/swing era of the 1930s, in the "bebop revolution" of the 1940s, and in the emergence of solo jazz artists throughout these eras and beyond. As music historian Eden E. Kainer notes, Amiri Baraka's omission of Fitzgerald when discussing the bebop scene in *Black Music*, relying instead on Billie Holiday as a representative for all jazz women, "reflects Fitzgerald's stance on the periphery of the academic jazz community, and the role of female jazz vocalist as a blanket category," despite Fitzgerald's long career as a scat singer who toured with bebop pioneer John Birks "Dizzy" Gillespie in the late 1940s and 1950s.[30] This chapter's focus on Fitzgerald displaces a bop/post-bop jazz virtuoso-driven narrative—which focuses regularly on black men—to add complexity to the portrait of the jazz profession and to reveal how some African American jazz women participated in the production of religious and racial sensibilities alongside their male colleagues in the profession.

Moving from explicit racial and religious irreverence to reverence, the fourth chapter places Duke Ellington's musical compositions into the early twentieth-century black Protestant narrative of an African American history emerging from, and connected to, a sacred African past that included both biblical scriptures and ancient African civilizations. Academic literature, black Protestant race record sermons, public intellectual engagement in the religious and nonreligious black press, and popular music represented collective African American Protestant efforts to make sacred both the ancient civilizations of the African continent and dark-skinned biblical peoples. These collective efforts also extended to rendering the enslaved African experience in the United States—with its eventual black Protestant institutions—as an extension of that sacred African history. Late nineteenth-century Pan-African engagement with West Africa, recent discoveries in archeology and Egyptology, and the cultural production of the Harlem Renaissance influenced popular black Protestant expressions of reverence for African American history and a reading of ancient biblical (and extra-biblical) civilizations as the record of African contributions to civilization. In this chapter, a discussion of Ellington's music, poetry, and prose accompanies an examination of other early twentieth-century black cultural producers who contributed to this sacralizing, reverential view of Africa and its ancient religious women and men.

Part 2, "Missions and Legacies," moves from thematic discussions of jazz as an artistic profession for racial and religious representation to more specific focuses on the religious thought and practice of two African American pianists and composers in the jazz tradition, Duke Ellington and Mary Lou Williams. Ellington and Williams fashioned public personae as race representatives and had significant religious statements to express in the late 1950s, 1960s, and into the 1970s. These musicians operated within a jazz profession that underwent a decades-long transition in social status, starting with its association with a vicious urban nightlife that corrupted black youth and ending with its treatment as a virtuosic art form conducive to progressive race representation. Key to these famous musicians' self-awareness as race representatives is the preservation of their documents in national and university archives, with Ellington's materials at the Smithsonian Institution's National Museum of American History and Williams's records at Rutgers University's Institute of Jazz Studies. Both Ellington and Williams produced sacred jazz music through album recordings and religious concerts, and their archives often reflected detailed thought processes and business organization required to manage and produce these professional endeavors. The chapters in part 2 rely on these musicians' archives to locate their religious practices and articulations of belief.

Two of the chapters in part 2 focus on Duke Ellington. Chapter 5 situates Ellington as a prominent African American race representative who served this role in white religious spaces, although the religious literature and influential conversation partners he enjoyed did not emerge from African American Christian denominations or thinkers. Ellington did not situate his sacred music in the mainline African American Protestantism of Washington, DC, in which his parents raised him. Rather, as we will see, he engaged an explicitly ecumenical religious project that brought him into the world of white mainline liberal Protestantism in the United States and Western Europe.

Moreover, while Ellington implicitly bore the task of representing African American Christianity in his new music, his primary familiarity with African American religious life stemmed from his childhood, when he spent Sundays between his father's AMEZ church and his mother's National Baptist Convention, USA (NBC) church. Engagement with the evolving expressions and theologies of institutional African American Protestantism in the first half of the twentieth century was absent in Ellington's adulthood, and he gravitated more toward white mainline Protestant leaders, thinkers, and religious spaces. His sister, Ruth Ellington Boatwright, a significant champion of Ellington's religious legacy and a congregant at St. Peter's Lutheran Church in Manhattan, was similarly situated between white mainline and white evangelical religious worlds.[31]

Gospel developed as a popular African American music form and industry in the years between Ellington's religious youth and his Sacred Concerts in the mid-1960s, spreading throughout African American Christianity (from Holiness-Pentecostal churches to the Baptist and Methodist mainline). Consequently, a significant temporal and theological gulf existed between Ellington's religious life and that of many African American Christians, despite Ellington's de facto task of serving as an African American racial and religious representative to predominantly white mainline Protestant audiences. In this light, the posthumous popularity of Ellington's sacred music in white American mainline and European Protestant churches is not an ironic outcome, and these are the congregations that continue to perform his compositions annually.

The sixth chapter interprets Ellington's theology through his recorded private thoughts about believing in God in relation to the religious practice of constructing and performing sacred music publicly. The theological reflections Ellington produced with his sacred musical compositions reveal not only his manner of wrestling with appropriate language to address and characterize the nature of God but also his noteworthy omission of language about Jesus Christ and the Holy Spirit. The chapter focuses squarely on Ellington's affirmation of religiosity while revealing that such a stance did not necessarily mean the total acceptance of any denomination's teachings about Christianity, even as he mostly navigated Christian religious spaces. However, we may qualify the "individuality" of Ellington's religious belief and expression not only by interrogating the religious literature with which he engaged but also by incorporating the people responsible for shaping (and responding to) his religious pronouncements. With this chapter, the notes that Ellington wrote on hotel stationery during his tours emerge as a unique form of literature for interpreting individual theological statements and commitments. Such literature allows for a portrait of "lay" engagement with and production of theology as a process of "working out" individual commitments. Ellington's particular linguistic concerns in voicing his theology represented his responses to the issues and discourses of liberal Christianity as a composer of sacred music who moved primarily throughout white mainline Christian religious spaces.

Mary Lou Williams was born with a "veil" and claimed that she had religious visions as a child. She likely had religious family members who encouraged the notion that she wielded spiritual gifts. But Williams did not explore "conventional" religious traditions until after the death of her friend, jazz saxophonist Charlie Parker, from years of hard substance abuse. The seventh chapter explores Williams's religious thought as she sought her personal calling following her embrace of Roman Catholicism. Before conversion, Williams had engaged in prayer and "ascetic" practices like fasting, meditation, and abstaining from purchasing luxuries. These habits followed an intense period of continued visions and accompanied close friendships with jazz trumpeter Dizzy Gillespie and his wife, Lorraine, a Catholic convert. Lorraine encouraged Williams's exploration of Catholicism, while Dizzy encouraged her to return to performing music. She viewed her music, and the music industry itself, as antithetical to her religious mission before meeting a black Catholic friar, Mario Hancock, who encouraged her to compose religious reflections as part of her calling.

The eighth chapter mines the business archive of Mary Lou Williams to reveal her religious commitments and labor. She envisioned and worked to establish the Bel Canto Foundation, a professional institution to care for jazz men and women. The pursuit of a Bel Canto Foundation was Williams's work to create a structure and facility to care for musicians struggling with substance abuse, as she had personally cared for many in her apartment. Biographies of Williams have examined her productive sacred jazz period and career revival extensively, but the absence of sufficient attention to her business pursuits in this period results in the dismissal of an arena of her personal and professional labor that exemplifies a novel form of intense religious work.

Williams's embrace of Roman Catholicism and production of sacred jazz did not constitute a conscious affiliation with an emerging "Black Catholic" identity in the late 1960s that reflected the Black Power era's performance of race consciousness, as religious historian Matthew Cressler has detailed. However, the 1960s and 1970s saw Williams composing many religious works that revealed her shared cultural interests with Black Catholics who "embraced what they took to be an essential Black Spirituality and learned how to incorporate the traditions of the Black Church (which they took to be singular) into the liturgy."[32] The Roman Catholic reforms of Vatican II afforded her a vehicle to promote the concept of "sacred jazz" by providing music "for the disturbed soul."

Her music for Catholic liturgy contained gospel influences, and Williams, as a champion of jazz education, sought to make clear to others the roots of authentic American music in spirituals and the blues. *Black Christ of the Andes* celebrated the seventeenth-century Afro-Peruvian Catholic saint Martin de Porres. "Dirge Blues" was a memorial to President John F. Kennedy (the first Catholic US president). And her concerts *Praise the Lord in Many Voices*, *Mass for Lenten Season*, and *Mass for Peace* saw Williams and her music circulating throughout Catholic churches in an attempt to get a male-dominated and formerly segregated religious institution to take seriously her musical talents, religious sincerity, and the general presence of Catholics who shared her roots. When Black Catholics acquired formal institutional presence, such as the National Office for Black Catholics and its Department of Culture and Worship, they called upon Williams and other prominent Black Catholic liturgists to offer "direct liturgical consultation for parishes across the country" in the 1970s.[33] Early in this decade, Williams articulated the sacred origins of jazz through a particular African American heritage: "Through our suffering God took pity on us and created the world's greatest true art: the 'Negro Spirituals' and from the Spirituals: Jazz was born in all its creative and progressive forms. . . . Jazz is also a healer of the mind and soul. God reaches others through it to bring peace and happiness to those who know how to listen to it."[34] Williams reiterated her belief about jazz music's divine origins in a 1978 interview, adding the notion that performing and listening to the music had spiritually therapeutic benefits: "God did blacks a favor by creating jazz especially for them. God helps people through jazz; people have been healed through it. It has happened to me."[35]

Lastly, the ninth chapter weighs the meaningfulness of African American jazz professionals' authority as religious and racial representatives by examining their posthumous legacies and celebrations. This chapter examines the "afterlives" of Ellington, Fitzgerald, and Williams by revealing practices of reverence for them in the late twentieth and early twenty-first centuries. Because of the United States' cultural purchase on jazz as a distinctive national art form, the professional music industry, academia, and those who celebrate African Americans in the arts have bolstered the effort to safeguard jazz as both America's classical music and a living art form. Musicians and fans worldwide have celebrated these jazz professionals since their passing, creating musical works, artistic testaments, research institutions, and landscapes both physical and virtual that mark practices of venerating prominent African Americans with spiritual and religious significance. This chapter also brings into focus African American celebrations of these jazz virtuosos, and black women's religious engagements, more specifically.

This book is a work of jazz history and African American religious history that adopts an expansive concept of sources and sites constituting the archive of race representation and religious expression. From this interdisciplinary effort emerge portraits of racial identity, humor, profession, and religion in middle-class black cultural production in the twentieth century. This book takes seriously the careers of jazz women and men, instrumentalists and vocalists, as artistic professionals with the authority to voice religious belonging, perform religious belief, and demonstrate religious practice for their vast audiences.

PART I

Representations of Religion and Race

1

"Jazzing Religion"

In the early 1920s, the attitude of at least one African American doctor reflected the sentiment that race representatives had no business indulging in popular entertainment. Writing for the *New York Amsterdam News* in 1923, the Harlem medical physician and Garveyite E. Elliott Rawlins characterized jazz music as an addictive intoxicant with the power to alter cognitive capability. While music was able to "soothe" and "stimulate," affording African Americans a "reflective mood, in which the mind ponders, thinks and reasons," music was also able to "overstimulate, confuse and finally paralyze the thinking and reasoning center of the brain, leaving you intoxicated and drugged." Rawlins claimed that jazz music, particularly "in these days of prohibition," often substituted for alcoholic beverages in producing this cognitive effect. Rawlins further claimed, "In the social life of the people today jazz music is king, and jazz music will reign until a spiritual awakening and reformation sweeps like a whirlwind over the land." The anticipation of another war, financial crisis, or "some devastating catastrophe" was Rawlins's only prospect for ending the American addiction to jazz music and beginning the work of spiritually reforming its citizens. Until then, popular black audiences were morally vulnerable as patrons of this entertainment form, for "the quick and staccato tempo of jazz music, with the plaintive and pleading notes of the violin and clarinet; the screeching of the horns; the moaning of the trombone; the calling and imploring tones of the saxophone; the rhythmic beating of the drums[,] all these send a continuous whirl of impressionable stimulation to the brain producing thoughts and imaginations which overpower the will."[1]

Rawlins moderated his opposition two years later, and he shifted his metaphor of jazz as an intoxicant to jazz as controlled substance: "Jazz as a drug is a benefit in its place, but it should not be used by the very young, or in copious amounts by the old. Jazz, like any other drug, should be used only when needed, in a specific dose, and by those who know how it should be used. A little jazz is all right and proper; an overdose is harmful."[2] Some religious race representatives agreed with Rawlins's disapproval of young black men and women's enjoyment of jazz, and they sought to oppose modern recreational forms. However, they worked to articulate their cultural opposition without appearing to champion an African American Protestant Christianity that was fundamentally opposed to the interests of modern youth.

Opposition to dancing as popular entertainment became the framework for religious race professionals initially to protest jazz. As the representatives responsible for shaping modern black youth into culturally well-rounded adults, these professionals, many of whom wrote in religious periodicals like the African Methodist Episcopal Zion (AMEZ) Church's weekly publication, the *Star of Zion*, debated the nonreligious black press concerning both the value of critical public religious voices and the worth of the religious recreation that they offered as alternatives. Moreover, they also confronted the "jazz religion" of charismatic itinerant ministers and emotional displays of worship, each a product of the Great Migration's emerging urban presence of Holiness-Pentecostal preaching and worship styles. "Jazz religion" challenged the reserved, refined, and educated atmosphere that middle-class black Protestants had forged with modern worship and sermonic habits in their effort to represent the race's modern propriety. Religious race professionals had settled well into their pulpits as authoritative cultural critics and aspired to maintain their status as race representatives. Popular entertainment's potential allure as an alternative, competing profession for race representation necessitated strong and dramatic language to criticize jazz and its effects on the morality of youth.

This chapter discusses the Afro-Protestant mainline in the era when jazz emerged as a distinct profession. In the 1920s and 1930s, religious race professionals provided editorial commentary on entertaining African American social gatherings through their denominational newspapers and the black press. Jazz competed with middle-class African American religious leaders for the minds, time, and even finances of African American youth. At the same time, these churches and clergy were already facing the criticisms of African American intellectuals who questioned the aims of their ministries as well as the moral and intellectual fitness of their ministers. As they faced various challenges to their authority as race representatives, religious race professionals articulated and constructed their Protestant ministries as credible professions for a modern era.

Jazz music, in their view, was an "intoxicant" both iniquitous and ubiquitous, and curiously appealing to African American professionals. Despite the contentions of a number of ministers, such professional enjoyment of jazz served as evidence that the music culture was not entirely conducive to personal destruction. If many African American Protestant churches in the early decades of the twentieth century were in actual competition with emerging forms of popular entertainment for the moral, social, and financial allegiance of African Americans, then the reality was that these working, middle, and professional black classes all found these forms of entertainment appealing.[3] Entertaining music, in particular, was not just a challenge to African American Protestant churches' religious authority within the race. Ultimately, jazz provided middle-class and professionally oriented African Americans with a competing venue for race representation.

The transfer of black middle-class social authority from educated black Protestant ministers to the world of black entertainment became possible with the emergence of jazz, the sounds accompanying and producing modern dancing in parties and nightclubs. However, this transfer did not entail the total shift of authority from a black ministerial profession to a black musical profession. As the music's clerical critics evince, the black Protestant religious profession comprised artistic performance, the fashioning of dramatic personae, and the cultural authority to make moral, social, or political pronouncements. Whether the members of a younger African American generation who were aspiring toward jazz music as a profession were dedicated church parishioners or not, they bloomed from a cultural garden that these religious professionals had tilled. Moreover, they inherited and brought into their entertainment profession the cultural leeway to fashion their work in such racially representative ways that were performative, dramatic or charismatic, and authoritative.

Middle-class black Protestants operated as religious race professionals: cultural critics whose pursuit of modern religious identities resulted in their debates to determine the appropriateness of recreation, entertainment, and theatricality in both the daily lives and religious aesthetics of black Protestants. These debates responded to the rise of popular entertainments and entertaining preachers, which middle-class black clergy deemed representative of a detrimental "jazz culture." Though middle-class black ministers and intellectuals offered strong criticisms of jazz, the music ultimately emerged as an alternative arena for the practice of interracial community, beyond the interracial ecumenism and fellowships that middle-class black ministers were working to forge.

Dancing in the Dark: African American Middle-Class Protestants versus Recreation

As Mrs. J. S. Williams wrote in the *Africo-American Presbyterian* in 1928, "There is no profession or class of men so much criticised as the preachers."[4] Ministers in the AMEZ Church often felt slighted by W. E. B. Du Bois in particular, as is evident in a 1921 article written by AMEZ clergyman Rev. W. W. Evans in which he addressed the prominent black intellectual's criticism of African American churches as too conservative and moralizing on matters of leisure and recreation, too encouraging of Christian prayer as a solution to worldly problems, and too dependent on religious revivals. While Evans found "such things as card-playing, going to theaters, and dancing" to be "innocent" pastimes, he distinguished between "members of the Church" and "members of Christ's body," with the latter group "dead to the world" and "crucified in the flesh," meaning that such amusements did not tempt them. While it was simply human for "members of the Church" to engage in such innocent amusements, Evans cautioned that Christians who remained susceptible to recreational temptations "have yet to work out their own salvation in fear and trembling"—although without the AMEZ Church's punishment. Evans also prescribed the use of religious revivals in moderation, writing that "they are essential to the spiritual awakening of the Church. Like everything else, like dancing, drinking, smoking, card-playing, they are subject to abuse and must be used discreetly, advisedly and discriminatingly."[5]

However, Du Bois referred to black Methodists as "the black wing of the Methodist Church" and accused them of being the sole obstacle to lifting bans on the worldly amusements of dancing, attending theaters, and playing cards. According to an article by Du Bois reprinted in the *Star of Zion*, this was "a singular fight in the Methodist Church in which

the black man is arbiter," because most white Methodists "have realized long since that it is false to say that all dancing, all card-playing, all
theatre going, and all 'worldly' amusements' are wrong." The adamant
opposition of black Methodists "is not only wrong; it is dangerous."[6] In
response to Du Bois, Rev. William J. Walls, then *Star of Zion* editor who
was consecrated an AMEZ bishop in 1924, wrote that "great men make
mistakes . . . when they attempt to speak with authority on subjects beyond and external to the world in which they have lived and wrought." In
his response, Walls claimed that Du Bois was incapable of instructing or
reprimanding African American Christians because the sociologist's understanding of Christianity failed to exceed mere academic investment:

> It is well that the Crisis whose editor is an authority in history and soci-
> ology confine its advice to the realm in which he is an authority. He has
> been accorded leadership by a large group of intellectuals in the race; but
> leadership in political and social matters. Nobody has ever accused him
> of being religious. Hard and dry and matter-of-fact with scarcely a little
> interest in the supernatural, Mr. DuBois [sic] comes forth to say that the
> Negroes of the Methodist Church are wrong because they have convic-
> tions from their observations and experience in governing the church. . . .
> . . . The trouble is, the writer has gotten beyond his realm. A man
> whose life is lived and whose deeds are wrought from such an angle and
> with such ability as his ought to know his limitation. He cannot advise
> religious leaders. He knows little about Christian practice. He studies it
> from the surface; he has small and compromising notions of Jesus Christ.
> Christianity is like any other convenient system in his way of thinking
> which should be moulded [sic] to suit our desires. . . .
> We would advise Mr. DuBois to stay out of church matters until he gets
> into the church, or gets the church into him. We invite him to the Methodist
> mourner's bench and when we are satisfied that he has humbled himself
> sufficiently at the foot of the cross we will thank him for his advice.

Walls identified the segregated white Methodist Episcopal Church,
South's opposition to recreation in order to cast Du Bois's criticism as an
unfair characterization of African American Christians, exclusively, as
anti-modern in their conservative stance and wholly at odds with their
white Methodist counterparts. "As a matter of fact," Walls wrote, "the

agitators for the repealing of the general rules in the Methodist Episcopal Church have been a blatant minority."[7] Importantly, Walls's editorial
response represented more than black Protestant leaders who questioned Du Bois's religious commitments, not to mention the substance
of his familiarity with Christianity. His response revealed the existence
of a generation of black religious leaders at odds with the black intellectuals who caricatured and criticized them. Black Methodist clergy's
antagonism toward Du Bois nearly erupted in public confrontation. The
summer of July 1922 saw Du Bois withdrawing from an AME engagement in New York, where senior AME clergy learned that several of
their ministers conspired to "hoot him down" at his planned address to
these churchmen. The AME bishops apologized to Du Bois, and Walls
concurred with their gesture in one of his *Star of Zion* editorials.[8]

Throughout the 1920s and 1930s, black mainline denominations expressed their frustrations with elite black intellectual criticisms, given
their efforts to cultivate a crop of ministers to serve as the race representatives black intellectuals and modern clergy both desired. African
American religious leaders shared with many of their white religious
allies concerns about the impact of modern entertainment culture on
professionally oriented black youth. Edwin Mims, a Vanderbilt University English professor, anti-lynching advocate, and Methodist, was a
white Protestant ally whom African American Protestants granted the
authority to lecture their race on the proper path toward social progress. Speaking at Tuskegee Institute's annual Founder's Day celebration,
Mims recalled the life of Booker T. Washington as exemplary for the
African American student audience while also offering maxims for them
to safeguard African American culture in the tumultuous jazz age: "We
need your Spirituals, but not your jazz; your faith, but not your supersti-
tion. Let your humor remain as a fountain of innocent joy rather than
cesspool of vulgarity. Let the school and the church retain your fealty
rather than the cabaret. Let the rhythm of your souls be the music of the
spheres and not the tomtom of the orgy."[9]

Religious race professionals considered the fate of their Protestant
congregations and denominations in light of the attitudes toward dancing they shared with their white religious counterparts. In 1921 the *Star
of Zion* quoted Reform rabbi Davis Philipson of the Rockdale Avenue
Temple in Cincinnati on the problem of dancing: "Dance halls are

crowded with the youth of both sexes; churches rarely see them. If the churches and their leaders are wise they will attack this most pressing problem and bring to bear upon its solution every resource at their disposal."[10] "The Fight Looming on Dancing" was *Star of Zion* editor Walls's discussion in 1924 of the backlash at Brooklyn's St. Mark's Congregational Church, a white congregation whose pastor, Rev. Charles W. Dane, banned the continued use of the church basement for dancing as an alternative recreational space to "the cabarets and public dance halls which do not furnish the right environment for future deacons and deaconesses," according to a St. Mark's Sunday school teacher quoted in the editorial. Walls remarked that the day's dancing was too promiscuous, and although their churches may have both dancing members and pious members, "we cannot have both at the same time." Protestantism, in black and white, faced a fight over dancing, and Walls urged Protestants to follow the Catholic parishes, which had banned the practice. Dancing was an "insidious evil to society" that threatened Christian piety: "It has lost us influence in this generation until our spirituality is almost paralyzed and our efforts at personal work in soul saving, shut off where we have a right most to expect positive and active assistance." Walls even deemed African American Protestant clergy especially culpable for losing authority over their parishioners.[11]

However sympathetic the nonreligious black press was to the antidancing cause of religious press editors, they reported on and engaged the opinions of black denominations in ways that reinforced and questioned these religious writers' standing as race representatives. *New York Age* editors responded to the "prophetic editor of the *Star of Zion*" by questioning the effect of wholesale condemnation that only pushed black youth further away from church adherence and attendance: "The trouble with such denunciations of dancing as conducted today is that the critics do not suggest a way to eliminate the evils and preserve the good features that may be found in dancing as an exercise and a diversion."[12] Walls responded to the *New York Age* by pointing them to previous *Star of Zion* editions where he advocated that churches open their doors to "clubs, boy scouts, camp fire girls, Sunday School athletic groups, healthy games, indoor for winter and outdoor for summer, for both old and young, but separate" to supplant the pursuit of worldly dancing. These recreational opportunities were to exist alongside churches' administration of "employment bureaus and classes to teach public conduct and every sort of organization to help save our earnings and extend ourselves into co-operative business, community protection, [and] education and religion." By doing so, churches would be able to fulfill the task of "directing the play of all the people, both young and old, that their lives will count for the most in carrying on the work of the kingdom of God." As black Protestant denominations expanded in the urban North, Walls and many other black Protestant ministers took this task seriously. He urged that they "take over the recreation work or lose thousands of our group who wind their ways into this bustling, congested Yankee civilization."[13] For their part, the *New York Age* editors responded to Walls by affirming "the broadening attitude of the church and authorities on the question of rational and proper recreation for the people. The increased consideration given to vital questions of community welfare by such established religious organs as the *Star of Zion* and the [AME] *Christian Recorder* is a hopeful sign of the times." The *New York Age* editors anticipated that these religious papers' editors "may yet devise a way to take the danger out of dancing," a step beyond the recent example of forty white Methodist bishops who recommended "the removal of the ban against dancing and other prohibited amusements."[14]

To provide recreational alternatives to dancing, some African American Protestants turned to the stage. The *New York World* writer Lester A. Walton detailed the work of Mount Olivet Baptist Church pastor William P. Hayes and St. Mark's Methodist Episcopal Church pastor John W. Robinson, who performed a production of *The Merchant of Venice* and played the roles of Shylock and the Duke of Venice, respectively. "Ministers of the gospel, donning sock and bushkin," wrote Walton, "are convincing overflow audiences that they can act as well as preach[,] can dramatically portray worldly characters as well as pray." More than two thousand persons attended the performance, designed "to minimize the public taste for jazz," and the rest of the cast comprised "members of the various Harlem churches—Protestants and Catholics." Attending the play cost seventy-five cents, resulting in the performance becoming "the biggest artistic and financial success in Mount Olivet's history." And for Walton, the most interesting aspect of the interdenominational event was its confirmation of a shift away from complete disapprobation of worldly arts: "In years past, many Negroes of the Baptist and Methodist faiths have been superlatively orthodox in their opposition to the theatre. That the two denominations have joined to make war on jazz does not surprise, but for them to walk hand in hand with the theatre and take theatricals seriously is nothing short of revolutionary."

The play's production represented a translation of performance skills for both black ministers and local church members, although it was not without dilemma for members who may have hesitated about religious adherents performing "worldly" fictional characters. After the play, according to Walton, some Mount Olivet Baptist members "engaged in a friendly discussion as to the propriety of their pastor depicting a character so unlike a minister of the gospel." They concluded that "for one so reverent to shine so brilliantly as Shylock was a compliment to his histrionic ability," an acknowledgment that dramatic performance was an essential asset for the black pastor as preacher.[15] While African American Protestant ministers debated the appropriateness of one form of entertainment within religious spaces, they also contested other practices within black congregations that blurred the performances of worship and entertainment. For many ministers, these more enthusiastic and charismatic ways of conducting worship and preaching comported with jazz music's corruption of African American recreation, and they sought to characterize entertaining religious expressions as bearing a jazz tarnish.

"Jazzing Religion": Protesting Provocative Protestant Preachers

As a race church we have been intolerant of all forms of amusement. Still we have gotten lots of amusement out of our religion. Our churches have been the scenes of performances that puzzle and astonish other races, while as a race we have sent all outside amusement to Hades. But we wink at performances ever more ridiculous in the worship and as much corrupt in church society as the vaudeville ever suffered to be so. Witness the holiness bands and some extreme practices of our boasted Protestant Churches.
—William J. Walls, "The Negro Church and the Stage"[16]

Black Protestants faced an uphill battle to capture the approval of the nonreligious black press outlets, where religiously invested individuals often dismissed their ministries as insufficient for combating the contemporary dilemmas of modern life for African Americans. In particular, the black press focused on what they and black middle-class Protestants regarded as a horde of lecherous black preachers. AME evangelist Ruth R. Dennis was affiliated with New York City's Bethel AME Church and regularly appeared on WGBS's radio station in the late 1920s to discuss biblical topics. She had previously engaged in evangelism and missionary work for a decade, and she was trained at Wilberforce University and completed coursework in theology and classical literature at Columbia University. Dennis also contributed articles to the *Pittsburgh Courier*.[17] In a column for the *New York Age*'s "Readers' Forum" in 1925, Dennis wrote in response to an AME minister's call for "Holy Ghost Preaching" in African American churches. She critiqued this as a call for the "noise" likely characteristic of the Holiness-Pentecostals and rural Baptists. Instead of advocating for more enthusiastic sermonic styles among Methodists, Dennis declared that what black Protestant Christianity needed were preachers of upstanding moral character:

> The ministry of today is regarded as depraved and immoral to the extent that preachers are not respected and in many instances not allowed to enter into the homes of parishioners. I am speaking generally; sensible, thoughtful readers know that if it were not for the few conscientious religious leaders working earnestly this would be a veritable hell on earth. There are some ministers who are led by the Holy Ghost but they are few.
>
> There are others who enter the ministry because it affords them an easy livelihood and ofttimes a rich and popular one. The name of this type is legion. Christ still rebukes them as He did the Pharisees, saying "Well hath Isaiah prophesied of you hypocrites, as it is written, this people honoreth me with their lips but their hearts are far from me." As lights of the world to be set upon a hill that they may give light to all, these who dare call themselves ambassadors of Christ are as weak morally as a jellyfish and excuse themselves with the plea that they are only human and therefore not responsible.

Dennis wrote of her attendance at an AME ministers meeting the previous year, where she "appealed to them to do something tangible in bettering conditions" of their parishioners. When one minister retorted that criticisms of preachers must cease because "they are the best God has," Dennis stated that African Americans were "better off" for "preferring to associate with the worst and remain out of the church." Black Protestants were in need of "a great revival among the ministers" instead of among the people, and "Holy Ghost preaching" would follow the emergence of true "Holy Ghost preachers," whose ministries would reflect, in Dennis's words, those of "John the Baptist, John Wesley[,] Whitfield [sic], Moody and others." "Spirit-filled" preaching was beneath black Methodists, and Dennis regarded these practices as unintelligent, irrational, and regressive in light of the direction in which African American Protestants must now take a modern Christianity.[18] These enthusiastic practices, coupled with perceptions of preacher immorality, dissuaded those African American physicians, lawyers, and academics who spent their Sundays enjoying modern recreations: "I have heard it said time and again that the most learned of our race, especially the professional people, seem to avoid the church. Of course they should not, but it is not altogether their fault; their intelligence is insulted by all the antics that are perpetuated in the name of religion." Dennis created distance between lower and higher forms of black Christian expression by comparing these "antics" to "the Indian or African war dance," implying that the latter examples were primitive but also less "ridiculous" than shouting and dancing preachers. The project of a modern black Protestant ministry, for Dennis, was to be in service of the race to "blaze our path upward and onward, intelligently and devoutly," without "noise" or questionable personal morality.[19]

In the previous year, *Star of Zion* editor William H. Davenport (1868–1936), who assumed the position following Walls's promotion to bishop, termed this noisy preaching style "whangdoodleism" and blamed its promoters for dissuading educated young African Americans from church attendance: "If we would save to the Church the youth who come out of our schools and college, we must raise the tone of many of our pulpits. Too often when we cannot interest or garner the young, we berate them and education in bitter and vehement language; but voluble vacuity has no charms for the thoughtful."[20] A decade later, AMEZ ministers who opposed emotional religiosity as the authenticator of being "deeply religious" employed the King James versions of James 1:27, Job 16:19, and Job 29:12–16 as the criteria for showing deep religiosity "in a practical way." With this selection of biblical verses, these clergymen emphasized Christian social responsibilities over bodily expressions of religious enthusiasm.[21]

Amusing theatricality and entertainment in black Protestant worship services were signs of the decadence of the Jazz Age. Black Protestants in the press and pulpits warned of a proliferation of "jazz evangelists," or those who were "jazzing religion," thereby employing the popular genre's name as an all-purpose pejorative. In 1930 the *Philadelphia Tribune* warned of "false prophets" who were "willing to desecrate the House of God in order to get the coin of the realm," replacing "thinking, ideas and ideals" with "the waving of arms and prancing legs" in that pursuit. Expressive worship represented the "antics of jazz vaudeville," which, like popular entertainments, sought "easy money" to reward its "oily-tongued speakers."[22]

In 1934 Henry T. McCrary, pastor of Philadelphia's Tasker Street Baptist Church, wrote of his fondness for jazz music but lamented what he saw as a jazz influence on Christian proselytizing, a practice he termed "Jazz Band Evangelism." While McCrary confessed that the music "always and invariably makes me feel like dancing, in spite of my religion and the fact that I am a Baptist preacher," he surmised that "jazz has become too prevalent in our religious services, especially in our evangelistic endeavors." Traveling revivalists were responsible for promoting such Jazz Band Evangelism. However, McCrary blamed church pastors for "allow[ing] their churches to drift along in a rut of spiritual inactivity" because they had not remained "alert to [their] soul-saving mission instead of free-wheeling along" until the next evangelist was to hold a revival. Whenever these lackluster churches depended on outside revivalists, their brand of evangelism "must be accompanied by a brass band or a jazz orchestra in order to rejuvenate the half-dead Christians and draw the sinners whom the church can at no other time attract." McCrary asserted that emotionalism and evangelism were distinct while also decrying "jazz music" and "blues singing" in religious services, likely indicating his opposition to the nascent influence of gospel music and Holiness-Pentecostal worship practices that accompanied southern black migrants entering the urban North's black churches.[23] In asserting the problem of emotional religion and the use of popular, jazz-like instrumentation, McCrary criticized ministers whose charisma became the source of excitement without dismissing the value of religious emotionality:

> In the first place, when people are worked up over jazz in religious services sung and directed by the waltzing and shimmying of some of our 20th Century high powered evangelists, these people are not religiously stirred; they are emotionally animated. They are not God-conscious; they are jazz crazy. I am not signifying that I do not believe in emotional religion; to a certain extent, I do. I think that religion concerns itself with the entire personality of man. But I do not think that emotionalism should be the sole object of our religious worship.[24]

To counter the supporters of emotional religiosity, whom he regarded as "attempt[ing] to justify their ultra-noisy and jazz-band-type of worship by referring to Miriam, David, and others in the Old Testament," McCrary leaned on higher biblical criticism to situate this interpretation of 1 Samuel 18:6 in line with the subsequent verse, 1 Samuel 18:7 ("Saul hath slain his thousands, and David his ten thousands"). He claimed that such poetic biblical narratives reflected "the early Hebrew's conception of God" as "a God of War" and that such a conception "was purely in keeping with the ethics and moral standards of that day." "Since the Hebrew's idea of God (Yahweh) was that of a military Deity winning battles for His people," argued McCrary, "his worship and praise to God was often characterized in the same manner in which many of the surrounding heathens expressed their religious feelings toward their gods—in tumultuous shouts—in war songs and dances." McCrary declared that Jesus offered a theological alternative, "not a God of war, and pillage and wrath; but a God of Love, of Peace, and of Good-will toward all mankind." He invoked John 4:24 to convey that the worship of Jesus's God "in Spirit and in truth," consequently, required a degree of reverence beyond jazz stylings and entertaining theatrics. McCrary concluded with colorful prose that questioned the propriety of popular musical sounds and dances for the reverent worship of God's presence in eternity:

> Music then in the church should be characterized by a spirit of sincere reverence; it should be devotional and sacred. It is the tunes of the soul that lift one from the common and ordinary spheres of life unto the sub-

lime relationship with the Infinite. It should enable one to so integrate his personality as to correlate it with the highest conceptions of the Divine.

Imagine the angels in Heaven playing jazz upon their harps of gold and the four and twenty Elders singing meaningless ditties in ragtime tunes, until Heaven is thrown into a frenzied state of emotional pandemonium. If such be our highest conceptions of the Divine, then: On with jazz until every rheumatic brother and sister in the congregation forget their aching joints and erstwhile lameness, and express their religious ecstasy by snake-hipping and buck-dancing.[25]

McCrary's relative appreciation of jazz music, coupled with his disapproval of its use to support emotional worship in black Protestant houses of worship, represented one form of extended response to "jazz evangelism" in the black press. Other black Protestant ministers evidenced less patience for "jazz preaching" and released statements banning various traveling ministers from their collective pulpits. The Ministers Interdenominational Alliance of Camden, New Jersey, produced a resolution to repudiate "'jazz preaching,' religious racketeering and all forms of commercialized religion." Rev. George E. Morris, pastor of Camden's Kaighn Avenue Baptist Church, chaired this ministerial alliance's fact-finding committee, and it echoed McCrary's stance that the Christian New Testament did not directly permit the expressive worship practices that these preachers encouraged. "Their appeal is made purely to the sentiment or excited nature of the members of congregations; they do their exploiting from the standpoint of the movies, jazz and minstrelsy. They give the people a false idea of preaching the Gospel, Divine Worship, and of the Christianity of Jesus Christ, for which they can find no example in the New Testament which sets forth sane, straightforward, practical Christly teaching, preaching and living." Ministers who continued to invite such "false prophets" would lose the alliance's recognition of their churches.[26]

These black clergymen often singled out popular independent ministers like Bishop Charles "Daddy" Grace for their ire. At the AME Church's denominational conference in Philadelphia in May 1934, Bishop N. W. Williams of the seventh district in South Carolina declared that "missions with spurious bishops like the self-styled 'Bishop' Grace are a reflection on the religious development of the race."[27] A 1938 article chronicled Grace's takeover of 20 West 115th Street—previously the home of Father Divine's Peace Mission—as the emergence of a house of worship comparable to Harlem's famous Savoy ballroom. Grace's House of Prayer for All People made it "hard to tell whether he was attempting to compete with Chick Webb beating it out at the Savoy," a reference to the ballroom's famous bandleader, whose group included vocalist Ella Fitzgerald. Grace even intentionally appropriated the fashions of the swing era's jazz bands, and the article declared, "The band members' uniforms, styled from [Earl] Snake Hips Tucker's famous dance suit, consist of black silk, wide sleeved shirts, white trousers, gold sashes and ties, while the upper bracket soldiers wore helmets, gold-braided green coats and white trousers." Those who attended Grace's House of Prayer were in for "an evening packed with swing—and perspiration," a deceptive musical style that produced dubious bodily evidence of sincere Christian worship, according to black mainline Protestants.[28]

Clerical Cultural Critics: Direct Opposition to Jazz

It is said that the Negro created jazz. If he did so he should be ashamed of it.
Jazz has about had its day among thinking people.
Experience has shown that this sort of music is exotic. It has this effect on the performers and the auditors. . . . Persons who are concerned with social progress, then, must take steps to restrict jazz and stamp it out as an evil.
—Carter G. Woodson, "Jazz Demoralizing, Creators Should Be Ashamed"

In 1933 Carter G. Woodson (1875–1950) penned an editorial in the *Philadelphia Tribune* titled "Jazz Demoralizing, Creators Should Be Ashamed," where the man considered the "Father of Black History" voiced the sentiments of a generation who found little value in this "exotic" form of youth culture that, unlike African American spirituals, provided no positive political or moral value for a race. "I have always felt mortified to see Negroes labeling themselves as 'Jazz Spreaders' and 'Jazz Hounds,'" confessed Woodson. "Well might they use the latter term, for I have never seen a group that reminds me more of the 'Hell Hounds' described by my spiritual adviser in Virginia when he used to try to frighten me into getting religion at the 'Anxious Seat.' The 'Jazz Spreaders' have run many a soul into a veritable hell."[29]

Given the popularity of jazz as a music genre in the 1920s and 1930s, many social leaders and academic elites in black and white America considered it a moral contagion, capable of rapidly reproducing the decadent habits of a reckless black urban youth. The hours of dedicated practice and repetition required to master the musical art of improvisation, or to perform convincingly the charismatic presence of a lead singer in command of her vocal talents, or to make the swing dancer's choreography seem effortless and innate did not capture the attention of the genre's cultural critics.[30] Instead, jazz music and its cultural practices represented for them the immature social habits of a younger generation. African American youth would be wise to spend leisure time refining the race's "higher" cultural arts, like African American spirituals (or at least creating new ones). Woodson used this editorial to decry both jazz culture and the more physically emotional aspects of African American Christian culture, represented in a religious leader from his youth preaching a revival sermon to compel persons with the fear of God's eternal punishment to "get religion" through the embrace of Christianity. Neither the "exotic" jazz music nor the frightful religious tactics of "low-church" black Protestantism appear to have captured, for Woodson, the sensible dignity and religious fidelity African Americans must represent, as modern subjects, if they were to engage in progressive intellectual, cultural, and ultimately political projects in the United States.

Woodson's criticisms aligned strongly with the middle-class black Protestants who shared his disdain for "jazz" in the previous decade. Jazz was the music of dancing in the 1920s, and earlier proponents of dancing in these debates sought to differentiate the healthy physical exercise from the immoral music that must require censorship. James G. Bland wrote to *Half-Century Magazine* in 1922 to express his desire to censor jazz for its encouragement of sexual impropriety: "Jazz music appeals to the lowest instincts. The most sober citizen loses some of his dignity when he listens to the moaning, groaning and wailing of a jazz orchestra. And most jazz dances are followed by 'petting parties,' joy rides and other orgies." Dancing, however, was an acceptable practice, but Bland believed that "an effort should be made to have better music."[31]

AMEZ bishop Thomas Walker Wallace took to his denomination's paper to respond to an Associated Negro Press report that a German musician sought to ban jazz from Germany because "Negro talent" was responsible for its production. Wallace did not rebuke the German racial bias; he chose, instead, to express offense at the suggestion that jazz represented African American talent:

> TALENT! Is not this a travesty? Millions of music-loving Negroes would have this abortive offspring of musical parody driven from the universe of music. Will these same Negroes be accused of denying to talent its production of genius? Now, dear little hare-brained brother, a succession of discordant sounds and a jumble of musical notes in syncopated time is not music nor is the ability to produce such a paroxysm of howls, moans, and groans, talent. Jazz, the Bunny Hug, the Bear Walk, the Shimmy, and all other detestable outrages of the poetry of sound and motion are fit companions and are the offspring of the disordered and lust maddened souls of the followers of the hideous ogre of mankind—EVIL.

Like most other African American Protestants, Wallace claimed that African American talent belonged to those who created and sang spirituals, and he listed "Swing Low, Sweet Chariot," "Roll, Jordan, Roll," "Steal Away to Jesus," and "Didn't Ole Pharaoh Get Drowned," along with the contemporary singers Harry Burleigh and Roland Hayes. These singers and songs were the evidence of a refined black musical tradition formed in suffering and representative of steadfast piety. By contrast, "jazz is but the pitiful parody of heart songs wrung from suffering souls."[32] Black Protestants in the print press world also sought to validate the spiritual tradition against jazz's popular emergence by identifying African diasporic authorities on music, like Nicholas George Julius Ballanta of Sierra Leone, "a man whose job it is to examine the relationship of jazz to the music of [Africa's] jungle tribes." Whereas Ballanta agreed that jazz had African roots, he declared that it was not the best modern representative of "a definitely painstaking system rooted in centuries of culture" that constituted African music: "The place where you may look for the real survival of African music in America is not in jazz—that has grown up too much in the western way—but in the 'coon songs' of the

South. Many of the 'spirituals' still heard in the South, too, may also be heard—the identical melody—in the jungles of Africa."[33]

Religiously invested individuals in the nonreligious black press also made more general and generational criticisms of different religious audiences, when not directly criticizing black Protestant clergy. A 1928 *New York Amsterdam News* editorial contained a lament that the Jazz Age youth wanted a "jazz religion"—with this phrase representing the paper's pejorative summary of a recent conference on religion at Harlem's St. Philip's Episcopal Church. The Young People's Fellowship of St. Philip's hosted the gathering, with "The Christian Religion—Is It a Sufficient Dynamic for Living in the Modern Day?" as the conference theme. The paper reported that the Young People's Fellowship "brought forth many opinions, some for and some against religion. The speeches, when analyzed, were found to deal with the churches rather than with religion itself." The editorial writer asserted, "The Christian religion is sufficient for this day or any other day, if it is lived up to. . . . The Christian ideal of pure living, high thinking, faithful work and the Golden Rule does not square with today's ideal of luxurious living, shallow thinking, slipshod work and the Brass Rule."[34] In responding to the opinions of the church's youth, however, the editorial revealed that this black mainline Protestant congregation permitted its younger congregants to express their criticisms of religious institutions, likely in the pursuit of reforms to suit St. Philip's youth who would come to take charge of the church as they matured. Nevertheless, to claim that the conference's discourse represented a preference for "jazz religion" also marked the name of the musical genre as one black mainline Protestant generation's efficient generalization of a host of different social and moral attitudes among African American Christians.

In 1929 the *Star of Zion* quoted Bishop Walls lamenting the effects of jazz and leisure on learned African Americans: "I am afraid that some of our educated men and women devote too much time to jazz, the dance, and the auto." To this concern, the column cautioned that "no people can jazz and dance and auto ride themselves to the top," framing African American progress as a modern competition. The *Star of Zion* also suggested that the educated class's excessive recreation may become an impediment to a race's collective advancement as a civilization: "The

Negro in play forgets that the Caucasian race had won its way to the top before it took the jazz and the auto. The instructors of our youth might be interested in this phase of our social problems."[35] The *California Voice* complemented this sentiment by criticizing educated African Americans as indulging in leisure instead of serving and educating fellow African Americans: "If our graduates would throw off some of their superior complex and devote a little time to uplift and inculcating the higher ideals of this life, how much better the race would be and those benefits would redound to the educated group. Education that does not mean service to humanity is the half-baked product."[36] Denominational leaders and press writers warned of popular entertainment's indirect effect upon the broader African American race when the talented tenth put its energy into the pursuit of recreation rather than of uplift.

Lastly, the black Protestant minister's recourse against jazz entertainment was the artistry of the sermon. By the late 1930s, when "swing" became the name for popular jazz music, Rev. Capt. D. J. Gilmer penned a sermon that reconstructed swing as a timeless concept representing humanity's ignorance. The printed sermon afforded Gilmer the opportunity to exercise blunt, preacherly humor against those he considered lost in the sin of swing. Gilmer offered "What is man?" as the divine, timeless, and unanswered question; for the swing era, Gilmer responded to this question by offering a comical anthropology that might strike readers as profane if he preached it aloud:

There is a coined word which has been used to describe man and what he is. This word is spelled "damphul." When Jesus was being crucified by this "damphul" class of men, these words were spoken about those who were trying to crucify him: "Father forgive them for they know not what they do." No, they did not know then and they don't know now what they are doing. At the crucifixion of Jesus men passed by as he was hanging on the cross in agony and death and scoffed at him and wagged their heads in rhythm. That was the first "swing" time of the world whose tragedy then may not have been as bad as it is today. "Swing," no reason, no knowledge, just "Swing." Yea, today, millions of years since God cried from blank space, "Let there be light," damphuls are still grappling in the dark swept on by "Swing."

Swing captured the vicious culture that swallowed modern youth. Gilmer spotted "hundreds of young girls and boys" smoking cigarettes while waiting in line for a swing band's show, evidence of the age's decadence. He determined that modern ignorance was fueled by its entertainment culture and the habits like smoking it promoted, bolstered by cross-promotion between the entertainment and tobacco industries: "The cigarette craze is only 'Swing,' and when Miss John Doe declares over the air that cigarettes protect her voice, it is the power of the dollar god behind swing." Beyond encouraging unhealthy habits, swing was responsible for mob violence, the destruction of homes, and the demise of nations. Swing was "on the throne" while truth was "on the scaffold, or before the firing squad, or in the death house to die." Gilmer lamented the sight of "young men and girls passing the church on Sundays in the suggestive attitude of wagging their heads at Jesus as the world swings," ignoring the righteous path God provided them, "swept on," instead, "by the inanities of swing."[37]

Conclusion: Ministers and Musicians

The enticing lurements of rag, the jazz, and the blues, find in Harlem either their origin or their home. The Negro funmakers, minstrels, theatricals and songsters thrive nowhere else as in Harlem. The ephemeral joys of Nineveh, Tyre and Babylon, stir the imagination on the lower level of fun and devilish excitation. While this may not constitute a characteristic of our orthodox Heaven yet these things appeal mightily to the imagination. Harlem is the center of the Negro dance, cabaret and night life. Negro art, music and poetry radiate from this center.
—Kelly Miller, "Where Is the Negro Heaven"[38]

When H. L. Mencken charged that African Americans failed to equal whites in the creative fields of art, poetry, and music, Bishop Walls wondered about the lack of response from the black jazz artists' community to Mencken's charge that others outside the race were refining their craft: "So far, we have heard no shouting chorus from either these or even from the jazz writers who Mencken says left it for George

Gershwin and Paul Whiteman to make a serious matter." Rather than speak for these popular black artists, Walls argued that the faults of black Protestants rested with preachers and the middle-class populace, with the former more interested in entertaining sermons and the latter more invested in popular entertainments: "We have not kept our vision apace with the present needs and trends. . . . The great majority find that money is most easily culled through the peoples' emotions. We have scarcely attacked the greater tasks of building a program that will commend itself to the newer and greater demands of the race in his advancing opportunity and complex struggles." This work required the educated black middle class's financial and time commitments to create, in Walls's words, social programs to attract "our high brows," "our everyday masses," and the youth.[39]

Black Protestant mainline ministers soldiered on as the race's representatives throughout the 1930s. One milestone achievement for this group came with the effort of Rev. Glenn. T. Settle, pastor of Cleveland's Gethsemane Baptist Church, to produce *The National Negro Hour* for broadcast over 107 CBS radio stations. Establishing the broadcast involved the efforts of "the National Baptist Conventions, The AME Church, The AMEZ Church, The CME Church, The ME Church (colored), The Negro Press, the outstanding Negro educators and schools of the nation, the Negro business and professional organizations, not to forget the Negro welfare and social workers and the various college fraternities of the nation." The program launched the career of the Wings over Jordan Choir, and its promotion in the black religious press emphasized its intention to counteract other popular narratives and representatives of African Americans: "The feature of the program is a message delivered on each program by some prominent Negro character revealing to the nation The Better Side of Negro Life. The speaker to be used on the program will join the chain during broadcast from their own city. This system is a guarantee that the most prominent people of our race will be heard as guest speakers." This national structure ensured for middle-class black Protestants a stronger vehicle for combating the popularity of jazz musicians, showcasing local race representatives in ministry, education, publishing, and law while providing their own entertaining musical traditions to black and white radio audiences.[40]

As cultural critics, these religious race professionals marshalled their denominational papers and allies in the black press against the powerful, popular songs and dances that a wayward generation of African Americans was forging in the 1920s and 1930s. As the music grew in popularity, the ministers saw it as a temptation leading black youth and emerging black professionals away from institutional religious commitments, as well as a symptom of gratuitous emotionality and materialism, a wider social epidemic that was infecting and corrupting modern black Protestant worship and preaching. Church associations, conventions, and religious radio programming served as venues to preach against the emerging jazz and swing cultures. Wholesome recreation and an educated black ministry that spoke for African Americans on pressing social and political matters also represented practical tools of combat. These middle-class black ministers sought to reform ministerial professions and the mission of Protestant churches as they faced criticisms from black intellectual elites, the black press, white cultural critics, and the very black youth their work targeted as they also sought the investments of black professionals in their local congregations and wider denominations. Additionally, the ministers articulated modern theologies to maintain interracial religious conversations as well as to provide racialized critiques of a white American Protestantism that sanctioned Jim Crow violence and segregation. To remain prominent race representatives, these religious race professionals balanced a progressive religious engagement with society and a critical religious discourse on popular culture. But as Rev. T. J. Jefferson's 1930 letter to the *Star of Zion* noted, "The preacher no longer monopolizes the privileges of the public speech."[41]

The emerging African American generation's attachments to popular music, dancing, and urban night life raised the question of whether the sounds of jazz as an art form drowned out the voices of these religious race professionals. The following chapter discusses Cab Calloway, a black male musician who emerged from the modern religious world these middle-class black Protestants created in the 1920s. Calloway elected not to follow their path toward sanctioned race professionalism and became, instead, a dancer-singer-composer-bandleader-entertainer whose comical jazz music often addressed African American Protestantism. But because of his celebrity, he bore the responsibility of race representation throughout his early career.

2

"Get Happy, All You Sinners"

A musical call-and-response between brass and reeds opens the 1933 composition "Harlem Camp Meeting." A voice asks, "What's this comin' off here?" and after a brief pause, reflects, "It's more like one of them good ol' revival days here. A camp meeting! Yowza, yowza!" Next comes a clarinet solo, and the inquiring voice assumes the role of a narrator in remarking, "There's a dear brother got happy on that clarinet, look at him. Greeeat day!" As the clarinet solo continues, the narrator interjects affirmative responses: "Tell me all about it, brother. Tell me all about it, now." The narrator then refers to the "brother" as "son" and tells him, "Get ready for this scat sermon I'm gonna give you here." The narrator produces a wordless vocal melody, accompanied by syncopated chimes replicating the sound of distant Sunday church bells. Another "brother" follows his vocal solo with a muted trumpet solo, and the narrator encourages this man to "get happy there, get happy" with responses of "uh huh," "yowza!," and "shout it, Elder, shout it, Elder." To this musical crowd, the narrator proclaims, "Get happy, get happy, all you sinners, and get happy here!" The percussion halts for a brass interlude, before the beat resumes with an antiphonal chorus of clarinet "sisters" swinging with brass "brothers." As the music climaxes, the narrator joyously proclaims with laughter, "This is the kind of camp meetins we have in Harlem, yeah, man!"

Composed for Cab Calloway and His Orchestra by the African American trombonist Harry White in 1933, "Harlem Camp Meeting" takes the (foxtrotting) listener on a tour of the exciting sounds of a black Protestant revival setting. The key sonic distinctions from a traditional black Christian worship experience, however, are the song's instrumental "testimonies," "yowza" exclamations, and the swinging sounds of a Harlem big band. When the narrator urges participants to "get happy," or when he recognizes a clarinetist who got happy on his instrument, he evokes the charismatic Christian practice of shouting, crying, and dancing

under the possessive influence of the Holy Spirit—but these participants
are to be happy as "sinners." The narrator speaks back to the soloists who
provide their musical testimonies, behaving as a church member who
vocally affirms the righteous speech of her or his sisters and brothers
in Christ. In this three-minute recording, the African American singer,
dancer, composer, and bandleader Cabell "Cab" Calloway III (1907–
1994) shifts rapidly from observer to interpreter to practitioner.[1]

Calloway's ascendancy to revival preacher comes with a "scat sermon"
in the middle of the song. This forty-second scat interlude is most interesting, for Calloway produces a rhythmic and melodic imitation of
the "whooped" portion of African American "chanted sermons" with it.
Scholar of preaching and preacher Martha Simmons describes whooping as "melody, one that can be identified by the fact that its pitches
are logically connected and have prescribed, punctuated rhythms that
require certain modulations of the voice, and is often delineated by
quasi-metrical phrasings."[2] The "chanted sermon," according to African
American religious historian Albert Raboteau, originated in the rural
South's revivals and prayer meetings, spreading into urban areas through
the United States with African American migrations in the twentieth
century. Calloway was familiar with the form, despite having attended
more elite middle-class African American churches in his youth, because the chanted preaching style as oral "folk" art was a "tradition of
preaching [that] remain[ed] popular among literate and 'sophisticated'
congregations." The chanted sermon contains three movements. The
first consists of conversational prose that is "occasionally grandiloquent."
The preacher then enters the "whooped" or "chanting" portion by speaking more rapidly, excitedly, and rhythmically. The third movement represents the sermon's climax, wherein the preacher's chanting "becomes
tonal and merges with the singing, clapping, and shouting of the congregation." The chanting preacher's musical performance of a sermon was
"compos[ed] on the spot" and "delivered in rhythmic metrical speech":

> The meter is not based on accent but on time, the length of time between
> regular beats. As the preacher moves into the chanted section of his ser-
> mon, he fits his speech to a beat. When necessary, he lengthens vowels
> or rushes together words in order to make a line match the meter. The
> regularity of the beat is accentuated by the preacher's gasp for air at the

end of each line. Sometimes he actually raps out the rhythm on the pulpit. The congregational responses . . . reinforce the beat and simultaneously fill in the space left by the preacher's pause for breath. . . .

. . . At a certain stage, the preacher's chanting takes on a musical tone, which indicates a concomitant rise in emotional pitch. The preacher's voice changes: the timbre becomes harsh, almost hoarse. His vocal cords are constricted; his breathing is labored. All the while he moves, gestures, dances, speaking with body as well as voice.[3]

Calloway's "growling" portion (from 1:28 to 1:35) most exemplifies the preacher's monotone chanting sound and audible gasps for breath. The shouts near its beginning emphasized his rising emotional pitch, and the moans represented the shouted singing that many preachers use to conclude their sermons, displaying their physical exhaustion by this point.

With "Harlem Camp Meeting," the musicians and composers intended to produce a hilarious and familiar representation of black Protestant religious practice. Unlike the chanted African American Christian sermon, however, Calloway's scatted message celebrates the jazz man's existence: a recreational life that is at times sexual, inebriated, and raucous. And as a nocturnal life on the weekends that resulted in partiers sleeping late on Sundays, Harlem's "camp meetings" were always in conflict with observing the Christian Sabbath.

As a bandleader, flamboyant conductor, composer, singer, and dancer, Calloway often crafted and inhabited the identity of a pastoral figure against the backdrop of New York's Cotton Club. The Cotton Club itself was a representation of a particular romantic pastoral image, namely, the antebellum southern slave mansion and plantation. This scenery was not visible to most African Americans, barred from the Cotton Club due to its segregated policy. If not the owners of radios, most African Americans encountered Cab Calloway's jazz through phonograph records, thereby accessing the sounds of his artistry absent the racist professional context in which whites consumed his performances. In the Great Depression era, the "Hi-De-Ho man" was the entertaining showman with a popular reputation for offering a jubilant, often irreverent musical message inviting partying club patrons and radio or phonograph listeners to partake in his celebration in their homes (see figure 2.1).[4] Calloway, once referred to as the "Satanic Sultan of Scat Singing" by writer and

New York Amsterdam News journalist Vincent L. "Roi" Ottley, employed irreverent humor to offer a clear alternative to religious calls for a return to "old-time" African American Christianity that traded on expressions of "low church" religiosity.[5]

Through his music, Cab Calloway articulated and portrayed *irreverence* as a distinctive mode of religious skepticism in African American religious history. His early career shed light on the impactful presence of black men and women's comedy that poked fun at African American religious life based on intimate familiarity with it. In the broader twentieth century, African American music, film, television, plays, literary works, stand-up specials, and radio/television sketch actors would create a comedic tradition. Comedic religious subjects generated a "knowing" laughter among African Americans with intimate knowledge of these irreverent caricatures because of their own experiences with religious life. Producing this laughter encouraged African Americans to embrace a kind of religious affiliation or participation that appreciated humor about matters that they had been instructed to treat with reverence.

Through humor, irreverence oriented African Americans toward religious affiliation in ways that differed from radical humanist critiques of African American Protestant Christian theology and practice. Atheist, agnostic, and theologically liberal African American playwrights created such critical dramas in the interwar era, with scenes and characters that directly challenged the theologies these playwrights determined were preventing African American progress in Jim Crow America.[6] In Cab Calloway's early career, by contrast, he made a concerted effort to produce humorous irreverence by replicating the sights, sounds, and behaviors of black Protestant church settings, characters, events, and experiences.

Accordingly, this chapter identifies the young Calloway's tensions with his respectable middle-class African American roots and religious upbringing, as presented in his 1976 autobiography, *Of Minnie the Moocher and Me*. Several Calloway musical performances in addition to "Harlem Camp Meeting" reveal Calloway's religious and racial irreverence: "Is That Religion?," "Miss Hallelujah Brown," "A Strictly Cullud Affair," and "Yaller" on record; and "St. James Infirmary" in an animated short. Calloway emerged as a de facto race representative in his early career, first through the ambivalence of religious irreverence with his performance in the 1936 feature film *The Singing Kid*, then through his perspectives on racial representation as an established musician. The early body of work of this "Satanic Sultan of Scat Singing" left a consequential irreverent legacy in black Protestant popular culture.

Respectable Roots, Sabbath Sacrilege

A summary of the answers submitted by the 135 youths of Baltimore will show several results. The majority attended church regularly, including the preaching services. On the other hand, they manifest less active interest in the Sunday Schools and the special young people's organizations. The majority attended a particular church chiefly because of family ties. The majority disapproved of the prohibition and limitation of amusements by the church, and in most cases as a result manifested a change of attitude toward the church which bordered upon either neglect, defiance or indifference. The belief of the Negro youth of Baltimore concerning Christianity was, on the whole, orthodox with a growing demand for practical religion—which was generally shared by some of their parents. The ministry as a career has fallen into disfavor among the young men. Only one student intended to study for the pastorate, the great bulk of the remainder preferring other professions.
—Charles H. Wesley, "The Religious Attitudes of Negro Youth"[7]

Against the wishes of his middle-class black parents, Cabell Calloway III pursued the life of a popular entertainer in the art form of jazz, which they considered beneath their son. His mother, Martha Eulalia Reed, was a graduate of Morgan State College who worked as a public school teacher. She was also a church organist who ensured that her children occupied their Sunday youth in regular services and Sunday school. His father, Cabell Calloway Jr., was a graduate of Pennsylvania's Lincoln University and was a lawyer who first worked in real estate in Rochester, New York. When the Calloway family moved to Baltimore, Calloway Jr. clerked in a law firm.[8] In his autobiography, Calloway remembered that his family "had status in the Negro community" as working professionals, even if that did not necessarily mean they were always comfortable financially, given that "Negro professionals were paid a hell of a lot less than white professionals with the same jobs."[9]

Two years after moving to Baltimore, Calloway Jr. suffered from mental health issues unknown to the young Calloway, having a "nervous breakdown" and being institutionalized. Calloway never saw his father again, who died shortly thereafter.[10] His mother then married John Nelson Fortune, whom Calloway and his siblings called "Papa Jack." Papa Jack had a series of jobs: department store employee, chauffeur for a white family, grocer (and gin bootlegger), and ad salesman for the Baltimore *Afro-American* newspaper. Most memorable to Calloway was Papa Jack's work as the first African American insurance salesman for the Commercial Casualty Insurance Company. Calloway wrote, "Papa Jack built up the insurance business in the black community. He was probably the first insurance broker to really educate black schoolteachers, doctors, dentists, and other professionals in Baltimore about life insurance. He says that within a couple of years he had over 80 per cent of the Negro teachers in Baltimore."[11]

Calloway remembered the roots of his parents in the black middle class, evident in the "three-story wood frame middle-class home[s]" of his maternal "Grandma Reed" and paternal "Grandma Calloway."[12] While in Baltimore during the 1910s and 1920s, Martha and Papa Jack's middle-class income afforded the family the choice to rent residences in Baltimore's emerging black suburban neighborhoods. When Calloway was a teenager, his mother and stepfather moved the family to "a small suburban development seven or eight miles outside Baltimore called Wilson Park." Harry O'Neill Wilson, an African American entrepreneur who founded the Mutual Benefit Society in 1903 to provide insurance to other African Americans, purchased and developed a few hundred acres to construct Wilson Park's homes for African American professionals to own or rent in the segregated city.[13] Calloway recalled, "[Wilson] lived out there, too, and his children were about my age. We rented a great big house on a corner. It had four bedrooms, a garage, a big lawn, and hedges all around. But it was the Wilsons who had the nicest house in the park. It was at the end of a long drive, up on a hill, with a swimming pool."[14] Renting a Wilson Park home afforded the family access to stable education, albeit far from elite primary school training. On his junior high education at the Lauraville School, where he played baseball and basketball and became valedictorian out of a class of four students, Calloway reflected, "I'm very proud of coming out of a school like that and going on to do the things I've done in life. The conditions for learning weren't very good—we had few books or supplies—but the teachers gave us attention and love and understanding. They were stern, too. They pushed us to learn, but they were sensitive to each child so that nobody ever felt left out or uncared for. The quality of education at that school was less important to me than the feeling of confidence and security that I got from it."[15]

Convincing Calloway to commit to his studies was a constant struggle for his mother and stepfather. They feared their son being labeled a "delinquent" and the attendant social embarrassment for respectable black parents (Martha was also a clubwoman who hosted meetings in her home). Calloway was inclined to skip school, he played craps on street corners or in the woods on Sundays, and he had a penchant for getting into fights.[16] Middle-class African American religious, educational, and social leaders attempted to address the delinquent "Boy Problem" through proscriptive literature, community building, and the establishment of civic and recreational spaces. For instance, the racial uplift manual *Floyd's Flowers* provided moral instruction for forging boys and girls into "good men and good women." Calloway's recreational habits and aversion to Sunday school would have qualified him either as rowdy or, worse, as a "Bad Boy" in black middle-class categorizations of youth.[17]

Around age fourteen, while Calloway was playing craps instead of attending Sunday school, Martha caught him on her way home from church. She later decided to send him to a church-run boarding school in Pennsylvania for African American young men and women. Downingtown Industrial and Agricultural School (DIAS) was founded around 1904 and 1905 by Dr. William A. Creditt, pastor of Philadelphia's First African Baptist Church and the brother of Calloway's maternal grandmother, Anna Creditt Reed.[18] With John S. Trower, one of the nation's wealthiest African Americans and a member of First African Baptist, Calloway's great-uncle sought to model the instruction of Atlanta's Tuskegee Institute for adolescents in a northern US city. DIAS became a state-funded institution in 1907, and it sat on a 110-acre campus with two dormitories. Each year the school enrolled 110 young black women and men, whose parents or guardians submitted applications on their behalf. DIAS was well known by the 1920s when Calloway enrolled, due to the school's advertising in major northeastern black press papers.[19] Calloway remembered a larger campus and student body at DIAS, writing in his autobiography that the school sat on about two hundred acres and enrolled about two hundred students. Beyond this estimate, Calloway recalled his daily tasks: "We were supposed to cultivate the farm, learn a trade, and take regular academic courses like reading and math and history. . . . Actually we were a mixture of students and truants. Like I said, it was more a reform school than an agricultural and industrial school." Calloway further recalled that classwork occurred two days each week, with manual work on the farm or training in shops for the rest of the week. The DIAS delinquency reform project, which African American middle-class race representatives instituted in their commitment to racial uplift, sought to instill a Victorian-era ethos of middle-class manhood characterized by "production (or engagement in the marketplace), character, respectability, and the producer values of industry, thrift, regularity, and temperance."[20] In the spring of 1922, after attending DIAS for a year, Calloway left the school without notice and returned to Baltimore, committing thenceforward to take his studies seriously.[21]

Martha and Papa Jack expected Calloway to follow his late father's example by studying law after completing high school.[22] Encouraging Calloway in this respectable direction also meant recognizing and cultivating his potentially respectable talent—singing. Calloway, a tenor "with a range from around C to B above C," often performed in church choirs, and his parents allowed him to take private voice lessons in his teenage years. Ruth Macabee, a family friend and former concert singer, instructed Calloway in opera and classical singing every Wednesday for two years: "She taught me the fundamentals; like how to breathe, place my tones, and use my diaphragm to get the sound that I wanted. I would spend hours holding my tongue with a handkerchief and singing the scale, up and down, up and down, until I could sing a scale with a handkerchief around my tongue as well as most people without one." To practice elocution, Calloway spent hours counting from one to ten "to get the execution of the sounds precise and correct," following Macabee's instruction that "it is not enough to be able to sing and hold a key, people have to understand your lyrics." Calloway continued his musical instruction in high school, taking voice lessons and basic music theory from Llewelyn Wilson.[23]

Calloway's parents and music instructors likely assumed they were preparing him for the performance of the respectable vocal arts: the singing of classical European music, Protestant hymns, and the concert-style arranged spirituals. However, he was intent on honing his talents for the non-respectable art forms of the early 1920s: popular musical entertainment like revues and vaudeville shows, in addition to singing and playing drums for Dixieland and "straight jazz" music in Baltimore bands.[24] Calloway recalled that Macabee considered jazz "below her" and forbade him to sing it.[25] Along with singing, Calloway had learned to play drums in high school.[26] Always "hustling" to earn additional income for himself and his family, he performed in Baltimore speakeasies without the knowledge of his parents and voice music teachers: "There'd be someone cooking ribs and barbecue and pigs' feet in the kitchen. Everybody would be laughing and dancing and hollering behind the music, which was always loud. We drank gin, wine, and whiskey, mostly old, hard bootleg rye. Mama and Papa Jack and my music teachers didn't know I was performing in these places. Jesus, they would have been mad as hell. They forbade me to go near them, but since they never went into them themselves, I was pretty safe."[27]

Despite the intentions of his black middle-class parents and teachers, the young Calloway appeared unable and unwilling to aspire to the respectable Negro ideal. The teenager had less than respectable professional goals and leisure habits centered around dancing and drinking. Although he had imbibed at parties at an early age, he first became intoxicated while serving drinks for one of his mother's club meetings. Additionally, he had already been helping Papa Jack sell bootleg alcohol.[28] And despite the presence of African American clergy in his extended family and a mother who was a church organist, Calloway expressed a lack of interest in African American Protestant church life and attendance. The older Calloway reflected on his adolescent days living with his paternal grandparents and his desire to avoid Sunday services and Sunday school. He characterized his younger self's admiration for his paternal grandfather, who was a "hustler" who owned a pool hall in Baltimore. Calloway regretted not seeing more of his grandfather, because his parents and paternal grandmother deemed the pool hall "off limits" for him. Instead, at the insistence of his mother and grandmother, the young Calloway and his siblings were to attend Baltimore's Grace Presbyterian Church services and Bible school "every damned Sunday, rain or shine, from early in the morning till late afternoon." This humorous recollection included the imagery of all family members "get[ting] dressed up and walk[ing] nicely to church together," possibly revealing the older Calloway's disagreeable memory of this required weekly routine. This may have also been his attempt to relate to readers who were also familiar with the apparently exhausting Sunday ritual to "keep up appearances" within the community, if not to sincerely enjoy Christian worship, sermons, and instruction. Alternatively, what stood out to Calloway as respectable was his grandfather's ownership of the pool hall, which he noted his family was "very open about" despite being "strong churchgoing people": "In fact, we were all proud of it. No one else in our neighborhood had a grandfather who went off to New York City for months at a time and owned a pool hall as well."[29]

Between the death of Calloway's father and Martha's remarriage to Papa Jack, she moved her children to live in her mother's home. Calloway remembered Grandma Reed as less strict than Grandma Calloway, explaining this moment in adolescence as his opportunity to break away from his regular church attendance and to appreciate leisure and hustling for employment with friends:

> At Grandmother Reed's I began to break out of the restrictions of Grandma Calloway's house. To begin with I stopped going to church, although my mother was always on me about it. But now there were more important things to do on Sunday morning, like selling newspapers. I guess I went from one extreme to the other. One year I was spending three or four hours in church every Sunday plus Bible classes during the week, Bible school every day during the summer, and singing in the junior choir, and the next I was a part of a gang of guys who were basically young hustlers. We had two interests—making money and having a good time.[30]

As noted previously, when Calloway, about age fourteen, skipped Sunday school to play craps, his mother decided to enroll him at Downingtown. When he returned from Downingtown and moved with the family to

Wilson Park, he returned to regular church attendance: "Going to church was like going to school—there was nothing else to do. Everybody went to church out there, so I'd get myself all dressed up and we'd walk down to the little church." Additionally, the teenage Calloway mainly looked forward to bonding with other adult men in his congregation on Sunday afternoons: "Then, after church, the men would go out into the woods to shoot craps. We'd have a hell of a crap game every Sunday. Papa Jack was one of the few men who wouldn't go. He didn't believe in gambling, but I took his place and shot craps right along with the men."[31] Likely gambling with the additional income he made from his various jobs (some of which he also gave to his mother to support their family), the teenage Calloway balanced religious and recreational time on the Sabbath, despite the disapproval of his parents.

The older, reflective Calloway framed his high school social habits as representing a tension between two social worlds—the "rather puritanical" family and music teachers who were "churchgoing, middle class, strivers" versus those who enjoyed the "rough and raucous Baltimore Negro night life with loud music, heavy drinking, and the kinds of moral standards or lack of them that my parents looked down on." With his narrative, he ascribed to his younger self an independent assertiveness that made him resist fully imbibing the night life's intoxicants or fully accepting the black middle class's respectable social script.[32] In evaluating his life and career, Calloway rendered his youthful desires for personal independence as instructive and indicative of later successes in life. In his writing, he qualified his respect for black middle-class ideals with a playful irreverence toward black Protestant religious life and the expectation that young black men must be in attendance dutifully and abstain from all other tempting leisure activities.

Calloway became sexually active around age seventeen—although due to a "wandering eye" this activity was not even with his "respectable" partner at the time. He had been dating Zarita Steptoe, the daughter of the pastor of Bethel African Methodist Episcopal Church in Baltimore. Calloway remarked, "In fact, the main reason that I was going to church at all those days was to be near Zarita. But like most boys that age, I had a wandering eye." He began a relationship with Zelma Proctor, and the two shared their first sexual experience. The result was Proctor's pregnancy. Calloway wrote that while he was "uncertain" about what to do, likely referring to continuing the pregnancy, Proctor informed Calloway that she would carry it to term. Calloway decided to marry Proctor, but she declined because she considered herself too young and him to be "too fly-by-night" for marriage. Calloway recalled his mother agreeing with Proctor about not wanting to marry her son. Because Procter "had a lot of boyfriends," as Martha reasoned, no one would find him at fault for not marrying her.[33]

Calloway did not provide introspective reflections on his early romantic relationships and sexual practices. Nevertheless, his late-adolescent leisure habits, active heterosexuality, and aversion to black religious moral instruction reflected some aspects of the cultural shift from a Victorian-era production ethos that defined middle-class manhood, to a modern, postwar American ethos of consumption that fostered a sense of middle-class manliness. With this latter ethos, "the goods one owned, the leisure practices one engaged in, and one's physical and sexual virility" supplanted aspirations to respectability.[34] However, Calloway's aspiration to participate in jazz culture professionally, as a producer of music for popular consumption, strongly suggests that he did not represent the stark opposition of a modern consumption ethos to the previous generations' Victorian-influenced production ethos. Instead, Calloway's musical performance and personal practices allowed him to represent one possibility of a modern, iconoclastic black masculinity in jazz.[35] His pursuit of jazz as a viable profession for black celebrity demonstrated to working- and middle-class African Americans an alternative (and lucrative) realm of race representation in the late 1920s and 1930s, one that promised broad national media exposure and existed independent of higher educational training, licensing, or ordination.

Without any money, Calloway and Proctor left Baltimore for New York. Calloway found regular pay performing in Atlantic City speakeasies, clubs, and restaurants. Proctor decided to travel to New York on her own to stay with an aunt, and they parted ways, with Calloway returning to Baltimore. Although he recalled regretting not being in the life of his daughter, Camay, he stated that he continued to support his daughter financially and that he had developed meaningful relationships as an adult with Proctor, Proctor's husband, his daughter, his son-in-law, and his grandchildren.[36]

Calloway completed high school in 1927 at age twenty, while continuing to perform in local Baltimore clubs. Calloway admired his older sister, Blanche (1902–1978), who had already entered the entertainment industry and had become one of the stars of the musical *Plantation Days*. Blanche lived and worked in Chicago, and Calloway intended to follow her after high school. She and his mother permitted Calloway's ambition for musical success only if he also promised to enroll in coursework at Crane College. Calloway agreed and moved to Chicago with his sister, where she arranged for him an audition for *Plantation Days* (he was cast as a high-tenor singer). Calloway attended Crane Junior College for free because he lived at Blanche's Chicago residence. After January 1928, about four months into schooling, Calloway returned to part-time singing: "It was a different kind of life when I started to sing again. I didn't really have time to study, so I started to cheat a bit. I had a little girl who used to do my work. She would write my papers and helped me to get ready for tests. Thelma Eubanks was her name. I needed her help because I was beginning to get into everything again, just like I had in high school."[37]

Calloway eventually made his way to New York City and Harlem by late 1929 after performing with several bands. Calloway's orchestra became the famous Cotton Club's replacement band for Duke Ellington whenever the latter musician and his orchestra were on tour. In 1931 he recorded his most famous tune, "Minnie the Moocher," which featured his "Hi-De-Ho" call-and-response with the orchestra that he would replicate with audiences for the rest of his career. The black press noted his sudden rise. A 1931 *Pittsburgh Courier* special feature on Calloway created a "respectable" narrative for his life by noting his church choir roots in Baltimore's Bethel AME Church, by portraying him as monogamous with the mention of his wife, Wenonah Conacher (mistakenly called "Denoanah Corey"), and by depicting him as a family man who "likes a nice medium steak cooked by his wife, smokes a pipe, and attends an AME Church whenever he can." The piece also noted that Calloway recorded two songs, "St. James Infirmary" and "Is That Religion?"[38] However, the messages and representations Calloway produced through such music conflicted with his press presentation as the respectable result of black Protestantism.

Musical Mimicry of the Ministry

In 1930 Calloway and his orchestra recorded a cover of "Is That Religion?," a comedic criticism of sexual impropriety in black houses of worship written by African American composer Maceo Pinkard and Jewish American lyricist Mitchell Parish. Duke Ellington and His Orchestra also recorded a version of "Is That Religion?" in 1931. This music composition entered a culture where images of black preachers and churchwomen were the constant fodder of comedic portraits. African American music scholar Teresa L. Reed notes that for a popular audience, Ellington's version, sung by a preacher character in "a highly theatrical, burlesque singing style," helped to reinforce the stereotype of African American churches as "place[s] not of devotion but of unbridled sexuality."[39] The Calloway version featured the bandleader as preacher (or elder), accompanied by "call-and-response" vocals from a chorus. His arrangement imitated the era's popular black phonograph preachers who employed a "staged and primed studio congregation" to enhance their sermons with "singing, clapping, shouts of affirmation, and popular music."[40] According to a *Chicago Defender* article in April 1931, the Calloway version of "Is That Religion?" was "adjudged one of the best discs of the month." *Pittsburgh Courier* reader Annette Brown wrote to the paper that "Is That Religion?," as performed by Belton's Florida Syncopators, was one of her favorite tunes.[41] With his version, Calloway performed a musical imitation of folk sermons that revealed his deep familiarity (and perhaps exhaustion) with this African American tradition.

The tune begins with Calloway the preacher calling and responding to his choir:

> Brethren
> Sisteren
> I got shoes, you got shoes
> All God's children got shoes!
> Brethren (*Yeah! Sing it, Brother!*)
> Sisteren (*Yeah!*)
> Oh, hear my preachin'
> Hear my preachin', do! (*Yes, Elder!*)
> Brethren (*Yeah! Glory!*)

Sisteren (*Yeah! Have mercy!*)
The Good Book teachin'
Ain't been reachin' you! (*Ain't it true, ain't it true?*)

Sisters strut the aisles
All dressed to kill with style
You wink your eye and smile
Is that religion? (*Oh, you've got me, preacher!*)
One thing I do despise
You catch my deacon's eyes
That's where the weakness lies
Is that religion? (*Tell 'em all about it!*)

You see, your parson's vexed [*churchwoman's response*]
Doggone it, you've got him so preplexed [*woman and man respond*]
Now, you know doggone well, my mind ain't on my text!
Now, tell me, is that religion? (*That's it, brother*)
You know there's gonna be some cheatin' did [*antiphonal singing*]
You all done took me off my lid
Tryin' to get your parson to skid
Now you know doggone well that ain't religion![42]

The remainder of this foxtrot tune contains an instrumental version of the melody, featuring a solo accompanied by the church sister saying "Amen, Amen!" to the muted trumpet. The initial, brief singing of the spiritual "All God's Children Got Shoes" indicates that this tune's object of humor is the southern African American Protestantism that Calloway's preacher represented. Parish's lyrics employ the term "parson" for the minister, and the black chorus's use of the titles Elder and Brother when responding to each of the preacher's lines locates the song firmly within black Protestant and Holiness-Pentecostal traditions. Calloway the preacher's rising and falling inflections in the lines "One thing I DOOO despiiiiiise / You catch my DEAcon's eyyyyyyes" serve as instances revealing his familiarity with the melodic whooping of black folk sermons. And the tempo of the song is well suited for dancing, so the contemporary hearer may imagine phonograph listeners dancing along to Calloway's sermon about ministerial promiscuity.

With the Ellington version of this tune, the sisters who wink and "strut the aisle" and the parson who is "so perplexed" appear to share equal blame for their sexual impropriety and moral hypocrisy.[43] With Calloway as the preacher, however, this character is clearly most deserving of ridicule—he blames the women of his congregation for arousing himself and his deacons, he implies that they are at fault if (and when) he or others pursue each other, and he is someone whose refinement and education are questionable, evident in his use of the colloquial exclamation "doggone it" and the pronunciation of perplexed as "*preplexed*." The responses of the church members become ironic, punctuating the preacher's lines as he vents his sexual frustrations and admits his carnal intentions. Calloway and the other voices structure this humorous performance for those familiar with Sunday sermons to enjoy. They focus on a recognizable instance where church settings appear to have latent sexual tensions. And they voice the suspicions of some regular (yet unenthusiastic) black churchgoers who may suspect that the ostensibly devout experience the same sexual desires as others.

According to Calloway biographer Alyn Shipton, this song performance was an artistic instance of using a record "not so much to satirize religion, but to use its familiar tropes as a new way to engage an audience." However, given Calloway's autobiographical reflections about his adolescent disdain for church attendance and fondness for the church sisters his age, it is probable that he enjoyed the opportunity to sing his opinion that he and the black clergy he encountered shared similar desires. And more so than Ellington's version, Calloway's arrangement of "Is That Religion?" conveyed the musician's familiarity with black Protestant "low-church" preaching through its imitation of prominent black phonograph preachers and their recorded sermons. So while it is accurate that Calloway employed black sermonizers' race record genre "as a setting for entertainment . . . in the very kind of nightclub most frowned upon by preachers of the type Cab was emulating" and that this was a "genuinely original" innovation in this era of jazz, his performance is more critical of a particular religious setting, cast of conventional characters, and muted sexual tensions for many black Protestants than previous interpretations have concluded.[44] To perform "Is That Religion?" in clubs on Saturday nights leading into the Christian Sabbath may have allowed patrons, alongside radio and phonograph listeners in their homes, to revel in a popular musician identifying with church experiences they anticipated witnessing the next morning in service—if they planned to be awake and to attend.

Desire "ain't religion" for Calloway. Nevertheless, the musician humorously celebrated desire and its unavoidable presence in the religious lives, practices, and associations of African Americans. In the early years of his career, Calloway and his orchestra performed "Miss Hallelujah Brown," with lyrics by Benny Davis and music by J. Fred Coots, and they recorded the song in 1938:[45]

[Male chorus] Hallelujah, Hallelujah!
[Calloway] Was the lady's name when she sang in the choir [Hallelujah]
[Male chorus] Hallelujah, Hallelujah!
Since she left the old church choir
Brother, she's a bowl of fire!

Who's got the fellas prayin'?
Who's turned things upside down?
Who goes without saying?
Miss Hallelujah Brown
Who's got the gals all squirmin'?
Who's goin' right to town?
Who's got a new sermon?
Miss Hallelujah Brown!

She don't do no preachin'
'Bout the Lord above
She confines her preachin' to
That precious thing called love

Don't blame the fellas, do ya
The way they hang around
Hats off and here's to ya
Miss Hallelujah Brown![46]

This Calloway arrangement follows the lyrical portion with call-and-response phrases between the horns and clarinet soloist, solos from trombone and tenor saxophone, and a reed feature with horns. It concludes with Calloway proclaiming, "Hallelujah! Hallelujah! / Hallelujah for Miss Hallelujah Brown!" Davis and Coots were prolific white vaudeville song composers and performers, and unlike Calloway's performance of "Is That Religion?," his arrangement of "Miss Hallelujah Brown" does not attempt to reproduce the familiar sounds of African American churches. Instead, his decision to perform this white songwriters' tune indicates a celebration of its lyrical depiction of an attractive, formerly pious, "fast" black woman (her racial identity presumed according to the given last name) who offers carnal excitement for men, engenders resentment from other women, "preaches" an erotic love, and does not regret backsliding.

Calloway's vocal presence in motion pictures also celebrated irreverent living in African American culture. In the 1933 animated Betty Boop short film *Snow-White*, Calloway voiced Koko the Clown for a performance of the popular tune "St. James Infirmary." Calloway's famous dancing appeared in the film due to rotoscoping, an animation technique that involved tracing over footage of his live "dance-walk" moves (and Koko the Clown transforms into a long-legged ghost). His version of the lyrics, substituting "hallelujah" for "hell" in one line, indicated what he considered a jazz man's appropriate funeral celebration: "Then give me six crap-shootin' pallbearers / Let a chorus girl sing me a song / Put a red-hot jazz band at the top of my head / So we can raise hallelujah as we go along."[47] Calloway's irreverence in this performance highlighted the gambling habits, women, and music he preferred as worthy of high praise rather than damnation. And while the Louis Armstrong recorded version of "St. James Infirmary" ended this verse with "Raise hell as I stroll along," Calloway's version substituted "hallelujah" for "hell" because the Motion Picture Production Code forbade the use of the latter word. To "raise hallelujah" further provided an affirmative spin on this popular dirge as a song to celebrate a jazz man's lifestyle and its material, carnal, and musical delights. Rather than support popular disregard for jazz living as socially and culturally adverse for African Americans, as with a "worldly" man's funeral procession that "raised hell" or created posthumous social disruption, Calloway's vocal performance and altered lyrics to "raise hallelujah" rather than "hell" in this jazz procession affirms a jazz man's passing as a "holy death" worthy of celebration.

Calloway wrote that he "converted in the 1930s" to the Episcopal church and was "still a firm believer in church and in God. I don't think of myself as a religious person. I love to live. I like the good life. I enjoy entertaining and I get as much satisfaction out of giving people pleasure as I do out of going to church. Maybe entertaining is my way of expressing godliness. Lord knows, there are worse ways."[48] But what was a "religious person" for Calloway? Was it someone inclined to "get happy" through ecstatic religious expressions, as "Harlem Camp Meeting" preached? Was his Episcopalian affiliation a signal that he wished to participate in a religious tradition that did not emphasize shouting or dancing as signs of holiness or devotion? If Calloway was not suggesting a direct rejection of certain African American worship practices, then perhaps to be a "religious person" was to avoid living "the good life" that he celebrated in his music. For Calloway the Episcopalian, providing joy to others through entertainment was personally gratifying and an acceptable vocational objective in lieu of dutiful church attendance. But with the suggestion that there are "worse ways" of "expressing godliness," is it possible Calloway was referring to types of religious worship he found either distasteful, insincere, or hypocritical? Ultimately, it is not difficult to misinterpret this brief reflection and overlook what Calloway offered: a constructive but vague appreciation for institutional religious life and a fundamental belief in the divine. He lived as if religious irreverence was compatible with religious belief and belonging.

From Comedian to Ribald Race Representative

Calloway's humorous takes on black Protestant church life became early models for African American artists who sought to produce critical black humor about shared cultural experiences, practices, and social figures as novel music for black buying populaces to consume and enjoy. But there was an inherent peril in this media's commodification. It was accessible to white audiences, offering tacit permission for them to deride and pathologize African American religious beliefs and practices, in addition to black sexuality—or to continue doing so, now with the music of Calloway and others as further black cultural data. As we have seen, modernist religious race representatives in the 1920s and 1930s criticized both "old-time" black Protestantism and black popular music for the very reason that white scrutiny and judgment of African American culture presented a constant impediment to their pursuit of social equality through race representation. And these preachers were likely to criticize black musicians who sang white lyricists' words about humorous aspects of black culture as complicit in the effort to maintain Jim Crow's system of racial discrimination. However, it is important to acknowledge that African American musicians may have written or composed this music, because whites in the professional music industry were often likely to receive songwriting credits and royalties for compositions by uncredited black composers. For instance, jazz publisher Irving Mills had a contract with Duke Ellington early in his career that permitted adding his name to Ellington's song credits; consequently, he received royalties for several compositions by Ellington and his orchestra musicians (whom Ellington often did not credit as sole composers or co-composers).[49]

Popular black musicians like Calloway faced a dilemma if they worked to create and perform musical expressions that celebrated and criticized aspects of African American culture. Musical celebrity, and the potential for cross-racial appeal, came with visibility for African Americans and the assumption that popular art captured representations of some ingrained cultural disposition. In other words, white audiences may have perceived racial performance to be coterminous with racial essence. Consequently, Calloway and others became de facto race representatives. One instance of this perceived representativeness occurred in 1932 when Rev. Dr. Christian F. Reisner, the white pastor of New York's Broadway Temple Methodist Episcopal Church, invited Calloway to perform on a Sunday evening to revive the "old-time religion." In the words of the *Philadelphia Tribune*, Reisner asked Calloway "to play some moving Negro spirituals for his cold-blooded white worshipers" because, in Reisner's words, "what we need is more of the old-fashioned thrill in religion."[50] If racially progressive white ministers regarded Calloway as the bearer of an African American religious music tradition, then there was no guarantee that the performer's intent matched popular receptions of what his career and cultural production through music represented.

To create comical musical performances about African American racial identities and religious practices, Calloway's fraught task was to present a form of humor about and for black people through jazz, but without permitting a designation of black people as essentially and enduringly ignorant and degenerate, as minstrelsy's mockery offered. And with minstrelsy, there was a history of songs mocking spirituals or African American respectability politics in light of material want.[51] As Calloway's career advanced, this tension became more pronounced as the singer and bandleader made groundbreaking professional achievements in motion pictures, where his racial representation existed alongside competing images of minstrelsy.

For instance, Calloway signaled his role as race representative during the filming of Al Jolson's 1936 film *The Singing Kid* when he and his orchestra clashed with Warner Bros. executives because they refused to don "whiteface" for a publicity photo with Jolson in blackface.[52] That the black press took note of Calloway's opposition in this instance indicated their support for him as a commendable African American entertainer. They counted his refusal to perpetuate certain racial caricatures as a professional achievement.

The Singing Kid represented Calloway's professional rise and the waning of Jolson's career. While this film was a commercial failure, it was also interesting—and ultimately incoherent—for its attempts to provide "an explicit autocritique of the old-fashioned content of Jolson's past while maintaining some of his modernist form and style" and also seeking "to both erase and celebrate boundaries and difference, including most emphatically the color line."[53] This film contains three scenes with Calloway and Jolson (as "Al Jackson") appearing together, a cautious attempt to present a social message of visual integration while elevating Calloway to the same status as Jolson in the entertainment world. At first, Calloway and Jolson sing opposite each other from "separate-but-equal" penthouses. Next, Calloway performs in a "Broadway" scene that includes the theme of religious revival, and the white actors appear as blackface characters among the African American singing and dancing club patrons. Finally, Calloway and Jolson sans-blackface appear together as white and black entertainers (of course, the all-white audience in this last scene reaffirms the film's visual sign of racial segregation). The Broadway scene is set in an African American nightclub and features the Calloway-written "Hi-De-Ho in Your Soul." Following this song are the Harold Arlen compositions "Who's the Swingin'est Man in Town" and "Save Me, Sister," which music and film scholar Arthur Knight classifies as a "mock sanctified" song—it contains a reference to the spiritual "Sometimes I Feel Like a Motherless Child."[54] Actress Wini Shaw's blackfaced-angel performance appears before "Save Me, Sister," and she and Calloway produce a sermonette that features "old-time" religious themes and melodic whooping:

[*Blackface angel*] Do you hear that thunder?
[*Black chorus*] Yes, we hear that thunder!
[*Calloway*] Well, that ain't thunder!
[*Black chorus*] Well, now we wonder, if that ain't thunder
Then what is thunderous thunder?

[*Calloway*] That rowin' you is hearin' in the sky-blue rafter
Is nothin' but the devil doubled up with laughter. [*whoop*]

He's puttin' on his top horn (Chorus: *Yeah!*)
Brushin' off his tail (*Yeah!*)
He's gonna throw you bachelors out like
Jonah from the whale!

[*Blackface angel*] Cuz there's too much sportin' and not enough
    courtin'!
[*Calloway*] [*whoop*]
[*Blackface angel*] There's too much high-life'n' and not enough
    man-and-wife'n'!
[*Calloway*] [*whoop*]
[*Blackface angel*] There's too much fancy turtledovin' and not enough
    real lovin'!
[*Calloway*] And the glutton who goes struttin' after every sportin'
    duchess
Will find himself a-wriggling in the giggling devil's clutches![55]

For Knight, this medley appears to "take seriously, if superficially, the potential in black culture(s) for interconnecting 'opposites'—in this instance the secular and the religious, 'swing' and 'spiritual,'" and he further concludes that both Calloway and Jolson appear to be "saved" in this performance as a result of "switch[ing] styles from the religious to the secular." Knight's primary aim in analyzing this film is to determine the musical and performative contrasts between Jolson-as-Jackson and Calloway, with an understanding that Calloway's purpose in the film was to introduce American audiences to a more vibrant, modern sound and style that African Americans were producing.[56] However, it is important to recognize that both Calloway and the angel are preaching—literally bringing a divine message into the nightclub—with Jackson alone as the attentive respondent and first-person voice in "Save Me, Sister." This performance of a stereotyped "fire and brimstone" sermon on (black) male sexual promiscuity and habits of enjoying urban nightlife, in lieu of faithful monogamy, renders this African American sermonic style and its typical messenger(s) a comically moralizing presence in modern American life.

This medley elevates a style of black religious parody to the national stage, albeit also as a racially deprecating display that likely affirmed preexisting disdain for black Protestantism as fundamentally unserious or foolish, in addition to disregard for African Americans as perpetually in need of salvation or reform. Additionally, the film had a white songwriter, producers, and blackfaced white actors who performed in front of one of the era's most popular African American swing orchestras and against the backdrop of the black club patrons-turned-choir—and in this film, like many others, the African American vocals are from the Hall Johnson Choir. Consequently, the question of who was permitted to laugh at these black characters stood alongside the question of who benefited from this religiously irreverent and racially derogatory performance. Ultimately, as Knight notes, the black press appreciated Calloway's performance in The Singing Kid as "a too rare opportunity to see a popular black performer on screen—and on screen for more than just a couple minutes or in a narrative role that straightjacketed him or her in a demeaning stereotype."[57]

The older Calloway offered autobiographical insights into his thoughts about race and racial identity in this earlier period of his career. Writing in an era when "black" became the preferred label for African American racial identity, Calloway recalled identifying primarily as "Negro" or colored: "To call somebody black was an insult; and, of course, to call me black, light-skinned as I was, was a triple insult." His performance of the

1932 song "A Strictly Cullud Affair" by Maceo Pinkard along with lyricist Allen J. Neiburg celebrated his generation's exclusively "colored" spaces that encompassed the variety of African American skin hues, which the song's lyrics highlight:

> When your spirits are low, there's a place you can go
> You never see white folks, at a strictly cullud affair.
>
> See 'em layin' 'em down, boys, they goin' to town
> You'll see a few light folks, but they all got cullud folks' hair.
>
> It's given by the cullud ladies' auxiliary
> Come on, brothers, check in all your artillery.
>
> Spend your nickels and dimes, have some marvelous times
> I mean it's too tight, folks, at a strictly cullud affair.[58]

As one of the many "light folks" with "cullud folks' hair" (although he straightened his own), Calloway remarked on others' (mis)perceptions about his skin tone: "Whenever people ask me where the white blood in my family is, I tell them, 'Hell, there was a nigger somewhere back there who jumped over the fence—and, man, something happened.'"[59] Labeling this interracial sexual practice "nighttime integration," Calloway offered the colloquial belief that many other white Americans who made assumptions about their racial identity without knowing their family history likely had ancestors who "jumped a fence and integrated them the quick way, without busing or anything," in comical reference to school integration practices. Because his Baltimore youth was racially segregated, Calloway did not encounter white racial hostility. When he entered the music industry, he was required to perform in segregated venues and travel through all-white areas.[60] However, Calloway recalled that his light complexion led him to experience some hostility from other African Americans:

> Even black people have given me a hard way to go sometimes. They've called me dirty yeller and poor white. That went on for years in the thirties and forties. Some people were bothered because they couldn't clas-

sify me easily; they thought I was Cuban or Puerto Rican. It's a horrible thing when people want to classify you or resort to name calling, but I've come through it because I've always known, from the day when I was a nigger kid selling papers and hustling shoeshines and walking hots out at Pimlico—hell, I'm a nigger and proud of it.[61]

Apparently, racial irreverence accompanied religious irreverence for Calloway. His use of the racial slur when recalling the "hustling" past that led to his successful and lucrative career signified the determined work ethic embodied by Calloway and others who often bore that pejorative label. But with this reflection, Calloway also indicated his experience with colorism, when people used his complexion to perceive his ethnic identity as other than African American. He sang the 1930 tune "Yaller," a composition by Charles M. Schwab and Henry Myers. "Yaller" was socially significant for its assertion that lighter-complexioned African Americans—regarded as "yellow" or "high yellow"—were disregarded by blacks and whites for not fitting this American racial binary. The song's melancholy lyrics reflected the "neither/nor" social place for African Americans of his complexion. The lyrics may have even indicated that lighter-skinned African Americans were utilized for race representation with their prominent positioning in black Protestant church services as prayer leaders or vocalists. Calloway reflected a sentiment of someone who had experienced social disregard mixed with token visibility in respectable social settings, both because of his skin hue. With the song's closing lyrics, Calloway offers a prayer to God to fit within American racial categories that are as radically opposed as the religious categories of sinner and saint.[62]

Of his racial identity, Calloway wrote, "I've always accepted the fact that I'm Negro. I don't know anything else. I've been kicked in my ass all my life because of it, and, hell, I've come through it and become a star. . . . The only difference between a black and a white entertainer is that my ass has been kicked a little more and a lot harder because it's black."[63] Speaking of "nighttime integration" may have been Calloway's method to use humor to deflect scrutiny of his perceived racial identity in his youth, given prevalent criticisms of individuals whose appearances did not comport with American racial constructs. Ultimately, Calloway confirmed his African American racial identity. His cultural production as an entertainer was a conscious project to present traditions of African American song, dance, composition, language, and humor that reflected his life experiences. However, in an early jazz era that was not entirely distinct from minstrelsy, a lighter-complexioned African American man satirizing other African Americans and receiving support from both black consumers and an industry that white music executives, producers, managers, and club owners controlled raises some questions. Which individuals were able to profit from humor directed at darker-skinned black populations, even if these people were the intended audience for the humor? Given his rise in the entertainment field and the further recognition he earned for jazz, to what degree was Calloway the beneficiary of racism because of his lighter complexion? Was Calloway perceived by white audiences as a racial intermediary, capable of interpreting African American culture, religion, and life through comical music in a manner that ultimately makes him complicit in racial stereotyping or possibly the racialized maligning of black religious habits? To what extent was his satire of African American Protestantism inherently (or inadvertently) racist? Calloway's religious irreverence, attendant with racial irreverence, was a fraught cultural undertaking for which he was socially responsible as a race representative in a popular music profession.

The social circles of Calloway's wife, Zulme "Nuffie" Calloway (née MacNeal) (1915–2008), reveal his ascent into the world of conventional African American middle-class respectability as a jazz entertainer who assumed responsibility for his cultural output (see figure 2.1). Nuffie was a Howard University graduate with a master's degree in sociology, and she studied with the African American intellectual Alain Locke. Her previous employment included working as an assistant to then NAACP attorney Thurgood Marshall, working as a civil servant for the Federal Housing Authority on race relations, and working as a typist and researcher for social scientist Gunnar Myrdal's influential study of race relations, *An American Dilemma: The Negro Problem and Modern Democracy*. She was an administrative secretary in the Department of Housing when she met Calloway in 1942. One of her friends was John H. Johnson, founder of the Johnson Publishing Company, which produced *Negro Digest* as well as *Ebony* and *Jet* magazines.[64]

As Nuffie recounted in her husband's autobiography, she was raised to avoid association with popular artists like Calloway: "I was taught

Figure 2.1. Zulme "Nuffie" and Cab Calloway arriving at Heathrow Airport. London, United Kingdom, August 18, 1955. (Photo care of PA Images / Alamy Stock Photo. Reprinted with permission.)

that show people are evil, low life, and inferior, but Mama also brought me up, as a Christian, to respect each individual as a person." She attributed this formation to her eventual acceptance of Calloway and his band members: "So when it came down to it, and these men turned out to be loving people and gentlemen, my better instincts prevailed and all my prejudices melted."[65] The two moved in different social circles, however, and Nuffie recalled her husband's apprehension to fraternizing with her friends:

> My world, the world of Washington's Negro intellectual class, was as different for Cab as his world was for me. And he was just as intimidated by my friends as I had been by his. I tried to get him involved in the parties and functions of my group[66] in Washington. He resisted; he didn't like the idea of parties where the people stood around making delicate, intellectual small-talk and smoking pipes and discussing politics. Cab was

a gambler, and while gentle, his natural milieu had been among rough, tough-talking, earthy folk.

In 1943 Nuffie eventually persuaded Calloway to attend a "typical DC Negro upper-middle-class party" with her. She recounted that at first, Calloway was drinking by himself in a corner; however, a group that included NAACP executive secretary Walter White conversed about racial discrimination. Calloway "had experienced some of the worst of it—his was the first major Negro band to make a great deep-South circuit." White invited Calloway into the conversation, and "just about every man in the place was huddled around Cab listening to his stories about traveling with a big band through the South." Nuffie's assessment was that these African American elites "had, in effect, acknowledged Cab's wisdom and intellect. . . . Walter did love and respect Cab greatly, and years later, when some of the Negro organizations protested the revival of *Porgy and Bess* as demeaning to black people, Walter White spoke out most strongly that *Porgy* was a folk opera and that it should be a source of pride."[67] Ironically, Nuffie would have been the ideal spouse for Calloway in the eyes of his mother, Martha, given her elite education, the commitment to African American progress evident in her professional work, and her social circles. As Nuffie and Calloway's social acquaintance, White was a prominent race representative who also advocated for the federal government to provide buses for black swing bands to travel through the South in the 1940s.[68]

Nuffie was likely responsible for encouraging her spouse to publish his thoughts on race relations in opinion editorials for the black press, like his November 1949 contribution to the *Philadelphia Tribune*. Calloway addressed the concern of an unnamed African American who was to make a speech on "The Negro's Place in Motion Pictures" to an African American audience. For Calloway, the place of any black person in the motion picture industry is "where he is suited. If he's an expert cameraman, his place is behind a camera. If he's a musician, he should be blowing a horn or leading a band. If he's an executive type with executive abilities, his place is as an executive." A push for "the equality of races" should trump concerns about any singular "place" for black entertainers, and Calloway noted that the film industry was becoming cognizant of African American talents in a variety of professions: "Hollywood is learning, slowly," wrote Calloway, "that a Negro actor need not necessarily play the part of a maid, Pullman porter (named George), or Zulu native. And Hollywood needs to learn a lot more about colored people. . . . One of the things which has made me most proud of my race is that many, many of our people have refused to admit that they were restricted in their efforts because of their color." The "invisible line" of racial distinction failed to discourage African Americans from pursuing a host of professional occupations, including scientists, executives, sports figures, bakers, and shoe clerks. Ultimately, Calloway expressed the hope that the nation would recognize the African American man or woman who treads into new professional territory as "an individual with a purpose and not a Negro with a 'place.'"[69] In these written moments, the comical musician advocated social integration in the same manner as his middle-class African American clerical contemporaries. Duke Ellington, Calloway's other contemporary, was also working to render jazz as an option among the black professional elite, while black ministers disregarded it as a vestige of the immoral and low-down, similar to the blues. With many jazz entertainers, America saw the emergence of race men and women unsanctioned by African American Protestant religious leaders, institutions, or press. However, did jazz men like Calloway and elite educated black preachers share an object of ridicule—the hypocritical, greedy, unlettered, promiscuous preacher—because they were both working to carve out a "New Negro" professional status and claim some prominent form of race leadership in public?

Conclusion

Cab Calloway tells of the time he sneaked into his daughter's bedroom to hear her say her prayers before retiring. The tiny girl's voice was barely audible and Cab interrupted with: "A little louder, dear, I can't hear you."

"That's all right, daddy," she replied. "I'm not talking to YOU!"

—Irv Kupcinet, *Chicago Times*[70]

The reflections of Calloway, a jazz musician who parodied others, ultimately reveal not so much a call to remove oneself from African

American religious practice, but more the option to take seriously the embrace of a less "intense" religious existence. To embody religious irreverence meant that one did not pretend to be highly devout, and one acknowledged that desire persisted for everyone, including preachers. Calloway's jazz profession poked fun at the African American religious subjects he knew well. His musical comedy was a form of entertainment that he found morally acceptable, given the hypocrisy he perceived to be widespread among religious folks. His anti-religious humor offered mockery for black audiences to enjoy without urging them to renounce or abandon their beliefs and practices.

In terms of showmanship and combined singing and dancing talent, Calloway's legacy is established through a lineage of entertainers like James Brown, Prince, Janet Jackson, Usher, and more. However, several of Calloway's performances demonstrate that he also prefigured more than five decades of twentieth-century African American entertainers who were familiar with black Protestant Christianity engaging in their own displays of religious and racial irreverence: Louis Jordan's popular 1944 record "Deacon Jones"; Langston Hughes's weekly short story column in the *Chicago Defender* from the 1940s through 1960s about Jesse B. Semple, along with his 1956 play *Tambourines to Glory*; Flip Wilson's performance as "Reverend Leroy" of the "Church of What's Happening Now" on *The Flip Wilson Show* in the early 1970s; Arsenio Hall's performance as "Reverend Brown" in the 1988 film *Coming to America*; and a host of stand-up comedians, represented perhaps most clearly and consistently in Rickey Smiley's act focused on black churches and his performance on stage and radio as elderly church member "Bernice Jenkins." In the twenty-first century, Aaron McGruder's television series *Black Jesus* as well as the YouTube comedy of religious entertainers like Lexi Allen and The Playmakers, as shown in Allen's "Things Black Folk Say at a Funeral" and The Playmakers' "How to Shout in a Black Church," sit within this comedic tradition on African American religion.

Preachers, and musicians like Calloway, are professional performers who have honed distinctive artistic styles. They may perform nostalgia for audiences by singing songs that evoke their audience's memories of childhood in both contexts. They may also perform nostalgia by adopting older and familiar dialects, colloquialisms, sayings, anecdotes, and metaphors. In the professional jazz arena, nostalgia operated to elevate the African American folk religious sensibilities that often provided comical fodder for Calloway's musical productions.

While embracing irreverence at times, some jazz women and men performed laudable race representations through other direct and indirect aspects, outcomes, and responsibilities of their profession as musicians. The following chapter on jazz vocalist Ella Fitzgerald explores the concerted work to render jazz a viable celebrity profession for race representation, resulting in Fitzgerald's emergence as a race representative with considerable "crossover" appeal and the ability to foster desegregation and to support activist civil rights organizations. These outcomes were shared pursuits with religious race professionals, who once considered it unthinkable for popular musicians in the jazz world to accomplish them.

3

"Tears of Joy"

Ella Fitzgerald is a great philanthropist. She gives so generously of her talent, not only to the public, but to the composers whose works she performs. Her artistry always brings to mind the words of the Maestro, Mr. Toscanini, who said concerning concert singers, "Either you're a good musician or you're not." In terms of musicianship, Ella Fitzgerald is "Beyond Category."
—Duke Ellington, "Portrait of Ella Fitzgerald"[1]

An arrangement for Ella is only a framework within which to move. She will do all kinds of things within that framework. Often she'll add a new twist or improvisation, even when we're actually on stage performing. She may lag behind the beat a bit or move ahead of it, but she always knows exactly what she is doing. What would be musically risky for other singers, she pulls off easily. She rarely sings a song exactly the same way she did last. But we've played together so long that no matter what she does, we are all right there together.
—Tommy Flanagan[2]

A major singer must swing, improvise imaginatively, and phrase instrumentally. But a major jazz singer must also make each song reflect what he has lived and experienced. Musicianship, however skillful, is not enough. And Ella, technically brilliant as she is, is not emotionally open enough in her singing to merit a place in the first rank of jazz singers. After all these years, do we know yet just who Ella Fitzgerald is? And if she has indeed revealed all there is to tell, there is not enough there for the best of jazz.
—Nat Hentoff, "Is Ella a Great Jazz Singer?"[3]

Ella Jane Fitzgerald (1917–1996) was very protective of the tragic details of her turbulent adolescence. Fitzgerald was born in Newport News, Virginia, to Temperance "Tempie" Williams Fitzgerald, a laundress, and William Fitzgerald, a transfer wagon driver. Tempie and William were not married, and Tempie eventually partnered with Joseph Da Silva, an immigrant from Portugal. The couple moved with Tempie's child to New York as part of the Great Migration, and Tempie and Da Silva had a daughter, Frances (whose son Ella Fitzgerald later adopted upon her sudden death). When Fitzgerald began grade school, the family lived in Yonkers in a poor, multiethnic community of black Americans and Italian, Irish, Greek, and eastern European immigrants. Fitzgerald attended Sunday services and Sunday school at Bethany AME Church, which moved to Yonkers in 1925. Annette Miller, a neighbor of Fitzgerald, recalled to biographer Stuart Nicholson that the children of her block attended each other's churches, broadening Fitzgerald's religious experience by lessening the degree of her exclusive involvement in Bethany AME's activities. In addition to singing, Fitzgerald enjoyed dancing and initially aspired to the latter as her profession.[4]

Fitzgerald's junior high school education was interrupted by tragedy and mistreatment. In 1932 Tempie died suddenly from a heart attack, leaving the teenage Fitzgerald and her sister in the care of Da Silva. Following suspicions that Fitzgerald suffered physical abuse at the hands of Da Silva, Virginia Williams (Tempie's sister) took Fitzgerald to live with her family in Harlem. Da Silva also died from a heart attack shortly after Tempie's passing, and Frances joined Fitzgerald in the Williams home.

Fitzgerald's school records showed that prior to her mother's death, she excelled as a student. However, these dramatic changes in her home life led to Fitzgerald becoming "fractious" with her Aunt Virginia and dropping out of school. For extra income, Fitzgerald became a numbers runner and a lookout for a "sporting house" or brothel. In April 1933, authorities caught Fitzgerald and placed her in a Hudson River valley reformatory, now known as the notorious New York State Training School for Girls at Hudson. The fifteen-year-old Fitzgerald's offense, according to the log book entry for the "General Record of Girls Committed to the New York State Training School for Girls," was that she was "ungovernable and will not obey the just and lawful commands of her mother—adjudged delinquent." In the week following Fitzger-

ald's death in 1996, *New York Times* journalist Nina Bernstein reported
that a state investigation of the reformatory in 1936 revealed that "black
girls, then 88 of 460 residents, were segregated in the two most crowded
and dilapidated of the reformatory's 17 'cottages,' and were routinely
beaten by male staff." The Hudson reformatory's English teacher, E. M.
O'Rourke, depicted Fitzgerald as a "perfectionist" and model student
who participated in the school's choir; however, the fact of the school's
segregation and all-white choir proved this to be a fabrication (Bernstein did determine that Fitzgerald and the school's other black girls
performed with a local AMEZ church choir at the time). Thomas Tunney, who became the reformatory's last superintendent in 1965 before
it closed in 1976, attempted to have Fitzgerald, by then an internationally famous jazz musician, return to the school as an honored guest.
Fitzgerald refused the invitation, and Tunney recalled his conversation
with her: "She hated the place. . . . She had been held in the basement
of one of the cottages once and all but tortured. She was damned if she
was going to come back."[5]

Fitzgerald ran away from the reformatory in the fall of 1934. Unable
to return to her Aunt Virginia's home because authorities were looking for her, she became a homeless adolescent in Harlem. Like many
Depression-era Harlemites, Fitzgerald earned tips by entertaining on the
street. It was in this environment that Fitzgerald and two of her friends
decided to enter the newly instituted Wednesday Amateur Night talent
competition at Harlem's Apollo Theater. On November 21, 1934, Fitzgerald entered the Amateur Night intending to dance; however, Fitzgerald stated in many later interviews that a popular dancing duo named
the Edwards Sisters intimidated her, and Fitzgerald instead performed
as a singer. Even though Fitzgerald won first prize that night and was
guaranteed a week's performance at the theater, the opportunity did not
materialize because of her disheveled appearance due to her homelessness. In December, Fitzgerald lost a competition at the Lafayette Theatre but won another amateur night competition at the Harlem Opera
House. Although she received the reward of a week's performance at the
venue, Fitzgerald received no pay, likely due to the Opera House manager deducting the cost of wardrobe he provided her because she had no
suitable clothing. Fitzgerald's young age, appearance, and homelessness
prevented her from securing paying work. It was not until Charles Lin-

ton, a singer for Chick Webb's orchestra, brought Fitzgerald to the Savoy bandleader's attention that her fortunes changed significantly.[6]

The jazz vocalist Ella Fitzgerald rose to superstardom as a racial crossover artist, and her early career was critical to securing jazz as a profession for race representation. Fitzgerald was a homeless, "delinquent" adolescent when she emerged as a popular vocalist for Chick Webb's swing band, and she became a symbol of a respectable African American woman to counter the negative characterizations of the jazz world as corrupting of youth. Her career in the late 1930s, 1940s, and 1950s became an effective vehicle for the desegregation of performance venues and the creation of integrated clubs, due to her popularity with black and white audiences. Fitzgerald's race representation included her status as a wealthy African American woman who provided for her extended family and who made charitable investments in civil rights organizations, particularly the Southern Christian Leadership Conference (SCLC). Importantly, Fitzgerald showcased the jazz profession in several aspects as a nonreligious vehicle for accomplishing the progressive, integrationist pursuits of religious race representatives.

In various ways, this highly visible race representation entailed constant black and white press coverage and critical assessments of Fitzgerald, requiring of the professional vocalist a carefully crafted public image protected by herself, her publicists, and her managers. Fitzgerald never divulged much of the early hardship she experienced in her youth. Instead, she chose to present a simplified or truncated "rags-to-riches" biography as well as a joyful and optimistic persona to the public. This persona, coupled with the nature of her vocal instrument and crossover appeal, resulted in two major and recurring debates: whether Fitzgerald constituted a legitimate jazz singer, and whether her perceived lack of emotion in performance disqualified her as an authentic black jazz woman vocalist. These debates, and Fitzgerald's public religious representations through her music—commercially innocuous, comically entertaining, and professionally serious—are significant even as they provide no detailed certainty concerning her personal religious beliefs and practices, given her decision to remain a relatively private public figure.

Fitzgerald's professional career allows for a focus on racial perceptions of black women in the jazz profession, in addition to the racial and religious representations black women produced. A complete portrait of Ella Fitzgerald is impossible, given that she produced no memoir and rarely granted interviews. Accordingly, four portraits of Ella Fitzgerald reflect aspects of her professional identity that various publics throughout her career engaged, appraised, and displayed proudly. Since she was a prominent black celebrity, these were inherently portraits of race representation. The first portrait is of Fitzgerald's coverage in the black press between the 1930s and early 1960s, through the black press writers who helped the maturing artist craft her professional image as a female race representative. The second portrait showcases Fitzgerald's contribution to civil rights activism. The third highlights the critical portraits of Fitzgerald's singing and the attendant questions over her vocal authenticity as a jazz artist and black woman. The last portrait showcases public representations of African American religion through some of Fitzgerald's studio recordings and live performances.

Portraits of Enchantment

Black press outlets in New York City presented articles claiming hometown pride in Fitzgerald's rise to fame, and they offered the public a rags-to-riches tale of Fitzgerald that placed Chick Webb as the savior who immediately recognized her talent, despite contrary recollections of Webb's initial lack of interest in Fitzgerald. A June 1937 story reprinted in the *Atlanta Daily World* lauded Fitzgerald through various popular and ostensibly intimate titles, including "First Lady of Swing," "the dusky peacock of rhythm," "the Dusky Maid of Rhythm," and "our little Nell," whom Webb heard "tearing her heart out over what was to be her last stand for theatrical fame." What followed was the enchanting tale of the orphaned amateur Fitzgerald's discovery by the bandleader who immediately identified her potential for fame:

> Turning to his personal manager, he said: "She has every quality I am seeking. She has youth, abundant vitality, and above all else—freshness. How I hope she is willing to be taught a few things." Webb's wish was granted. When he talked with her, he found her not only willing, but eager to learn the musical ways of this strange little man who had waited many years for such a voice personality as hers. In her, Webb knew that he had found the queen to do right by his kingly syncopation.[7]

Other scholars of Fitzgerald and Chick Webb's orchestra have already discussed this fabricated account of his initial encounter with the young singer. However, this narrative—likely circulated by Webb's manager, Moe Gale, or Decca Records—plays on themes of royalty seeking and identifying the perfect companion, a tale that established the bandleader as both a tastemaker for a legitimate musical profession and a responsible mentor to a younger musician. Webb's romantic enchantment is not erotic in this tale, and this presentation reflected the reality that his paternal role for Fitzgerald entailed keeping potential male suitors and their marriage proposals away from the young vocalist.[8] Instead, Webb's objective was to protect Fitzgerald and to cultivate her young, vital, and fresh professional talent into something greater.

Webb was from Baltimore, and black press pride in his successful orchestra meant other writers covering the rise of his new vocalist. Lillian Johnson's piece for the *Afro-American* in October 1937, titled "Ella Fitzgerald Hasn't Let Success Spoil Her," implicitly assured black audiences that Fitzgerald's involvement with Webb was thoroughly beneficial. Johnson profiled the twenty-year-old vocalist in a manner that distinguished the jazz artist as a respectable woman, one whose sensible taste in professionally minded young men indicated her aspirations to black middle-class notions of social stability. The interview occurred while Fitzgerald had an appointment at the La Blanche Beauty Parlor (Johnson conducted other interviews with Fitzgerald during salon appointments), and she quoted the singer as preferring "men in conservative, well-fitting clothes" while also seeking "a pretty little home, somewhere in the suburbs of New York State" more than she cared about owning fancy vehicles or fur coats. She was a modern artist who was able to read music without the need for extensive practicing, who played, in her words, "a little harmonica and a little piano," and who "doesn't have the superstitions that most theatrical folks have, although she respects the opinions of others on broken mirrors, peanuts, etc." Fitzgerald did not smoke or drink, but she "didn't think it was harmful if it didn't go to excess." The jazz vocalist was also fond of pets and children, and she informed Johnson of her intention to produce a children's broadcast in New York City "not so much for the purpose of discovering talent as for the purpose of giving the children something interesting to do and keeping them out of mischief." Johnson affirmed succinctly Fitzgerald's personal tastes and aspirations, stating, "All of [this] bears all the earmarks of a trend to domesticity." Despite the singer's admitted penchant for extravagant hats, Johnson wrote, "Ella does make an effort to keep the Fitzgerald budget tidy, although she admits that if something comes into view that she likes, the budget suffers—for that time anyway." Financial responsibility included Fitzgerald managing her own bank savings account and US Postal Savings account, from which she made no withdrawals. Johnson worked to convey to the black press readership that Fitzgerald and Webb constituted a socially and financially responsible pairing, with the young vocalist demonstrating the qualities of a proper black role model.[9]

A discussion of Fitzgerald's "shyness" on stage led to a conversation about the band's national travels, revealing Fitzgerald's (and Johnson's) progressive optimism concerning racial integration:

> She's traveled everywhere these last three years, sometimes by bus, sometimes by train, East, West, North, and South. She has seen a lot of color prejudice, but it never worried her much.
>
> "I sometimes hear that colored people are not allowed to go here or there, but if we're supposed to go, the manager usually arranges so that we get in with no embarrassment," she said.
>
> "For instance, a group of white college boys came to the show and invited me to come to the Delta Rho fraternity dance at the Lord Baltimore Hotel Sunday night."
>
> "Someone told me that colored people weren't allowed to use the front entrance and the elevators, but when I got there, a group of the boys met me, and we went in, and nobody seemed to take any notice of it."
>
> All through the South, she found that people, white and colored were friendly, and even in Texas, Mississippi, and Alabama, they came backstage to congratulate her and talk to her when the show was over.
>
> Seriously, she thinks the prejudice is not as strong in the younger generation as it was in their elders, and that given time, it will die out.[10]

Fitzgerald reiterated her optimism concerning integration by supporting Benny Goodman's decision to hire two African American jazz musicians, guitarist Charlie Christian (1916–1942) and pianist Fletcher Henderson (1897–1952), for his orchestra. *Down Beat* magazine reported

Fitzgerald's endorsement of Goodman's actions in October 1939: "I believe the hiring of colored musicians in a white band is really mutually beneficial. Both races have a lot to offer each other. It would be hard to understand the advisability of racial distinction where artistry in musical advancement is concerned. The interchange of musical ideas between both races surely must be broadening in influence."[11] Whether the *Down Beat* quote came directly from Fitzgerald, from her manager, Moe Gale, or from her publicists, it comported with Fitzgerald's commitment to desegregation that she expressed in other interviews and racially integrated performances.

Fitzgerald's later experiences with racial segregation and discrimination marked this interview content as ominous. Nevertheless, her celebrity activism continued to reflect her optimistic commitment to racial integration as she matured. What Johnson's profile provided black readers was an "intimate" portrait of the popular black female vocalist. Here, she was devoid of any trace of the social corruption that black and white critics attributed to jazz music, swing culture, and urban nightlife. And she was on a sure path toward laudable race representation through celebrity, motherhood, and interracial progressivism.

The notion of a constructive, professional relationship between Webb and Fitzgerald proved valuable for the black press as writers promoted these jazz musicians' work as legitimate and morally innocuous, particularly when tragedy befell the swing orchestra. The death of Chick Webb in 1939 led to the black press's portrait of Fitzgerald as a genuine, appropriate griever. By rendering the lyrics of a popular song as a mourning tune, Fitzgerald's participation in Webb's funeral service exemplified a jazz professional's understanding of proper affection within a religious space. Waters AME Church in Baltimore hosted Webb's service, where Fitzgerald performed the 1922 song "My Buddy" by Walter Donaldson and Gus Kahn. The *New York Amsterdam News* reported that Fitzgerald's attire and demeanor were appropriate for the black Protestant environment: "Dressed in black, Ella had been at the side of Mrs. Sallye Webb, widow of the orchestra leader from early Tuesday morning until late last night." The paper noted that Sallye Webb "was in constant distress" and that Fitzgerald set aside her own emotional distress to console others: "Despite her grief, however, Ella Fitzgerald had gone about comforting other members of the Webb family and steeling herself for the ordeal she

Figure 3.1. Ella Fitzgerald and an unnamed nurse assist Sallye Webb at Chick Webb's funeral in Waters AME Church. Baltimore, Maryland, June 20, 1939. (Photo care of Bettmann / Getty Images. Reprinted with permission.)

was to face that afternoon at the church." The press portrayed Fitzgerald's moral commitment in aiding Webb's grieving survivors as evidence of the late bandleader's proper mentorship of the young jazz vocalist. Although she inhabited the licentious realm of Harlem nightlife, she revealed mature commitments to family and community through comfort and memorialization (see figure 3.1).

"Grief wracked every muscle in the supple body of this brownskinned girl" was the paper's characterization of Fitzgerald as she held the microphone in front of the Waters AME funeral congregants, composed of "brown, white, black, and yellow" faces. Showcasing the interracial appeal of Webb, Fitzgerald, and the band afforded a simultaneous recognition of the integrated funeral ceremony as a social achievement that Baltimore's black Methodists hosted. This moment revealed a shared commitment between jazz and religious professionals—racial integration and the valuation of African American life and talent by the broader society. But the paper reiterated Fitzgerald's commitment to honoring her musical mentor in a socially appropriate manner, despite the "heartless cameramen from daily and weekly papers [who] flashed their bulbs in her face" while she sang. The funeral of this jazz musician was a private and public event, with "thousands milling like refugees in Aisquith street in front of the church" able to hear Fitzgerald's "heart-broken message over the amplifier." In this moment, Fitzgerald demonstrated the authenticity of her relationship with Webb and of her commitment to her professional craft by singing through her tears to honor him. The paper reported debates over the appropriateness of having Fitzgerald sing, with a response from an unnamed musician claiming that her participation confirmed her professional chops:

> Some criticism was heard that she shouldn't have been permitted to sing such an emotional song. Others contended she had been hurt enough by the death of Webb and shouldn't have been called upon to appear on the program at all. However, one musician declared:
> "That's what Chick would have wanted. It takes tests like these to see if you've got it in you to be a real performer. She's true blue!"[12]

Webb's death put the band's tour through the South on hold, but this narrative portrayed Fitzgerald as emerging from this loss of her friend as a mature vocalist. Her resolve compelled her authentic performance during his ceremony. Fitzgerald had proved herself viable in the black press and beyond as a reliable young race representative, respectful of religious spaces, and as a jazz vocalist who was a legitimate black musician of the highest caliber.

With Fitzgerald's emerging status as a legitimate jazz professional and race representative came visibility for her service to others. During her engagement at the Howard Theatre in Washington, DC, in September 1941, she reserved one Saturday night to perform at the Twelfth Street YMCA for a United Service Organization (USO) program.[13] She devoted three weeks in March 1947 to providing a free "song clinic" for four younger African American women who worked to become jazz vocalists. While not promising their employment, she guaranteed the women recommendations to various bands. Fitzgerald's motivation for her clinic experiment was to be charitable to those who could not afford the cost of singing lessons: "Opportunities are so limited for our ambitious girl singers to get any assistance whatever. The situation is even more difficult for these who can't afford to pay for training. I feel that perhaps we who have made our mark can do a wise and charitable thing to lend them some encouragement."[14]

Fitzgerald also affirmed and made legitimate the aspirations of other black celebrities to religious vocations. Bill Bailey (1912–1978), the tap dancer who was one of the stars of the 1943 film adaptation of *Cabin in the Sky*, turned away from the entertainment profession in order to become a minister. Bailey was also the brother of Fitzgerald's friend, singer and actress Pearl Bailey (1918–1990), and he set out to build a Harlem church. In October 1949 the *Pittsburgh Courier* announced that after four years of preaching, Bailey was to have "a mammoth Gospel revival at the Golden Gate Ballroom" on October 23 to raise funds for a "Church of Christ." Scheduled to perform that day were "Ed Sullivan, Sugar Ray Robinson, Ella Fitzgerald, Madeline Greene, Willie Bryant, Josh White and Pigmeat Markham."[15] For her jazz profession, Fitzgerald symbolized a moral presence by supporting her fellow entertainer's Christian ministry.

Fitzgerald's value as a race representative to black press writers was evident in E. B. Rea's "Uncompromisingly Yours . . . What Price Glory in Filmdom" in April 1942, which defended Fitzgerald against a Hollywood press release that attributed racist stereotypical speech to her. Fitzgerald's motion picture debut occurred with the 1942 Abbott and Costello comedy *Ride 'Em Cowboy*, where she played Ruby. As Ruby, Fitzgerald performed her signature song, "A-Tisket, A-Tasket," up and down the aisle of a bus. The scene maintained visible segregation by having Ruby return to her seat in the bus's rear, behind all of the white riders, at the close of the song.[16] Ruby had various subservient roles, including a cook and a rodeo clown, but Rea remarked that Fitzgerald "portrayed the part creditably." A press release recounted the interaction between *Ride 'Em Cowboy* director Arthur Lubin and Fitzgerald, following Ruby's appearance in a rodeo scene that contained live animals. Rea provided the offensive excerpt:

> Ella Fitzgerald . . . got her camera baptism while surrounded by thirty wild steers used in a rodeo sequence. Everything was all right with Miss Fitzgerald except for the behoofed steaks, of which she wanted no part.

When the scene was finished, Director Lubin congratulated the badly frightened newcomer on her performance.

"Mr. Lubin," she replied, "but I'se glad I done okay, this job sho am going to change my mode of livin.'"

Rea remarked, "This writer has conversed with Ella Fitzgerald enough to know that those words were expounded by the white man." She criticized "the language of Hollywood's publicists" that belittled black entertainers in order to ensure their films' profitability among white audiences that were ill-disposed toward any messages or scenes of racial equality in motion pictures. The quote that the press release attributed to Fitzgerald was an insult "to a star revered as 'America's queen of swing vocalizing,' and embarrassing to all who know that Ella Fitzgerald couldn't be such a composer, rave-exponent of song, and such a public figure without a better mode of expression—unless the script called for this reversion to illiteracy."[17] Since Ruby's dialogue did not reflect the attributed quote, any association of Fitzgerald with such speech was possibly credible only with audiences unfamiliar with the famous vocalist.

In the early years of performing, Fitzgerald benefited from favorable black press portraits that posed her promising career and its racially progressive prospects as a stark counterargument to criticisms of a youth culture invested in swing entertainment as leisure. Her career also posed a response to criticisms of jazz as a purportedly immoral and racially counterproductive vocation. Optimism and responsibility—interpersonal, social, and professional—appeared inherent to Fitzgerald's character. Additionally, they were essential to progressive racial projects to showcase black talent and social propriety in the pursuit of desegregation in all social aspects.

Following her years with Chick Webb's band, Fitzgerald emerged as a solo artist. With the assistance and guidance of new professional management, she built a career that solidified her national prominence as a race representative. As part of Chick Webb's orchestra, Fitzgerald had Moe Gale as her manager since her career began in the 1930s. Following a series of performance tours with Jazz at the Philharmonic (JATP) in the 1940s and 1950s, which jazz impresario Norman Granz (1918–2001) arranged, Fitzgerald left Gale and Decca Records and selected Granz as her new manager in 1956. Granz proved consequential to shaping the rest of the vocalist's prominent career. Granz committed to raising the profile of the vocalist he considered "the greatest singer of our time," seeking to move Fitzgerald into more prominent performing venues beyond the clubs and ballrooms she toured under Gale's management. This increased popularity also meant moving her financially beyond what Granz deemed the "Fifty-second Street money" of her career performing solely in New York City clubs.[18] This objective also involved Fitzgerald's presence as a musician who desegregated performing venues and fostered the establishment of integrated ones. Most notably, Marilyn Monroe (1926–1962) advocated for Fitzgerald to perform at the Mocambo in Los Angeles in 1955, and 1956 saw the establishment of Pandora's Box, the Purple Onion, the Crescendo, and the Renaissance as integrated nightclubs in Hollywood.[19] Granz's management of Fitzgerald's life was controversial. Her professional and personal acquaintances deemed Granz too controlling of the singer, with Granz deciding to remake Fitzgerald as a "pop-jazz" singer while also vetoing opportunities for her to record with certain established jazz musicians, including her friend Frank Sinatra (1915–1998). What came from their partnership was the symbol of Fitzgerald as a success story for the promise of racial integration in America, and Granz framed his overbearing managerial role positively when recalling that he secured Fitzgerald a Hollywood residence by bypassing de facto segregation standards.[20]

Fitzgerald, now the owner of a mansion, added a domestic dimension to her public portrait—she had become a wealthy black jazz woman who lived in her Beverly Hills home with her son, Ray Brown Jr. (b. 1949). A November 1961 *Ebony* magazine article by Louie Robinson, titled "First Lady of Jazz," showcased Fitzgerald's economic stability as the head of a household and the wealthy provider for an extended family.[21] By the 1960s, Fitzgerald was a symbol of black professional success, and her public image became that of a jazz vocalist who toured (inter)nationally while maintaining a normal and relatable domestic life. Her career represented a celebration of racial integration, both in her commercial appeal and in her domestic residence. The prospect of her positive influences upon future generations provided a prominent public case that African Americans' ongoing battles for desegregation and increased economic opportunity were wholesome, critical domestic endeavors for the nation. And because of professional experiences with discrimination, Fitzgerald also made visible her financial commitments to activist organizations working toward desegregation.

Portrait of Engagement

Jazz musicians participated in civil rights organizations as a general support of their work and not necessarily to endorse one organization's ideology or tactics over those of another. These artists "seemed to respond to particular events in the civil rights movement rather than show exclusive loyalty to particular organizations," revealing that "practical political action often carried greater weight than ideological purity, especially in times of crisis."[22]

Participation in charity benefits had been a consistent practice for many jazz professionals, and Fitzgerald had been making these performance appearances since the early years of her career. With Chick Webb's orchestra, Fitzgerald participated in the Savoy Ballroom's "Scottsboro Defense Ball" from 10:00 p.m. Friday, February 21, to 4:00 a.m. Saturday, February 22, 1936. Partying patrons paid either seventy-five cents in advance or a dollar at the door to support the fund of the National Committee for the Defense of Political Prisoners, a civil liberties organization working to acquit nine African American teenagers falsely accused and convicted of raping two white women in 1931. Other entertainers that night included jazz vocalist Mildred Bailey (1907–1951) and blues vocalist Bessie Smith (1894–1937).[23] In this instance, urban nighttime recreation and entertainment served to benefit social activism. In 1947 Fitzgerald suggested that a national union of all social and charitable agencies should exist to "serve as a clearing house and accrediting agency for the endless stream of demands on performers for benefit concerts." The Norfolk Journal and Guide reported that because Fitzgerald knew that she and many other musicians were unlikely to refuse charitable performance requests, "very often it turns out that the so-called 'benefits' are nothing more than promotions by unscrupulous operators." New York's Theatre Authority held sanctioning power over these events in order to check their validity, and Fitzgerald advocated the establishment of a central body for touring musicians. The Chicago Defender reported that the head of New York's Theatre Authority endorsed Fitzgerald's call.[24] The next year, Fitzgerald headlined at Chicago's State

Lakes Theatre for its inauguration of a new policy to feature the "integration of artists in all future bills without regard to race, religion, or nationality." The *Philadelphia Tribune* reported, "Miss Fitzgerald cut short an engagement at Bill Berg's in Hollywood in order to accept the engagement at the State Lakes. She felt that such a progressive experiment deserved the fullest cooperation of every forward thinking artist."[25]

Firsthand encounters with segregation influenced Fitzgerald and many others in their financial support for civil rights organizations and activism, proving that prominent entertainers were not immune from racial discrimination. Fitzgerald had scheduled a first-class Pan Am flight on July 19, 1954, from San Francisco with her cousin Georgiana Henry (also her personal assistant) and Modern Jazz Quartet pianist John Lewis (1920–2001) for performance dates in Australia. During the flight's stopover in Honolulu, Fitzgerald, Henry, and Lewis were removed from their seats to make room for white patrons, forcing them to remain in Honolulu for three days and causing the cancellation of the Sydney concerts. Granz took legal action, and the suit "was eventually settled out of court for an undisclosed sum."[26]

While touring with JATP in Texas in October 1955, Fitzgerald and trumpeter Dizzy Gillespie were set to perform in Houston, the home of tenor saxophonist Jean-Baptiste Illinois Jacquet (1922–2004). Jacquet refused to play to segregated audiences in his hometown, and he had witnessed the role of Catholic churches in Texas, New Orleans, and Kansas City in hosting both integrated dances and traveling jazz bands.[27] JATP had previously performed to raise funds for the NAACP, and this group of musicians set out to provide Houston with its first major desegregated concert. Granz recognized that Fitzgerald was a major draw for JATP concerts, and he used her audience demand to ensure Houston Music Hall's desegregation that evening. Granz removed the "white" and "black" signs from the restrooms, and he refused to pre-sell tickets in order to prevent white patrons from purchasing self-segregating seat sections.[28] Following the musicians' first set of the evening, five armed officers from Houston's vice squad entered Fitzgerald's dressing room in plain clothes, and they arrested the vocalist, Henry, Gillespie, and Jacquet without a search warrant.[29] Hearing the arrest, Granz entered Fitzgerald's dressing room and saw a police officer entering the bathroom. Granz suspected that the officer intended to plant narcotics in the bathroom, and he confronted him, stating, "I'm watching you." The officer put his gun on Granz's stomach and responded, "I oughta kill you." They arrested and charged the group, including Granz, with gambling (Gillespie and Jacquet were playing craps in the dressing room corner at the time of the arrest). The vice squad booked the group, made them pay a fine, asked for their autographs, and released them in time for the second concert set that night. There were reporters and photographers at the police station when the group arrived, indicating that the police encounter was a sting operation. The humiliation and publicity of the incident led to more integrated concert performances, and Jacquet performed in Houston the next year to such an audience without police interference.[30]

Experiencing racial discrimination led musicians to support activist civil rights organizations. The previous year, on May 28, 1954, Fitzgerald joined Harry Belafonte (b. 1927) and Steve Allen (1921–2000) at the Eastern Parkway Arena for a concert to benefit the Brooklyn NAACP. During the summer of 1960, Fitzgerald appeared at the Stamford, Connecticut, home of Jackie Robinson (1919–1972) along with Duke Ellington, Joe Williams (1918–1999), Sarah Vaughan (1924–1990), and Carmen McRae (1920–1994) for an "Afternoon of Jazz" to benefit the student sit-ins of the Congress of Racial Equality (CORE) and the Southern Christian Leadership Conference (SCLC).[31] Jesse H. Walker's May 18, 1963, "theatricals" column in the *New York Amsterdam News* named Fitzgerald, along with soul singer Jackie Wilson (1934–1984) and actor Frederick O'Neal (1905–1992), as three eager financial and moral supporters of the "Back Our Brothers" movement to aid the Birmingham civil rights effort. The nature of their support included contacting President Kennedy, donating money to the movement, and contacting five other prominent or celebrity acquaintances to do the same.[32]

Fitzgerald appeared partial to supporting the SCLC, and she used one of her scheduled stays at Hollywood's Crescendo Supper Club in 1963 to perform a one-night benefit for Martin Luther King Jr.'s organization. Fitzgerald, with trumpeter Roy Eldridge (1911–1989) and the Tommy Flanagan Quartet, agreed to donate the musicians' normal proceeds for the two performances that night, and the club owner Gene Norman agreed to donate all other proceeds.[33] A spokesperson for Fitzgerald announced that the engagement netted $5,000 for the SCLC (more than

$41,000 in 2018 dollars). The Associated Negro Press reported that the
Los Angeles City Council cited Fitzgerald for her civil rights efforts, and
the press quoted Fitzgerald on the event: "'Even the musicians donated
their pay for the night to this crucial cause,' Ella said, 'and everyone went
out of their way at added expense to make sure that the Crescendo was
packed that night so that I could show my deep support.'"[34]

Fitzgerald composed few songs during her career, but her modest description of a 1968 song she wrote as a tribute to King offers one of her
assessments of the slain civil rights religious leader she admired:

> FITZGERALD: I composed a little thing up in Vancouver about Martin
> Luther King. . . . I've had so many requests for it, called "It's up to me
> and you, to make this dream come true." It's very simple, it's nothing
> jazzy or nothing fancy like that. . . . They all seem to like the melody,
> and it's simple enough that it's not a whole lot of mush.
> BILLY TAYLOR: Well, it's the way you felt.
> FITZGERALD: Yeah, I didn't put too many things in it, because he was
> not the type of man that believed in too much fiery things, so the
> song I didn't feel should have been like that. It felt like it should just
> be soft.
> TAYLOR: Well, he was a very gentle person.
> FITZGERALD: Yes, well to me, that's the impression I had.[35]

The official title of Fitzgerald's song was "It's Up to Me and You," released
on Capitol Records, with Fitzgerald composing the lyrics and music and
with Benny Carter (1907–2003) conducting and providing the orchestral
arrangement. Fitzgerald's sentimental delivery and Carter's orchestration highlighted the emotion with which she sought to honor King's
memory and to advocate the nonviolent pursuit of social justice and
racial integration. Additionally, Fitzgerald's simple, politically mainstream lyrics revealed her straightforward appeal to general American
audiences that no doubt included all age groups.[36]

In what is the only known recorded live performance of "It's Up to
Me and You," at the Chautauqua Institution in New York on July 11, 1968,
Fitzgerald revised her lyrics to "So down with hate and let's not wait,"
indicative of the vocalist's more assertive appeal when singing for her
audiences on the road.[37] Later that year, the Martin Luther King Foun-

dation named Fitzgerald its honorary chairman, and all proceeds from "It's Up to Me and You" were to benefit the organization established in honor of King's legacy.[38] At "Ella's Night," a ceremony in December of that year, Fitzgerald received New York City's first "Cultural Award" for "exceptional achievement in the performing or creative arts." She also was the first entertainer to become an honorary member of the Alpha Kappa Alpha (AKA) sorority. As part of the ceremony, the blind pianist and composer Valerie Capers (b. 1935) played and sang "It's Up to Me and You" as part of a medley of songs associated with Fitzgerald. AKA sponsored "Ella's Night," and all receipts went to the sorority's scholarship fund and to the King Foundation. *Jet* magazine quoted Fitzgerald upon receiving her honors that evening: "This is like a dream that I didn't believe would ever happen. It only shows that love is such a beautiful, special thing, love all over the world. This is a memorable night for me; I hope I live up to it."[39]

Granz and Fitzgerald both recognized her role as race representative for black audiences and to non-black audiences. But this cross-racial appeal as a popular entertainer also meant that some critics questioned Fitzgerald's placement within the jazz tradition, evincing assumptions about racial essence in music consumption.

Critical Portraits

Concurrent with becoming Fitzgerald's manager, Granz established Verve Records, the label that chronicled her transition from recording primarily singles for Decca Records to recording the "Great American Songbook" standards that helped to define her international prominence in the 1950s and 1960s. This beginning period with Verve in 1956 and 1957 also saw Fitzgerald recording three landmark albums with Louis Armstrong, including *Ella and Louis* in 1956, *Ella and Louis Again* in 1957, and *Porgy and Bess* in 1957.

There was an unintended consequence of casting Fitzgerald as a pop-jazz singer. In this role, she produced a massive songbook catalog of American musical standards with orchestral backing. These recorded studio performances contained less vocal improvisation from Fitzgerald herself, as opposed to the liberties she took while on tour, where she deployed more melodic improvisation, scatting, and varied tempos while a jazz trio or quartet accompanied her. Based on her studio albums, critics scrutinized the authenticity of Fitzgerald's vocal performances and declined to consider her a genuine jazz singer. This chapter's third epigraph is from a column by jazz critic Nat Hentoff (1925–2017) in the 1962 debate-editorial "Is Ella a Great Jazz Singer?," which he wrote for *Hi Fi/Stereo Review* with Leonard Feather (1914–1994), who affirmed Fitzgerald's status as a jazz singer. Jazz critics and audiences expected musical performance, especially performance recorded and reproduced on albums, to reveal authentic existence, not simply musical skill and training. Hentoff regarded Fitzgerald as "an above-average pop vocalist but a minor jazz singer" and an "accomplished stylist" similar to two white jazz musicians, Frank Sinatra and Peggy Lee (1920–2002). Hentoff declared that Fitzgerald appeared unable to convey or to access the emotional depth that he expected to serve as the link between a jazz vocalist's lived experience and the lyrics of a jazz tune, whether her own or by a professional lyricist.[40]

Hentoff's full qualifications for a vocalist to be a "complete, full-strength jazz singer, like Billie Holiday, Louis Armstrong, or Jack Teagarden" included swinging and phrasing, instrumental singing, and timbre. In these three categories, Hentoff claimed, Fitzgerald exuded technical virtuosity but lacked a proper conveyance of (or the physical ability to convey) some musical essence. With swinging and phrasing, Fitzgerald "appears unconcerned with the meaning of a song's lyrics" and "swings in an emotional and intellectual vacuum . . . neither remain[ing] faithful to the original nor creat[ing] a new story." With instrumental singing, the vocal approximation of jazz horns, reeds, and percussion, Fitzgerald was strongest as a scat singer but often "sound[ed] like an extraordinarily fluent but dehumanized horn." She exemplified vocal acrobatics that "[were] brilliantly sustained, but they have less to do with self-expression than with mechanics." Hentoff again contrasted Fitzgerald with Billie Holiday, claiming that "there was not the slightest doubt about the complex nature and uniqueness of a human personality when Billie sang." Concerning timbre, Fitzgerald's voice was "naturally rather thin and lacking in intensity." Although Hentoff compared Fitzgerald to Mildred Bailey in terms of similar vocal range, he deemed Fitzgerald deficient because of Bailey's ability to personalize her vocal performances through improvisation and to convey a "maturity" that Fitzgerald's voice lacked. Fitzgerald "too often sounds like a child, and although much popular music is based on the fantasies of actual or arrested adolescents, the essence of jazz has certainly never been for children."[41] Hentoff concluded by asserting that authentic jazz had its basis in lived experience, quoting bassist Milt Hinton ("What makes a great jazz-man is experience") and Charlie Parker ("If you don't live it, it won't come out of your horn"). Hentoff added a hypothetical comparison of Fitzgerald performing two landmark jazz songs: "Imagine, if you will, Ella Fitzgerald singing *God Bless The Child* or *Good Morning Heartache*, and then compare Billie Holiday's approach to the same songs. The difference is rather like that between paintings by Norman Rockwell and Ben Shahn."[42]

Considering Hentoff's assessment, it becomes ironic that Fitzgerald recorded "Good Morning Heartache" with the Lou Levy Quartet for the 1961 studio album *Clap Hands, Here Comes Charlie!* and performed the song into the 1970s to honor Holiday. Fitzgerald also recorded "God Bless the Child" for the 1982 studio album *The Best Is Yet to Come*. But in Hentoff's estimation in 1962, Fitzgerald was childlike in voice, purely technical in proficiency, devoid of sufficient vocal emotionality, and seemingly lacking a genuine dramatic jazz man or woman's lived experiences. For these reasons, she lacked vocal jazz virtuosity and authenticity.

Nat Hentoff and the jazz critic Gunther Schuller (1925–2015) both "positioned Fitzgerald as a cheerful singer of trivial music, rather than as a soulful and serious vocalist."[43] Fitzgerald's voice placed her within a category containing other popular black singers, like Billy Eckstine (1914–1993), Chuck Berry (1926–2017), Jimi Hendrix (1942–1970), and Dionne Warwick (b. 1940), who "[did] not perform musical racial personae as expected."[44] In the mid-1930s, Fitzgerald was invaluable to Chick Webb's band as the group's vehicle for garnering commercial (meaning white mass audience) success. It was in this capacity that (white) jazz critics implicated Fitzgerald "in the process of 'whitening' and thereby compromising the integrity of the band, even as her great talent was recognized."[45]

When popular music criticism emerged in the 1930s, it was "related to the strongly leftist, anti-capitalist project of social transformation with which those constructing the nascent field of critical jazz discourse aligned themselves." These white male critics represented an elite group of jazz fans with the economic, social, and intellectual means to launch magazines and newspapers in the United States, England, and France. They valued ultimately a progressive political project of defining black artists as the creators of culture from positions of oppression. They provided accounts and analysis of live and studio performances for a readership of record-collecting fans of jazz and swing music. And some of these men, namely, John Hammond, Leonard Feather, and Norman Granz, became impresarios with the industry power to shape public perceptions of musicians. They defined a jazz canon through their control of performance and recording opportunities.[46] Consequently, Fitzgerald's career began in the swing era against a "discursive backdrop in which ideals of artistry were set in opposition to commercialism," and black jazz musicians who achieved viable livelihoods through profitable, national careers inevitably became subject to scrutiny for their music's racial authenticity.[47] Jazz criticism privileged the instrumental over the vocal, attendant with the industry reality that men dominated the instrumental realm and women were the genre's few, prominent vocalists.[48] The criticism that Fitzgerald drew as the overwhelmingly popular black singer fronting Chick Webb's band revealed her disruption of the traditional vocal role of a "girl singer" for female band performers and demonstrated "the rigorous cultural work that built and policed the masculine aesthetic of 'pure jazz' and the homosocial space it maintained."[49]

For critics, Fitzgerald established her evolution from the role of a "girl singer" fronting a big band to a "serious musician" who was able to jam with male instrumentalists through the use of "scat" vocals in her singles recordings of the mid-1940s, particularly her very popular recordings of "Oh, Lady Be Good!" and "Flying Home" in 1945 (released in 1947). Her tour of the American South with fellow bebop pioneer Dizzy Gillespie further established this musical credibility.[50] "C-Jam Blues," a 1972 jam session performance with Count Basie and his orchestra as well as instrumentalists named the "JATP All-Stars," demonstrates a live "battle" from Fitzgerald's later career decades. This performance recalled her JATP concerts in the 1940s and 1950s, in addition to her international tour with the Ellington orchestra in the mid-1960s.

But as a solo artist in the late 1940s, and during her continued ascent in the 1950s, Fitzgerald also weathered shifting criticisms that again relegated her professional style and output to the periphery of jazz, now regarded widely as artistry distinct from a popular commercial endeavor. The universal consensus was that Fitzgerald was not capable of being a blues singer, having a light voice instead of the "low, hoarse, or twangy sound" of the genre's classic singers, and she fell victim to the conflation of "the musical idiom of the blues with a performer's personal sense of tragedy."[51] Fitzgerald's disinclination to sing the blues entailed the dissociation of her particular black female public presence from notions of sexual suggestiveness, an outcome that also meant critics referred to her as "a non-erotic companion, either a mother figure or a little girl." Because of her scat recordings, some critics occasionally refrained from accusing her of performing inauthentic jazz or musical "whiteness"—but even this form of vocal improvisation was not sufficient to locate Fitzgerald firmly in the category of black women's authentic, emotional musicality.[52]

In the jazz profession, it became a dilemma if an African American woman did not conform to audiences' cultural expectations about how black women should sound and *which* emotions they should convey, based on preconceptions about black jazz musicians' biographies. For Fitzgerald, "the cheerful, joyful affect of many of her performances distanced her style from common tragic conceptions of the blues idiom, which are so intimately linked to an ideal of musical blackness."[53] Illustrative of this affect and its stylistic distancing is Fitzgerald's performance of "I Can't Give You Anything but Love" at the Newport Jazz Festival in 1957. Her immediate vocal improvising for each of the three choruses—the first her own rhythmic and melodic style, the second imitating the "Chee-Chee Girl" Rose Murphy (1913–1989), and the third imitating Louis Armstrong—meant that no chorus reproduced the song's original melody in this vocal jazz performance. Although each chorus represented a different African American vocalist, the comedic effect of the latter two impersonations, evident in audience laughter, was Fitzgerald's self-representation of a joviality well distanced from conceptions of a more serious, blues-inflected, and tragic musical blackness.[54]

Fitzgerald's critical and popular listeners developed an "aural understanding of a white middle-class voice" from her specific vocal qualities.[55] Indeed, beyond Fitzgerald's specific vocal qualities, songbook recordings of lyrics espousing the cosmopolitan vacationing of Harold Arlen's "Let's Take a Walk around the Block," the leisure itinerary of Richard Rodgers's and Lorenz Hart's "Manhattan," familial relations as with George and Ira Gershwin's "My Cousin in Milwaukee," or the cultural touchstones referenced in Cole Porter's "You're the Top" certainly made Fitzgerald's vocal instrument the soundtrack for white middle-class sensibilities and experiences to which most African Americans in the 1950s and early 1960s would not have related. Norman Granz may have helped Fitzgerald accomplish a racially significant statement by situating her, an African American woman, as the major vocal interpreter of popular American lyricism in the twentieth century through her exhaustive recordings. However, the cultural cost of occupying this prominent professional position was the dissociation of Fitzgerald the jazz vocalist from a black aural and cultural identity, at least from one of the sanctioned public performances for black women that critics within the profession determined.

In reality, Fitzgerald was a major female jazz vocalist whose personal hardships were evidence of a tragic, racialized existence. She had experienced the death of her mother in her youth, physical abuse by her stepfather, homelessness, institutionalization, and the torture associated with black women in reformatories. Fitzgerald was unable to conceive her own children, likely from a medical procedure early in her career. At age twenty in 1937, Fitzgerald had a relationship with Vido Musso (1913–1982), an Italian tenor saxophonist in Benny Goodman's orchestra. By December of that year, she was rumored to be pregnant and was not on tour with the Webb orchestra. Whether from the pressures of the musicians' professions and management, taboos against interracial unions, or both, it is likely that Fitzgerald sought an abortion. The medical procedure apparently went awry, leaving Fitzgerald unable to conceive.[56] She was also the victim of physical assault by a "rabid" male audience member during a performance.[57] Additionally, several romantic relationships Fitzgerald believed to be genuine were actually motivated by financial exploitation; her first marriage, to Benny Kornegay, resulted in an annulment.[58]

Fitzgerald attempted to keep these biographical details from the public; some became known right before and after her death. To arrange her biography around these traumatic life details might have led critics to a different assessment of Fitzgerald's fit with conceptions of musical blackness and its emotional modes of conveying racial authenticity. Instead, joy was the principal emotion Fitzgerald elected to convey vocally. Frenetic tempos, which she embraced during the bebop era, breathed improvisational life into jazz standards for her decades of performance. And a "girlish" voice was her natural instrument, often conveying a youthful existence that suggested she had not weathered the racial, emotional, physical, and sexual frustrations expected of a black woman emoting musically in public. Audiences often equated singing with genuine emotion for public consumption, and Fitzgerald's voice and vocal choices both belied the reality of her experiences and signaled her mission to offer a joyous message to audiences. Up-tempo, ecstatic, scat-filled performances, like "Stompin' at the Savoy" at the Los Angeles Shrine Auditorium in 1957, represented the exuberant emotional performance and improvisation that Fitzgerald elected to present to live audiences (and the record's audio indicates that the Shrine audience more than welcomed her musical offering).[59]

For critics and audiences, expectations of black women vocalists' emotionally heavy performances echo "the reality of the sweating brow," a phrase by jazz composer and multi-instrumentalist Anthony Braxton (b. 1941). Guitarist and historian of American religions Jason Bivins has theorized Braxton's phrase as "the palpable field of racialized expectations audiences have when engaging 'jazz,' often understood to be music played by sweating, cathartic, emotionally exuberant black performers." The history of jazz discourse is subject to frameworks of religious and racial essentialisms that emerged with turn-of-the-twentieth-century white academic discourses of the religions of African-descended peoples in America:

> "Race" came to depend on "religion" as one of its fundaments, and the racial taxonomies central to American public life took shape in part via a discourse that posited black religion's innateness, emotionality, primitivism, and irreducibility. Both attraction and revulsion turned on these imagined traits, their wildness, their excess, their merging in spectacle. Jazz was born amid and took shape in these very conversations linking racial imaginaries with religious naturalism and its sociopolitical implications. So too have jazz audiences persistently recapitulated these tropes, theorizing black creativity for the creators.[60]

The expectations for black women to convey an authentic musical emotionality reflected a spectrum that encompassed the history of

performances of spirituals and the blues—and gospel music by extension, as it emerged in the mid-twentieth century. In the 1970s, Fitzgerald
spoke with pianist Billy Taylor (1921–2010) about audiences' musical
expectations for singers and deployed the term "soul" as the measure-
ment of black vocal ability, deeming herself inferior in comparison to
singer Aretha Franklin (1942–2018):

> FITZGERALD: Aretha's got her bag going with that soul. Oh boy, she's
> got so much soul, she could lend me a little of it, you know. I never
> had that kind of soul . . .
>
> TAYLOR: I can't let that statement stand unchallenged. To me, soul is
> many things. And Aretha certainly has what is the current way of
> putting it. She is directly related to the gospel feeling in music. But to
> me, I think to hear you sing the blues, for instance, or to hear you do
> some of the things that are more in the Negro tradition, then I hear
> the same quality, but in your way. And to me, it's the same as—well,
> Charlie Parker and Art Tatum had soul, but I don't think you would
> compare what they did—you wouldn't listen to them in the same way
> that you would listen to Ramsey Lewis, for instance.
>
> FITZGERALD: Right, thank you for helping me. Well, you got me out of
> that! [*Laughs.*]
>
> TAYLOR: When you do "Misty," there is no mistaking that this is Ella
> Fitzgerald's kind of soul going into a very beautiful composition by a
> jazz pianist.[61]

Fitzgerald's apprehensions in this conversation with Taylor reveal the
importance that African American women's public emotional religious
expressions maintain for assessments of racial authenticity in nonreligious vocal genres. Franklin was an exemplar of many twentieth-century
African American musicians who emerged from the black gospel tradition and translated its idioms into soul and R&B music. In her 1974
live performance of Carole King's "You've Got a Friend" at Ronnie
Scott's Jazz Club in London, Fitzgerald's call-and-response reprise playfully echoes Franklin's rendition of the song, a medley combined with
Thomas Dorsey's "Precious Lord, Take My Hand" for her landmark
1972 live gospel album *Amazing Grace*. Even though Fitzgerald's vocals
and the quartet's accompaniment provide a gospel feel for "You've Got

a Friend," as she omits the Jesus-centered message in Franklin's reinterpretation, both her improvisations and her wishing of divine blessings to the audience at the close of her set reveal the joyful intent of her public performance.

Beyond her "gospel" of joy, Fitzgerald's public "soul" was difficult to identity. The following discussion highlights performances and recordings where Fitzgerald presented her versions of religious (and racial) identity for consuming audiences.

Portraits of African American Religion

NBC reporter Bobbie Wygant interviewed Fitzgerald around 1980, and the singer reflected in modest language on her belief that divine favor was responsible for her career: "I'm happy today and I feel that all of the things that have happened have happened for a reason. And I believe in faith, and I believe in the man above, and I guess this is the way it was supposed to be." Fitzgerald also remarked on the importance of the love she felt from those who appreciated her music, even volunteering herself as an asset to the US government for resolving America's immediate hostage crisis: "As long as I've got the love of people. And that's the important thing. I think love—if I could go over to Iran and sing, and if they would let me sing, and I thought that would bring the people back, I would go over there and sing 'How High the Moon,' anything! [Laughter.]"[62]

Although Fitzgerald's religious commitments beyond a belief in God and in the value of love in human relationships remained unknown to the public, she did produce "religious" representations of African Americans in studio and live performances that arguably provided more a cultural portrait than genuine reflections of her own beliefs and practices. Fitzgerald recorded two singles with the Ray Charles Singers and Sy Oliver and His Orchestra for Decca Records in 1955.[63] With the first single, a cover of a country hit titled "Crying in the Chapel" by Artie Glenn, Fitzgerald performed a religious testimony of fulfillment and commitment that casts the song's title at odds with its mood and content, were the album's purchaser to expect a jilted lover's lament with this single. The Ray Charles Singers act as a choir to introduce Fitzgerald's explanation of her experience with a house of worship, clarifying that the emotionality that one witnessed was not the singer in distress but her religious delight. An interlude by a Hammond organ associates this arranged jazz tune with African American gospel styles; but rather than conveying a shouted religious ecstasy, the song's slower tempo and Fitzgerald's vocal delivery represent a religious commitment marked by modest prayer for daily existence, the pursuit of personal peace, a quiet and reverential awe, and intimate harmony with a religious community. Following the organ interlude, Fitzgerald attests that the listener will also find the same solace and pleasure that she found in this religious community.[64]

Fitzgerald's vocalization and Glenn's lyrics evoke a chapel without denominational particularity, although the instrumentation lends the tune some association with African American Protestant worship. And Fitzgerald's testament to the chapel reveals a valuation of a religious institution that requires a different degree of commitment, in terms of one's time and finances, than the degree of commitment a member gives to a church or denomination. A generic affirmation of divine belief and engagement in communal worship make this single palatable to various audiences of religious listeners, exemplifying music artists' attempts at both racial and genre (religious versus nonreligious music) crossover appeal.

The second single, "When the Hands of the Clock Pray at Midnight" by Mann Curtis, is a song with lyrics that capture Fitzgerald yearning for romance without a sense of an erotic commitment. Beyond the imagery of clock hands pointing upward as prayer, the lyrics illustrate that the objective of prayer is for Fitzgerald and her lover to be reunited. The Ray Charles Singers provide a more responsive choir in this song, and it contains a Hammond organ solo following a trumpet solo. Nevertheless, the song appears to have a purpose of further introducing the listener to the various musicians as a supplement to the record's first side, rather than providing even a general musical message of (African) American religiosity.[65] Milt Gabler (1911–2001), who worked for Decca Records during Fitzgerald's contract and selected "Crying in the Chapel" for her in an attempt to garner black and white crossover appeal, stated that despite her dislike of the song, the single became Fitzgerald's biggest hit for Decca in the 1940s.[66]

Fitzgerald's decision to release an album of Christian music in 1967 followed the success of Duke Ellington's Sacred Concert recording and tours. Fitzgerald initially hesitated about recording religious music, telling the *Washington Post*, "I thought it was wrong. I felt like jazz and religion didn't mix." She admired her friend, gospel singer Mahalia Jackson, and she felt incapable of following in her gospel lane: "I don't think anybody sings those songs like Mahalia Jackson. When she gets through, everybody puts them aside." However, the *Post* wrote that an unnamed preacher convinced Fitzgerald to record the album: "He told me, 'This is your talent God gave you.'"[67]

Brighten the Corner appeared from Capitol Records in 1967, when Fitzgerald and Granz briefly parted ways before formally reuniting under the Pablo label in 1973. The album was decidedly not a jazz album and featured little vocal improvisation or embellishment from Fitzgerald. Its song selections incorporated nineteenth- and early twentieth-century white Protestant hymns (including "What a Friend We Have in Jesus"), white evangelical songs (including the title song, "Brighten the Corner Where You Are"), and African American spirituals and gospel ("I Shall Not Be Moved" and "Just a Closer Walk with Thee"). These choices possibly reflected Fitzgerald's early twentieth-century AME upbringing, wherein church music consisted more of hymns and spirituals than of the emerging black gospel tradition. With the backing of a white singing unit, the Ralph Carmichael Choir, Fitzgerald signaled again her attempt at racial crossover. For the era, the album represented an imagined racial integration—in this case, an integrated, nondenominational Protestant worship experience.[68]

By contrast, comical takes on black gospel, especially evident in live concert performances, comprise Fitzgerald's playful and joyous representations of African American religious music for national and international audiences. Fitzgerald recorded "Hallelujah I Love Him So," her masculine-pronoun version of the Ray Charles 1956 debut single "Hallelujah I Love Her So," for her 1962 studio album *Rhythm Is My Business*. Like other Ray Charles recordings, this song was a romantic play on black gospel music—Fitzgerald's version opens with the organ of the album's arranger, R&B pianist Bill Doggett (1916–1996)—and it necessitated joyous shouts of "hallelujah!" from Fitzgerald.[69] Fitzgerald's "Hallelujah" and the other studio orchestra recordings on *Rhythm Is My Business* presented a stylistic departure from her songbook interpretations, mainly of white composers and lyricists besides Duke

Ellington and Billy Strayhorn, in part because she chose to work with Doggett, an African American arranger. She worked with other African American composers and arrangers in the 1960s and 1970s, including Quincy Jones (b. 1933) for the 1963 Verve studio album *Ella and Basie!* with Count Basie and his orchestra, Gerald Wilson (1918–2014) for the 1970 Reprise studio album *Things Ain't What They Used to Be (And You Better Believe It)*, and Benny Carter for the 1979 Pablo studio album *A Classy Pair*, also with the Basie orchestra. While not reaching the popularity of her songbook albums for white composers, these albums, like the songbook entry for Ellington and Strayhorn, showcased the popular musical compositions of black jazz musicians and composers.[70]

On tour, Fitzgerald also performed the 1958 song "I Can't Stop Loving You" by country musician Don Gibson (1928–2003), a song that Ray Charles also popularized with his 1962 version. Fitzgerald's live orchestra versions, as heard in May 19, 1968, Cave Supper Club and 1972 Santa Monica Civic performances, lacked the strings of Charles's "sweet" version. She imitated a chanted sermon in the 1968 performance, enabling a humorous call-and-response interaction with the Tee Carson Trio drummer as well as the Canadian club's patrons:

> Here we are in the Cave,
> And I'm preachin' this mornin',
> I'mma tell you all about my man.
> Have you ever loved a man like I love my man?
> If you'd have, you'd know how I feel this mornin'. (*Preach, preach, preach!*)
> Awwwww, yeah!
> All I want is respect in the mornin',
> In the evenin', all night long.
> TREAT me right, baby! Just treat me like a woman, like a lady.
> Call me Miss, Miss Ella to you.
> Yeah, yeah, yeaaaaaah, I'mma tell 'em.
> Tell it to the judge! [*laughter*]
> Yeaaaaaah, sock-it-to-me, sock-it-to-me, sock-it-to-me, baby!
>   [*laughter and applause*]
> [*Blues vocal run, scat run*][71]

This humorous interaction was part of Fitzgerald's set in 1968, as evident in a 1968 concert broadcast at the Deutschlandhalle in Berlin that includes a variation of her preacherly interlude with the Carson trio's verbal and musical responses.

Beyond "I Can't Stop Loving You," Fitzgerald's 1975 Montreux concert version of "'Tain't Nobody's Bizness if I Do," a 1922 blues standard by Porter Grainger and Everett Robbins, features the vocalist and the Tommy Flanagan Trio performing the tune with a comical gospel inflection. When Fitzgerald says at 1:50, "And if I go to church, church on Sunday," the tune switches recognizably to a preacherly tale of romance with Tommy Flanagan's staccato gospel piano lick, followed by the Montreux Swiss audience's evidently knowing laughter as a response. In her verse, "And if I go to church, church on Sunday / Come home and bawl all night Monday / 'Tain't nobody's business / If I do, if I do," Fitzgerald may have even revealed her personal habits, given that other renditions by Bessie Smith and Billie Holiday follow the church line with a verse suggesting the enjoyment of worldly nightlife on Monday. Tommy Flanagan (1930–2001) produces gospel riffs throughout the song's remainder, and Fitzgerald preaches through humorous stanzas, like "Three times seven! Three times seven makes twenty-one! / Add one more, add one more and that makes twenty-two! / 'Tain't nobody's business / If I do, If I do!" She appears to use a basic ABCB rhyme scheme to highlight the particular black Protestant musical and vocal style more than any of its conventional theological or lyrical content.[72]

While Fitzgerald chose to leave no introspective public record of her personal religious practices, it is probable that she relished showcasing her eclectic appreciation of various (African) American singing styles through the performance of songs like "I Can't Stop Loving You" and "'Tain't Nobody's Bizness if I Do." Additionally, Fitzgerald may have simply displayed through humor the incongruity between the mode of emoting in gospel vocal performance and the modes that she had honed in jazz and popular song over her career, perhaps playfully signifying the amusing inauthenticity of her own gospel-inflected performance. Moreover, Fitzgerald's playful appropriations demonstrated the cultural currency that African American religious music had achieved internationally by the mid-twentieth century. Cultural or racial irreverence may be at play with these recordings, while her vocal delivery on *Brighten the*

Corner may have represented the reverent style of religious music she preferred in her personal life. If the latter case is true, then Fitzgerald effectively accomplished the objective of the century's earlier religious race representatives who actively pursued interracial religious fellowships. Whether through her playful or reverent vocal choices, however, Fitzgerald conveyed a disposition of joy as the gospel she offered to listeners and live audiences.

Conclusion

Personal decisions and tastes combined with professional management and early press exposure to produce a career of prominent racial crossover. This career symbolized the cultural virtues of racial integration, while it also compelled desegregation and enabled the construction of new desegregated spaces. Ella Fitzgerald represented personal, domestic, professional, charitable, and activist aspirations for African American women. At the same time, the quality of her voice, eclectic song choices, and joyous disposition created critical reservations regarding the sanctioned possibilities for the performance of authentic black womanhood in public. In her commitment to offer a joyous disposition, Fitzgerald constructed a public persona adamantly devoid of the disclosure of personal tragedy and hardships. Coupled with her particular vocal instrument, her singing abilities and self-representation enabled questions about her racial, gendered, and professional authenticity. Despite questions from critics, Fitzgerald was, and chose to represent, a black woman offering joy publicly to consuming audiences.

Such joy, for Fitzgerald, could entail both respectful and irreverent religious representations, while descriptively thick personal "confessions" remained private. In examining Duke Ellington's compositions that signify black racial and religious identity and history, the next chapter returns to the respectful mode of representation of black middle-class Protestants in the early twentieth century. These men and women offered narratives of a sacralized African history and a racialized biblical past through popular culture and artistic practice.

4

"Royal Ancestry"

He looked up at the sky and it seemed to say:
Boola, look at the sun, you're not alone.
How warm and friendly it has ever been.
Do you need more than other men to comfort you?

Look, now, is this not the same golden sun
Which fired your brain along the calm Euphrates?
And smiled upon your seeking, searching sorties
As you followed the course of the Ganges
Absorbing here poetic, soaring folklore,
Leaving there a part of you . . . a rhythmic song?
Yes, it's the same. The same old sun which smiled
Upon you as you pushed along the Nile and planted
Seeds. Seeds of the first civilization
Known to man!
Drink them in . . . their glowing stories
Of Babylon and all her glories
Knowing well her culture sprang
From black men. Forgotten long ago . . . Meroë . . .
From whence the first bright light flamed up
In Ethiopia to guide mankind along the way.
—Duke Ellington, "Black" manuscript text

Edward Kennedy "Duke" Ellington (1899–1974) grew up in Washington, DC's black middle class at the turn of the twentieth century. His mother, Daisy Kennedy Ellington, took him to at least two churches every Sunday: Nineteenth Street Baptist and John Wesley AME Zion, the family church of his father, James Edward Ellington.[1] The young Ellington was educated in an environment that saw the staging of historical plays and pageants by civic groups, schools, and churches. Washington, DC, and other American cities saw pageants such as W. E. B. Du Bois's *The Star of Ethiopia*, which purported to cover "10,000 years of the history of the Negro race and its work and suffering and triumphs in the world." These pageants began with a conception of black world history inaugurated by a classical, African period. This classical Africa was a civilizational analogue to ancient Greek and Roman civilizations for whites in the modern Western world. It contained the histories of Egypt and Ethiopia and extended to African American life at the start of the twentieth century.[2] Other pageants, such as *The Evolution of the Negro in Picture, Song, and Story*, similarly encouraged musical and visual dramas that captured a history of an African American slavery that produced "sorrow songs" (a form of spirituals that transition from somber themes of despair to themes of hope and joy), outlined Emancipation and the socioeconomic promises of Reconstruction, and concluded with the present "Day of Opportunity."[3] Christine R. Gray wrote of these pageants' participatory value for African American communities: "Making costumes, painting sets, posting notices, practicing musical or choral scores, researching the characters and history portrayed, and working on stage and backstage . . . those participating were closely involved not only communally but also culturally, intellectually, and emotionally, for the history to be presented was *theirs*."[4]

"When we went out into the world," wrote Ellington in his 1973 memoir, *Music Is My Mistress*, "we would have the grave responsibility of being practically always on stage, for every time people saw a Negro they would go into a reappraisal of the race. . . . As representatives of the Negro race we were to command respect for our people." Ellington's reflections on his early education in African American history, which was "crammed into the curriculum, so that we would know our people all the way back," reveal an early twentieth-century culture of instilling racial pride and the responsibilities of race representation through programs crafting artistic, historical narratives of African American social progress.[5]

Don George (1909–1987), a lyricist for Ellington in the 1940s, wrote that he "musicalized" African American history. The first three decades of his career saw conscious attempts to assert an appreciation for blackness in music that includes "Black and Tan Fantasy" (1927), "Black Beauty" (1928), *Symphony in Black: A Rhapsody of Negro Life* (1935), "Black Butterfly" (1936), and in *Black, Brown and Beige* (1943), Ellington's extended symphonic "tone parallel to the history of the Negro in America." George recalled how Ellington "told me about the invasion of Africa by Portugal, shortly after Columbus discovered the New World, when the Portuguese set up the slave system as we knew it." Ellington's additional history lessons for George included Crispus Attucks, "the first casualty of the Boston Massacre," the underground railroad, Harriet Beecher Stowe, and the work of Marcus Garvey and George Washington Carver.[6]

For Ellington and many other African Americans, to know and herald black history in the Americas was to invest oneself in a sacred racial narrative that extended into the African continent's ancient past. But as a sacred racial narrative, this history incorporated biblical narratives that black Protestants read as confirmation of their racial pride and contributions to humanity's history. They followed the precedents of nineteenth-century black Protestant discourses of ancient Africa's sacred significance. Historian of African American religion Curtis J. Evans has discussed sacred treatment of Africa in the address of AME bishop Benjamin William Arnett (1838–1906) at the World's Parliament of Religions in 1893. Evans writes that Arnett deemed Africa "the cradle of civilization, the home of Moses, and the asylum of the infant Redeemer" in his formal remarks, noting that this redeemer contained "African blood in his veins."[7]

Popular methods of African American scriptural interpretation formed the early religious context that Ellington represented through his jazz artistry. In these biblical interpretations, African American Protestants in the twentieth century's early decades read the Hebrew and Christian scriptures in concert with constructing their own history as descendants of the African continent. Ellington brought into his musical profession a relation to the Bible as a sacred African document. Its collection of tales recounted African and black people as the great founders of ancient civilizations and as contributors to the foundation of modern civilization.

For black religious readers, biblical scriptures chronicled a sacred racial history both directly and indirectly. These interpretations reveal that middle-class black Protestants, along with black academics who studied ancient North Africa, the Near East, and East Africa, invested their intellectual and artistic energy into racializing sacred Hebrew figures and sacralizing non-Hebrew peoples as venerable contributors to the development of religion. This twentieth-century Afro-Protestant cultural work echoes what historian of Africana religions Tracey Hucks identifies in her study of nineteenth-century African American religious nationalism: the "revolutionary efforts to racialize the divinity of God

and sacralize black humanity in the midst of American social demoni-
zation and violence."[8] However, these Afro-Protestants' racializations of
sacred texts and ancient religions, alongside their sacralizations of African identity, involved their embrace of *both* monotheisms and polythe-
isms. Historian of African American religion Craig Prentiss has noted
that even for Carter G. Woodson's effort to construct and disseminate
a narrative of "Negro history" in the early twentieth century, "not only
redeeming the message of Christianity but rehabilitating the African
characters of biblical narrative from the clutches of European and Euro-
American exploitative exegesis made common cause with the task of educating African Americans about their noble ancestry."[9] These religious
constructions of "royal ancestries," to borrow an Ellington phrase that he
employed to characterize Ella Fitzgerald's racial heritage, responded to
"the lived contexts of entrenched Anglo anti-blackness" by "provid[ing]
counternarrations and countertheologies to the deprecating images of
blackness, black humanity, and divinity."[10]

By publishing and promoting books on history and biblical interpretation, writing editorials, answering reader questions in regular black
press columns, staging pageants, and even through long- and short-
form jazz compositions, African Americans declared that the Hebrew
and Christian scriptures revealed an African history that encompassed
the earliest Hebrews and Christians. Importantly, this work reveals a
tradition of African American Protestant Christians who incorporated
African ancestors, beyond Hebrew and Christian traditions, in their reverence. For Ellington at midcentury, in particular, this racialized reading
of the Bible and sacralized reading of African history implied an essentially "classical" religious nature for African Americans. The musical
works over his career promoted a complex representation of African
American history that appreciatively wedded his folk's sacred and "sin-
ful" practices. As Ellington wrote in the "Beige" manuscript section for
his *Black, Brown and Beige* composition, "Harlem! For all her moral
lurches / Has always had / LESS cabarets than churches!"[11]

Ellington arrived in Harlem in 1923 formed by a family and class of
African Americans who viewed racial uplift as a professional duty. The
Ellington who matured as an artist in the 1930s fit perfectly Alain Locke's
jazz archetype, because he "came to embody the ideals of the New Negro
artist in his dignified manner and cultivated persona, his social con-

sciousness, his use of vernacular sources as the basis for original compositions, and his deep pride in the Afro-American heritage."[12] Ellington articulated his music's social importance as representative of a racial and cultural experience. Additionally, he offered his music as the emblematic representation of African-descended people who claimed an American identity. By declaring that his music was essential "Negro folk music," he presented jazz as an important vehicle for a romanticized concept of African American religious history. His "classical" musical portrait of African American Christianity was necessarily a depiction of racialized religiosity, one confined mainly to the past in service to the Harlem Renaissance project of addressing social inequality without recourse to political advocacy. However, there were others within African American Protestantism who fostered a view of their race's ancient religious history that cultural producers like Ellington promoted.

This chapter first explores African American Protestant cultural practices of racializing scriptures and constructing narratives that made the ancient African world sacred. Ellington's composition "Come Sunday" situates his representations of the history of African American religious fidelity within broader racially essentialist concepts of black belief. Beyond "Come Sunday," other Ellington compositions reflected and complicated his appraisal of the West African past that was the immediate ancestry of many African Americans.

"Three Black Kings": The African World of Hebrew and Christian Scriptures

God honored the black man by allowing some of his Ethiopian blood to flow in the veins of His only Son Jesus Christ, and I unhesitatingly assert that Jesus would in America be classed a NEGRO.
—James Morris Webb, *The Black Man, the Father of Civilization, Proven by Biblical History*

Ellington came from and participated in a black Protestant culture that signified African countries such as Egypt and Ethiopia as ancient examples of mighty and formidable black civilizations. His people traced the racial lineage of African-descended peoples throughout the Hebrew Bible.

In 1958 Ellington had the opportunity to meet with Queen Elizabeth II (b. 1926) and offered to compose "a real royal suite" for her. *The Queen's Suite,* by Ellington and his co-composer and arranger Billy Strayhorn in 1959, consisted of six movements, one of which bore the title "Apes and Peacocks." The title comes from a verse in the Hebrew Bible, 1 Kings 10:22b: "Once every three years the fleet of ships of Tarshish used to come bringing gold, silver, ivory, apes, and peacocks" (NRSV). Ellington wrote that this song "was inspired by reading the Bible about the Queen of Sheba and all the gifts she brought to King Solomon." When the English jazz historian Stanley Dance asked Ellington the significance of this title, Ellington instructed him to "reread the Old and New Testaments."[13] Ellington participated in what historian of American religions Laurie Maffly-Kipp defines as a narrative of African American history that signified many biblical characters such as the Queen of Sheba as Ethiopian and the Hebrew King Solomon as the presumed descendant of dark-skinned Ethiopians.[14] The present Ethiopian monarchy also attests to this belief in their claim that Solomon and the Queen of Sheba produced a son together who founded the ancient Ethiopian empire. One earlier Ellington composition in 1941, titled "Menelik, the Lion of Judah," revealed the composer's celebration of Menelik II, the late nineteenth-century Ethiopian emperor believed to be one such descendant of King Solomon and the Queen of Sheba. Ellington later reiterated the concept of Solomon's blackness in his final composition, *The Three Black Kings* (*Les Trois Rois Noirs*) in 1974, completed by his son, jazz trumpeter Mercer Ellington, for jazz band and symphony orchestra and scored for the Alvin Ailey American Dance Theater by Luther Henderson Jr.[15] The suite's three movements are named for different black royalty: "King Balthazar" (a name for one of the biblical Magi/Wise Men who visited the infant Jesus), "King Solomon," and "Martin Luther King, Jr." The selection of biblical characters, titles, and themes for his jazz compositions represented one of Ellington's practices for advertising—overtly or with subtlety—his intention to create music that was both beautiful and racially inspiring.

Civilization's Black Foundation

Black religious leaders and academics provided African Americans with approaches to racializing Hebrew and Christian scriptures, establishing narratives and arguments that informed the dissemination of this ideology through cultural and artistic production. James Morris Webb, a Seattle-based "Evangelist of the Church of God," published *The Black Man, the Father of Civilization, Proven by Biblical History* initially in 1910. He designed this text as a supplemental guide for African Americans studying the scriptures. Webb proclaimed his profession as "a Minister of the Gospel of Jesus Christ" who did not have "malice and hatred or any ill feeling toward my white brethren" in authoring this text. Instead, his writing represented both "that meek and humble spirit" of true Christian commitment and "a gigantic pride in my race, which I hope, pleases God."[16] *The Black Man* includes a dedication that reads, "In Memory of Paul Lawrence Dunbar, Famous African-American Poet," who died in February 1906. It also includes a reprint of "The Regeneration of Africa," a speech delivered at Columbia University on April 5, 1906, by Pixley Ka Isaka Seme, who founded the African National Congress in 1912. It also contains a reprint of W. E. B. Du Bois's February 13, 1907, address on education and civilization at the University of Chicago. As a member of Garvey's United Negro Improvement Association (UNIA), Webb was active in Seattle, San Francisco, and Los Angeles.[17] As Judith Weisenfeld notes, Garvey "contributed to the intellectual, cultural, and theological currents that fostered the emergence of alternative religio-racial narratives among blacks in early twentieth-century America. Garvey proclaimed that blacks were a transnational, global, and connected people and promoted a black nationalism focused, in part, on reclaiming Africa as a spiritual and political homeland."[18] African American clergy like Webb and others embraced the UNIA because they found in Garvey's political philosophy an articulation of Pan-Africanism that comported with emerging popular histories of Africa's religious significance.

Webb's approach to racializing biblical accounts as African history in *The Black Man* began with the premise that the Hebrew and Christian scriptures were historically authoritative. He named the Bible "the first and only true account of the origin of mankind." According to Webb, the Bible was "a dispassionate record of man's creation and progress, untrimmed, unshaped, and unvarnished, to suit prejudice" that charted humankind's progress toward civilization. What made the Bible a "complete record" was that it also revealed "the origin of the black man" and confirmed that he was "the father of civilization."[19] The Bible, then, served Webb as a text that African-descended peoples were to read to uncover the original race responsible for civilization; its principal purpose went beyond the unveiling of a salvation history through the New Testament's life and ministry of Jesus. Because of Egypt's importance as a civilization that Webb urged African Americans to claim with pride, his reading of the Bible even went beyond the existing black Protestant tradition that cherished the theological comparison of Israelite enslavement and freedom from Egypt to black enslavement in the United States, which situates the latter nations in each narrative primarily as antagonists. And in the case of reading the Book of Revelations as portending future events, Webb related African American enslavement and oppression to the American government as one of the "beasts" that Revelation's John of Patmos beheld.[20]

Webb set out early in *The Black Man* to undermine the notion of the Curse of Ham (more specifically, Noah's curse of Ham's son Canaan). In popular interpretations of the Bible's constructions of racial history, this curse rendered black skin as a sign of God's disfavor. Webb noted that Canaan fathered "seven prosperous nations, foremost among them were the Canaanites, Phoenicians and Sidonians." Webb stated that King Solomon built his temple with the labor of the Sidonians, "'black men' [who] were the only men possessed with anywhere near sufficient skill to take charge of and successfully complete the artistic timber work on 'His' Solomon's temple." Webb referenced 1 Kings 5:6 for this assertion and concluded that "Solomon knew the black race was a superior, not an inferior race."[21] Webb offered a larger conclusion that the very idea of efficacious human curses was incompatible with biblical scriptures. Not only did these ancient, non-Hebrew black peoples participate in the construction of sacred places critical to biblical history, but they also represented God's gifts as civilizations in their own right.[22]

This section's epigraph illustrates Webb's stance on the heritage of Jesus, whom Webb believed "will have His head covered with woolly hair when he comes to judge the world," according to Daniel 7:9–10.[23] Contemporary portraits of Christ conveyed "an erroneous conception of Him, by the artists," because they neglected to depict his woolly hair and a darker skin color.[24] Jesus descended from the tribe of Judah, whose

"The Birth of a Nation" Is Answered by.
The Black Man's Part in the Bible

"Moses was found by a black woman." "Moses was educated in a black school." "God allowed Moses to marry a black woman." "Moses' black father-in-law was the author of our system of courts, from the city to the supreme court," that we have today. "Solomon declared he was a black man." "Solomon employed black men to work on the Temple." "Solomon sent to Africa for his black bride." "Jesus was rescued and rocked in the black man's cradle in Africa." "God ordered it to be done." "The black man wore the first Christian badge by helping Christ to bear the Cross up Calvary." "Jesus was a black man by blood." And when he comes to judge the world His hair will be woolly and not straight. THE BLACK MAN'S PART IN THE BIBLE is two books, price $1.00 Will send them C. O. D. by mail. Write ELDER JAS. M. WEBB, 3545 Prairie Avenue, Chicago, Ill. The biblical facts in the matter are worth $5.00 in gold to any one, especially to the black race.

Figure 4.1. Advertisement for James Morris Webb's writings on Moses, Solomon, Simon the Cyrenian, and Jesus. From *Chicago Defender*, November 13, 1915, 3.

wives (the daughter of Shua, and Tamar) were descendants of Canaan, "a black man who was the son of Ham (Genesis 10th ch. 6th v.)." Webb located Mary, the mother of Jesus, in the lineage of Judah, and he referenced Jesus as the "seed of David" (according to Romans 1–3), thereby proclaiming that Jesus descended from another noteworthy biblical character "who had Negro blood in his veins" due to descent from Ham and Canaan (see figure 4.1).[25] And the story of Jesus's birth was significant to Webb for Egypt's role in sheltering the infant Jesus from Herod's infanticide decree.[26]

Beyond an African heritage for the Christian savior, Webb signified the heritage of Jethro, the Midianite priest whose daughter Zipporah married Moses, as "the Ethiopian or Negro father-in-law of Moses." Jethro "gave Moses the foundation of what is today our system of graded courts for pronouncing judgments," according to Exodus 18. The Egyptian upbringing of Moses was also significant because of "Pharaoh's daughter," the black woman who raised him, and because of his Egyptian education. Consequently, the examples of contemporary black male educational leaders like Booker T. Washington, Du Bois, and W. S. Scarborough should not have seemed novel to African American readers of the Bible, for these men were "descended from fathers who ruled Egypt centuries ago and with their great wisdom layed [sic] the foundation of learning."[27]

Webb concluded *The Black Man* by anticipating that when God summoned humankind at the end of time, the black man "will be found heading the line" and will hear from God, "Well done, thou good and faithful black servant, thou, My instrument, the Father of Civilization," a modified version of Matthew 25:21 and 23.[28] Following this conclusion to the book were various endorsements that provide evidence of the mainstream appeal for Webb's readings of scripture among prominent black Protestants, including an undated letter from AME bishop Henry McNeal Turner extolling "Elder Webb" and the lectures that produced this book.[29] Webb also included an undated comment from the *Seattle Daily Times* that regarded the African racial heritages of Israel's wisest ruler and the Christian messiah as Webb's most significant assertions.[30]

Webb's *The Black Man*, along with his 1919 tract *A Black Man Will Be the Coming Universal King Proved by Biblical Prophecy*, represented influential approaches to scriptural interpretation among Garveyites.[31] However, Webb's work likely resonated among black Protestants, evidenced by a clerical endorsement from AME bishop Turner. Webb also produced a race record sermon, titled "Moses Was Rescued by a Negro Woman," to preach his theological content from *The Black Man* by employing the popular three-minute phonograph format.[32]

The 1924 pageant "Ethiopia at the Bar of Justice" by Edward J. McCoo, pastor of St. Paul AME Church in Lexington, Kentucky, from 1926 to 1942, participated as well in the dissemination of popular black Protestant Ethiopian narratives.[33] McCoo presented this pageant with the help of John R. Hawkins, former professor of mathematics and business manager at North Carolina's Kittrell College as well as former education secretary and financial secretary for the AME denomination.[34] "Ethiopia" was one of the main characters in McCoo's play, and she represented the transhistorical presence of Africans in world history as well as her more explicit presences in scripture. "Opposition" represented the principal antagonistic voice or spirit in this pageant. Opposition responded to Ethiopia's apparent advancement over time and demanded of "Justice" that Ethiopia receive judgment because "she is doing too much; she is becoming too ambitious; she is flying too high; [Justice] must clip her wings."[35] The character named "History" attested to other nations' esteem for Ethiopia: "Ethiopia reigned upon the throne of Egypt for many years; to Ethiopia is Egypt indebted for much of her early civilization; in Egypt Ethiopia built many monuments, which still exist. . . . Homer sings the praises of Ethiopia, calls her blameless, and the favorite of the gods." History relays the Ethiopian heritage of the Cushite king Tirhakah, who aided the Hebrews against the Assyrians (according to Isaiah 37:9 and 2 Kings 19:9).[36] When Justice calls the character "First Slave" before him, McCoo's writing extolled this character's perduring theism by simultaneously disregarding and rationalizing (in appreciative language) its non-Christian and non-monotheistic forms in West African traditional religions: "I am the First Slave brought from Africa to this land, where sorrow and despair have been my portion. Opposition lured me here and has continually dogged my steps. In my primitive home, my morals were pure. Opposition corrupted them. All that Opposition could purloin she robbed me of, but my faith in God she could not dethrone; I overcame at last."[37] For twenty-five cents per copy, McCoo made his pageant available to African American performers of all ages, most likely within black Protestant religious congregations among other community organizations.[38]

Citing the claim of French Egyptologist Gaston Maspero, George Wells Parker (1882–1931) used his 1918 booklet *The Children of the Sun* to provide African American readers an argument against those he considered armchair scholars who asserted that Egyptians "must have been something other than African" because of their religious resemblances to other ancient nations. Parker regarded "the old idea of man having been created in the image of his Maker" as a universal religious trait that was indicative of a people's gods being "ever representative of their worshippers." Therefore, it was reasonable to conclude that black depictions of Egyptian gods were, in fact, indicative of a black worshipping populace. Moreover, it was unreasonable to ignore that this ancient civilization envisioned a high god whose skin color and features proudly reflected their own:

> If, then, the black skin was in any way despicable to the old Egyptians; if men of that color were known to them only as servants and slaves; if they themselves were white-skinned Libyans or yellow-skinned Semites,

it will be difficult to persuade a fair-minded people that the Egyptians would so far depart from the ideals and traditions of their race as to give Negro features and a black skin to the personification of the highest conception of the human mind—that infinite and unfathomable power that rules omnipotent to all men and gods, whose empire encompasses the earth and seas, the eternal stars and everlasting suns, and stretches to the uttermost confines of this mighty universe![39]

Parker viewed the Egyptian and Canaanite peoples surrounding the biblical Exodus tale as the African or black races that likely mixed with the Semitic Hebrews over the centuries: "The legend that Israel was in bondage in Egypt for five hundred years would presuppose that considerable mixture took place, but surely if it had not done so, it did so after the Israelites came to their promised land, Canaan. Here was another nation almost purely African and among them the Hebrews made their home." The evidence for the black wives of Moses and other biblical figures was sufficient to infer widespread ethnic mixing, for "what the greatest men did is but an index to what others might have done." And beyond the Exodus narrative, Parker noted that the Hebrews' "chief god, Jahve," chastised the people for "associating too intimately with the black trash of the neighborhood," with King Solomon even "go[ing] so far as to forsake the gods of Israel for the gods of Canaan" by building temples for the latter group of deities.[40]

Published writings like Parker's *The Children of the Sun*, which examined different ethnicities in the Exodus narrative and insisted on the reliability of these scripture passages for promoting positive racial narratives, also impacted the dramas that Harlem Renaissance playwrights created for black audiences. *Graven Images* was a 1929 play for eighth grade students by May Miller (1899–1995), a theologically liberal member of Washington, DC's Fifteenth Street Presbyterian Church and daughter of Kelly Miller. May Miller's play dramatized the adolescent life of Eliezer, the son of Moses and Zipporah, whom Moses's sister Miriam mistreats for his dark complexion. *Graven Images* is based on the story of Miriam's curse in Numbers 12:1–16. Miriam's skin becomes whitened through leprosy after God hears her and Aaron speaking against Moses "because of the Cushite woman whom he had married." Miller's drama attributes this curse to color prejudice against Eliezer and racial or ethnic prejudice against Zipporah. Miller presents a theme that Eliezer's blackness results from his creation in God's image, and as Craig Prentiss notes, Miller's play held social value for African American performers in churches, schools, and colleges: "By casting Miriam as a representative of white supremacy, complete with modern concerns of so-called miscegenation, 'blood purity,' and fear of 'contamination' through the dilution of 'whiteness' as it came to be imagined, Miller's African American audiences were reassured not only of their worth but of God's favor as well."[41]

Parker, one of the founders of the Hamitic League of the World, also produced an Associated Negro Press column, "Questions and Answers in Negro History." This series solicited correspondence from the black press's readership. If readers enclosed return postage, Parker even offered to respond personally to questions involving longer replies.[42] African American religious papers like the *Star of Zion* carried Parker's column in 1925, a fact that revealed the interest of African American readers in the histories of ancient civilizations linked to biblical narratives. "Mrs. A D. F." asked Parker, "Was the Queen of Sheba a Negro and where was Sheba?" Parker responded that the Queen of Sheba "was of Ethiopian blood and a Negro according to modern usage of the word."[43] J. M. Patterson asked for the distance between Sheba and Solomon's Temple, and Parker replied that the ancient city, "ruled by Ethiopians," lay "about 1,500 miles from Jerusalem."[44] Parker also assured F. R. T. of Chicago that St. Augustine "was a Negro" born in Africa "as were many others of the early Christian prelates."[45]

Parker fielded questions from African Americans who disagreed with portrayals of ancient Egyptians in popular culture. G. W. W. of Chicago wrote to Parker, "I have recently seen the Ten Commandments, by DeMille, and in this picture the Egyptians are represented as white," asking Parker how he accounted for this racial (mis)representation. Parker replied that this was "simply that the American subverts the truth to his own devices" and that the consensus among contemporary Egyptologists was "that the Egyptians were Negroid and that those of the Upper Nile were wholly black."[46] D. B. N. of Kansas City asked Parker whether Jesus was "of African blood," to which Parker replied that the New Testament's genealogy of Jesus confirmed his ancestry, in contrast to the "forgery" of popular depictions of Christ with "blue eyes and blonde hair."[47]

Parker did not respond exclusively to questions concerning Christian religious history. The *Star of Zion* included his response to F. G. N. of Alton, Illinois, on the veracity of claiming that "black scholars composed the Koran." Parker identified Abu Bekr [*sic*] as "a full-blooded Negro, a rich merchant of Arabia and the keeper of the records of his tribe" who preserved Muhammad's sayings.[48] For the readers of Parker's syndicated column, including the Christian clergy who edited the *Star of Zion*, pride for an African past transcended their denominational religious commitments.

Concepts of a black or nonwhite Jesus endured in the black press and performance art in the following decades. In preparation for Easter in 1924, the Sunday School Publishing Board of the National Baptist Convention, USA, offered scripts of Willa A. Townsend's *"Because He Lives"*: *A Drama of the Resurrection* for fifteen cents per copy. The black Baptist churches that purchased these dramas were able to witness congregants—and in particular, their "ambitious young people"—performing "the trial, death and resurrection of our Lord as witnessed by the most intimate of his disciples and followers." Additionally, Townsend's drama featured "the return of the Ethiopian Wise man, whom Tradition says was one of the first Gentile worshippers at the Manger-Cradle." The advertisement in the *National Baptist Voice* also stated that the drama was for use at any time of the year.[49] *The Story of Baltasar, the Black Magus*, was Eva Jessye's oratorio for a 1932 Christmas broadcast for NBC Radio in New York. Jessye created a narrative and made use of spirituals for African American listeners to envision their race's participation in sacred history. As Weisenfeld notes, Jessye's production centers "Baltasar of Ethiop" as a man who followed Hebrew messianic prophecy, thereby celebrating Baltasar for trusting "a faith not [his] own." Weisenfeld concludes, "African peoples were there from the beginning of Christian history, *The Story of Baltasar* asserts, and, represented in the person of Baltasar, they recognized the significance of the combination of divinity and humanity in the infant whom Christians believe was the Messiah."[50]

Beyond merely fashioning visual representations of a "Negro" Christ and biblical characters, it was because of Townsend's drama and Jessye's oratorio that black Baptist youth and black radio listeners were able to portray and to imagine, respectively, a cast of biblical figures and their messiah who were of African origin and descent. Through these creative theological productions, Townsend, Jessye, dramatic actors, and vocalists of spirituals evinced the cultural resonance of black religious nationalism within Afro-Protestantism. As Hucks has defined one of black religious nationalism's major characteristics, these Afro-Protestants "subvert[ed] the association of blackness with deified evil and [made] a deliberate attempt to theologically realign blackness with divine essence."[51]

A letter to the editor of the *Star of Zion* from Rev. Richard Alexander Carroll of the AMEZ Church in 1930 demonstrated the attitude of a black minister who related Ethiopian and Canaanite ancestry to contemporary African American identity. Carroll noted that the Ethiopian and Canaanite presence in maternal ancestries, coupled with Semitic paternal ancestries, would nevertheless render many of the Bible's characters black according to America's system of racial classification: "There are many Biblical characters whose mothers were Ethiopians or Canaanites, etc., and fathers were Shemitic or many other races, who, if they were in America would be called Negroes, or Ethiopians according to the 'closed door' religion manifested in America, which makes you a Negro if you have one drop of Negro blood in your veins." But like Webb, Carroll listed several biblical names and verses to indicate the Bible's Negro heritage, while rendering Jesus's race Negro but also deeming him a racially universal figure:

> It may be interesting to our people to know that Simon the Cyrenian was a Negro (Ethiopian), and that his son Rufus assisted the Apostle Paul in his missionary work while his son Alexander was contemporary with Peter at Jerusalem (Acts 4:6) and also assisted in ordaining him. (Acts 13:1, Rom. 16:21). That Jether, David's brother-in-law was a Negro (I Chr. 2:17, I K. 2:5–32). That the Syro-Phoenician woman was a Negro, a (Canaanite) woman, (Mat. 15:22, Mk. 7:24–26). That Rahab was a Negro woman (Canaanite) and that all races are represented in Jesus Christ and that he is more easily traced through the Negro race than any other because Adam was not white—red, as the word implies, neither white or black, and "in his own likeness he begat a son," from whom the earth was replenished through a direct line to the flood, when all else were drowned but Noah and his family; out of which came the seed for replenishing the earth in the new day which followed in direct succession to Tama, a Canaanitish (colored) woman, the beginning of his earthly lineage. Gen 3:25–26, 5:3, 6:10, 9:1, 38:6–30, Mat. 1:3, Lk. 3:33.

Closing his letter with "Yours for racial development," Carroll indicates to the paper's readership more than the likely content of his sermons or Bible lessons as pastor of several AMEZ congregations over his career. He also confirmed and authorized for other black Protestants an approach to reading biblical history that situated Hebrew and Christian scriptures as records of African and "Negro" history.[52]

"Come Sunday": A Race's Essential Religiosity

> Thru all the bloody, burdened years
> Boola has clung to the Word of God.
> Boola believed.
> His faith remained the Kindly Light
> To lead him safely through the darkness
> Of despair, misery, hunger, pain.
> God was good, but in His infinite wisdom
> Would allow one blessing at a time.
> And he answered honest prayers.
> He opened Boola's mouth
> And made those Golden sounds come out.
> He touched Boola's heart
> And gave those golden sounds a lilt . . .
> A depth . . . that no one else could duplicate.
> He nudged the whites
> And said to them: "LISTEN!"
>
> They listened and were lifted up
> Those golden tones were lulling tones.
> Their consciences were glad. Glad the slaves
> Had found the Bible . . . Singing to their God . . .
> Reassuring, too, it was. Calming. Healing.
> Harsh words abandoned. A happy medium!
> The spiritual was soothing to singer
> And slavemaster, too![53]

The claims that black religiosity was innate, which even Ellington represented in his music, emerged not solely from perceptions of enslaved black Christian fidelity in the antebellum South. In the nineteenth century, Pan-Africanist religious thought promoted the concept of the race's steadfast piety that stretched from the ancient past to the post-Emancipation present. In the 1887 work *Christianity, Islam and the Negro Race*, the West Indian educator, writer, and prominent Liberian émigré Edward Wilmot Blyden (1832–1912) wrote of "Africa's service to the world" from antiquity to the present.[54] Blyden recorded "the fidelity of the African" based on missionary experience. He declared, "There are no atheists or agnostics among them." This orientation toward supernatural belief, according to Blyden, had led ancient Greek writers "to regard the fear and love of God as the peculiar gift of the darker races." As these ancients regarded Africans "the only fit associates for their gods," the modern distribution of Africa's descendants in the West—"in all the countries of their exile"—bore the same enduring truth of their "unswerving faithfulness."[55]

The self-trained historian and journalist Drusilla Dunjee Houston (1876–1941) wrote that African-descended peoples had an essential belief in God because of their ancient Ethiopian or Cushite past (named for Ham's eldest son, Cush), and it was one that contemporary "New Negro" leaders could not unsettle. Writing for the Associated Negro Press in 1930, Houston contended that New Negro leaders were fundamentally mistaken in "attempting to represent and voice ideals, hopes and aspirations" for modern African Americans while having no understanding of "Ethiopian nature." There were "deep underground currents" that ethnology, paleography, archaeology, geology, and anthropology were uncovering that confirmed the ancient African parentage of monotheistic societies. These currents also explained for Houston an essentialist racial impulse toward supernatural belief among African Americans:

The Negro can not be led to discard God because the nations of antiquity co-eval with Egypt received their conception of the Deity from Ethiopians. Before the decadent civilization that recorded history reveals in Egypt, there had flourished a superior knowledge of God on the Upper Nile. This was in the ages when Egypt was but a colony of Ethiopia. This older Cushite empire had spread its first impulses of civilization to Egypt, India, Chaldea, and to the Aegean through black colonists.

Houston stated that the Cushites were the "favored people" whose "intimate knowledge of God" predated the biblical accounts of the Hebrews. Houston dismissed the historical polytheism of Egypt as a devolution from the "earlier purer form" of monotheism, which she asserted was the Ethiopian gift to the ancient world.[56] The black masses were "the poorest of soil in which to plant the seeds" of communism and atheism, which Houston identified as the "fantastic theories" that some contemporary black leaders attempted to offer, because "Negroes are religious by nature." Black leaders skeptical of this assertion of racially essential piety—what Houston termed the "early race concept of deity"—ignored what white scholars were teaching as "the mainspring of ancient mythology" in white colleges. In concluding her article, which the *Africo-American Presbyterian* reprinted, Houston reflected on her mixed racial heritage and how it impacted her relationship to the perceived greater, innate religious fidelity of other African Americans: "I look in wonder at the passing throngs of these faithful black people to their churches. You and I may not attend, but they will be there to the last day of their human existence. They 'shout' because they have a communion with God from which you and I of colder and mixed nature are shut out." Houston lauded this religious "constancy" and declared that African Americans "would retrograde" if their religiosity declined.[57]

Houston's romantic observations and claims in 1930 may have represented widespread racial essentialism about religious belief—namely, that African Americans who also had white or European ancestry displayed a diluted religious temperament in comparison to their phenotypically darker siblings. If her primary objective was to oppose the influence of atheism and communism in African Americans' concerted, progressive political efforts, then her work for this Associated Negro Press piece was to marshal claims to an ancient racial history that connected African American readers both to the African continent and to a biblical—and pre-biblical—past. It was this past that indicated the race's enduring purchase on divine belief. From Houston's perspective, it was the responsibility of learned race leaders, regardless of hue, to safeguard this orientation or face the prospect of their people's moral and social degeneration.

The *Star of Zion* quoted the white Unitarian theologian Charles Francis Potter on the Egyptian origins of monotheism in 1930, incidentally one year after Potter had founded the First Humanist Society of New York. Potter's book, *The Story of Religion*, was of value to the AMEZ editors because it affirmed the belief of many African American Christians that, in editor Davenport's words, "'Hebrew genius' was not the first to conceive the monotheistic thought." Before Moses was ever "startled by the phenomenon of the burning bush," the Egyptian ruler Akhenaten offered for a brief period a religion that was, according to Potter, "a bright spot in the darkness of the superstitions of the Egypt of the second millennium BC." The editorial speculated that Moses must have been aware of this monotheistic history, given that he was "trained in all the wisdom of Egypt."[58]

The 1930s also saw the Pan-African historian and educator Willis N. Huggins (1886–1941) produce *An Introduction to African Civilizations, with Main Currents in Ethiopian History*. This 1937 book, which Huggins co-wrote with his student John G. Jackson (1907–1993), seconded the assertions that Webb the minister and Houston the historian made in claiming African precedents, contexts, and persons for shaping what would become the Hebrew people and religion. Huggins appealed to historical studies of events chronicled in the Hebrew Bible, despite his lack of clear investment in promoting a Christian identity for African Americans, particularly in light of Italy's invasion of Ethiopia.[59] Huggins associated the Egyptian Queen Hatshepsut, the "first great queen in history," with the Hebrew Exodus narrative. He stated that the Exodus "appears to have taken place circa 1440" after the death of Thotmes (Thutmose) III, and he marshalled contemporary Egyptological arguments to frame the characters surrounding the founder of Hebrew religion as essentially comprising an ancient Negro tale: "Recent discoveries tend to show that Hatshepsut was the one who found Moses in the bulrushes and later it was her favor, that brought him to power and finally her death that made it necessary for him to flee from Egypt to Midian where he married Jethro's daughter, Zipporah, the Midianite (Ethiopian) woman."[60] Lastly, Huggins also wrote of Shishak (Shoshenq I), the "Black Lybian [*sic*] King of Egypt," who oversaw "the dissolution of Israel and Judah" that began in 978 BCE.[61]

Through the collective intellectual efforts of Houston, Potter, Huggins, Jackson, and others, the first half of the twentieth century saw the maintenance of black religious nationalist endeavors in which "Africa is often revalued and historically honored as a sacred source of philosophies and traditions," now extended through the circulation of sacred African histories and racialized scriptural performances and interpretation in popular culture. For the collective American populace, the optimal outcome of this ongoing work was that, in Hucks's words, "the image of Africa and African humanity [were] deprimitivized and rescued from pejorative European typologies."[62]

African Antiquity's Pious Antebellum Descendants

Among the African American academics, religious leaders, press writers, and artists who rooted this religious and racial essentialism in an African and biblical past, many also encouraged similar sentimental portraits of African Americans that focused on antebellum religious piety. According to the original script for Ellington's 1943 performance of his symphonic composition *Black, Brown and Beige*, the composer began to tell the audience the history of African Americans through the mythical journey of a Boola, an enslaved African who travels through three hundred years of history, including the African slave trade, the colonial era, Emancipation, and the "Black Metropolis" of Harlem, and finishing with World War II.

Ellington's poetry in this chapter's epigraph reveals through the composition's first section, "Black," that Boola's African history before the transatlantic slave trade extended back to the earliest ancient civilizations of North Africa, the Horn of Africa, and the Near East.[63] Ellington listed other great ancient nations in this poetic introduction to expand the geography of African American race pride beyond North and East Africa:

> Before the great white horde pushed out
> Across the seas to your peaceful, plodding shores,
> The Bantus in South Africa had long since learned
> To till the soil . . . And bartering
> Was their medium of exchange that did not
> Blacken men's souls with greed and hate!
> Your people of the [African] Great Lakes mined the gold
> And silver, traded precious stones and built

Their homes. They fashioned lovely things
Of pottery and metal, developing a craftsmanship
To this day unexcelled! In the kingdom of Songhay
There flourished a system of agriculture, law,
Literature, music, natural sciences, medicine,
And a schooling system, too. As early as the
Eleventh century you were weaving cotton. . . .
In the Sudan![64]

Boola's experience on a southern slave plantation in "Black" portrays African American religiosity in the Sunday experiences of black slaves. Ellington's poetry introduced the audience to spirituals by detailing the peace they sought against the lashes of their forced daily labor:

Came Sunday. Boola was irresistibly drawn
To that pretty white house with the steeple
So tall, shining there in the sun. Everyone
Who entered there was scrubbed and polished
And all dressed up! How happy they seemed!

When the white voices inside rang out
In triumph . . . the blacks outside would grunt
Subdued approval. When the white voices inside
Were raised in joyous song, the blacks outside
Hummed along, adding their own touches. Weaving
Gorgeous melodic, harmonic, rhythmic patterns.
Thus the spiritual was born. Highly emotional
Worshipping of God in song.[65]

An early manuscript version of Ellington's introduction detailed the composer's prosaic construction of enslaved black religious life on southern plantations. This prose provided the imagery of religiously receptive African American slaves "huddled" beneath a tree. The slaves whispered the Word of God to each other, each of them "sipping the reverent purity / Of each trembling word till he was filled / To bursting with the joy it brought!" Ellington emphasized the African American slaves' embodied inclination toward belief in their conflicted responses to hearing the white worshippers proclaim the Christian Gospel. Simultaneously, they restrained their expressive, emotional reverence for God and identified the moral hypocrisy of their enslavement:

> Thrilling, puzzling, strange it was . . .
> They spoke of love of all mankind. . . .
> What then was this? Did they not hear:
> "A false balance is abomination to the Lord;
> But a just weight is his delight." . . .
> "When pride cometh, then cometh shame;
> But with the lowly is wisdom."
> "The integrity of the upright shall guide them:
> But the perverseness of transgressors
> Shall destroy them."
>
> In turn they trembled for the transgressors,
> Their joy knew no bounds when words of hope
> Renewed in them their faith and trust in God.
>
> HUSH! Don't shout about it! No! No!
> Keep it down! Down! Enjoy your sweet suffering
> Of this profound upheaval of love and joy
> In aching silence.[66]

The enslaved blacks "trembled" in "aching silence" over the prospect that their white "transgressors" would one day meet some form of divine justice. For Ellington, the joy that they embodied (and which they had to subdue in the presence of white Christian masters and mistresses) represented an essential African American religious response to the material and spiritual freedom they understood as a promise from biblical scriptures. And with his gifted ability to sing the spirituals like no one else, Boola, who personified African American history, represented the inherent and steadfast religious nature of African American people that allowed them to endure the suffering of Jim Crow inequality following Emancipation.

"Come Sunday," originally an instrumental composition, stands as Ellington's musical rendering of the history of the "soothing" spirituals in black America. When Ellington recorded "Come Sunday" for a 1958 album version of *Black, Brown and Beige*, he recruited gospel singer Mahalia Jackson, who sang lyrics that captured the notion that African Americans relied on God in the face of daily hardships:

> Lord, dear Lord of love, God almighty, God above
> Please look down and see my people through.
> Lord, dear Lord of love, God almighty, God above
> Please look down and see my people through.
>
> I believe the sun and moon will shine up in the sky
> When the day is grey, I know it's clouds passing by
> He'll give peace and comfort to every troubled mind
> Come Sunday, oh, come Sunday, that's the day.
>
> Often we'll feel wearied, but He knows our every care
> Go to Him in secret, He will hear your every prayer.
> Lilies of the valley, they neither toil nor spin
> And flowers bloom and spring time birds sing.
>
> Often we'll feel wearied, but He knows our every care
> Go to Him in secret, He will hear your every prayer.
> Up from dawn 'til sunset, men work hard all day
> Come Sunday, oh, come Sunday, that's the day.[67]

The first stanza of "Come Sunday" illustrates the individual's appeal to God for the protection of an entire race. The next stanza turns toward a spiritual rendering of the natural world, one in which the symbols of sustenance and guidance ("the sun and moon") can be depended on to reappear, even when that provision seems obscured (in this case, by heavy overcast). God's gift of "peace and comfort"—when Sunday comes—allows believers to endure the psychological devastation of a people's existence in America, less to heal the wounds of the physical traumas of slavery and Jim Crow segregation. With the third stanza, God is for these people an intimate confidant, aware of life's woes and interested in listening to the individual who elects to give voice to suffering. Ellington then references in the Christian Gospels the instructions

Jesus gave his disciples that they must not worry about tomorrow's provisions, that they should take lessons from natural flora and fauna, and that they should instead "strive first for the kingdom of God and his righteousness."[68] The last stanza speaks to the specific daily reality of enslaved labor, an experience soon replicated in the dawn-to-dusk workdays of black sharecroppers post-Emancipation. The final line captures the African American slave's anticipation of the one day of respite promised by the antebellum South's Protestant religious culture.

With "Come Sunday," Ellington captured the universally familiar in the weariness of daily labor. However, he presented this common experience in (and for) a particular racial story: this was the narrative of a compensatory African American Christianity, an expression of the belief that the divine assuages the spirit in response to the abuses inflicted on the body. Here, Ellington's reverential musical portrait framed African American religious history as a set of well-established cultural practices. For Ellington to contemplate African Americans' enduring religiosity was to think reverently about a history of always-enduring ancestors. When the individual faces the world's travails, she may appeal to the same religious concepts as her ancestors. Weariness with the world's ills finds its salve on Sunday.

Whereas Ellington's 1943 poetic introduction to the spirituals celebrated the improvisational creativity of his ancestors in the face of hardship and exclusion, his later 1958 lyrics relegate a concept of religious experience to the weekly practice of a racialized memorialization. In this weekly ritual, the mode of being religious involves an essential practice of reflecting on one's racial ancestors as they had lived religiously. The construction of these lyrics echoed Ellington's embrace of "the [Harlem] Renaissance project of memorializing the black folk inheritance."[69] For the listener, Ellington's music and lyrics stir up romantic, pastoral imaginations of long-suffering African Americans. Ellington's musical and poetic reflection on African American religiosity suggests that the utility of one's religious life is in one's capacity to think fondly and reverently on the faith of one's mothers and fathers and to practice their brand of piety in order to endure society, and one may entertain that idea of relief—only, apparently—come Sunday.

Understood in this light, the lyrical content to "Come Sunday" suggests that modern African American religious belief and practice are essentially traditional and customary. For Ellington, the individual practices religious devotion by taking his or her woes to the divine for relief once a week—and not much else. There is no room to capture prosaically or lyrically, for instance, more than a century of (in)visible institutional practices and spaces of theological training, professional education, or political activism in African American religious history. Ironically, these practices were inherent to Ellington's middle-class black Protestant upbringing that shaped the world of his religious race representation. They are implicitly nonessential to the romantic historicization and romantic practice of African American religion. Ellington rendered this history thus, likely because his early life and professional career did not require that he spend time in any of these institutional contexts. Ultimately, Ellington's appraisal of African American piety is that it bears an inherently classical quality.

Sacred West Africa?

With his music, Ellington rendered a "classical" African American Christianity as distinct from a primitive rendering of pre-Christian enslaved African religiosity and the West African drumming and rhythms regarded as the progenitor of modern American music. Importantly, Ellington reflected other Harlem Renaissance figures who appreciated West African culture and history by prizing the notion that his African ancestors exuded a primitive sensuousness. Ellington introduced his 1940 composition "Ko-Ko" at his 1943 Carnegie Hall concert as "a little descriptive scene of the days that inspired jazz . . . think it was in New Orleans, and a place called 'Congo Square' where the slaves used to gather and do native and sensuous dances, religious dances."[70]

Furthermore, seemingly in response to criticisms of primitivist representations of African-descended peoples and their history, Ellington even qualified his usage of the word "primitive." In the 1957 musical allegory *A Drum Is a Woman*, he narrated the journey of Madam Zajj, the "African enchantress" who was the personification of rhythm, as she traveled from the West African coast throughout the Americas. On the track "Congo Square," Ellington narrated the scene commonly associated with ecstatic African religious expression and generative of African American musical rhythm:

Congo Square. Here the crowd has congregated. They all have such strange, far-away looks in their eyes. You can almost smell violence and fear, maybe afraid to be there, or maybe afraid not to be there. [*Woman screams.*] Stage is set. We await the rising of a curtain that is not down or even there. Ah, there on the fringe of the clearing, a girl. Her face is pretty and childlike. The rest of her is pretty, too, but not childlike. Her feet are so motionless, you get the illusion that the tree stump in the center of the clearing is inching itself toward her. She's oblivious of the waves of desire generating in the crowd, thrilling to every gentle touch of the drum. Another drum, and another drum. Many drums in counter-rhythm, and for every drum we hear, there's a woman to see. Their gyrations accelerate to a frenzy and a sudden stop, and they all go scurrying out of the clearing. [*Sax solo.*] Eh-heh. [*Sax solo continues.*] One by one, every head turns to the entrance of the most primitive woman. This, of course, does not mean simple or elementary. She is an exciting, ornately stimulating seductress with patterns of excitement and the power to hypnotize and enervate the will toward total abandonment. This, if anybody, must be none other than Madam Zajj.[71]

In keeping with Ellington's musical romanticism, this album track certainly presents an exoticized portrait of Congo Square's African-descended ritual participants in an arena and atmosphere where both physical and spiritual security were uncertain. And Ellington's narrative portrait of Congo Square's women participants renders them not only unconscious conduits of desire but also physical instruments for male drummers.[72] Nevertheless, Ellington's method of divesting "primitive" African-derived rhythms of negative connotations was to describe them as foundational, complex, and holding efficacious sway over bodily responses. Ellington made their consequential historical presence significant, even as they maintain persistent social and cultural complications that accompany this descriptor (not to mention the feminine gendering of rhythm versus the presumed masculinity of the person who produces or possesses the rhythm). Moreover, Zajj was an inversion of the word "jazz," the "most primitive" genre of Africa's descendants whose stimulating, seductive, will-enervating music Ellington not only cherished as a sacred gift of his people's history but also composed in order to move listening and dancing patrons toward similar "total abandonment" of their social composure.

Further complicating the notion that Congo Square's musical participants were mindlessly primitive is Ellington's choice to narrate the women's accelerating gyrations, which come "to a frenzy and a sudden stop" before the ritual participants scatter from the center. This statement indicates on its surface that the music of West Africa's descendants produces ecstatic (religious) bodily responses. What Ellington also suggests, however, is that the music engenders and interacts with expressive, emotional dances that are the participants' thoroughly regulated performances with the deceptive appearance of chaos. While Congo Square's collective practitioners convey the superficial appearance of mindless frenzy, they are indeed conscious of their ritual's temporal and spatial boundaries. Ultimately, Ellington's descriptive work for primitivism serves to sophisticate a category often deployed to deride African and African American people and cultures.

However, the "primitive" rhythmic Africa for Ellington stood alongside Liberia, the West African nation that African American Protestants championed as civilized. Ellington's 1947 production *Liberian Suite* celebrated the African nation's centennial following its independence from the American Colonization Society. Liberia was the home of descendants of enslaved Africans in the Americas who founded a black Christian nation—joining Ethiopia as its younger religious sibling. The Liberian government had commissioned Ellington to compose and perform this suite to commemorate its founding. *Liberian Suite* lacks any of the instrumentation Ellington commonly employed to convey romantic notions of a primitive West Africa, such as the drumming in songs like "Wild Man (aka 'Wild Man Moore')" from *First Time! The Count Meets the Duke* in 1961, "La Plus Belle Africaine" from the live album *Soul Call* in 1967, "Afrique" from *The Afro-Eurasian Eclipse* in 1971, or the "shouting" horn solos in "Moonbow" from the album *Afro-Bossa* in 1963.[73] Instead, Ellington chose to present a triumphant musical portrait of Liberia as a modern nation, and *Liberian Suite*'s first song, "I Like the Sunrise" with vocals by Al Hibbler, contains lyrics heralding a "new day" that brings "new hope" after a very "weary" night—a promise that Africa's inhabitants seeking decolonization and Africa's descendants in the United States pursuing civil rights certainly desired.[74] When compared to *A Drum Is a Woman*, Ellington's race pride had far less complicated representation in the *Liberian Suite*. This representation was indicative

of the Christian nation's purchase on the religious and racial imaginations of African American Protestants.

Conclusion

Throughout his career, Ellington's jazz reflected the established corpus
of African American folk culture—the elements of African American
life already considered worthy of status as folk expressions and rendered
in a fixed sense. He joined the singers, dancers, anthropologists, historians, and African American Protestants in these professions as well as
within the arts as one of many performers and compilers of an African American national culture. As the Ellington chapters will reveal,
Ellington's personal sexual practices may have put him at odds with
the clerical representatives of African American Protestantism, whose
race pride through investments in sacred racial narratives and esteem
for a "classical" ancient Africa he shared. Additionally, Ellington's personal theologizing, beyond conventional ministerial guidance or regular
church attendance, reflected his confidence in grasping the teachings
of Hebrew and Christian scriptures. This confidence is attributable to
both his frequent middle-class black Protestant churchgoing in adolescence and the cultural world that black Protestants shaped and fostered
in broader black professional and artistic production. Professional artists like Duke Ellington and others owed their production of righteous
representations of their race to African American pageant culture,
long-standing narratives of Ethiopianism, Pan-Africanist and Garveyite
political investments, Harlem Renaissance appreciation and romantic
construction of a classical black "folk," and the popular dissemination of
academic and theological arguments along with artistic performances
that racialized scriptural narratives and sacralized a non-Christian and
non-Hebrew African ancestry.

Ellington's later sacred compositions in the 1960s and 1970s journeyed beyond the romantic narratives of African American people and
their religiosity. The next part of this book uncovers archives of complex,
thick, and at times private religious beliefs and practices in the personal
lives of Ellington and fellow jazz pianist/composer Mary Lou Williams.

PART II

Missions and Legacies

5

God's Messenger Boy

At a November 2, 1969, concert in Copenhagen, Denmark, Duke Ellington introduced the vocalist Toney Watkins (1947–1986) to perform his
classic 1943 composition "Come Sunday." With this version, Watkins
sang a Hebrew translation of Ellington's English lyrics, just as he had performed the song three years earlier for an Ellington concert at the Reform
Jewish congregation Temple Emanuel in Beverly Hills, California. This
Hebrew version of "Come Sunday" represented the composition's transformation from Ellington's original wordless tribute to spirituals in 1943,
to a lyrical version with the voice of gospel artist Mahalia Jackson in 1958,
and then to Ellington's offering as a solo vocal or choir song for a series
of interfaith occasions in the late 1960s and early 1970s. The first December 1966 Temple Emanuel concert was significant because it contained
"an integration of audiences and forces that rarely united in American
society, particularly in this period, with black separatism on the rise
and the formerly strong links between blacks and Jews, which proved so
important years earlier in the civil rights movement, fraying."[1] Featuring
classic and new Ellington compositions as he explored musical structures
to convey his reverence for God and the concept of belief to religious
audiences, this concert was the first in the composer's series of Sacred
Concerts in his final decade. Following the December 1966 evening concert, Temple Emanuel's newsletter celebrated the "standing ovation" that
the performance received from "more than 1200 cheering congregants,
friends and neighbors of all races and religions."[2]

Earlier, Ellington allowed for this song's interpretation during the touring of his First Sacred Concert. He, his orchestra, and a host of soloists
traveled to various churches to perform at their requests. Theologically
liberal white congregations, like the Fountain Street Church in Grand
Rapids, Michigan (an independent, formerly Baptist church that favored
affiliation with the Unitarian Universalist Association in the 1960s), re-
arranged "Come Sunday" when Ellington performed in their houses of

worship.[3] The Sacred Concert tours became local events by including local choirs in the performance of "Come Sunday" and other compositions.

Ellington and his orchestra traveled to predominantly white, socially and/or theologically liberal worship spaces in the United States and Western Europe to showcase the promise of ecumenical and interracial fellowship. These occasions served to affirm belief in God in the late 1960s. In this moment, the public questioning of God's existence animated the anxieties that many of these mainline and liberal religious communities expressed in denominational conventions, seminary colloquia, theological literature, and interfaith festivals. For instance, Ellington headlined a *Reader's Digest*-sponsored symposium at Union Theological Seminary titled "New Religion" (also called "New Time Religion"). This 1968 event was an interreligious gathering of two hundred clergy and seminarians to discuss methods of modernizing religious worship and the purpose of "God is dead" religious discourse. Featured clergy speakers included Yale chaplain William Sloane Coffin Jr., Episcopal priest Malcolm Boyd, and Reform rabbi and "death of God" theologian Richard Rubenstein. Ellington's participation came at the encouragement of the Lutheran pastor John Garcia Gensel of St. Peter's Lutheran Church, the congregation that Ellington's sister, Ruth, attended.[4]

Duke Ellington's three Sacred Concerts were interfaith projects in which his musical professions of faith lived and came to acquire religious authority due to his prominent celebrity status. His personal religious reflection ultimately resulted in the production of religious music for public consumption. Ellington was a professional elite, as evidenced by the accepted title of "Duke" in the jazz world; however, elitism may not precisely characterize his authoritative religious standing. As an African American race representative who composed sacred music, Ellington came to enjoy associations with elite white mainline/liberal Protestant ministers, rabbis, Catholic priests, and to a lesser extent some African American Christian ministers. Although he was never truly a student of a particular religious denomination to appropriately bear the title "layman" in his adulthood, Ellington's theological explorations marinated in a world saturated with popular religious literature that he studied to compose his Sacred Concerts. Moreover, the presence of Ellington in houses of worship across theological and racial lines also revealed differences in the ways that black and white religious audiences were receptive to his musical work.

Curiously (and likely coyly), Ellington considered himself "God's messenger boy," perhaps embracing an evangelical task with his music and the notion that he lacked seniority or authority within any specific tradition.[5] "Boy" could have also indicated his fondness for the faith of his youth. It may have also revealed his insistence that one should approach faith and belief with simplicity, not from a place of high theological training and deftness, but from a posture of openness to contemplating the source, guidance, and destiny of existence. As he wrote in his autobiography, "Like a child, I had always believed that nothing was impossible until it could be proven impossible."[6] When Ellington composed music to represent the simple embrace of faith, he produced simplified lyrics—and some critics like Nat Hentoff maligned his words for their apparent naïveté. However, the composer's lyrics often belied the mature artist's wrestling with matters of ultimate concern that he worked to express religiously through music.

Additionally, Ellington expressed no interest in evangelizing "people who have never heard of God, but those who were more or less raised with the guidance of the Church."[7] This statement appeared in a program booklet for his Second Sacred Concert at North Avenue Presbyterian Church in Mount Vernon, New York. A 1966 interview revealed that he did not make an effort to ensure that all musicians performing with him embraced any particular faith: "Some of the other performers weren't believers, Ellington admitted, but 'I never got to the point of saying "if you don't believe, we don't want to have you perform." I just let it go along.'"[8] Importantly, there is no salvation narrative or record of a conversion experience, or baptism, with Ellington. His primary intention with these concerts may have been to relate his own religious orientation to other people who had inherited a religious tradition from youth, rather than to people who had converted to one.

The Sacred Concerts: Interfaith and Interracial Performances

After New York's Fifth Avenue Presbyterian Church voted to host the East Coast premiere of Ellington's First Sacred Concert in November 1965, at the request of the Protestant Council of the City of New York, Rev. Bryant M. Kirkland hailed it as "an important religious and cultural event" for the church members. Kirkland announced that the concert would serve as "outreach into the city of New York as a gesture of our mission to declare the supremacy of God over all human life and as a symbol of our desire to proclaim God's grace to all the world." As he assured Fifth Avenue's members that the traditional Bach and Handel Christmas music would appear in the services, he promised that Ellington's music represented the offering of praise to God "in new tonal forms of subtlety and delicacy." Kirkland's letter did not mention Ellington's compositions reminiscent of modern black gospel music, a genre capable of accommodating delicate, subtle, and complex harmonies but often presented at volumes matching the high degree of emotionality its artists wished to convey. Neither did Kirkland mention Ellington's vocalists, like Toney Watkins and Queen Esther Marrow (b. 1941), who came from gospel church traditions. Instead, he chose to frame the Sacred Concert for white mainline religious audiences as an opportunity to experience new music that gave voice to modern anxieties and that served as a bridge to connect individuals: "Modern music catches the melancholy of contemporary life and the paradox of communication; built-in answers keep some from hearing their brother's cry of loneliness. When communication takes place in honesty and courage without fear or bitterness the miracle of understanding transpires."[9]

The Sacred Concerts also served the racially progressive purposes of white mainline congregations following Martin Luther King Jr.'s assassination and the social unrest in America's urban centers. For the 1968 convention gathering of the Wisconsin-Upper Michigan synod of the Lutheran Church of America (LCA) in Milwaukee, Ellington's Second Concert inaugurated a series of resolutions to confront "the racial situation and the urban crisis." The LCA's communications official, Richard Sutcliffe, told the convention, "You are doing what Duke Ellington told us so beautifully Tuesday night—'make a joyful noise unto the Lord.'" The convention approved nine resolutions, including calling for members to lead in open housing campaigns, approving of interracial marriages, opening LCA congregations to all races, and disapproving of racial discrimination in the calling of pastors to LCA churches. Additionally, the convention reacted to concerns about police brutality by "commending" fair and honest policemen and expressing "sadness" about police "mistreatment." The delegates also posed several questions about race relations in local church communities:

How do I treat my neighbor of a different race or color or class?

Do I refuse to walk beside him? To be seen with him? To eat at the same table with him? To go to the same school or the same church?

Do I begrudge him fellowship in my congregation?

Do I put "the most loving interpretation" on what he does? Do I refuse to sleep in the same building with him? To share recreation with him? To employ him or to work with him? Do I refuse help to him who needs me?

Do I patronize him? Use force against him? Do I refuse him full membership in any organization to which I belong?[10]

Ellington and his orchestra's presence in multiple white religious spaces in the United States and Western Europe over eight years symbolized an implicit mission to be an evangelist for racial integration among religious institutions. However, recalling Ellington's statement that he was "God's messenger boy" to those who had grown up within a religious tradition, it is important to note that he was not the sort of evangelist who sought to change the minds of nonbelievers concerning the existence of the supernatural. The emergence of the "death of God" rhetoric in the late 1960s struck Ellington as a national dilemma in which it was more often popular than sincere to state adamantly one's certain disbelief in God. "Now and then," wrote Ellington, "we encounter people who say they do not believe. I hate to say that they are out-and-out liars, but I believe they think it fashionable to speak like that, having been brainwashed by someone beneath them, by someone with a complex who enjoys bringing them to their knees in the worship of the non-existence of God. They snicker in the dark as they tremble with fright." These remarks were printed in the North Avenue Presbyterian Church's booklet for its 1966 Festival of Religion and the Arts. This ecumenical event also included a performance by Indian sitarist and composer Ravi Shankar (1920–2012), a viewing of the documentary *A Time for Burning* on white Lutherans in Nebraska and resistance to integration, a "Religion and Jazz" discussion with the Catholic "jazz priest" Norman O'Connor, and an "African crafts exhibit" on the day of Ellington's concert.[11] Inasmuch as this event served as an interracial and interfaith practice, it also represented a symbolic unity among religious Americans as they rallied against the perceived threat of atheism and agnosticism. The religious declarations of Ellington, a senior artist in an ostensibly secular musical genre, provided additional weight for the cause of generally theistic citizens.

Ellington also expressed that it was not his intention to compel new believers to join specific religious denominations or congregations: "I was brought up in a religious household, and I went to my mother's church and to my father's church; it wasn't the church that mattered, it was the feeling of believing in something, having faith." Visiting multiple congregations every Sunday of his youth resulted in his lack of commitment to denominational distinctions, and the current social moment simply required people's reinvigorated sense of faith and commitment to belief in God: "The current ecumenical movement is the thing that will save us by stressing the importance of faith rather than rules or the type of church we happen to attend."[12] As a member of this ecumenical project, Ellington was encouraged by Roman Catholic, Presbyterian, Unitarian, Lutheran, Episcopalian, Christian Science, and Reform Jewish ministers.[13] Reciprocally, these various denominations influenced the choir vocals he incorporated into his concerts—Ellington included the "Litany of Reconciliation" from the Anglican Coventry Cathedral in England as "Father Forgive" in his Third Sacred Concert. They also provided liberal Protestant denominational literature to Ellington, and he relied upon these texts in his daily religious study.[14]

Within the broader white American Protestant world, the path was already paved for Ellington's sacred music performances in religious spaces. The theologically conservative Lutheran Church—Missouri Synod's Concordia Publishing House produced *The Christian Encounters the World of Pop Music and Jazz* by William Robert Miller, a "reviewer of jazz records acquainted personally with leading performers" who worked as the religious editor for the grade school textbook publishing company Holt, Rinehart and Winston. Part of Concordia's *Christian Encounters* series, Miller's 1965 book set out to "analyz[e] a modern issue with the tools of Christian truth" based on his perspective as a jazz aficionado. He worked to provide a Christian readership a set of "basic values for determining the creative and spiritual contribution of modern performers and types of popular music."[15] Although published by the conservative Missouri Synod denomination, *The World of Pop Music and Jazz* also evidenced its author's embrace of the theologies of Karl

Barth and Paul Tillich when discussing the modern Christian's responsibility to ensure that cultural production reflects the will of God and must be judged accordingly.[16]

For Miller, jazz had the potential to demonstrate "a creativity and depth that both express and transcend its norms and traditions," particularly evident in recent compositions by jazz artists addressing civil rights struggles in the American South. Among Ellington's works in this discussion, he cited the symphonic composition "Nonviolent Integration" and "King Fit the Battle of Alabam," an adaptation of the spiritual "Joshua Fit the Battle of Jericho," which celebrated the "freedom riders and the struggle of nonviolent church people against police dogs and fire hoses." Moral integrity was evident in modern jazz because of the social statements many musicians made with their music despite the pressure to "go commercial" and only make popular recordings. These creative jazz artists contradicted the "lurid view of jazz often peddled by slick journalists" who characterized the music as "originating in whorehouses, flourishing in speakeasies, and played today by narcotics addicts in night clubs."[17] Because of Ellington's nearly forty years of composing racially significant extended form music that "parallels the work of classical composers," Miller's writing defined Ellington as the exemplary jazz composer.[18]

For his Christian readership, Miller stated the critical importance of jazz as an African American art form integral to American cultural history. Miller signified American cultural creativity as the product of interracial fellowship, wherein African American involvement was principal. Miller advocated the perspective of Arnold Toynbee that "nations have achieved greatness through the intermingling of diverse cultures," and he noted the social and cultural exploitation, exclusion, and omission of African Americans in history. "As in popular music," wrote Miller, "the contributions of Negroes to American civilization . . . are quietly absorbed by a culture that continues to think of itself as white. Jazz by its whole history punctures this illusion." If white Americans were to refute the narrative of jazz history as a lineage of white male innovators (from Paul Whiteman to Benny Goodman to Dave Brubeck) and, instead, "begin to touch the creative sources, we are face-to-face with a challenge to the myth of white supremacy by which we live (whether we believe in it or not)."[19]

As he indicated his support for the pursuit of racial integration, Miller wrote against the tendency to minimize or erase African American hand-prints in the fashioning of American culture. If "the earth is the Lord's and the fullness thereof," argued Miller while quoting Psalm 24:1, then music constituted one of the creative arts that are "part of that fullness which man has fashioned from the bounty of God's creation." Such an art, as a divine gift, is "part of God's covenant with man, and . . . it is given to man for his rightful and beneficial use as an intelligent and responsible steward." Miller wrote to convince Christian readers that there were many contemporary jazz musicians who were making proper use of this divine gift, particularly in an era when religious jazz compositions were becoming popular. The valuable history of African American cultural production, coupled with the expressed need to address social issues with creative art, required of white Christians that they embrace jazz as an American tradition and pay attention to religious currents in jazz music.[20]

Miller closed *The World of Pop and Jazz* with a set of fifteen discussion questions, most likely designed for church Bible study groups debating the place of popular music in individuals' lives or the place of popular and jazz musical styles in religious music. Miller posed a question that represented his attempt to tie white churches closer to the world of jazz musicians: "12. Is there anything that local churches can do to help provide alternatives to the night club as a place where jazz musicians can earn a living?" The final question referenced Ellington directly, addressing a recording that Mahalia Jackson performed for his 1958 *Black, Brown and Beige* album: "15. Do you think jazz has a legitimate part to play in worship services today? In the future? Is this good or bad? What about hymns for congregational singing, such as those written by Edgar Summerlin? Is there a place in *your* church for Duke Ellington's setting of the Twenty-third Psalm or similar pieces?"[21] Such literature set the stage for Ellington to feel welcome presenting his religious music in many white American Protestant churches.

The Sacred Concerts: Complications with African American Churches

By contrast, Ellington's sacred musical offerings found only a lukewarm response from African American Christian congregations, if they weren't rebuffed outright. What explained the minimal use of African American worship spaces for his Sacred Concerts? An Associated Negro Press feature column, titled "No Duke Soul in Colored Churches," presented a perspective of African American Protestantism in which the acceptance of popular music and musicians in religious spaces was not as simple or permissible as with a white Protestant congregation operating under the models of cultural appreciation and racial reconciliation—the model of white Christians like William Miller. The column presented the writer, Jim, having a fictional conversation with a character named Big Mouth, who employs a stereotype of black English. Big Mouth wondered why Ellington was not performing his Sacred Concerts in African American churches:

"I have dug in the New York Times, which Sara Lou reads religious, that Mister Edward Kennedy Ellington is making gigs in big, fine, rich white churches—blowing them sounds. Now, I am not one to knock any cat's hustle but, Jim, I do not dig how this have come about." . . .

"You do not want to understand, Big," I retorted impatiently. "You are a prejudiced person. You do not like to see new things happen. Actually, the use of jazz in religious institutions is not new."

"It is new to me," Big persisted. "Even so, if Duke can play his music in a big, rich church, how come Ray Charles cannot give a concert at Second Baptist? Or why can't Ella Fitzgerald work out at Gethsemane AME? They both has soul, just as Mr. Ellington has and it would be great for collections."

"I am beginning to see your point," I said. "You are more prejudiced than I realized. You do not really object to Duke playing jazz in church. Your objection is that he plays it in rich, white churches. Now, I cannot tell you why he has not done so in colored churches."

"I bet I know why," Big mused. "I bet no colored churches ever asked him. You are correct, man. Duke has soul and colored churches is really soul churches. But I bet they never asked him."[22]

Although this February 1966 piece would prove inaccurate with Ellington's performances in African American churches that year, its humorous cynical tone reflected the perception that Ellington was not seeking out less affluent, black venues for his performances and, thereby,

neglecting black Christian congregations. This perception met the competing impression that the majority of African American churches were
uninterested in popular performers in their houses of worship. For the
column's author, there was a perceived cultural disconnection between
the worlds of the most successful African American entertainers and
black Protestant congregations. Ironically, this disconnection contrasted
with the ability of both worlds to produce "soul," a signifier of an essential set of modern black musical innovations.

The strongest outright opposition to Ellington's sacred performances
in religious spaces came from the Washington, DC, Baptist Ministers
Conference (BMC), an association of African American church leaders
representing nearly 150 local black churches. The BMC passed a near-
unanimous resolution "against endorsing the Ellington performance,"
and anonymous reports to the Washington-area press indicated that
conference ministers urged their congregations to boycott Ellington's
performances of the First Sacred Concert. Indicating that Ellington's personal habits were the target of the ministers' ire, John D. Bussey, pastor
of the Bethesda Baptist Church, stated before the concert that Ellington's
life "is opposed to what the church stands for" given his "worldly" professional music and its common setting, the nightclub. One month after
the concert, Bussey reiterated his opposition, stating, "We think the man
himself is incapable of writing sacred music," because of the "worldly
beat" of Ellington's jazz music (and contemporary gospel music) and the
claim that Ellington's life "does not commend itself to the sacred."

Harvey Cohen references John Bussey's interview with Kenneth Dole
of the *Washington Post* in January 1967, where he elaborates on his opposition to "worldly beats" that were making their way into church music.
Seemingly unfamiliar with Ellington's sacred music that premiered the
previous year, Bussey assumed that the jazz artist's compositions would
bring an emotionally responsive tempo and rhythm to worship music
that would incite the worshippers to respond with "over-emotion."
Bussey's specific criticism of gospel choirs was that when they begin
singing, they "[don't] give the pianist a chance to start playing before
they are jumping and jumping and jumping and clapping, clapping,
clapping." Such highly emotional displays, for Bussey, were anachronis-
tic for educated African American Christians in the middle of the twentieth century. Cohen points out that Ellington's Sacred Concerts lacked

the emotionally conducive stylistic, verbal, and musical elements of gospel music. However, Cohen overlooks part of Bussey's criticism. Since Ellington's jazz rhythms came from "the beat of the world," they had the potential to evoke enthusiastic responses from "the uninformed Christian who is just moving by the beat," instead of the sincerely worshipful Christian, who "is not necessarily moved by the beat so much as by the message of the song." Bussey's criticism, echoing the criticisms that religious race professionals made in the 1920s and 1930s, offers a distinction between the emotionalism offered by "worldly" music and gospel that emerged from Holiness-Pentecostal African American Christianity, on the one hand, and the emotionalism produced by responding intellectually to some gospel songs but mainly standard Protestant hymns and spirituals, on the other. The latter songs more likely constituted the musical offerings in Bussey's Baptist congregation. Despite Bussey and the BMC's opposition, which kept the December 1966 performance at Constitution Hall from completely selling out, Ellington had the endorsement of many black churchgoers and E. Franklin Jackson, pastor of the John Wesley AME Zion Church (his father's congregation).[23]

The opposition to the Sacred Concerts, based on the claim that Ellington's personal life did not conform to Christian teaching, was likely rooted in the popular image of Ellington as decidedly non-monogamous, in addition to his close association with his younger male co-composer.[24] Ellington's womanizing was notorious, particularly given the fact that he remained separated from his wife, Edna, without ever divorcing. His close relationship with the openly gay Billy Strayhorn (1915–1967), his "writing and arranging companion," likely raised issues for those who found neither man's sexual practices morally acceptable. Ellington and others remarked on the closeness of his musical relationship with Strayhorn, sometimes ascribing a telepathic quality to it. In an hour-long 1970 television special, Ellington recalled that when Strayhorn was in the hospital, Ellington asked him to prepare a theme for "In the Beginning, God" "to keep him busy": "His theme had six syllables or six tones, and mine had six syllables or tones, naturally, 'In the Beginning, God,' and there were only two notes that were different. Now I don't remember which of his notes were different . . . [*Ellington plays six notes*] . . . His started in the same place and ended in the same place, and only two of the notes in between were different. So it was a very,

very close thing." In the same television special, after playing Strayhorn's "Lotus Blossom," Ellington remarked of Strayhorn's companion, who was also a pianist, "I'm sure Aaron Bridgers plays it better than I do," possibly indicating a closeness to Strayhorn that Bridgers had but Ellington could never obtain.[25]

Given Ellington's immense grief after Strayhorn's death from esophageal cancer, Strayhorn's publicist, Joe Morgen, produced a likely fabricated interview in which the younger pianist is "uncharacteristically tough-talking" about his presumed bachelorhood ("his apartment was too sloppy for any gal to stomach") in order to deflect rumors about a possible sexual component to Ellington's relationship with him. Additionally, at least one recounting of a conversation with Ellington presented the composer affirming Strayhorn's sexuality as natural, given its historical presence in West African societies. Strayhorn biographer and Duke Ellington Society president David Hajdu addressed the constant speculation surrounding the deeply intimate relationship between Ellington and Strayhorn in a 1999 *Vanity Fair* article, including the perspective of Ellington's son, Mercer. Hajdu wrote:

> As for Duke, Mercer said—with no hint of spin—he had always simply assumed that his father's bond with Strayhorn, his legendary sexual appetite, and his seemingly boundless sense of adventure likely led to some experimentation with Strayhorn. "I don't know for a fact—I didn't watch them," he said. "I just presumed as much. So did the cats [in the band]. One told me he walked in on them one time. I never pressed the issue. It seemed like a given."
>
> A few of those close to Duke Ellington discussed homosexuality with him directly. According to Sam Shaw, producer of the 1961 film *Paris Blues*, scored by Ellington and Strayhorn, "Duke talked to me about Billy and the whole subject of homosexuality. In certain [African] tribes, the priests wore blue robes, which were the symbol of their status. They were considered holy, and they were bisexual—part of the African culture. Duke accepted that as part of nature."
>
> Some of Ellington's personal beliefs, feelings, and preferences— including for instance, his habit of wearing blue clothing—are more than just subjects of gossip because they had a significant effect on what he brought to the public .... Duke Ellington accepted, nurtured, supported,

and empowered a small, shy gay man whom he loved as a soul mate, and he gave voice to that man's music through his own.[26]

It is worth noting that Mercer Ellington's reflections in this *Vanity Fair* publication caused controversy for Hajdu: "'It was as if I had printed the worst conceivable thing about Duke Ellington,' [Hajdu] says. Nobody seemed to mind reading that Ellington was 'a misogynist who treated women like interchangeable body parts,' Hajdu notes. 'But the suggestion that he might have had a physical relationship with a man—that was horrific.'"[27] The *Star of Zion* editor William Davenport produced editorial commentary on male same-sex intercourse as "vile affections" in 1929, declaring that homosexuality was the result of "disease" or of "a sort of cult of abnormal vice" whose perpetrators should be quarantined from the rest of society. This condemnation coincided with Abyssinian Baptist Church pastor Adam Clayton Powell Sr.'s work in Harlem to expose and suppress African American men's same-sex practices, particularly sexual relations among black clergymen.[28]

These examples of anti-gay social discourses and practices occurred during the rise of jazz culture and alongside the emergence of Ellington's professional popularity as a composer and bandleader. Whether protective secrecy or genuine agnosticism characterized others' beliefs about the type of intimacy existing between Strayhorn and Ellington over their decades-long musical partnership, Ellington certainly expressed no religious opposition to (or condemnation of) his beloved friend's sexuality. Aside from the perception of Ellington as a womanizer, his reported acceptance and affirmation of homosexuality may have also put him at odds with the church leaders who opposed the performance of his sacred concerts and doubted his religious sincerity.

Additionally, Pastor Bussey expressed to *Jet* magazine that Ellington's religious sincerity was questionable, because people who became Christians "stop worldly ways."[29] Ellington had no evangelical conversion narrative—no tale of transformation in a religious revival, no embrace of Jesus Christ on a mourner's bench, no theophany or religious vision in a dream of the sort that was common to nineteenth-century southern African American Christianity, no record of a private confession of Jesus as savior. Ellington presented his religious status as someone who was raised within churches and, more importantly, as a "believer." While in Bangor, Maine, he penned "I Have Sinned—Yes / But Do I Pray as a Sinner[?] No / I Pray—Yes—I Pray—Yes / I Pray as a Believer" as potential song lyrics, although they remained a private reflection.[30] Ellington wrote and spoke as an individual who inherited a religious tradition, rather than as an individual who underwent the conventional practices of status transformation within a religious community. The basic assertion of belief, during a perceived age of disbelief, was the ecumenical religious project that he promoted. However, if Ellington ever claimed "Christian" as the appropriate label for his professions of faith, the primarily wordless musical language that he used to convey a journey toward that position of belief, coupled with his sexual practices, would inevitably fail to convince some American Christians that he was one of their sincere brethren.

Despite this opposition from some black Baptists, Ellington enjoyed support for his concerts from several African American Christian congregations. He performed his First Sacred Concert at the First AME Zion Church of Brooklyn, a congregation within his father's denomination. To address the controversy surrounding black ministers opposing Ellington and his orchestra's performance in religious spaces, Ruben L. Speaks (1920–2001), First AME Zion's pastor and later a senior bishop of the denomination, wrote an introduction for the concert program booklet. Speaks stated that black Christian music initially emerged and continued to serve "as a bridge linking the sacred and the secular," given the history of professional choirs touring internationally and performing spirituals: "When all other avenues of expression and communications were closed to him [sic], the Negro sent his plea for freedom around the world on the wings of song." For Speaks, Ellington's concert remained in this tradition of African American sacred music that connected such ostensibly disparate realms. Speaks also argued that Jesus, who connected with the nonreligious world, served as a model for their church as well as Ellington: "Christ never attempted to compartmentalize or segmatize [sic] life; rather, He sought to spiritualize the whole of life. There is no rhythm, tune or melody that is unacceptable to God; if it is an honest attempt to glorify His Name. If it is acceptable to God, it is true worship." To concur with Ellington that he was using God-endowed musical talent for a worshipful purpose, Speaks quoted Psalm 150—as Ellington would in his Second Sacred Concert, when his song "Praise

God and Dance" used this biblical text. To further sanction Ellington's compositions, the program contained additional sacred music by First AME Zion's choir, which performed Bach's "Now Let Every Tongue" and Alberto Randegger's "Praise Ye the Lord." Additionally, the church's combined choirs performed Ellington's "Come Sunday."[31]

Ellington also performed the First Sacred Concert at a predominantly African American congregation in Boston that was not part of a historic African American Protestant denomination. Union Methodist Church's pastor, Gilbert Haven Caldwell (b. 1933), sent Ellington a telegram expressing interest in hosting a concert at his church, seeking to meet Ellington following a concert at Boston Symphony Hall on March 18, 1966.[32] In Union's program booklet for the concert, Caldwell hinted at controversy surrounding the church's decision to host the concert while ardently favoring it as Ellington's sincere religious performance: "There may be those who still find it difficult to accept the presence of an outstanding, world-famous Jazz Orchestra presenting a concert in a Church Sanctuary. I understand your reservations because unfortunately we have made a great division between the sacred and the secular. As a Clergyman I accept my share of guilt for perpetuating this division." However, the concert was to demonstrate that "all that we have has come from God. Tonight Mr. Ellington, The Orchestra and The Choir are making an offering unto God through the presentation of their music." Caldwell, then a thirty-two-year-old pastor, further stated that he had a "love affair" with jazz music and that it came from "the agony, the striving, the joy my people have known in this land. It represents one of the many contributions the Negro has made to this great country." Generational and denominational differences between Caldwell and other African American ministers in black Protestant churches likely accounted for his appreciation of jazz as a black art form. Caldwell expressed pride in the fact that he was able to "present to all of Boston this Sacred Concert" as representative of African American culture, for "in a very real way jazz had its beginning in the Negro church."[33]

As a minority presence within a predominantly white Christian denomination (and city), Caldwell inhabited the role of religious race representative. In this moment, he marshalled African American history to determine that Ellington's musical production was religiously sound. With Speaks, Caldwell framed the jazz musician's musical offerings as a bridge between "sacred" and "secular" realms. These ministers marked a departure from earlier religious race professionals' discourse about jazz music and culture. Whereas jazz had defined for them the realm of sin far removed from all sacred matters in the 1920s and 1930s, the history of the art form's professionalization and musician representatives resulted in its shift to the "neutral," nonreligious realm of labor and leisure, now with immense potential for religious significance.

African American religious participation in Ellington's First Sacred Concert also came from non-ecclesial organizations. A letter from Alma C. Hawkins, president of the International Church Ushers Association of Washington, DC, referenced Ellington's performance at Constitution Hall on December 5, 1966. Her letter indicated the service and support of African American ushers at this event, despite the disapproval of the concert by several Baptist ministers.[34] The Martha Chapter No. 10 of the Order of the Eastern Star sponsored a performance of the Second Sacred Concert at the T. A. Willett Auditorium in Portsmouth, Virginia, in February 1968. This date featured a "surprise appearance" by famed actor and choreographer Geoffrey Holder (1930–2014) for Ellington's "Praise God and Dance" climax. Holder performed a "ritualistic dance" on stage while wearing a red toga.[35] The Tougaloo College Choir appeared in the Carnegie Hall performance of Ellington's Sacred Concert on April 4, 1968 (and the program was interrupted to announce the assassination of King and to pause for prayer). The predominantly black Tougaloo College in Mississippi was sponsored by the predominantly white United Church of Christ and the Christian Church (Disciples of Christ). The Tougaloo Alumni Association of New York was a sponsor of the Carnegie concert, and the college president presented an honorary degree to Ellington.[36] The Alpha Nu chapter of the Omega Psi Phi fraternity sponsored a performance of the Second Sacred Concert at Boyle Stadium in Stamford, Connecticut, in June 1968, and the chapter affirmed Ellington's "growing sense of his vocation and his awareness of an ecumenical tide in religion."[37]

The First Sacred Concert won widespread acclaim, and Ellington's "In the Beginning, God" earned a Grammy for Best Original Jazz Composition in 1966. Ellington's Second Sacred Concert received greater support from African American churches, Protestant and otherwise. The premiere concert at the Cathedral Church of St. John the Divine in New

York City, on January 19, 1968, featured the choir of the Mother AME Zion Church in Harlem.[38] Eve Lynn, reviewing a performance held at Enon Baptist Church in Philadelphia, considered its potential to "open an entirely new world of dramatic music" for churches, an apparent confirmation that the concert's overall sound was quite distinct from either spirituals or gospel.[39] The Second Sacred Concert was performed as a benefit at St. Augustine Presbyterian Church, an African American congregation in the Bronx (to finance the church's summer camp) and three days later at Bethany Baptist Church in Newark, New Jersey. Performing the concerts to raise funds for black congregations signaled the Ellington Orchestra's financial security and, perhaps, the socioeconomic distances between black and white mainline Protestantisms.[40] Additionally, in November 1968, the Second Sacred Concert appeared "under the auspices of Christ Unity [now 'Universal'] Temple at the Auditorium Theatre" in Chicago, and the "Friends of Unity" choir performed the spiritual "Ain'a That Good News" in the concert.[41] Johnnie Colemon (1920–2014), the "first lady of the New Thought Christian community," founded this African American New Thought church in 1956.

The Sacred Concerts: Jazz in Sanctuary Spaces

On most occasions, the Sacred Concerts featured the participation of local church choirs, whether in black or white congregations. Thomas J. Whaley, a composer and arranger who was Ellington's chief copyist, was responsible for rehearsing the choirs of the congregations that hosted Ellington's performances in the United States and Western Europe. When performing the Second Sacred Concert in Barcelona, Spain, the accompanying choir was Roman Catholic. In his memoir, Ellington reflected on the interracial and interfaith significance of the concert occasion when performing with a Catholic choir in the Roman Theatre of Orange, France: "When I heard them singing in the ancient Roman amphitheatre in Orange with Alice Babs from Stockholm, Toney Watkins from Philadelphia, and our band of musicians from all over the USA, before a perceptive and very appreciative French audience—then I felt the ecumenical spirit was really working."[42] This "ecumenical spirit" in a welcoming, Cold War-era Western Europe had been made possible by the State Department's program of cultural diplomacy. The State

Department had sent African American musicians like Ellington and his orchestra abroad, ideally as evidence of the social and cultural promise of capitalism and representative democracy.

The sacred concert occasion also called for the momentary modification of worship space, or at least the unsettling of its normal appearance and intended purpose to accommodate an unusual religious event. The concerts required the running of microphone cables along the sanctuary floors in order to capture the voices of the musicians and vocalists as well as the precise sounds of the drum set. As a broadcast religious event at the Fifth Avenue Presbyterian Church, Ellington's concert brought television cameras, camera operators, and even more cable equipment into religious space. The drum set, seating (and portable stage risers) for the trumpets, trombones, saxophones, and a tap dance mat all required space. The performers, dancers, and instrumentalists were certain to generate plenty of sweat—and Ellington's horn and reed players needed to empty spit valves during the performances (see figure 5.1). On the cross-sectional schematic of the sanctuary for the concert performance and setup, the architect recorded the following instructions: "NOTE— CHURCH ENVIRONMENT TO BE COMPLETELY ADHERED TO."[43] Whether these instructions were for the audio-visual crew, or Ellington and his orchestra, they indicated a recognition that to stage a televised concert performance in this worship space was potentially to trouble its sanctity. In the interest of evangelizing with an ecumenical message, Fifth Avenue Presbyterian needed to welcome into its sanctuary an audience that extended beyond its regular parishioners to include the press and Ellington fans who may not have had a primarily religious interest in his performance. The Ellington concerts occasioned interfaith and interracial moments in liberal religious spaces. However, there was also a suspicion about the capacity of "outsiders" to behave appropriately in these progressive fellowships.

Some aspects of Ellington's musical reflections on God would never completely translate for audiences, given the acoustic hostility of some religious spaces, including cathedrals, to the sounds his instrumental musicians had honed over the years. A *Down Beat* review of the First Sacred Concert's premiere in San Francisco's Episcopalian Grace Cathedral lamented the building's inhospitable architecture for the jazz musicians' performance. The reviewer surmised that "Ellington may have

Figure 5.1. Duke Ellington rehearsing his Second Sacred Concert, with Toney Watkins directing the Gustav Vasa Church Choir (*left*), Alice Babs and dancers (*rear*), and the Ellington orchestra (*right*). Stockholm, Sweden, September 18, 1969. (Photo care of Roger Tillberg / Alamy Stock Photo. Reprinted with permission.)

been unaware that much of his musical statement had been lost high in the arched ceiling of the large church. Most of the low tones Ellington's men produced rumbled and blurred into an impenetrable mass—and to appreciate fully the beauty of Ellington's music, the lines must be heard clearly." The reviewer stated that the band's location behind the altar "may have added to the cathedral's built-in acoustical problems." Grace Cathedral's "devilish acoustics," combined with a poor sound system, became especially noticeable when vocalist Queen Esther Marrow sang Ellington's "Tell Me It's the Truth" and "fell victim to the lo-fi public-address system (it sounded like something the cathedral people had borrowed from a store-front church)." Vocalist Jimmy McPhail (1928–1998) was also "dealt a blow by the sound system and acoustics, making it impossible to understand much of what he was singing."[44]

Marrow, a soul and gospel singer, and McPhail, a jazz and blues singer, faced acoustic difficulties in Grace Cathedral's sanctuary. It became evident that the vocal traditions they represented and performed, in addition to Ellington's orchestral jazz, did not emerge from within the large communal spaces of elite American mainline Protestantism, where constructing high, ornate ceilings was within financial reach for these denominations. These vocal and instrumental styles emerged from alternative black religious and social spaces: rural churches, urban storefront churches, apartment rent parties, and dance halls. In these spaces, the sounds were less likely to reverberate down long sanctuary halls or to dissipate among the rafters. Consequently, social distances became evident in the unintended sonic dissonances. And ironically, cathedral performances that occasioned racially significant candid photographs to promote the Sacred Concerts commercially and religiously belied the acoustic difficulties present during live performances. These unanticipated problems with sound may have muffled Ellington's interreligious and interracial messages.

Conclusion

Over the course of the three Sacred Concerts, Ellington would modify the tones, tempos, and voices he used in his music to create sounds more audible within these elite white religious spaces. As Ellington worked to speak about, to, and for God through his music, the theology he conveyed over the three concert tours also reflected personal changes in tone over time. Endowed with the trust of many ministers and religious institutions to present a statement of faith, Ellington made use of these public settings to serve as an African American representative of religious fidelity who was privately in the constant process of working out the nature of that belief. Although he was granted a unique opportunity, Ellington's wrestling reflects the individual lives of many religious adherents. It troubles the easy assumption that an individual's commitment to religious institutions, assent to doctrinal statements, or participation in religious rituals implies a shared, uncomplicated understanding of those spaces, languages, actions, or objects of reverence.

6

"Is God a Three-Letter Word for Love?"

There have been times when I thought I had a glimpse of
God. Sometimes, even when my eyes were closed, I saw. Then
when I tried to set my eyes—closed or open—back to the
same focus, I had no success, of course. The unprovable fact
is that I believe I have had a glimpse of God many times. I
believe because believing is believable, and no one can prove
it unbelievable.

Some people who have had the same experience I have had
are afraid or ashamed to admit it. They are afraid of being
called naïve or square. They are afraid of being called unbrain-
washed by the people who brainwash them, or by those they
would like to be like, or friendly with. Maybe they just want to
be *in*. Maybe it's a matter of the style, the trend, or whatever
one thinks one does to be acceptable in certain circles.

There was a man who was blessed with the vision to see
God. But even this man did not and does not have the power
or whatever it takes to show God to a believer, much less an
unbeliever.

—Duke Ellington, "Seeing God"

Duke Ellington sympathized with any effort to affirm God and to affirm
believing in God. While on the road, in preparation for his Sacred Concerts, he used hotel stationery to make personal notes that contained
potential lyrics for his sacred music. In the process of crafting prose and
poetry for his songs, Ellington transcribed his efforts to verbalize what
it meant to express belief in God. A reflection at the Detroit Hilton hotel
became a driving assertion of his Sacred Concerts: "Every Man Prays in
His Own Language & there is No Language GOD Does Not Understand."
On the opposite side of the stationery, Ellington explained that music

was "My Language," that it "Got Me into Church," and that it was "Possibly My Most Eligible Form of Semantics—if I am to Speak to GOD."[1]

Historian of religions Charles H. Long contemplated the emergence of African American religion and culture as modern phenomena birthed in the Middle Passage. Specific to this emergence was the practice of prayer, "an orientation, the initial deciphering of a way to be in the world" that did not depend on "words or postures" to come into being. Rather, both the form(s) and object(s) of the enslaved African's prayers on the slave ships were yet indeterminate, or disoriented:

> To whom does one pray from the bowels of a slave ship? To the gods of Africa? To the gods of the masters of the slave vessels? To the gods of an unknown and foreign land of enslavement? To whom does one pray? From the perspective of religious experience, this was the beginning of African American religion and culture. In the forced silence of oppression, in the half-articulate moans of desperation, in the rebellions against enslavement—from this cataclysm another world emerged. This other world was a correlate of, simultaneous with and parallel to the other Atlantic world. Africans' first expressions of the meaning of the New World took place in the experience of the daemonic dread as they were forced into history as terror—the modern world-system.

For Long, wordless prayer was "a basic turning of the soul toward another defining reality." It was the foundation for "another world" of religions that enslaved human cargo expressed as ships transported Africans into the Americas.[2] This emerging Afro-Atlantic world of religions and cultures eventually produced the Afro-Protestant institutions that Ellington met in his childhood church life. Now, the wordless prayers that he embraced through music constituted his language to engage his "GOD"—not in the bowels of a slave ship, or hush harbors, or segregated churches, but in the sanctuaries of the Western world's elite houses of worship.

The constantly touring Ellington made sense of God on the road without a regular church home. He theologized as he read the Christian Bible and engaged primarily liberal religious literature. When he finally attended houses of worship, it was without adhering to their specific doctrinal commitments. It was as a celebrated musician, similar to an honored guest preacher, but bearing a primarily musical and nondenominational message. In these moments, the famous composer bypassed lay status within any denomination. As a professional African American artist who enjoyed more than forty years of career success, he enjoyed a relatively exalted status in white religious spaces and in the black religious spaces where ministers and congregants respected his jazz career. In this light, Ellington embraced the authority to speak about God that listening audiences afforded him. He sought to do so publicly so that Protestants, Jews, and Catholics would accept his musical messages. However, Ellington's private reflections in hotels reveal that the composer and his God were never exactly Protestant, Jewish, or Catholic.

Ellington's private lyrical writings expressed belief in God, his frustrations with language to refer to God, and his appeal to the very act of believing. His undated hotel stationery writings, in conversation with his engagement of religious literature and ministerial friends, exist as the unexamined arena of his personal religious exploration, reflection, and contention in the process of crafting music to make public expressions of belief. Ellington's ultimate aspiration was to use his preferred language of music to express wordlessly the proper reverence for God. In that process, however, he wrote lyrics to convey his frustrations that language was inadequate for articulating what it meant to believe in and to speak of God. Ultimately, the concepts of God and of love became synonymous for Ellington, and he articulated these most vocally in his final Sacred Concert. The primary context for examining Ellington's expressions of belief and conceptions of God is the composition of specific songs for performance in his three Sacred Concerts, premiering in 1965, 1968, and 1973. These Sacred Concerts also served to revitalize Ellington's career as he entered his seventies.

As the chapter epigraph reveals, remembrances of "seeing God" stuck with Ellington throughout his adult life and compelled his commitment to believing in God, rather than a statement of faith tied to the variety of possible Christian confessions.[3] His music lyrics were not likely to represent Christian communities that required conversion experiences from members or elicited their conversion narratives—and Ellington similarly lacked such a conversion narrative. Ellington reflected on his attempts to describe God and his expressed frustrations with existing language to describe the divine in his private writings and his annotations of religious literature. He ultimately composed several songs that he selected for public performance to reflect his characterization of the divine. In private, Ellington expressed his belief in the declaration and practice of believing, he engaged regularly with liberal Christian literature, and he affirmed certain teachings about Jesus in relation to God, even though there was a near-total absence of references to Jesus in his Sacred Concert music. And toward the end of his life, Ellington posed a musical question equating "love" and "God."

With Ellington's private writings and public professions, his thoughts stand as prominent examples of theological wrestling. They complicate any conclusion that the profession of belief and performance of praise for the divine, within sacred spaces, serves to affirm wholesale the teachings about the divine within those theological communities.

"In the Beginning, God": Duke's Divine Descriptions

For Ellington's First Sacred Concert, the opening of the King James Version of Genesis 1:1 represented his musical theme, "In the Beginning, God." It begins as a wordless, "personal statement" with six tones symbolizing "the six syllables in the first four words of the Bible" that Ellington and his ensemble repeated "many times . . . many ways" throughout the performance.[4] In a 1968 Sacred Concert program text draft, Ellington wrote that these four words had greater ecumenical and individual value as a "personal statement" than if he had chosen any specific denominational creed: "I base the major theme of these sacred programs on the first four words of the Bible: 'In the beginning God. . . .' Because whatever church we're appearing in, the people there can understand these words and the feeling they give. It becomes a personal statement, not a doctrine. / Personal things are the important things in life: love is personal, music is personal, communicating is personal."[5]

Following the instrumental performance of this theme on the album version is the voice of Brock Peters (1927–2005), the African American actor recently famous for portraying Tom Robinson in the 1962 movie version of Harper Lee's novel *To Kill a Mockingbird*. Peters sings:

> In the beginning, God,
> In the beginning, God,
> In the beginning, God,
> No heaven, no earth, no nothing.[6]

After this statement, the song takes an up-tempo swing beat, and Peters provides a list of objects and concepts familiar to the audience that were not yet in existence. This act of listing effectively requests that the concert attendee (or album listener) pause to contemplate an original state of existence where God is the sole presence. For AMEZ bishops in the mid-1920s, "In the beginning, God" encompassed "all that Moses knew, and that is all anybody knows about the beginning: God. And that is the sublimest fact in history."[7] For Ellington in the mid-1960s, to stop at the words "In the beginning, God" and its implication of pre-primordial divine existence was to capture an assertion he found sufficient for religious reflection, praise, and worship. The double negative at the end of "No heaven, no earth, no nothing" conveyed both a colloquial African American phrasing and the belief that even nothingness or nonexistence was absent when God was the only being.

Following the Peters section, the choir shouts the names of the books of the Hebrew Bible alongside a solo by alto saxophonist Paul Gonsalves. Ellington biographer Janna Tull Steed writes that his listing of Hebrew Bible and New Testament books indicated "the likelihood of an early Bible memorization assignment—as does the chanting, in order, of all the names of all the books of the Bible in the development of the piece."[8] Such verbalized memorizations of the books of the Bible in his youth lend to a portrait of Ellington's participation in what Bible scholar Vincent L. Wimbush has termed the culture of "scripturalization." "Scriptural" subjects are those who have viewed the compilation of the Hebrew and Christian texts in the English (or King James) collection as "the Bible" (or "the Scriptures"). They represent a dominant Protestant culture's regard for this specific religious literature as the "fetishized center-object" that came into being with the establishment of British North America.[9] This modern Protestant view of a specific edition of Christian and Jewish religious texts endured through the birth of the United States in the form of evangelical narratives of self. The King James Bible bears a "fetishistic" imprimatur, because one may gain cultural authority through rhetorical invocation of "talking" scripture passages—as in the example of an individual who declares, "the Bible says . . ." to make her case.

One also acquires cultural authority through a "biblical" narrative of one's own conversion, or through naming the individual books, as in Ellington's sacred music. Historian of American religions Seth Perry frames scripturalization as a "co-constitutive operation" that privileges biblical text and its citation against all other forms of text in American culture: "Biblical citation—through oral quotation, physical performance, written imitation—is a way of distinguishing some speech or activity from the usual, as special. At the same time, scriptural citation marks the cited text itself as special, worthy of citation."[10] Through his vocal choir, Ellington's mere recitation of the Bible books marked himself, through musical prose, as an authoritative bearer of consequential American religious content. In this composition's live performance as well as through its preservation on record, he reinforced the sacred status of scriptural texts in American religious culture.

After a pause to applaud Gonsalves, a dramatic fanfare introduces an ascending trumpet solo by William "Cat" Anderson. After Anderson's final high note, Ellington states, "That's as high as we go," to audience laughter and applause for Anderson. This trumpet solo captured Anderson's sonic limits—despite his virtuosic gifts—as a reflection of human limitation in praising, approaching, or even apprehending the divine.

Neither the biblical acts of creation nor God's creative capacities are Ellington's principal foci with this opening personal statement. Simply to contemplate God's eternal existence aside from any other created order engenders Ellington's musical celebration. In a rough copy of his Sacred Concert program text, Ellington wrote, "In the beginning, we only existed in the mind of GOD, and so GOD, very graciously, shared with us a life of our own."[11] These notes and Ellington's hotel stationery reveal that while traveling, he made constant attempts to characterize God in his own language. He debated the precise language others employed to capture the nature of God for his songs. In one private hotel moment, Ellington expressed a definition of God through personal experience with the natural world: "I Can Hear GOD Anytime / I Can Feel GOD in the Sun Rise / the Smell & the Taste / of the Wind & the Sea / MAKES ME See GOD When I Close My Eyes."[12] At other times, Ellington turned to religious literature to encounter other conceptions of God within Christian traditions. Some of this literature he acquired from clerical fans, and he sustained an engagement with it in the process of composing his three Sacred Concerts.

As a public representative of receptivity to religious belief, Ellington became a repository or vessel for others' more pronounced and firm religious commitments. Clerical friends, religious fans, and evangeliz-ing strangers sent him religious materials as gifts in order to persuade him to join their religious communities. For Ellington to express divine belief without adhering to any particular Christian denomination meant that others were willing to send him scriptures and religious literature to compel him in particular theological directions. Ellington's appar-ent openness left him vulnerable to accusations of insincere piety and superficial belief, as previously explored. But such openness also made him likely to forge new religious relationships that became friendly ex-changes of letters and telephone conversation, some of which fed into the Sacred Concerts. Ellington's collection of religious literature reveals that one's profession of religious commitment in twentieth-century America did not seal the individual off from the reality of competing religious commitments, which may even have appeared as the well-intentioned proselytizing of others who admired the popular jazz musi-cian and sought to welcome him into their fellowships. Nevertheless, Ellington wrote that he interpreted these gifts from clergy as encourage-ment to create sacred music "not as a matter of career, but in response to a growing understanding of my own vocation."[13]

Several religious books that Ellington received during his Sacred Concert years simply served as gifts of appreciation following concert performances, bearing no visible markers that the composer had read, annotated, or even opened them. He received a copy of *Sabbath Songs for Congregational Singing*, adapted from the Central Conference of American Rabbis' Union hymnal. The Christian Science writer Frank A. Salisbury sent a copy of Mary Baker Eddy's *Science and Health with Key to the Scriptures*. From the Unitarian minister Richard Gilbert and Presbyterian minister Kenneth Neigh, Ellington received a copy of *The Blue Denim Bible: The New Testament in Today's English Version: Good News for the Modern Man* with the inscription, "To the Duke—who is the real 'Good News' to men and music! Agape." From the Canadian Roman Catholic priest Gerald Pocock, Ellington received copies of F. C. Happold's *Prayer and Meditation: Their Nature and Practice*, *Good News for Modern Man: The New Testament in Today's English Version*, *The Psalms of the Jerusalem Bible* (a birthday gift in 1969), and *The Catholic Hymnal and Service Book*. Following the 1968 premiere of El-lington's Second Sacred Concert at New York's Cathedral of St. John the

Divine, Episcopal bishop James A. Pike sent a copy of his book *A Time for Christian Candor*, addressed to "Duke and Evie" and signed by Pike, his family, and friends praising Ellington's musical statement about his faith. After a November 1970 concert performance, Ellington received a copy of *The Jerusalem Bible: The Psalms for Reading and Recitation* from Rabbi Meyer Heller of Temple Emanuel in Beverly Hills, California. Ida Joseph Atwood, a Chicago minister in the National Spiritualist Association of Churches, sent Ellington a copy of *Divine Remedies: A Textbook on Spiritual History* from the Unity School of Christianity, with creased page ears for sections dealing with throat and lung ailments (likely her attempt to aid Ellington in the early 1970s after his battle with lung cancer became public knowledge).[14]

Of the religious literature in his collection, Ellington read *Destined for Greatness*, a booklet by Life Messengers, "an evangelical non-profit organization" based in Seattle, Washington. Life Messengers, a publishing ministry founded in 1944 by Moody Bible Institute graduate Ray W. Johnson and his wife, Vera, also published *The Last Days Bible*, which focused on premillennial evangelical concepts of the impending apocalypse.[15] *Destined for Greatness* is an apologetic narrative tract, with a scientist named "Dr. Fronkby" at the center of the encounter over proof of God's existence and the literal reliability of the Bible. Dr. Fronkby is convinced of God's existence and biblical infallibility, and he engages a group of students who challenge his rationale behind evangelical Christian commitment versus modern science's presumed opposition to it. A student named John asked, "If there is a God and He created everything, who made God?" followed by "'But *why* didn't God reveal something about how He came to be?' John persisted. 'If He does exist why hasn't He explained His existence? Maybe I could believe if He would explain His own beginning'" [emphasis in original]. Ellington drew a question mark and circled it next to this passage. In response to Steve, who asked, "But *why* is God so secretive about His beginnings?," Ellington wrote, "HOW DARE WE" at the page bottom, and at the top of the next page he wrote, "WE DON'T UNDERSTAND ALL THINGS ON EARTH— TANGIBLE." In his response to this series of questioning, Dr. Fronkby speaks of God's beginning: "What He has chosen *not* to reveal is none of our business." Here, Ellington bracketed this sentence and wrote "GOD" on top of "He." With this action, Ellington placed the sentence, which he considered a compelling response, in his preferred theological language.[16] Similarly, Susan's question to Dr. Fronkby about the concept of the Trinity and God permitting Jesus Christ's substitutionary atonement ("Why didn't He show His great love for us by coming Himself instead of sending His Son to suffer? Why didn't *He* suffer for us instead?") irked Ellington. He added a question mark to the paragraph and wrote, "STU-PID" after Susan's question.[17]

As expressed in his writings on hotel stationery, precise language to address directly and to speak about God was a paramount concern for Ellington. An Ellington stationery writing at the Hilton in Jacksonville, Florida, adds texture to his expressed frustrations with the exchange between the fictional Dr. Fronkby and the students:

> What Made You Think ^(That) You Can Use the Word HIM
> Why Do You Refer to the Almighty as HE
> When You Pray ^(First Person) How Dare You Address the
>   LORD as YOU
> Him, You & He
> Are Correct When Addressing Me[18]

Ellington's private writing, which addressed an unspecified believer as the subject, reveals a tone of frustration with the commonplace usage of masculine pronouns and titles to refer to God. Ellington even made an attempt to craft lyrics for a tune, titled "There Is No Pronoun Good Enough for GOD," which expressed his belief that regal addresses like "His or Her Majesty" and "Your Highness" for royals or "Your Honor" for a judge fall short of adequacy when speaking to the divine.[19] A Washington, DC, reflection expressed his lament over the absence of sufficiently exclusive language: "With So Many ^(Educated[,] Brilliant) People (Scholars) With Such Highly Developed Vocabularies—In So Many, Many ^(Sophisticated) Languages & Not One, Who Think[?] of a Worthy Pronoun." When referring to God, the archaic "thou" and capitalized masculine pronouns were apparently insufficient for Ellington. At the end of this note, Ellington declared, "GOD is Beyond Gender."[20]

To identify the supreme deity as "beyond gender" was a clear statement with which Ellington relegated gendered language to the created, material world. However, this exact phrasing is likely significant in El-

lington's usage, given his history of considering others "beyond" standard classification. For other artists, to be "beyond category" in the jazz
world was to bear Ellington's highest praise. Fellow musicians Mary Lou
Williams and Ella Fitzgerald received this veneration, with the latter artist receiving a musical tribute when Ellington and Billy Strayhorn composed "Portrait of Ella Fitzgerald" with a third movement titled "Beyond
Category." It is likely, therefore, that this assertion of a deity's genderless
identity is simultaneously Ellington's insistent assertion of God's superi-
ority to gendered descriptions and an expression of high religious praise.

The evidence of this descriptive theological assertiveness would not
appear as an explicit message in any of the songs from Ellington's three
Sacred Concerts. However, Ellington created a symphonic composition titled "New World A-Comin'," inspired by Roi Ottley's *New World
A-Coming: Inside Black America*, a Peabody Award-winning book on
African American society. Ellington's "New World A-Comin'," with the
composer's spoken-word introduction in the 1970 orchestral album recording, envisioned a future where "there will be no war, no greed, no
categorization, no nonbelievers, where love is unconditional, and there
is no pronoun good enough for God."[21] A testament to this composition's long-standing religious significance for Ellington is that he included his solo piano performance of "New World A-Comin'" in his
First Sacred Concert series.

Historian of African American religions Wallace Best has examined
the religious liberalism of Ellington's contemporary, the African American poet Langston Hughes (1901–1967). Hughes shared with Ellington
"a deep affection for many aspects of the church of his youth, mainly its
worship."[22] Hughes wrote that "no single word or language is big enough
to contain God." This statement meant that "no name for God is ad-
equate and all names for God are equally valid." As Hughes surmised,
"Maybe another name for God is Mystery, or Love, the Holy Spirit or
Father Divine, Unity or Universal Power, Buddah [*sic*] or Allah, or Jehovah, or names I have never heard of."[23] By contrast, Ellington began to
pursue the use of terminology to address and describe God that would
not apply to any other subject or concept. This must have been a constant thought process for Ellington while traveling, for his poetic reflection in San Antonio, Texas, describes his ongoing pursuit of such elusive
language:

My Dear GOD I've Been Searching
Searching For the Word or the Phrase
that Cannot Be Use[d] [for?] any Purpose
& Has Not ~~Been Used~~ Through All the Universal Days

My Dear GOD I've Been looking,
Listening, looking & Trying to Find
An Eligible light of Semantics
that's Right For the One God Divine

When Speaking to or Of My Dear GOD
There's Not One Pronoun
that Hasn't Been Used for Others
~~& Not One That Hasn't Been Used I've Found~~ No Not One I've
Found[24]

With music, Ellington was able to find or create a phrase, theme, or melody to express a concept, mood, person, or group of people. But he appeared frustrated by his inability to do likewise with existing language about the divine. Additional reflections in Greensboro, North Carolina, and Baltimore, Maryland, indicate that Ellington momentarily considered the exclusive use of the first-person pronoun by God—and God alone—acceptable. In one instance, he declared "The Only Pronoun Good Enough for God is 'I' When used in the FIRST PERSON." In another, he wrote, "There is only ^(the) ONE Pronoun / good Enough For GOD / & It Can only Be Use[d] By the ONE / GOD—I AM."[25] To relegate the address of God to God's self may have served to convey the essential ineffability that Ellington felt in his reverence for the divine. The practice of generating such written statements about God may have even served as acts of private worship for Ellington. However, this work would not suffice for Ellington's attempt to capture the worshipful rhetoric of believers in the God of the Hebrew Bible for the songs he was composing. The Baltimore reflection in which Ellington referred to God as "the ONE" reveals his attempt to employ a numerical pronoun to address the Almighty. Another reflection in Honolulu, Hawaii, reveals Ellington's seemingly meditative attempts to spell out this form of reverence.[26]

Ellington had used "the One" to refer to God in a composition that predated his three Sacred Concerts. In 1963 he composed a stage play, *My People*, a "social significance" work intended for a children's audience during the height of the civil rights movement. *My People* was reminiscent of the pageants from Ellington's childhood, including Du Bois's *The Star of Ethiopia*.[27] This play was broadcast so that black children, the larger white American viewership, and a wider European audience would know that "there are Negro doctors, lawyers, businessmen, nurses, teachers, telephone operators, policemen, and housewives" worthy of admiration.[28] One of the religious compositions for this broadcast was titled "Ain't but the One," which Ellington's orchestra performed with the lead vocals of Jimmy McPhail and the backing vocals of the Irving Bunton Singers. By employing the familiar call-and-response singing of black gospel music, "Ain't but the One" reflected Ellington's strident monotheism through the lyric's listing of God's activity as chronicled primarily in the Hebrew Bible. These lyrics invoked events that would have been familiar to any African Americans who were attached to the tradition of music derived from spirituals. But the lyrics for "Ain't but the One" made use of implied pronouns (and interrogative pronouns) when describing God. They effectively served Ellington's frustration by evading gendered usage altogether. McPhail and the Irving Bunton Singers alternated choruses of "Ain't but the One (just One)" when describing the "one good Lord above" or the "one great God of love." McPhail spoke of a God who "made a serpent wiggle from a walking stick / made a snake out of a cane," and he asked, "who set the stars (sun and the moon)?" and "who knows the judgment (just who)?" without the use of "He."[29]

McPhail's line "Snatched Jonah, yes He did, from the belly of the whale" contains the masculine pronoun to refer to God. However, Ellington's manuscript lyrics for this song do not include "yes He did" and appear, instead, as "Snatched Jona / From the belly of the whale." While this instance indicates McPhail's original improvisation of the line, the inclusion of such exclamatory speech nevertheless acknowledges the importance of this African American Protestant manner of testifying about God's greatness. Aside from the performance of the 1958 version of "Come Sunday" in his concerts, which includes masculine pronouns to refer to God, McPhail's exclamation is the only instance of the use of "He" in Ellington's original Sacred Concert lyrics.[30] Ellington incorporated this song into his First Sacred Concert, thereby conveying to religious audiences nationwide his appraisal of the African American Christian musical tradition. But it was with subtlety that he omitted the use of the masculine pronoun that most Christians associated with God.

Besides use of "the One," Ellington composed "Supreme Being" for his Second Sacred Concert, an epic song similar to "In the Beginning, God" in its focus on the Hebrew Bible's Genesis creation narrative. Following an arranged instrumental opening, "Supreme Being" relied primarily on the choir and soloists' spoken word:

> Supreme Being!
> Supreme Being
> There is a Supreme Being
> There is one, only one, one Supreme Being
> Out of lightning, thunder, chaos and confusion
> The Supreme Being organized and created
> Created and organized heaven and earth. . . .
> Supreme Being.
> The immortal creator and ruler of the universe, eternal and
>   all-powerful
> Supreme Being
> Called God![31]

To speak repeatedly of one "Supreme Being" allowed Ellington to marshal many familiar religious descriptors for this divine concept. The lyrics contemplate this being and its attributes for over four minutes, before the chorus builds to the revelatory exclamation that it is also "called God!" The phrase "Supreme Being" also facilitated Ellington's declaration that the capitalized word "God," which many English-speaking monotheists use to refer to this divine being, inevitably fell short of fully capturing the divine object of reverence. In this instance, more words, rather than fewer, were necessary for Ellington to represent to the listener the detailed, epic biography of this entity of utmost existence.

Why was "Jesus" an insufficient noun for Ellington's description of God? Language about Jehovah, Yahweh, the Holy Ghost (or Holy

Spirit) is absent from Ellington's hotel stationery reflections. Similarly, Jesus's name appears only once. One undated piece of hotel stationery writing (without a location) reveals that Ellington similarly thought about the proper address of Jesus Christ as God's son: "People Who Have the Honor to Be Presented to a prince or Princess—[the] Son or Daughter—of a King is addressed ∧(or referred to) as your ∧(or His) Highness—Not He or She / But Not Jesus Christ—& Jesus is the Son of GOD / Why is Proper Protocol ∧NOT Provided [to?] the Son of GOD— Jesus Christ—" Although Ellington's pursuit of exclusive language to appropriately address the "Son of GOD" may reveal a significant place for Jesus in his theology, it does not indicate conclusively that he held God and Jesus (alongside the Holy Spirit) as equal deities, or that the "Son of GOD" was also "God the Son."

A 1958 interview revealed that Ellington regularly wore a gold cross under his shirt but also that he "almost never spoke about Jesus Christ directly, either in conversation or in the lyrics for his sacred compositions."[32] In his First Sacred Concert, Queen Esther Marrow sang in "The Lord's Prayer" that she was "beggin you, Jesus, to give me more grace / I need your power to help me to run this race" before she improvised on the New Testament "Our Father" prayer. It is likely that Ellington granted Marrow the improvisational freedom to use her preferred divine language. Nevertheless, the almost total absence of the name Jesus or the title Christ from Ellington's compositions is significant.

Two exceptions are possible allusions to Jesus in "Ain't but the One" and "Tell Me It's the Truth." In "Ain't but the One," McPhail's line "Made the cripple [sic] walk and the blind men to see" refers to two acts of Jesus that the New Testament Gospels provide, although this lyrical presentation also allows for attribution of the healings to the power of God. "Tell Me It's the Truth" references "the Gospel truth," because "the truth is the light and the light is right"—and to Marrow's "right?" Ellington answered, "right." Wilbert Hill writes that "Tell Me It's the Truth" is an example of Ellington incorporating characteristics of 1950s and 1960s gospel music in his First Sacred Concert, namely, "use of the tambourine, triple meter, a simple harmonic progression, call and response, and idiomatic orchestration of the gospel style accompaniment part supporting the melody sung by a contralto."[33] However, Marrow appears to sing, "Tell me it's *a* truth" in the Grace Cathedral premiere and on the album version, despite the album version's song title and versions by other Sacred Concert singers since.[34] Throughout the song, the singer appears in need of assurance that something is either true or "the truth," and the allusion to Jesus as either the biblical "truth" or "light" is possible but unclear. In both cases, Ellington elected to avoid direct mentions of Jesus or Christ.

A rhyming reflection written in Houston, Texas, serves as Ellington's attempt at a proverb, imitating a Shakespearean line from *The Merchant of Venice*: "It's a Wise Man Who Knows His Father / It's a Wise Man Who Knows His Son / It's a Wise Man Who Knows that GOD / & that GOD is the *One and Only One*."[35] A *Christianity Today* profile of Ellington possibly sheds additional light on these theological absences in his Sacred Concert lyrics:

> His Washington, DC boyhood was filled with sermons and Sunday school, but Ellington has rarely attended services during his career and never joined a church. At 23, with a jazz career beginning to bloom, "I began to read the Bible for myself, to see what there was. I have my own idea, and I think it makes sense." This idea strays from the orthodox belief on the Trinity, but he is conservative about the Bible itself. "I believe the whole story," he said. "I am always in a position to have it out with people who say the Bible contradicts itself. I'm not a formal Bible student, but I can correct people on things like that."[36]

The profile offered no specific stances Ellington may have had regarding the doctrine that God existed simultaneously in three persons. However, it conveyed the musician's confidence in his own ability to comprehend, interpret, and defend biblical scriptures without conventional clerical guidance. The article glossed the prospect that Ellington's personal theology was unitarian, which may have explained his frustration with the fictional student questioning Dr. Fronkby about God suffering in Jesus's crucifixion. Rather, the article's focus was on Ellington's affirmation of the existence of God. *Christianity Today*'s mission was to promote a more conservative evangelical Christian voice in print magazine culture than the mainline Protestant magazine, the *Christian Century*. Ellington's Sacred Concerts proclaimed belief. The defense of believing was sufficient for those religious participants who elected to operate

within an interfaith world as he had. However, the lyrics of his compositions never expressed clearly a belief in the resurrection, atonement, or
divinity of Jesus.

Like the religious booklets and pamphlets that easily accommodated
his itinerancy as a traveling musician, hotel stationery captured momentary religious exclamations, assertions, and attempts to work out convincing poetry and prose about God for a musician whose career was
anything but stationary. Additionally, pamphlet and booklet religious
literature suited women and men who were confident in their ability to
interpret religious scriptures, or to confirm religious authors' interpretations. These two vehicles served Ellington as he fashioned himself an
evangelist for the idea of believing. His Second Sacred Concert further
demonstrated this relatively assertive support for belief.

"Something 'bout Believing"

"Do you," a questioner probed, "consider yourself a religious
man?"

"I don't know what a religious man is," [Ellington] replied.
"There are a lot of people in the world who demonstrate
their religious belief more than I do but I don't know any
who are more serious in it than I.

"I say my prayers regularly, I believe in them and I believe
I am helped."
—Russ Wilson, "Jazz and a Cathedral"[37]

Was Ellington certain about the existence of God? Ellington represented
a conception of divine belief in his Second Sacred Concert. But this
statement about belief followed his engagement with Christian religious
literature. His reading habits represent his attempts to characterize the
meaning of having faith, or to commit to matters ultimately unverifiable
or not yet confirmed by human experience.

In private moments, Ellington played humorously with the idea of explaining the limits of certainty (and of cognition) regarding faith. At the
Detroit Hilton, he wrote, "I Know that there is So Much that I Know I
Don't Know . . . But I Don't Know How Much There is that I Don't Know
that I Don't Know I'm Ignorant of."[38] As Ellington reflected during one

stay in Fort Wayne, Indiana, "Any ^(SO CALLED) GOD That Can Be Proven or Identified By Shape, Size, Colour, Sound, Action or Reaction is Not a GOD at All—or Rather is Not GOD—"[39] Here, he appeared to embrace a basic uncertainty attendant with the limits of human knowledge, despite the prospect of scientific advances. Perhaps, then, to locate God in the historical Jesus was, for Ellington, to mistakenly or imprecisely identify God with a finite, material, gendered body.

Ellington elaborated on his belief with a draft of his text for the Second Sacred Concert's booklet in 1966. With respect to God's existence, "that which is possible is possible until proven impossible."[40] In this reflection, Ellington provided God a location within the universe that affirmed his previously mentioned doubt about anyone defining God empirically: "Not a little bit here, or a little bit there, God is Total, everywhere." Consequently, he argued that it was logically fruitless for a finite human being to profess the nonexistence (or demise) of God, or to interrogate another finite human being to prove God's presence:

> There is no such sentence as "GOD is dead." Anyone who says the first word immediately nullifies the balance of the sentence. GOD is all-specific—nothing can be added, positive or negative. Nobody can make GOD—nobody can make GOD prettier, better-larger-more powerful—nobody has eyes good enough to stand and look at GOD. GOD causes things to happen that we can see—hear-smell-taste-or feel—GOD causes things to happen that make all the other—I don't know how many—sensitivities react.
>
> Believing is a matter of profound intent, so, don't say to me "Show me GOD"—because I can't, and neither can anybody else. Such talk and questions, the most ridiculous stupidities. There are many things that most everybody believes that they cannot see.
>
> God and the enemy subversive—we can't see either one, but we know they are here in the USA.[41]

These statements about the impossibility of a perfect God's nonexistence did not end up in the Sacred Concert program booklets in Ellington's archival collection. However, Ellington's lyrics for "Something 'bout Believing" express this same sentiment that God is coterminous with existence. In one song section, the vocalists are monotone and emphatic:

"The silliest thing ever read / Was that somebody said, 'God is dead.' / The mere mention of the first word / Au-to-ma-ti-cal-ly e-li-mi-nates the se-cond and the thiiiiiird."[42] Ellington's confidence in his musical form of theological reasoning became evident when he included this portion of "Something 'bout Believing" in the text for his annual Christmas card—a recurring practice for sending holiday greetings to his family and friends in the music profession and beyond.[43] Ellington's Third Sacred Concert in 1973 included a composition, "Ain't Nobody Nowhere Nothin' without God." In this song, vocalist Toney Watkins cautioned, "One more word / Before I am dismissed / If you don't believe in God, / Then brother, you don't exist," and repeated the phrase "Ain't nothin' nothin' without God."[44]

Ellington kept a clipping of "The Greatest Gift Man Can Possess," a column by newspaper writer and Christian author Jim Bishop that the Hearst-owned King Features Syndicate originally published in 1958. Bishop's column addressed the very concept of faith in God in the absence of proof of God's existence: "Faith implies an absence of proof. You have [faith] or you do not. If you do not, then you have cancer of the soul and you will end up believing in nothing, including yourself." Bishop's concern in the piece was to reflect on coping with the death of a loved one and being uncertain of the existence of heaven. A general concept of faith in all human relationships was to flow from faith in God. And Bishop advocated reliance on the biblical accounts of God's promise of eternal life that required the individual's belief: "It's not necessary to be a divine to understand God and what He expects of us and what He has promised. All one needs is a small degree of literacy and an open mind." Adopting mainly a persuasive tone, Bishop also conceded the limits of proving divine or eschatological existence: "Faith is the most easily reviled of all the virtues. I can read the Bible and you can tell me that it is phony and I cannot prove that you are wrong."[45] While Ellington did not mark this newspaper clipping in any manner, it comported with his statements about faith and he kept it inside one of his many religious pamphlets.

Ultimately, message tone mattered to Ellington. A ripped-up score sheet from 1969 reveals an attempt to rebuke those without faith like Ellington. He wrote in capital letters, "IF YOU DON'T BE-LIEVE WHAT THE BIBLE SAYS SHAME ON YOU" and "YOU DON'T BELIEVE THAT

GOD'S IN HEAVEN SHAME ON YOU."[46] Ellington decided against reprimanding his potential audience, opting to employ a tone in songs like "Something 'bout Believing" that affirmed the feeling that faith produced within himself and his eager anticipation of encountering fully God's presence one day.

But what about God's heavenly abode, central to Christian tradition in anticipation of a resurrected future for a faithful humanity? Ellington addressed the concept of heaven with two songs he wrote for Swedish vocalist Alice Babs (1924–2014) in his Second Sacred Concert. His description appears to be rooted in how he personally imagined heaven to exist as if he were to inhabit a child's youthful, imaginative anticipation of this afterlife. In "Heaven," Babs sang eight lines twice (while alto saxophonist Johnny Hodges played the melody in between her verses): "Heaven, my dream / Heaven, divine / Heaven, supreme / Heaven combines / Every sweet and pretty thing / Life would love to bring / Heavenly heaven, to be / Is just the ultimate degree to be."[47] Another Alice Babs performance in this concert, titled "Almighty God," featured clarinetist Russell Procope playing the melody after her verse, with Babs providing her soprano scatting over the melody as it continued through the choir's verse:

> Almighty God has those angels a-way out there above,
> Up there a-weaving sparkling fabrics just for you and me to love.
> Almighty God has those angels up in the proper place,
> Waiting to receive and to welcome us and remake us in grace.
> Wash your face and hands and heart and soul, 'cause you wash so
>   well,
> God will keep you safely where there's no sulfur smell.
> Almighty God has those angels as ready as can be,
> Waiting to dress, caress, and bless us all in perpetuity.[48]

Together, these two songs may reflect Ellington's effort to reflect his childhood imagination and eager anticipation of life beyond earthly existence—and perhaps children were Ellington's intended audience for these songs.

In a televised 1969 performance at the Gustav Vasa Church in Stockholm, Sweden, Alice Babs sang the lyrics to "Heaven" with eyes closed, appearing to inhabit the role of the believer who imagines with joy the prospect of eternal existence. While Hodges played, Babs also smiled and gazed upward and around the cathedral, appearing as if she was picturing the celestial place that Hodges articulated with his saxophone solo.[49] The lyrics for "Heaven" and "Almighty God" are fanciful, and at times comical in "Almighty God," wherein a particular reference to hell as a place with a "sulfur smell" is the only allusion to the concept of damnation in any of Ellington's three Sacred Concerts. But the "Almighty God" lyrics speak of a God who provides guardian angels, tasking them with fashioning a beautiful paradise and refashioning the souls who come to inhabit it. These poetic lyrics register less like Ellington providing a statement of belief in the afterlife and more like Ellington employing a playful tone with his musical descriptions.

One of Ellington's personalized Christmas cards after 1970 suggests that he may have believed in an eternal existence after life on earth. This "Season's Greetings" card contained a general pronouncement about all human inclination toward religious feeling. In the card's interior, Ellington identified "the validity of the foundation of religion" in the "HEAV-ENLY ANTICIPATION OF REBIRTH"—a phrase he borrowed from a prayer the Roman Catholic priest Gerald Pocock wrote for him.[50] The card's interior described the eleven movements that form *The River*, Ellington's suite for an Alvin Ailey ballet that premiered in 1970. With this suite, he anthropomorphized a river that begins as a spring and ends up in the sea, only to evaporate, condense, and precipitate as a reborn spring.[51] For Ellington, the cycles of genesis, transformation, dissolution, and material reformation in the natural world reflected and anticipated the remaking of human existence in another realm. When paired with Ellington's more playful "Almighty God," this was humanity's remaking by God's angels "in grace."

To add weight to the stance that Ellington entertained seriously the concept of heaven, there were hotel stationery lyrics that likely served as an initial draft of "Almighty God": "All the Angels Rejoice / When a Sinner Repents / & they Are Waiting / to ^RECEIVE Greet & Welcome / Him to Heaven."[52] Ellington's regard for himself as both a "sinner" and a "believer" may be evident with these lyrics that address heavenly reward as the outcome for personal repentance. Additionally, the absence of specific language about the nature and form of this confession would

have left it open enough for a receptive interfaith audience that consumed his Sacred Concerts. However, if Ellington had used these lyrics,
it would have also left unknown what he considered the precise meaning
and form of repentance.

Ellington's annotations of his religious texts revealed his affirmation, questioning, or frustrations with an author's claims. Ellington owned Paul S. McElroy's *Quiet Thoughts*, published in 1964 by
the Peter Pauper Press. In a section titled "The Providence of God,"
Ellington underlined passages on faith: "To believe in the providence
of God means to be anchored in those realities which are timeless."
And "Rather than being an optimist or a pessimist, the man of faith is
a realist, a man with the strength to look at the changing world and see
God at work bringing renewal and healing in the midst of decay and
suffering." Ellington drew a large X over a subsection titled "How Big
Is Your God?," writing, "This is *Not* to be *questioned*!" Despite McElroy's contention in this paragraph that human conceptions of God
have changed over time, the mere stating of the question appears to
have annoyed Ellington. An assertion of certainty marks Ellington's
marginalia in *Quiet Thoughts*, and he substituted "is" for "comes" in
McElroy's sentence, "There comes a time when we have to accept on
faith the things about which we lack knowledge."[53]

When Ellington did engage with formal Christian theology, he did
so through the literature of James Thayer Addison (1887–1953), Episcopalian author and comparative religion scholar. What resonated with
Ellington in the Episcopal prayer tradition was its emphasis on the forgiveness of corporate sins. Within Addison's writings on the Episcopal
"General Confession" in *The Living Sacrifice*, Ellington underlined "We
speak as a corporate group confessing in common a weight of sin that we
bear in common—all the ugly evils of society. They are evils for which
I am not responsible nor *you*, but evils none the less for which before
God *we* are answerable." In this instance, he indicated the importance of
shared responsibility for social transgression. Ellington also underlined
several "corporate sins in penitence" that Addison listed: "Dangerous or
unhealthful housing conditions that breed disease, ill managed prisons
where cruelty hardens criminals, remediable poverty and unemploy-
ment with all their waste of potential human values, the whole festering
business of prostitution, the kind of destructive insanity that war has

now become." This underlining indicated the appeal of Social Gospel Christianity for Ellington's conception of confession.[54]

It is also with Addison's work that evidence of the nature of Ellington's appreciation of Jesus emerges. On the Christian New Testament and its essential teachings in relation to following the Liturgical calendar, Addison wrote:

> They are not planned according to a system of thought because Christianity is not a set of ideas. They unfold the birth, the life, the death, the resurrection, the ascension, and the coming in power of the Lord Christ because Christianity is an historical religion growing out of the "mighty acts" of God in Christ and expressing and perpetuating itself in a Church which is the Body of the living Christ. While the *teaching* of Christ and His apostles is an indispensable factor, apart from which faith would be blind and conduct without a guide, what is unique and essential in Christianity is the Incarnation, and that is a supreme fact embedded in history. So it is not merely for its pedagogical or psychological value that in the Holy Communion the New Testament comes to us under the form of the Christian Year. It is because the Christian religion is centered in a *Person.*
>
> The New Testament, then embodies not a philosophy of life, but a Gospel, and a Gospel means good news, and news is always about events that have happened. Thus it is that Christianity is here presented in an historical framework so that every year we follow from humble beginning to triumphant end the course of His life in whom dwelt the fullness of the Godhead bodily. And the culmination at Pentecost is the good news that an ascended Christ is not a lost Christ, but a Christ who lives within His Church and irradiates it with His divine energy.[55]

A lack of annotation does not necessarily indicate Ellington's opposition to this framing of Christian teachings. However, Ellington's selective underlining likely reveals what he thought essential about the Christian religion. While Ellington did not underline the passage about the resurrection of Jesus or the statement that dwelling within the life of Jesus was "the fullness of the Godhead bodily," he did affirm the centrality of incarnation earlier in the text, possibly indicating an appreciation for the concept of Jesus as "God the Son," or the more general idea of the incarnate God existing among humanity.

Ellington underlined a later passage where Addison argued for the distinctiveness of God in the Christian tradition, in contrast to Judaism and Islam: "The God we adore so loved the world that He gave His only-begotten Son to suffer death upon the Cross for our redemption."[56] Hasty annotating may explain reasonably Ellington's omission of "we," "His only," and part of the word "Cross" from his underlining, for these words appeared at the ends and beginnings of new sentence lines. Nevertheless, this annotation demonstrates Ellington's appreciation of the central Christian narrative of the crucifixion for humanity's salvation. It is also noteworthy that there are no visible markings to indicate that Ellington took issue with Addison's use of masculine pronouns to address God or Jesus. Lastly, Ellington appreciated passages on the Eucharist, and he employed a similarly inconsistent but potentially unproblematic underlining of the middle of sentence lines in these paragraphs: "For salvation is a *process* in which the activity of God in Christ is continuous and which calls for cooperation on our part. In other words, what Jesus of Nazareth did for us on Good Friday must be realized and brought to fruition by what the living Christ does in us today and tomorrow. In this Sacrament, therefore, remembrance grows into participation."[57] What appealed to Ellington here was Addison's characterization of Christian salvation as a call for Christians to become like Christ when he existed as the human Jesus. The potential appeal of this phrasing is that it places Jesus and the Christian onto the same plane of human activity, with God tasking both subjects with implementing God's will on earth. In Communion, Jesus as Christ serves as the "radiant presence" symbolically passing the charge of God's earthly work to successive generations of Christians. In this Episcopalian light, Ellington's affirmation allowed him to commit to Christian ethical practice and ritual without necessarily resolving, for himself, the nature of the divinity of Jesus.

A clearer picture of the Ellington who had reverence for God and Jesus emerges from his study of Episcopalian literature. Why Jesus remained absent from Ellington's song lyrics and themes remains an interesting question, given the clearer articulations of God and God's angels in the composer's messages. Moreover, the Holy Spirit suffers the same omission. It is possible that Ellington held a Trinitarian-like appreciation for the other two persons in the Godhead, but decided to present his music in an ecumenical and interfaith mode by focusing on the monotheistic commonality that Protestants, Catholics, and Jews maintained. It is equally possible that God truly was "the One and Only One" for Ellington, and he wrestled with revering the life and ministry of Jesus in his private religious study while intentionally omitting the mention of Jesus from his sacred compositions.

In the 1969 edition of the publication *Forward Day by Day: A Manual of Daily Bible Readings* (from May 1 to July 31), which Addison also edited, the Friday, May 16 reflection resonated with Ellington. This text focused on Matthew 8:8–10, in which Jesus heals the centurion's servant because of his faith. The passage conveyed that the centurion sought Jesus as an act of faith, despite presumably knowing little about him. The passage then cast a skeptical gaze upon avowed agnostics, with Ellington underlining, "Though we sympathize with honest agnostics there is a point at which agnosticism becomes selfish." From an Episcopal viewpoint, the teaching asserted that acting out of love makes an individual receptive to faith in other unproven concepts, like the existence of God. Ellington underlined passages that comported with his disdain for a lack of faith, and he revealed his embrace of the supremacy of love in existence ("The only way to find out whether love is really at the heart of the universe is to base one's life on the ultimacy of love").[58] For Ellington, love is ultimate in existence. Consequently, love becomes synonymous with God. The next day's passage on Matthew 8:13 continued the centurion story, with Jesus pronouncing the servant healed in this verse. In this reflection, Ellington underlined the statement "love led to faith and faith led to more love," which claimed that the centurion's initial love for the servant compelled him to seek out Jesus, who "used the man's faith to manifest the love of God."[59] The Episcopal articulation of this account presented it as a socially just tale. Ellington's personal appreciation of the commentary may have been that it offered a connection between love and belief when acting.

The Sunday, June 29 passage on Matthew 25:31–46 conveyed that whenever Jesus taught about a future Judgment Day, he related it to the "here and now" to teach lessons for the disciples' lives. God's concern on Judgment Day would not be about theology, purity, morality, or respectability; the concern would be the way one treated and cared for those in need. Ellington drew a double border around the last paragraph, isolating its message that love was God's means of connecting earthly life to existence beyond it: "How quickly did Jesus bring us down to earth! If Judgment Day, if the after-life, if heaven and hell, if eternity mean anything at all that meaning is directly related to those immediate earthly lives we are living out together here and now. Love is the only link between time and eternity—the love which is aware of hunger and thirst and poverty and loneliness and gives of itself to assuage all suffering."[60] At this stage, Ellington must have looked forward to the prospect of eternal life. The Wednesday, July 9 passage on John 15:7–10 saw him affirming the words of Jesus when he promised, *"you will dwell in my love."* Ellington underlined a portion of the passage's last sentence, "'I love you as the Father loves me,'" placing special emphasis in this moment on the God who loved Jesus.[61]

Conclusion: Three-Letter Word?

By 1973, Ellington's "personal statement" about God had become a musical question, with the composer asking, "Is God a Three-Letter Word for Love?" in his Third Sacred Concert. This concert premiered at Westminster Abbey in London, in part as a tribute to the United Nations. But because of Ellington's declining health due to lung cancer, he did not tour it as extensively as with the first and second concerts. For the concert performance at the African American St. Augustine Presbyterian Church in the Bronx on December 23, 1973, the program booklet contained the song's lyrics—normally sung by Alice Babs, but regularly by DeVonne Gardner (b. 1945) in the concert's US tour:

> Is God a three letter word for love?
> Is love a four letter word for God?
> When Love is in the air, do you know that God is there?
> When roses bloom in May, didn't God plan it that way?
> Is God a three letter word for Love?
> Is Love a four letter word for God?
> God Almighty, whether former or latter really doesn't matter.
> 'Cause Love is of God, and God above is the King of Love.[62]

For a song whose major improvisational voice is Ellington's piano (primarily in the background), the explicit vocal message presents the interchangeability of two concepts: the supreme deity and an affective state of being. Ellington's lyrics suggested that the composer felt no extreme difference between love and God, or that uttering either one word or the other in conversation was effectively the same speech act. He wrote in one of his private reflections, "When ~~You~~ WE Call a Friend Love Are We Not Wishing them GOD's Blessings[?]" In another, he provided a rhyming couplet: "The Domain of GOD / is Universe Beyond End / the Beginning is LOVE / & Only GOD Knows When," followed by a definitive statement, "NO SHADOWS."[63] If the earlier Ellington of 1965's "In the Beginning, God" urged people to focus on the moment when God was the sole existent presence, was this later Ellington of 1973 asking that believers imagine that the supreme, originating presence is conceptually equivalent to love?

Gerald Pocock authored Toney Watkins's speech in the song's second part, supported by the choir vocalizing the tune's melody:

> Questions, answers, strange replies,
> Proclamations, truth and lies
> Let me ask, and tell me now
> What's important? Why? And How?
> Is God a three-letter word for love
> For all that is goodness below and above?
> Some seek a new life, but who will reply?
> Who cares if the truth will live or die?
> The best of all treasures we have is today
> On the time, and the life, the truth, and the way
> So why should you think that this question is odd?
> Is love a four-letter word for God?

Pocock later repeated this message, "The best of all treasures we have is today," in his lengthy written condolences to Ellington following the November 1973 death of Arthur Logan, his longtime friend and personal physician since 1936. Pocock provided the familiar cross symbol he used in several of his letters to Ellington, closing with "GOD/LOVE bless you always, Gerry." Pocock's signature revealed that the Roman Catholic priest and the African American jazz composer shared private reflections where they blessed each other by employing this conceptual manner of speaking.[64] This message became so important to Ellington that he chose the GOD/LOVE cross for one of his holiday cards in the early 1970s.

"Love" may have allowed Ellington to avoid the linguistic frustrations he felt in his earlier attempts to address his God properly. Ellington ultimately lifted the idea from his Ambassador Hotel stationery writings for another composition, "The Majesty of God." Sung by Alice Babs and the John Alldis Choir, this composition's lyrics reveal Ellington as he voiced an apophatic theology with three negative declarations (of divine ineffability, invaluableness, and inconceivability). Ellington's song offered the luminous universality of divine truth, posited divine limitlessness, and resolved in the contemplation of an originary divine love:

> The beauty of God is indescribable.
> The power of God is unappraisable.
> The sight of God is unimaginable.
> And one should know that the light of God is Truth
> And does not a shadow throw.
>
> The wonder of God is the future of futures.
> The splendor of God is the Heaven of Heavens.
> The Domain of God is universal beyond end.
> The beginning is Love and only God knows when.[65]

This later Ellington focused more on physical demise and the possibility of an afterlife following the deaths of several close friends and musicians, and his own failing health. The music tempos for Ellington's final Sacred Concert were not as fast as some of the joyously exuberant numbers of the first and second concerts, like "David Danced before the Lord" and "Praise God and Dance." The mood of many third concert songs appeared much more subdued and pensive.

As the circumstances of Ellington's life changed in the 1970s, so did his musical temperament and apparent attitude about expressing the idea of God. His sacred music represented an attempt to craft new religious sounds, and his presence in various houses of worship indicated the prospect of interracial fellowship and the creativity it was able to produce if more Americans committed to integration and welcomed

African Americans into their religious spaces. He championed a general belief in a supreme deity, and this musical artistry reflected his genuine commitment to ecumenism. This work also revealed his deep engagement with defining and representing belief in such a divine concept in private. For Ellington to pose an ultimate question about love was to pursue a divine connection that was not necessarily mediated by an engagement with the atonement of Jesus. To proclaim divine ineffability in public songs and private writings was both a product and practice of his personal religious wrestling.

7

Jazz Communion

I was in my hotel room alone and all of a sudden it seemed as though everything I had done up to then meant absolutely nothing. I was despondent because everything seemed so meaningless and useless.

Even my beloved music, the piano I played, all seemed to have lost their appeal. So had my former associates in show business, the musicians, the night club owners and the wealthy men and women who were my patrons and who had been dining and wining me—none of them seemed important any more. . . .

. . . In my efforts to get through to God, I felt great relief. For the first time in days, the cloud lifted and I began to feel like living again. I asked God which way I should go. I told Him I was tired of the life of sin I was living and of trying to make my way without divine guidance. I told God that day of prayer that I wanted to do something for Him, to serve Him, even to giving up my music and all else I was doing that was ungodly in His sight.

—Mary Lou Williams, "What I Learned from God about Jazz"

Despondency and meaninglessness, emotionalism and discontentment. These were the states that the jazz pianist, composer, and arranger Mary Lou Williams (1910–1981) described in her 1958 article for *Sepia* magazine, "What I Learned from God about Jazz." With this writing, Williams, born Mary Elfrieda Scruggs, articulated her pursuit of religious transformation six years after her hotel experience in Paris, France, in 1952. Before Williams's Paris sojourn, this African American female jazz instrumentalist enjoyed consistent professional success over nine years. She began her career as a member of Andy Kirk's otherwise all-male big band and then as a successful solo artist and head of a trio.

This fame included the "after-dark beat" of the musician who claimed she had done it all, "the hustle and bustle, the drinking and balling, the staying out all night" in the jazz clubs that served as the spaces of her artistic profession.[1]

Williams expressed that she was ill at ease with herself. In this *Sepia* article, for an African American readership whose interests included stories of black culture and leadership, she narrated a process of religious transformation that covered time (three and a half years), travel over two continents (the United States and Europe, through France, England, Switzerland, Holland, and "other Low Countries"), and solitude (relatively reclusive habits of intense prayer). Williams's successful jazz career presented a moral dilemma for her in the 1950s. She now claimed that God was revealing that she no longer belonged in this professional realm. The nightclub was where her profession lay, but its temptations were what she sought to avoid. There must be a reforming of the self in order to navigate this space and her compatriots. Williams decided to reconsider the worth of her professional output in order to make it worthy of her personal devotion to God.

Williams was also personally frustrated with the death of jazz saxophonist and composer Charlie Parker (1920–1955). Parker was her friend, and she encouraged his musical creativity in forging "bebop," along with trumpeter Dizzy Gillespie and pianist Earl Rudolph "Bud" Powell (1924–1966). Williams returned to the United States from Europe in 1954 and knew about Parker's heroin addiction. She received word in 1955 about Parker's declining state from her brother, Jerry, who spotted him leaving Harlem Hospital. Since she often cared for musicians in her Hamilton Terrace apartment, Williams relayed to Parker through Jerry that he should "come by the house."[2] After she stopped performing at Café Society, Williams regarded her apartment as "a headquarters for young musicians." She stated,

I'd even leave the door open for them if I was out. Tadd Dameron would come to write, when he was out of inspiration, and [Thelonious] Monk did several of his pieces there. Bud Powell's brother, Richie, who also played piano, learned how to improvise at my house. And everybody came or called for advice. Charlie Parker would ask what did I think about him putting a group with strings together, or Miles Davis would ask about his group with the tuba—the one that had John Lewis and Gerry Mulligan and Max Roach and J. J. Johnson in it. It was still like the thirties—musicians helped each other, and didn't just think of themselves.[3]

Unfortunately, Parker died a few days later. According to Williams biographer Tammy Kernodle, this loss made Williams despondent about the state of the jazz community and its music, given its demonstrated inability to provide care and safety nets for others: "[Charlie Parker's] death symbolized for Mary everything she thought had gone wrong with the jazz scene and the larger black community. Personal accountability and responsibility to the community had been replaced by an attitude focused on the individual and on personal advancement. Apparently no one had considered intervening with Parker; those around him simply distanced themselves when his behavior became too much to bear. Some fed his chemical demons in order to anesthetize or control him."[4] For Williams, personal tragedies led to her belief in God, her entrance into Roman Catholicism, and her initial articulations of a unique calling to religious leadership within that tradition.

This chapter charts Mary Lou Williams's decision to become a Roman Catholic. As she made this religious journey, she engaged in several critical conversations: with God, with Hazel Scott (1920–1981), with Lorraine Gillespie (1920–2004), with two jazz-loving white Catholic priests, and with several other jazz musicians. Williams also engaged in conversations with various publics: a black public, through African American print publications; and the professional jazz public, whose musicians she claimed had lost their creativity in the modern musical era. This first group of conversation partners compelled her return to performing and composing music. Aiding them were her new Catholic clergy friends, who urged her to reconsider the jazz profession as remaining worthy of her divine musical talents. Williams expressed the hope that her conversations with the professional jazz world would prompt meaningful conversions for them. She argued that the fruits of this labor would be the revival of black musical creativity.

Williams testified that any musician who established a conversational relationship with God would receive creative musical inspiration: "If you want to do anything, build a house, be a good parent, earn a decent living, play jazz or classics or religious music, you have to have inspiration through prayerful communication with God because the gift of creativeness comes from Him." Communication with God was a resort for those black musicians who may have lacked creativity but, more importantly, lacked employment and playing opportunities: "Our musicians who complain that they cannot find jobs and that everything is blacked out for them, should pray and then watch things open up for God answers all prayers."[5] Unrealized creativity for jazz musicians, and the material insecurities it produced, became Williams's chief concerns, which she sought to remedy through religious care. To safeguard God's gifts of creative African American music and musicians, Williams called for practices of care and accountability within the jazz community.

Personal Journey toward Roman Catholicism

Williams cared for fellow musicians upon her return to the United States in her period of religious exploration prior to an embrace of Catholicism. During this period, Williams also called others to encounter God through her street evangelism alongside her friend, the African American dancer Laurence "Baby" Jackson (1921–1974). Williams recalled: "I was working with [Jackson] who became a preacher at 15th Street and Seventh Avenue in a church there. He was snatching people off the street baptizing. You know what really happened during that period? A lot of musicians and dancers became preachers and they began to preach. They must have gotten the same thing."[6] Jackson had his own personal struggles in and out of prison and maintained a correspondence with Williams while incarcerated. He sympathized with her disdain for the music industry throughout the early 1950s. Jackson's prison writings to Williams reveal personal correspondences that entangled expressions of personal friendship, romantic admiration, assessments of musical mastery, and beliefs that they both enjoyed divine inspiration and guidance.

Studying several photos Williams mailed to him, Jackson told her that he believed that "the 'God Head' . . . destined you to be a profound figure in the field of musical expression." Her "independence of mind and soul" equipped her "with the immoveable ability to meet fate and circumstance on equal terms and laugh at the threat of self-destruction from over-passionate indulgence in temptation. Where I have been weak, you have been strong." The power Jackson found in Williams's work came through suffering. He was discovering that one cannot understand life without such struggle. Nevertheless, he optimistically quoted Romans 8:18 to her: "For I reckon that the sufferings of this time are not worthy to be compared to the glory to come."[7]

Williams left Jackson and evangelism "after I began praying in the Catholic church."[8] Before Williams became an official Church member, however, she carried into her encounter with Catholicism a sense of individual religious authority. She had explored "several religions" and fostered conversations about God and professional talent with musician confidants like Jackson and others. Williams maintained a correspondence with Gérard "Dave" Pochonet (1924–2000), a French drummer who convinced her to cease performing while she was overseas and to join him at his grandmother's countryside home.[9] In a lengthy romantic (but ultimately unrequited) correspondence with Williams in 1955, Pochonet pleaded that despite their subjective concepts of God, they shared a sense of religious duty and practice that he felt made them truly compatible:

> Please be kind; and don't worry, I do believe in Him. But how [could] two persons of different age, education, or whatever makes them different . . . have exactly the same conception of Him? You depend on your own feelings for a great part in this conception. To me, God is great, good, and helpful. He has built me the way I am, I try to use his gifts to be a decent people [sic] in my life.
>
> And I do consider that it is not the mere profession of a creed, but righteous conduct, along with sincere praying, which is true religion.[10]

Although Williams did not pursue a romantic relationship with Pochonet further, this correspondence reveals that Williams took seriously her dedication to praying long hours in addition to her questions about the religious tradition most suitable for her prayerful practices. Years later, writing in her personal notebooks, which included Catholic prayers, Williams reflected on the impactful role of Pochonet, his grandmother, and her friend Hazel Scott, the African American pianist, singer, and actress (who was also married to Adam Clayton Powell Jr., pastor of Harlem's Abyssinian Baptist Church and Harlem's congressman). These confidants helped her to pursue prayerful communication with God: "You see God works in his own strange way to save our weak souls. He sent two soft spoken people to tell me to pray—these I rejected until arriving in Paris—next approached by H.S. to pray—went straight to store and purchased Bible and stayed with it. She only could have made me really."[11]

Barry Ulanov (1918–2000), the jazz critic, academic, and convert to Catholicism, introduced Williams to Father Anthony S. Woods. Woods was a white Jesuit Catholic priest and jazz fan who Ulanov hoped would compel Williams to embrace Catholicism fully, to manage (and reduce) her ascetic prayer practices, and to cease caring for musicians in her apartment, a habit her friends regarded as fraught with danger. Williams comforted musicians dealing with substance abuse by providing them "prayers and music," or Psalms to read along with music parts to write and play:

> Like I had a drummer that was on [heroin] and his wife timed him. It took him 5 minutes to go home. He'd come [to Williams's apartment] 8 o'clock in the morning and I'd just keep him in the house. See, a dope addict, anyone on heroin they're like a baby. So I'd keep them with me all day. . . . This guy, it must have been in his mind or something because he was cured so very fast, but later on I had to take him to someone for injections and whatnot to counteract what he was doing. The first night I had him here in the house and he began to want a fix and I said, "I just wrote a drum part." I wrote and I wrote and I said, "Dig this." He said, "Yeah." I said, "Well, play it." He had a pad, and he played it and he forgot. Every time that happened I said, "Hey," and I'd write something else. That worked on him I noticed that night because it took his mind off completely, or else the stuff they gave him was so weak. . . . The other person was a dealer but they told me what they were and I kept them. Father [John] Crowley said to me, "Listen, what you're doing is very dangerous." I said, "I don't care as long as I'm helping them, a poor person." This other one he got away from it completely.[12]

Eventually, at the urging of Ulanov and her friend Lorraine Gillespie, Williams and Lorraine began to attend Our Lady of Lourdes Church in Harlem and took classes in religious instruction.

During this period of instruction, Williams wrote a letter to Ulanov in February 1957 that likely exemplified Father Woods's assessment of her as "an emotional thinker, a disorganized thinker" in need of proper religious instruction and guidance to dispel her more "fanatical" expressed beliefs.[13] However, her writings contained not only key statements that reflected popular theological beliefs in African American religious history, inclusive of and extending beyond those in black Protestant Christianity that this book has already noted. Williams also voiced convictions that foreshadowed her principal concerns about African American musicians and music over the next decade. She expressed to Ulanov her certainty that "the Negro is the chosen people" with divine gifts, and African-descended peoples were "Jewish before being stricken" by a curse "through their sins of envy, evil thoughts & jealousy." She conveyed a sense of individual hermeneutical authority over religious scriptures by declaring her certainty that earth and hell were the same place and that "the Bible is one-fourth man written—no book is true to form." Williams also asserted that black musical creativity was evidence of the race's divine gifts, now in jeopardy because of the lack of creativity she perceived to be the mark of contemporary jazz music. Anyone who possessed a divine gift like music would retain it for "all eternity." She stated that she came to know these truths because her prayer "enabled [her] to receive many gifts of the Holy Ghost (1 Corinthians Chapt 12)."

Because Williams interpreted a divine mission for African Americans in the middle of the 1950s, she professed that the cultivation of black musical talent was critical. Aware of the stark presentation of her convictions, she justified to Ulanov her practices of prayer while presenting her aspiration for a structure to institutionalize her aid of others:

Forgive me for saying that I know all that is in the books Father Woods had us to buy—sounded terrible after I said it—but Barry I only meant that if one prays the right ^(way) God will do the rest. That is (I forgot) ^(you also) have to learn to eliminate evil thoughts (the worst), help the poor, do not listen to or gossip about anyone. Well there's a crazy routine along with ^(the) prayers.

I have tried for the last 2 years to lay the story of Noah and the ark on friends and they cannot hear anything (Satan ^(is) on his last chance, the end is soon & entire America is blocked to good sounds). Whenever God heals or perform[s] a miracle they say I'm crazy, fanatic, a witch[,] anything evil.

Do you understand anything? I had told Father Crowley about a big deal that I'm sure you'd be interested in to help bring back creativeness, healing of mental patients, cancer, and many other diseases. I'd like to stay in the background 'cept for my music. I have an idea that is if John Hammond's friend Mrs. [Alice] DeLamar would donate her estate. Helping others is another gift I have always had—cannot write or play if there's no one to help.[14]

"Good sounds" was a multivalent refrain in Williams's writings. At times, "good sounds" expressed her conviction that the musician's sonic environment must be conducive to a contemplative peace with the self, and that American social unrest was its primary obstruction. At other times, "good sounds" expressed the religious messages she received in her life, during prayer or in conversation with others, and the religious truths she sought to convey to others. But "good sounds" also came to reflect *good* creative music—in this sense, Williams was adamant that contemporary jazz musicians must produce uplifting music that maintained the creative tradition of African American music.

On May 9, 1957, three months after writing this letter to Ulanov, Williams and Lorraine Gillespie were baptized and confirmed as Roman Catholics.[15] They followed a religious trend of the post–World War II period that saw an increase in African American affiliation with Roman Catholicism, from nearly 300,000 to more than 900,000— what historian of African American religions Josef Sorett describes as an "Afro-Catholic moment" with internationalist reverberations. In this thirty-year period, a Catholic embrace by people of African descent "facilitated key points of exchange between black artists and intellectuals in the United States and those within decolonizing Francophone African and Caribbean nations." Sorett counts Williams as "perhaps the most famous of these Afro-Catholic converts" in this era.[16]

According to religious historian Matthew Cressler, the distinct Catholic practices that Williams and a host of other black converts experienced and embraced included "Daily Holy Mass, Daily Communion, the Rosary, the Way of the Cross, weekly confession, constant direction of a priest, and the practice of the spiritual and corporal works of mercy."[17] Through this regular religious engagement, Williams and other Catholic converts "became something new as they learned (and were taught) to feel, imagine, and experience the world in new ways."[18] A later interview asked Williams about her reason for becoming Catholic: "But then you finally decided on the Catholic church because it was open, was that the reason?" Williams replied, "Yes, that was the only reason. Well the other reason is that was the only church that I felt good in, that I could meditate without vibes hitting me in the head."[19] What mattered most to Williams at this time was a tradition that permitted her unhindered prayerful connection to the divine—in this tradition, God in the Holy Trinity and the multitude of Catholic saints who interceded on humanity's behalf. And as her embrace of Catholicism changed over the years, she sought to maintain her energy and determination to produce a structure for struggling jazz musicians, even against the wishes of her Catholic companions.

Jazz Philosophy for Reconstituting Community

I have known so many people in Jazz. Everybody from Jelly Roll Morton to Baby Laurence. Great, great artists. Sometimes unmanageable, sometimes incorrigible, but so very gifted that [it] is a sin to have neglected them. So many of our great people in music have died sad, unsung deaths. Red MacKenzie, Leo Watson, Clarence Profit, Frankie Newton, Jelly Roll, oh so many that it behooves us to look after those who are left.
—Mary Lou Williams, press release[20]

For Williams, the argument that jazz music represented an art form and that African American women and men bore artistic gifts had triumphed. "Certainly," Williams wrote in an initial fundraising letter, "it is acknowledged that one of America's chief contributions to culture is jazz, and certainly the jazz player is one of today's creative virtuoso[s]."[21] She declared that it was important to guarantee the continued creative energies of African American musical artists. This commitment meant that others must provide resources and atmospheres conducive to jazz musicians' flourishing whenever they faced dwindling playing opportunities. Reminiscent of the patronage support for Harlem Renaissance-era artists in the mid-1920s, jazz musicians who were not part of well-paid, traveling orchestras like Duke Ellington and His Orchestra, or lucrative small groups like Ella Fitzgerald and her trios or quartets, lived precariously when their business was not gainful. "Times have not changed since the days of Hayden, Bach and Mozart," Williams opined. "Like the musician earlier in the history of music, the creative musician of today needs help and that help must come from the society he benefits."[22]

To Williams, the musician's gift was joy, the emotional result of innovative, creative jazz: "I think it is pretty well recognized by now that Jazz Music is contributing lots of joy to many people." Williams made the critical assertion that the production of jazz music established relationships between jazz professionals and jazz consumers. She declared that people were responsible for reciprocating a gift to musicians: "some happiness and fulfillment must be brought *to* the Jazz Musicians and the others in that group." Upon her return from Europe to Harlem, Williams encountered the reality of her fellow jazz musicians who were unsuccessful in their pursuit of happiness, in terms of both their state of mind and their material insecurity. As a jazz collective, "it is a sadly misunderstood group. They disappear and nobody knows what becomes of them. Many are in hospitals, in jail, in all kinds of unhappy situations." Williams regarded it her goal to alleviate musicians' poverty and personal suffering. She deemed them "our people" and worked to counter the propensity for many to resort to the unnamed "extremes that lead to their trouble."[23]

Williams's professional community contained meaningful relationships beyond blood relations. Before she transitioned into what would become her interracial Catholic religious community, she had always been attached to her immediate family and other relatives whom her professional success supported. Consequently, she rethought the nature of her relationship to her professional community. Within the community of instrumental jazz artists, Williams diagnosed a professional neglect of those musicians who needed material sustenance or psychological support. Williams identified a communal remedy when she determined that the jazz community consisted not simply of musicians, managers, critics, and recording executives; the community included fans—particularly, those who could prove sufficient financial benefactors. The music was a gift with emotional potential, and to give music was to provide a service to others. In turn, a community of beneficiaries must provide for its creative element to prevent financial insecurity, alleviate emotional despondency, or nurse and combat hard substance abuse.

Williams sought to instill her jazz community with a sense of accountability. Her orientation toward the communal responsibility of wealthy individuals mirrored her personal habits as a celebrated artist, given her desires for luxuries, on the one hand, alongside the need to provide financial support to her relatives on a weekly basis, on the other. Her care for family members represented her sense of accountability to kin, and now was the moment to establish an ethos of accountability by institutionalizing the care of marginalized musicians.

Williams proclaimed a new mission to institutionalize care and accountability in her local jazz context in the establishment of the Bel Canto Foundation. Her first effort was to arrange a benefit concert at Carnegie Hall, scheduled for September 20, 1958.[24] Prospectively, the concert was to feature Williams, jazz pianist John Mehegan, jazz vocalist Anita O'Day, the sixty-piece Xavier Symphony, and others. However, the list grew to encompass many more of Williams's fellow jazz professionals.[25] The day of the concert, the "Theatricals" column in the *New York Amsterdam News* promoted her event and vision for a foundation home: "The idea seems to be gaining support and it's important to note that the musicians, in devoting their energies and time Saturday night[,] are helping themselves as others would help them. . . . the idea is sound and deserves support."[26]

Williams crafted several messages to send to prospective financial backers. One letter, titled "Bel Canto Foundation," proclaimed the name she chose for her organization and listed the many tangible forms of care for these musicians that she worked to provide: "Helping musicians . . . may mean merely offering food and shelter. It may mean providing a congenial and creative atmosphere in which to both work and rest. It may mean giving moral support and encouragement during a period of struggle for recognition. It may mean medical aid. Perhaps, all of these things."[27] Struggling jazz musicians required material, emotional, and medical support, through means that conventional social service avenues at the local level of government did not provide adequately—particularly for African Americans.

"The foundation must get started," wrote Williams. Her prospects for the Bel Canto Foundation included acquiring and constructing "a home in the country" to serve as space removed from congested, tempting, and deleterious city life. Williams urged this distance so that "musicians, regardless of race, color, or creed may go for a time to find peace and whatever 'HELP' they may require to bring *us* the music *we* require." She envisioned a sacred respite "staffed with medical personnel, and equipped, with all home facilities, as well as work rooms with pianos and sound proofing," a practical monument to demonstrate a community's appreciation of its musicians.[28] The gift of a physical foundation would provide the musician rest, healing, and "a workshop away from the city where he can work and experiment with his creative ideas." Williams lamented that the creative artists and her musical world were "becoming extinct," given the social and professional pressures they faced.[29] The center she proposed for solving these problems must be far removed from the social pressures of urban America.

In a handwritten document draft, titled "Why Creative [*sic*] Has Disappeared," Williams reiterated these concerns for seeking to establish her Foundation. Her professional world "is an entity of its own, and because of their sensitiveness, musicians are more susceptible to the outside pressures (and the evils of the 'rat race') than other professional groups."[30] In her correspondence with Ulanov, Williams conveyed to a fellow creative artist (since Ulanov was a writer) that "a musician, writer—well—anyone in the art world is now exposed to a dangerous enemy in the form of corruption, wicked people etc. which makes it quite difficult to be able to create anything or try and make it in a nowhere world."[31]

In a 1973 interview, Williams recalled an instance where she aided bebop pianist Bud Powell. One of her fellow "over-sensitive" musicians, Powell became particularly difficult beyond the excessive alcohol or narcotics abuse that usually impeded his performance:

> Bud Powell was really gone; he was out of his mind. Something happened—it wasn't his drinking or smoking or anything else. I think from my feelings and Bud being around me I think he was over-sensitive, you know. He felt everybody, felt everything because he was so terrific in his music. Usually when he'd get into these things I'd take him home and make him take a hot bath and just put him in my front room and make him sleep. When he got up he'd play like mad and he'd go like mad.... At

one time Birdland offered me $75 a week to take care of him and all that. I said no, I have to work myself. . . . I couldn't even have a little baby around the house; he kicked at my little nephew. He let nobody come near me. I said to him, "All right, I'm going to tell Monk what you did." Then he'd straighten up. I don't care what he was doing, if I told him I was going to tell Monk, he'd straighten up.[32]

Williams attested to Powell's creative gifts when unhampered by substance abuse or issues of mental and emotional wellness. Powell wrote Williams a poem in the 1940s, titled "The Great Awakening." She held on to the poem, "pray[ing] that some day, Bud will know how straight he was" when he wrote it for her.[33] Beyond his music, Powell's poem represented creative possibility, attendant with his professed commitment to God and the avoidance of temptation. Williams sought to communicate to others that they must help create a resource for musicians like Powell to foster their creative energies, rather than exacerbate the struggles she attributed to their personal demons.

Soul Comfort and Social Sounds

For Williams, a musical world as a community must expand to encompass beneficent fans. However, those non-musician fans must also recognize that the musicians represented a specialized class, one that required a unique environment conducive to their creativity. Essential to this environment was its isolation. A space for contemplation, healing, and musical creativity would necessarily be a space removed from matters of local and national importance that could just as easily influence the content of a jazz musician's creative production. In this respect, Williams possibly reflected her personal testimony to the benefits of adopting ascetic practices—and her fondness for Catholic retreat homes, an appreciation for the convent life of Catholic nuns without ultimately the pursuit of becoming one herself. She expressed the belief that her jazz community required such a detachment from contemporary society.

But in her notes and interviews, Williams also voiced her concern that musicians who were susceptible to the disorienting sounds of the city ultimately produced music that was not healing. Rather, theirs was the sound of social discontent: "Some musicians have allowed them-selves to be taken for a ride thru outside 'sounds' such as politics, racism, and constantly shifting cults for nondescript fads."[34] She stated her fear that "a strange foreign sound would enter into the strains of jazz and would destroy the heritage, would destroy jazz completely."[35] There was a social cacophony that came with the city and its racialized citizens' politics. The musician diminished her art if she allowed local or national matters to determine her musical output. The enticing "sounds" of new religious movements for many jazz musicians in urban black America, such as the discourse of the Nation of Islam (NOI), struck Williams as another form of noise, albeit an expression of struggles against racism. In an apparent response to the rhetoric of African American religious movements like the NOI and the varieties of groups identifying with a Semitic/Hebrew/Israelite heritage, Williams wrote, "Often we speak of the Negro being brainwashed . . . yet we may do some of it ourselves." Williams was responding to the ideological influence of more radical African American religious rhetoric in the 1960s upon a generation of black jazz musicians who composed musical representations of the de-sire for social change.[36]

While Williams's entire career and activist social circles in Café Society demonstrated that she resisted the circumstances that produced racism in America, she disdained musicians whose *music* evinced social pro-test: "What with all the lust, greed and hate we're confronted with in the world, let's remember that music was given to us to make others happy (not to hate). . . . Creative music cannot be born of hatred and prejudice, even with the excuse of a suitable (and perennial) scapegoat."[37] Williams did not deny the reality of anti-black racial prejudice. However, she cau-tioned that Jim Crow was not a suitable muse for creating music that uplifted others. "It is not wrong to fight for justice, to fight for freedom," wrote Williams in a 1965 *New York Amsterdam News* article. What was wrong was "to absorb the evils that progress," and people must instead "rid ourselves of evil by becoming charitable."[38] At the moment when the modern civil rights movement's televisual imagery, songs, and discourse captured national and worldwide attention, Williams's religious discourse urged jazz music to be free of that discordant social noise.

For Williams, euphony was at the heart of a jazz musician's personal healing. In her account of the history of jazz, the music evolved from the "lighter and happier side" of African American expression that commenced with enslaved black recreational culture. She anticipated that African American critics would regard her as an "Uncle Tom" for speaking of jazz as "happy music," and she expressed her belief that "for every soul no matter how burdened, there is some happiness. God in the gift of love sees to that."[39] "Sorrow songs" and "happy music" were equally divine gifts. Williams found it imperative to maintain the emotional distinctiveness of the jazz heritage. She sought to control which social "sounds" surrounded the jazz musician, because her goal was to eliminate the "talk of no value" that "destroy[s] him and his music" in addition to "making his listening audience neurotics."[40] To transform the disposition of racial angst into music was to tune jazz audiences' ears poorly to music—and social matters. "Whatever is inside regardless whether love or hate will reach your audience and show you up as you are," Williams cautioned.[41]

The exact date of these remarks is unknown. It is unlikely that they represented Williams's sentiments in the late 1950s and were likely more indicative of her stance toward civil rights and racial discourses in the late 1960s. This discourse may belie the progressive civil rights leanings of her earlier performing years, as a supporter of local black causes and a reliable benefit concert performer at New York City's Café Society beginning in the 1940s. Farah Jasmine Griffin's study of Williams's political activism in this decade includes her reflective 1973 oral history interview, in which she declares, "There's not one musician I think [who] would be in any kind of political anything if they weren't disturbed about the race, as being abused and whatnot, [and] trying to help the poor." Griffin assesses that "Williams's passion for racial and economic justice was as spiritually driven as it was politically motivated. In fact, one cannot separate her spiritual quest from her philanthropic activities."[42] A messenger who articulated a new and urgent calling in the 1950s and 1960s, Williams carried into her religious mission a concern for marginalized others that she had manifested earlier in socially and politically activist music performances.

However, it would be equally problematic to ignore the possibility that this writing also represented messaging directed toward a largely white and wealthy potential donor base for her fundraising appeals. This expression of sentiments about racism and social progress for African

Americans exuded no sensibility of social radicalism. In part, it reflected popular disdain toward groups like the NOI, which was frequently derided as a militant, pseudo-religious challenge to Christianity in the United States. Consequently, Williams may have viewed this messaging as strategically advantageous.

The assertion is more likely representative of Williams's genuine concerns for the well-being of musicians. Her personal notes reveal her consistent claim that their physical healing required a retreat from the polluting atmosphere of urban America. Williams reflected on her own susceptibility as a professional musician in a 1958 letter to the attorney Herbert J. Bliss. At the recommendation of Father Woods, Williams contacted Bliss for assistance in establishing her foundation. She conveyed an awareness that others perceived her as "crazy[,] eccentric, ignorant, a fanatic, fool, pest and a goof" for her habits of nursing musicians in her apartment, handing out her money to persons in need, and persistently preaching to those around her. These pursuits militated against her return to the regular performing and recording habits of a professional jazz musician of her stature. She stated that other musicians had stolen her compositions, causing her to become bitter by 1952. This bitterness over her profession lasted throughout her European sojourn until she "reached God" and "got a sound to pray." Williams also attempted to convey to Bliss the reasonable motivations for her personal charitable behavior, which were counterproductive to her own financial stability and to the wishes of her Catholic friends and clerical advisers. These confidants pointed her toward more feasible Catholic outlets for charity. Because "no one 'cept an aunt had tried to teach [Williams] about God," she was thankful that institutional religion had not thwarted her perception of a gift to intuit God's immanence and direction for her life: "Not being forced into religion or church, I have great experiences and am fortunate enough to feel and see many important things about loving God, first."[43]

Catholic prayer practices supplemented Williams's stated perceptual connection to God. In her letter to Bliss, she mentioned that she had been reading *Sanctity's Mother Tongue: An Examination on Silence and Use of the Gift of Speech*, likely at Woods's recommendation. M. Cecilia Koehler, Mother Superior of the Ursuline Sisters of Paola, Kansas, and author of *Sanctity's Mother Tongue*, wrote the booklet's thirty-one daily meditations to address women religious "in very noisy and distracted times." Meaningful communication and union with the "Divine Spouse" required attention to habits of speech and practices of silence to work against "this life of ever increasing speed, of radio and video, in a world where everything seems to be designed to keep the mind from reflection even of the simplest kind."[44] For Williams, this meant wrestling with the place of prayer and serenity in her life against her inclination toward "still talking, I'm sure too much," and "doing the same things as far as helping others" that made her "a very bad risk" for agents who could not predict "when I'll stop to help an unfortunate guy." Williams was determined that "in helping others, we strengthen ourselves" and that "God works through unselfish people." However, whenever God worked through the unselfish, "the other bad sound comes through the weaker ones to destroy the good in the strong . . . and majority of times I've had it to reach me through my closest friend, husband or relative."[45]

Evident in Williams's explanation of her personal practices was this emphasis on sounds: signals to engage in prayer, or voices of negativity. Thus, the meeting of her established charitable habits and her new Catholic contemplative practices produced the pursuit of a foundation geared principally toward the alleviation of African American musicians' material insecurity and physical suffering. However, her solution to aid jazz musicians diverged fundamentally from the era's "noisy" political pursuit of broader socioeconomic change. Williams chose to tread where there were "good sounds," not the wave of "Freedom Sounds" that captured many other activist jazz artists who, as Ingrid Monson meticulously details, forged musical, political, and spiritual identities through deep engagement and travel within the African diaspora.[46]

Conclusion

In a 1978 interview, Williams reflected on her assertion that jazz is "God's gift to the downtrodden people of this world" while responding to a question about her religiosity:

> I became a Catholic several years ago, and that changed me a great deal. I used to bemoan the fact that so many of my friends were dead, like Ben Webster and Bud Powell and Errol Garner, but I found out that religion

can bring peace to the soul and dedication to the talent that God has given. Now we don't know if there's a heaven or a hell or what, but I know that certain things are going to happen in life, and you shouldn't be lazy about a challenge. You shouldn't waste the talent that God has sent to you.[47]

At age sixty-eight, Williams entertained the question of the ways older people deal with loneliness. She responded, "I often pray when I am alone, and I often play music. I used to get very upset to see my friends pass away, but since I became a Catholic, I don't cry that tune anymore. Religion is very comforting."[48] Reflecting from the vantage point of several decades of religious commitment, Williams described prayer as a religious practice concerning comfort and consolation, not necessarily an experience of the identifiably miraculous. For Williams, the problem of human mortality was not in wrestling with comprehending resolutely the eternal fate of individual souls. The death of her friends and fellow musicians was loss that disrupted her contentment with life. Soul comfort was not in hoping her deceased loved ones were now enjoying heavenly paradise; it was a matter of acquiring the resilience, endurance, and creativity to continue pursuing life. Divine gifts, like musical talent in the jazz world, exist to be practiced, shared, and celebrated in this world. Similarly, if blessings are "divine" in any sense, they were to come from others around the self.

The next chapter reveals Williams's attempt to restructure a community of African American jazz artists and their supporters by pursuing charitable social work as the institutionalization of personal accountability. She labored to institutionalize her personal habits of supporting others in order to aid musicians who experienced many of the frustrations with their profession that she knew well. This was a translation of personal practices, prior to her Catholic conversion, into the language of charitable organizations, following her Catholic conversion, as recognized by the governmental bureaucracy—a strategy not unfamiliar to many Christian denominations in the United States. In her charitable endeavors, Williams's ultimate goal was the production of "good sounds" for rehabilitated, creative African American jazz professionals.

8

Accounting for the Vulnerable

Following Charlie Parker's death in 1955, Mary Lou Williams served as a co-chairperson of the Charlie Parker Foundation, established to support the late musician's children. A memorial concert for Parker, featuring Williams, Dizzy Gillespie, and others, raised $10,000 (over $94,000 in 2018 dollars). This success inspired Williams to establish an organization for struggling musicians and children, which she named the Bel Canto Foundation.[1] To raise funds for the foundation, Williams opened a thrift shop to sell secondhand goods, including luxury items, to New York City's low-income patrons (see figure 8.1). As Williams reflected in an interview, the thrift shop came to occupy a place in her daily routine, at first alongside nursing musicians in her home and attending Catholic worship services: "I'd meet the musicians and like if anybody was hung up I'd take them into church and I'd teach them to pray, how to do the rosary beads. I used to sit in the Lady of Lourdes. I'd go to the mass in the morning, 7 o'clock mass, and sit through all the masses. I'd get out about 9 or 10." Following Mass attendance, Williams returned home to make lunch for "all the poor people" she was sheltering. She then returned to Lady of Lourdes to "meditate a couple hours" before returning to her apartment.[2]

In 1964 Williams revealed to the *New Yorker* her initial habits for housing and rehabilitating musicians:

> I put the worst cases in a room down the hall from my place I rent cheap from a neighbor. They stay a couple of weeks, and I talk to them and pray with them and help them get a job. But I can be very hard in my charity, and sometimes I tell them, "You've got to be a *man*. Stand up and go downtown and get a job. No use lying around Harlem and feeling sorry for yourself." Sometimes they come back in worse shape and ask for money, and sometimes they get on their feet. One boy I've been helping has a job at Gimbels, and he's doing just fine. I've also sent musicians to the Graymoor Monastery, near Garrison. Brother Mario [Hancock] there has been a lot of help to me.[3]

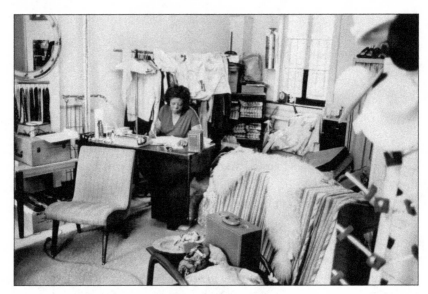

Figure 8.1. Mary Lou Williams at work in her thrift shop on Amsterdam Avenue, which she ran for her Bel Canto Foundation. New York, New York, ca. 1965. (Photo care of the Mary Lou Williams Collection, Series 2C, Institute of Jazz Studies, Rutgers University. Reprinted with permission of IJS and The Mary Lou Williams Foundation, Inc.)

Eventually, Williams ceased housing musicians in her apartment to focus her efforts more fully on fundraising for her foundation and managing the store, although she continued to provide for their convalescence elsewhere.[4] In part, the Bel Canto Foundation story centers an African American woman managing a business, attentive to her income and influence. Other narratives of Williams have represented the Bel Canto Foundation as a story of failure, due to her insufficient income and lack of experience managing a charitable effort. Critics of Williams's efforts to establish the Bel Canto Foundation regarded the thrift shop she managed as "more a place to socialize than to do business." Even Williams's friend and later manager, Father Peter O'Brien (1940–2015), stated, "She was not tough enough to run a business."[5] Biographers have characterized her donation standards and practices as unfeasible and unwise: "All an applicant had to do was give his name and address to receive a small check from Mary. This of course could not, and did not, last long."[6] These critical assessments stemmed from the negative reflections of Williams's friends and fellow jazz musicians, who watched

Williams care for other musicians with extreme devotion but found her religious exhortations off-putting. Miles Davis "respected Mary's musicianship . . . but he also mockingly called her 'Reverend Williams'" behind her back. Lorraine Gillespie recalled that people "started running when they saw her coming" to take them to church. And Williams's niece Helen Floyd said that her aunt "was like a bag lady—not crazy, but odd, running here and there with bags of groceries, trying to help these strung-out musicians," with an apartment "like a homeless shelter."[7]

Undeniably, the Bel Canto Thrift Shop failed as a sustainable business. However, the overwhelmingly negative assessments of Williams's work on this project from the late 1950s through the 1960s deal insufficiently with the worth of her daily effort. Williams worked tirelessly to manage her shop, to account for her finances, and to aspire to realize a support system for musicians in need. With this work, she strove to forge a new sense of community between jazz artists and broader societies. The sources for analysis of the foundation effort and management of the thrift shop have not included the musicians who were recipients of Williams's charity. The primary voices are those who financed Williams's initial mission efforts, ultimately at a loss, and those who sought to refocus her attention on composing and performing new jazz music. Ever the meticulous recordkeeper, Williams extensively documented her foundation efforts. These business papers reveal moments of promise, setback, progress, and failure. They also add to the Bel Canto story a record of several musicians who experienced Williams's charity, regardless of the foundation's ultimate fate.

Williams was a professional jazz musician, a Catholic convert, and an African American woman who worked with persistent diligence to establish and maintain the Bel Canto Foundation. She was an entrepreneurial (and religious) newcomer. Her primary musical profession likely prevented established social service organizations, prospective financiers, and Catholic authorities from taking her efforts seriously enough to support her mission robustly. Her effort to establish the Bel Canto Foundation created tensions for Williams. There was the fundamental tension in managing her professional output, which involved constant travel to perform and produce new music, versus managing her Bel Canto Foundation's daily affairs, which involved the local operation of her thrift shop and the maintenance of correspondence with potential donors. However, there was another tension for Williams the *successful* African American jazz professional. While she was a newcomer to the Roman Catholic faith, she was anything but a novice in her musical profession. Williams had charted a path to prominence within one jazz community. She was confident in her ability to manage a substantial project like her foundation because she had secured revenue for herself through the ongoing retrieval and management of her composition copyrights. Consequently, she strove to become more than a regular parishioner in her new Catholic community.

Williams attracted the friendship of many Catholic priests and enjoyed retreats with Catholic women religious, like the Cenacle Sisters Convent in Lancaster, Massachusetts.[8] These were relationships where Williams sought conversation and prayer partners about matters mundane, grave, and lighthearted. She also actively worked to convince the Catholic hierarchy that her moral work, which she had begun prior to her formal conversion, must be made legitimate. This would be possible if the Church invested financially in her entrepreneurial efforts. However, the Catholic authorities she befriended were fans of Williams the prominent jazz artist, not necessarily Williams the charitable organization executive. They encouraged her to put her full energies into developing her music—in particular, her "sacred jazz"—rather than treading this unfamiliar professional territory.

Williams's archive contains the materials to chart the incorporation and management of the Bel Canto Foundation, the bookkeeping and daily operation of the Bel Canto Thrift Shop, and the members of the jazz community Williams relied on for fundraising and material donations. As Williams faced challenges in managing her foundation and worked to construct a system of accountability in her aid to others, she left a record of her business correspondences with charitable professionals and those in need of Bel Canto's charity. Williams's rigorous daily activity becomes tangible through the exploration of her business archive. This record contests the portrait of her work from 1958 to about 1966 as insufficient, amateurish folly and a distraction from her more laudable, musical pursuits. This material provides an account of how Williams practiced and articulated her personal beliefs—it makes one African American, Catholic convert, jazz woman's meticulous labor visible while also making her business records legible as a brand of print culture documenting her religious work.

Previously, Williams's pursuit of the Bel Canto Foundation has been isolated and excised as an eccentric preoccupation during her years of religious maturation. Now, her daily labor comes to light as the outworking of her conception of a divine call—during the period that she and her Catholic friends contested the specific nature of this call.

Diligent Daily Devotion

With the legal assistance of Herbert Bliss, Williams incorporated the Bel Canto Foundation.[9] The fact that Bliss rendered his services pro bono was to serve as a testament of one legal professional's trust in her overall efforts. Additionally, he crafted letters that rendered Williams's period of religious exploration both intelligible and palatable to others outside her personal circle. Writing to the Internal Revenue Service in 1960, Bliss conveyed a condensed sense of the time between Williams's initial pursuit of God and the realization of her new mission, while also muting the sense of religious fervor others perceived Williams to have: "Mary Lou strove to find the peace within herself that jazz had not given her. She gave up music entirely . . . not touching a piano, composing a note or even listening to records. She became a devout Roman Catholic, spending many hours in prayer and meditation. And she translated her faith into action by helping dozens of down and out musicians get back on their feet. Thus did she find the serenity she was seeking."[10]

Bliss's narrative presentation erased the more socially problematic aspects of Williams's street evangelism and muted the intense asceticism of her prayer practices. It overlooked the possibility of theological complexity along a journey that settled with her embrace of Roman Catholicism, which was evident in her personal letters and correspondences expressing statements about divinely gifted African Americans. It also concealed the actual nature of her care for intoxicated musicians wrestling with mental instability in her apartment. Ultimately, this representation of Williams's religious journey reflected Bliss's effort to secure the government's legal blessing of Williams's pursuit through federal recognition of her social service project. With this condensed narrative portrait, Bliss conveyed this critical period of her life factually, without calling attention to decisions or habits that might cause others in his legal world to question her judgment.

The Bel Canto Foundation's charter stated the following primary purpose: "To voluntarily assist in relief of every kind and nature to those
persons suffering from or exposed to alcohol or drugs in any degree, but
primarily to musicians whose health or work is affected by alcohol or
drugs."[11] As of August 8, 1958, Mary Lou Williams had established a Bel
Canto bank account. The total deposits to the account were $851.75 by
August 28. She counted personal withdrawals from this account as loans
to herself.[12] A September 23, 1958, bank deposit statement recorded that
the Carnegie Hall benefit concert raised $2,922.75 (over $25,500 in 2018
dollars), excluding sizable and minor donations totaling $690.00 from
jazz pianist Erroll Garner, Dave Brubeck (who could not attend but contributed $10),[13] the noted jazz patroness Baroness Pannonica de Koenig-
swarter, Evie Ellington, and various judges and doctors whom Williams
knew.[14] This total existed against a cost to Williams of $3,211.42 (over
$28,200 in 2018 dollars) for promoting and holding the concert, a sign
for several of her invested friends that the foundation effort was a wash
and should not proceed further.[15]

Williams intended to record a live album of the Carnegie Hall concert, with all proceeds benefiting her foundation. At her request, Bliss
contacted the American Federation of Musicians for permission to record the volunteer musicians. However, Bliss received the response that
"unless the performing musicians are paid recording wage scales," the
union could not grant recording permission.[16] The unintended consequence of the musicians' charitable gesture, in forgoing payment for the
concert, was that the profession's established labor practices prevented a
potentially lucrative source of revenue and avenue for broader publicity
for Williams's foundation.

Nevertheless, Williams continued to navigate America's charitable
landscape through publicity and fundraising letters.[17] Some of the larger
initial donations to her foundation represented group ticket purchases
of seats in Carnegie Hall for the concert, like the request from the American Society of Composers, Authors and Publishers (ASCAP) for their
$100 gift to secure "a first tier box of eight seats."[18] And instead of im-
mediate financial support, noteworthy colleagues in the jazz profession
provided their names as currency for Williams to use in promoting her
mission and as a public testament to their trust in her vision. In lieu
of his appearance due to another engagement, Sammy Davis Jr. (1925–

1990) granted permission for his name to appear as a sponsor on Williams's official Bel Canto Foundation stationery.[19]

Not all respondents to Williams's fundraising appeals readily granted her requests. One reply came from Howard Sanders, who expressed that some quid pro quo form of entertainment would serve as a welcome enticement to accompany her charitable effort: "Dear Miss Williams, Your long experience with the public means that you do *not* send out such request without suggesting a complimentary ticket. Truly yours, Howard Sanders." Williams wrote at the bottom of this letter, "Mr. Sanders, This is zero hour. Please help me on the hour every hour to make this concert a success. Very truly yours, Mary Lou Williams." However, it does not appear that she mailed this reply to him.[20] Sanders represented a minority sentiment about the Carnegie Hall concert as a fundraising vehicle, and the publicity Williams gained for the foundation effort confirmed for her the vision she had to support others. Immediate friends, professional colleagues, and musical networks were willing to part with varying amounts of income, persuaded by these initial steps to reframe their conception of professional and personal accountability around Williams's prospective institutionalization of care.

Williams continued to send fundraising letters over the next few years as she devised new efforts to foster a sense of accountability between musicians and audiences. She organized rummage sales, offering "new items from Saks Fifth Ave" that included "children's clothes, shoes, dresses, books, house ware, dishes, antiques, men's clothes, original paintings, [and] lamps." She advertised the location of her rummage sales at 310 and 318 East 29th Street in New York City, with weekly operational hours from "10 [a.m.]–till."[21] Advertisements for the rummage sales were her hand-drawn leaflets, reproduced through mimeograph, and Williams likely distributed them throughout her neighborhood. Despite the Carnegie concert's publicity, Williams was perhaps the only person truly convinced of her ability to establish the foundation. But the rummage sales served as a charitable concept that Williams maintained into the following decade.

Successful musicians and socialites enjoyed an excess of material goods with which they could easily part. And even though all of these items were perishable in the long run, wealthier individuals had the means to buy sturdier, more durable goods that would be of great use, even through secondhand ownership. Williams and her successful friends donated their own luxury clothes, household items, and antiques in the ongoing effort to raise money for the Bel Canto Foundation. The rummage sale fostered the (re)circulation of material goods, within a local community, between two financially disparate socioeconomic classes, and for cheaper than original costs. This stood as an alternative to the conventional circulation of economic resources between these two classes, such as money dispensed through an hourly wage employment system. For her ultimate goal of benefiting jazz musicians on the social margins, Williams came to rely on a charitable commercial practice that linked the most marginalized of New York City's working class with its successful elites whose friendship, favor, and admiration she had earned over several years.

In 1959 Williams chose 308 East 29th Street as the location of a thrift shop to continue her practice of selling donated goods from musicians, socialites, and others to fundraise for her foundation. In the long effort to realize her dream to support musicians by holding others accountable for their care, Williams encountered the reality that in American society, the institutionalization of care required its own measures of accountability with which she had to become familiar. There were three related aspects of Williams's accountability: her personal bookkeeping, the maintenance of federal and state licenses to operate as a tax-free charity in the city, and establishing and maintaining her professional trustworthiness to (re)negotiate contracts and terms with her creditors. Official legal forms, bureaucratic liaisons, and constant personal correspondence served as the modes to institutionalize trust and credibility through accountability and transparency. To maintain her thrift shop in its more unprofitable moments, Williams also became responsible for drafting requests to revise payment terms and explaining insufficient funds for overdue bills, justifying her store's viability in order to renew licenses. Additionally, she was responsible for the diligent accounting of daily expenses alongside continued appeals for funds and advertisements.

Initially operating in her Hamilton Terrace apartment in New York City, Williams recruited others to assist at various stages of establishing the shop. To secure a location, Williams enlisted Irene Phillips as the chairman of the "Bel Canto Foundation Rummage Sale." Writing to "Mr. Weinberg," a potential landlord with property on East 29th Street, Phillips crafted a persuasive framing of Williams's mission by restating it in more conventional charitable terms: "The Bel Canto Foundation is an organization to raise funds for a Rest Home and/or Convalescent Home for Professional Musicians." Phillips then had to "sell" the idea of the shop as a viable venture, based on the current inventory of celebrity donations: "We have donations of clothes from many many professional musicians and to mention a few: Mr. Louis Armstrong, Mr. Dizzy Gillespie, Count Basie, Lena Horne, Nat King Cole, and many others too numerous to mention." The prospective viability of the thrift shop was to serve as evidence to secure a physical location for its operation, given that the foundation did not have immediate financial resources to acquire a store: "We are a new organization with no funds on hand but in need of a place to raise funds for this worthy cause. We are a duly authorized licensed charitable organization by the State of New York and our Lawyer (handling our affairs gratis until we get under way) is Mr. Herbert Bliss, 250 Park Avenue, N.Y.C. Telephone YU-6–7420." Lastly, Phillips requested that the landlord waive the immediate rental costs, assuring timely payments in the future: "We would appreciate it very very much if you or your organization would see fit to grant us 2 months rent gratis with the understanding that we would pay rent from there on." She also assured Weinberg that the maintenance costs of the rental space would occur at the foundation's expense.[22]

On Williams's personal part, her detailed expense books recorded the donations, sales, and personal finances she put into the thrift shop. Regular expenses in 1959 and 1960 included travel (train cost, cab and bus fare, tolls, parking tickets), transportation of materials (shipping, car rental), meals (for herself, relatives, and others), repairs (for the shop, the shop's car), shop maintenance (hardware, personal care products, cleaning supplies, office furniture and supplies), care for donated clothes (hangers, dry-cleaning), publicity (stamps, paint, posters, cardboard, printing), the shop's bills (telephone and gas), rental payments for the shop, and Williams's personal loans to the shop, for which she also recorded the shop's repayments to her. These expense books were also essential for holding her accountable about her own daily expenses, serving at times to check the degree to which her time and resources went toward personal errands and spending. Williams consistently recorded payments for her sister, Grace Mickles, who struggled with alcoholism, and for Grace's children.[23] Other expenses included her performance trips to other cities, the onetime services of an accountant, and the annual cost of a post office box. Total receipts for the shop from September 1 through December 31, 1960, amounted to $1,035.32. Against $357.38 in expenses for that quarter, the total gain amounted to $677.94 (more than $5,700 in 2018 dollars).[24]

Williams maintained inventory records for thrift shop donations. She informed potential donors that item prices would be low, given that "the territory in which the store is located is a poor one" and potential shop patrons "are on home relief with limited funds and therefore not able to pay too much."[25] The inventory book covering December 1959 through September 1960 lists the source (using donor initials) and costs of items: dresses, gowns, shirts, coats, skirts, scarves, girdles, hats, ties, shoes, slippers, pajamas, children's clothes, radios, irons and ironing boards, watches, vases, purses, cigarette holders, lampshades, books, photo albums, glassware, dishes, curtains, vinyl albums, a microscope, a periscope, and a Bible. Williams listed no entries for July through September 8, 1960, since she had no permit during that period to sell merchandise from her shop.[26] Williams kept track of the jazz musicians and composers who made donations to her foundation in 1960, including pianist Billy Taylor, trumpeter Lee Morgan, drummer Art Blakey, alto saxophonist Lou Donaldson, and pianist Lou Levy. Williams even experimented with issuing Bel Canto membership cards, attendant with $5 membership fees (about $43 in 2018 dollars).[27]

Naturally, financial accounting was central to participating in any institutionalized system of accountability. For the year ending May 31, 1960, Williams filed the New York State Department of Social Welfare's Annual Report for Charitable Organizations, declaring an income of $3,260.63 ($727.30 from the rummage sale and $2,533.33 in donations) and $1,952.50 in expenses ($973.74 for the rummage sale, and $978.76, possibly related to fundraising donations), for a total net income of $1,308.13 (nearly $11,200 in 2018 dollars).[28] Williams filed a financial report on February 15, 1961, a required submission to New York's Department of Welfare, Division of Public Solicitation. She declared $3,322.19 in receipts ($1,531.77 from the thrift shop sales and $1,790.42 in donor contributions) and $1,599.64 in total expenses, for a net income of $1,722.55 (nearly $14,400 in 2018 dollars).[29] On the form's reverse page, she indicated that the foundation's bank account contained $1,806.20

(over $15,000 in 2018 dollars) for the purpose of "helping needy and deserving musicians." She also needed to explain two other expenses she titled "Loan repaid to M. L. Williams" and "Aid $62.38" in writing on the reverse page:

> Aid: Check in the amount of 47.38 was given to Diane Coles to pay back room rent and to rehabilitate herself.
> Aid: George Gordon, Musician, had heart attack on job. Took care of him by letting him watch thrift shop. Gave George Gordon 1 check for $10.00 and 1 for $5.00.
> $100.00 of $165.00 loan made to fund by Mary Lou Williams.[30]

With this financial form and others, there were obvious descriptive limitations on what Williams could classify as "care" for individual musicians. Fifteen dollars (about $125 in 2018 dollars) for George Gordon may not have been enough to cover his health care costs, but the relatively insubstantial amount obscures the degree of William's actual involvement when she "took care of him" in her shop. Her "care" may have involved constant communication with Gordon over his period of recuperation, errands she may have run for him, recruiting others to check in on his progress, preparing meals for him, and even regular conversations with him about life, music, and future goals beyond his immediate illness. The checks may have even represented the official amount that Williams provided Gordon once he was well enough to leave the shop, concealing her unofficial investment of time and finances to ensure his recovery. Such matters of personal care are not as easy to quantify on federal forms, particularly when time was constantly a precious and limited resource for the busy Williams. Additionally, the George Gordon Singers performed for one of Williams's albums of religious jazz in 1964. This performing arrangement was evidence that her relationship with Gordon extended well beyond what one individual form was able to capture.

Contrasting Visions of Charity

Williams closed her thrift shop location on East 29th Street in 1963, after not having operated it for eight months (but continuing to make its rental payments). Performing and recording commitments made it increasingly difficult for her to oversee the shop's daily functions. Additionally, she declared that the store operated at a loss and "the Bel Canto Foundation is indebted to me for several thousand dollars."[31] She determined that her foundation required restructuring, and she settled on a new location at 1667 Amsterdam Avenue. At the request of Joseph Wells, owner of New York City's Wells Restaurant and an acquaintance of Williams, Waldo E. Parrish (1933–2014) contacted Williams on September 27, 1963, to assist her in acquiring a tax-exempt status for the Bel Canto Foundation. Parrish, executive director of the Adam Clayton Powell Foundation since its inception two years earlier, sought to recast the Bel Canto Foundation's mission statement in order to provide the tax exemptions that Williams's celebrity friends like the jazz vocalist and actress Pearl Bailey requested, given that her donations to other thrift shops were deductible.[32] Parrish offered Williams his experience as "Director of one of the, only four or five, Negro Foundations in the United States" in the effort to make her foundation viable.[33]

By November 13, Parrish had met with Herbert Bliss to determine "the feasibility of instituting specific programs and projects that might 'IMMEDIATELY' fit within the scope of the Bel Canto Foundation, Inc., Charter." One recommendation was to alter the foundation charter with a provision "to help—by befriending, assisting, and counseling—'WAYWARD YOUTH' (whose age category has not yet been determined)."[34] Parrish also evaluated the goals of Williams's mission as she rearticulated them. He became another resource who translated her ministerial aims into terms legible to the federal government.

Parrish assessed that the foundation's Carnegie Hall concert incurred a financial deficit and that the rummage sale, from his "personal evaluation, was not a financial success—in terms of the potential that it carried" with Williams's celebrity attached to it. Parrish evaluated the foundation's IRS application for tax exemption, noting its failure to define clearly the envisioned resources for helping "narcotic addicts" that fit this type of "Social Service Project." Parrish suggested that Williams use the word "REHA-BILITATION" instead of "treatment" to ensure federal approval of her next application, which "must include soundly structured projects in the areas of vocational rehabilitation in the musical field for these individuals." Parrish indicated that providing a professional staff of "psychiatrists, clinicians, medical personnel (both doctors, nurses, and clerks)[,] social workers and social leaders in the community, clergymen, and the professional public" would not occur at a substantial cost to the foundation, because he would secure volunteer services by recruiting persons with established connections to the arts community. With this approach, the foundation would rely on, expand, and call to accountability the very type of musical community that Williams had already imagined. For Williams's other goal to assist "wayward children," Parrish offered his own "project which will fit into the areas of counseling, vocational training and youth employment— all which can be funded."[35]

Williams decided against Parrish's practical experience and advice. By February 1964, Parrish had spoken with Williams on several occasions at length and reported to Bliss that "she may not be aware of all the ramifications involved in the operation procedures of her Foundation." By this point, Williams had committed to producing an album, following the advice of her friends Father Anthony Woods and Dizzy Gillespie. *Mary Lou Williams Presents Black Christ of the Andes*, released on her label, Mary Records, was a collection of original compositions (and some jazz standards) celebrating the seventeenth-century Afro-Peruvian Catholic saint Martin de Porres. The album's liner notes framed Williams's return to music as the implementation of her talents for the purpose of helping others:

> Finally, several years after she had joined the Catholic Church, her teacher, the Jesuit Father Anthony Woods, persuaded her to go back to music. For one thing, the Bel Canto Foundation she had started to rehabilitate sick musicians needed funds. But Father Woods was aware of something else. He told her, "Mary, you're an artist. You belong at the piano and writing music. It's *my* business to help people through the Church and *your* business to help people through music.
>
> Part of the proceeds from this album will be turned over to the Bel Canto Foundation. After more than a decade, Mary Lou Williams' music is heard again—a beautifully authoritative, truly moving experience.

Additional liner notes by drummer Gérard Pochonet indicated that 10 percent of the album's proceeds "will be used for the rehabilitation of musicians." According to Williams's friend and eventual manager, Father Peter O'Brien, Eustis Guillemet (b. 1934) was one of the African American jazz artists she supported financially at the time. Described in the liner notes to *Black Christ of the Andes* as "an up and coming bassman," Guillemet was the inspiration for Williams's composition "Dirge Blues."[36] According to Williams's 1965 income tax files, he received at least $172.76 from her (over $1,300 in 2018 dollars).[37]

Parrish deemed this method laudable but financially unfeasible. More importantly, he considered this reoriented revenue source a strong deviation "from the intent of the Certificate of Incorporation" that would make it more difficult for the government to approve the foundation's tax-exempt status. Parrish reiterated his suggestions for restructuring the application that he outlined in November, and he stressed that offering the services to youth and adults "will allow for dual-funding under the same programs." To suggest alternatives, he identified immediate federal government projects that could yield funding sources for Williams's foundation.[38] Parrish expressed a fine line between asserting his credibility as a consultant in designing projects close to Bel Canto's ideal mission and insisting that Bliss and Williams essentially appoint him manager of the foundation's future projects. Parrish reminded Bliss that he was a "Professional Consultant" whose fee for a memorandum of this length was normally $100 (over $800 in 2018 dollars).[39]

Was there an issue of mistrust between Parrish and Bliss, or between Williams and Parrish? Did Williams ultimately have a fear of the Powell Foundation's co-optation or absorption of hers? At the end of his memorandum, Parrish attempted to assure Bliss that a strong commitment to Williams and her foundation's aims drove his assertiveness: "I have met no other member of my race so devoted to helping others, by this method."[40] Parrish's relative youth, assertiveness, and an expression of bureaucratic meticulousness may have dissuaded rather than convinced Williams that he was suited to assist her foundation, despite the concern that these two black professionals shared for the plight of fellow struggling African Americans. Perhaps Williams, the established musician with her convictions about the scope of her mission, had committed to controlling her foundation and its path toward institutional recognition and stability. If music was her gift, then her music would prove a solution to aiding jazz artists in need.

In a March letter to Bliss, Parrish reiterated his concern to support Williams's foundation, reasoning again that since "Miss Williams is an artist and not a Foundation executive," she did not comprehend "all of the technicalities and ramifications involved in obtaining a Federal tax exemption." Williams was one of the recipients of a carbon copy of this letter, and she may have perceived Parrish's insistence as patronizing.[41] Williams and Bliss ultimately agreed to meet with Parrish to discuss his proposals further. Bliss requested that Henry R. Williams, lawyer to Adam Clayton Powell Jr., review Parrish's suggested changes to the foundation's Certificate of Incorporation. Communication between Bliss and Henry R. Williams indicates that Mary Lou Williams considered the suggested changes an unacceptable alteration to her foundation's principal concern for aiding musicians. Bliss submitted a copy of the Certificate of Incorporation to Henry R. Williams, stating that while he should make all necessary changes, "Mary Lou is primarily interested in musicians and wants this to continue as the main purpose. Changes to be acceptable to her must not alter this primary purpose." Bliss continued, "Mary Lou objects to the use of her name. I sincerely believe that there is more to it than people asking her for money. . . . Mary Lou is not too encouraged. She has dreamed of this terrific idea for so long, I am convinced she believes it will never get out of fantasy land."[42]

Bliss continued to communicate with Parrish as late as August 1964, and it is likely that the relationship between the Bel Canto Foundation and the Adam Clayton Powell Foundation ceased at this point.[43] If Williams narrowed her professional resources for institutional support following this series of memorandum exchanges and in-person meetings, she may not have appreciated the well-intentioned condescension of youth and the prospect of masculine legal professionalism (white and black) deciding the direction of the foundation. This demonstrated lack of trust in Williams's facility with institutional matters neglected recognition of her work to establish Mary Records, a "grassroots label" to sell her music, and Cecilia Publishing Company, which secured royalties from artists who performed her many compositions.[44]

It was important for Parrish to establish professional credibility and personal trust with Williams, but a palpable absence of deference to her decisions may not have endeared him to her. Williams already had fellow musicians, close friends, business and legal advisers, and Catholic compatriots whom she trusted and who trusted her. This trust and accountability took years to establish. And given that Williams's best friend, Hazel Scott, was the former wife of Reverend/Congressman Powell, there simply could have existed a personal distaste for any personal or institutional cooperation with him or his associates. Perhaps the hurried assurance of a young professional consultant, eager to restructure her long-held vision, failed to assure Williams that he was the right person to navigate her through hazardous legal bramble.

Forging Relationships of Accountability

A December 1963 *Christian Science Monitor* article briefly described Williams's support for musicians and her foundation effort: "Eventual goal of the foundation is a rehabilitation home for musicians in need of care. Presently the foundation provides short-term financial aid to musicians until they can find work. And work, in Miss Williams's vocabulary, means washing dishes as well as blowing trumpet."[45] In a May 1964 *New Yorker* profile, Williams discussed the contents of a letter that she received from a prison: "[The inmate] says he's about to get out, and wants to know if I can help him get a job. He saw a piece in *The Christian Science Monitor* about Bel Canto. I'll write him and tell him to pray and call me when he gets here. I receive letters like this all the time."[46] Several incarcerated men wrote to Williams as they sought her support upon their impending release.

Although it is unclear that she hired from among these gentlemen, Williams included in her foundation files the applications of several inmates for employment at the Bel Canto Thrift Shop in 1965 and 1966 at its 1667 Amsterdam Avenue location. Upon receiving application forms, supplied by institutions like Green Haven Prison in Stormville, New York, and Auburn Prison in Auburn, New York, Williams had the opportunity to complete the "Employer's Inquiry" form. Based on each man's application letter, she was able to signal to the Board of Parole that he was well suited to "make a fresh start as a useful member of society."[47] In a relatively impersonal way, this system allowed strangers to testify on behalf of strangers to secure their release from prison—to trust a person's testimony of rehabilitation, to forgive as a proxy for the broader society's forgiveness, and to guide the person's re-entry into the moral relationships of a free society (codified through its laws) in the role of employer. If the men ended up in Williams's employ following release, they now entered a relationship with her where they were morally accountable to her business and her mission.

The employment application letter by Jerry Hemphill attests to this transitory network of accountability that carceral officials of the state, potential parolees, and prospective employers worked to establish and maintain. Hemphill's letter expressed an appreciation of Williams's professional accomplishments, recognition of their shared identity as African Americans, and the promise that her goodwill inspired him to move beyond his past mistakes.[48] If hired, Hemphill owed Williams his relative personal success and social propriety, as a young black man starting life anew. His professed lyrical talents must have also resonated with Williams, given her work to aid disaffected musicians. It is also possible that Hemphill listened to Williams's music while incarcerated. Williams had established personal relationships with several Catholic prison chaplains in the 1960s, clergy who expressed admiration for her music and her charitable mission. She maintained correspondence with Rev. Thomas Jackson, Catholic chaplain at Pittsburgh's State Correctional Institution, and with Father Andrew P. Marinak, Catholic chaplain at the US penitentiary in Lewisburg, Pennsylvania (and, in 1967, chaplain of Lewisburg's "Christ the Prisoner" Holy Name Society). Consequently, someone like Hemphill may have become aware of her work through conversations with religious authority figures in the prison system.[49]

If they were successful, both as parolees and as applicants, employment at the Bel Canto Thrift Shop placed these men into a community of accountability. Rather than entry into "normal" society, however, they entered a community that encompassed the commercial transmission of (black) upper-class goods to a (black) working-class clientele, the constant reminders of the racially inequitable world of punitive incarceration, and the financial instability of charitable subsistence-wage job opportunities. It is also likely that Williams required their employ as one of her strategies to maintain a tax-exempt status. In her efforts to publicize her mission and to promote the thrift shop, she maintained accountability to an institutional system alongside the added responsibility of maintaining enough revenue to pay her employees' wages.

If the names of Hemphill and applicants did not appear on official Bel Canto employment paperwork, the likely case is that if hired, they received direct cash payments or they were the recipients of Williams's check made out to "cash." In the 1960s, several musicians appeared in Williams's checkbooks as the recipients of payments for performances (in addition to personal loans): bassist George Tucker (1927–1965), who performed for her trio along with drummer Andrew Cyrille (b. 1939);[50] drummer Berisford "Shep" Shepherd (1917–2018); drummer, arranger, and singer James "Osie" Johnson (1923–1966); double bassist and photographer Milton John "Milt" Hinton (1910–2000); and drummer Percy Brice (b. 1923).[51] These musicians likely had stable enough employment to maintain bank accounts, whereas the thrift shop employees and struggling musicians Williams encountered most likely received "out-of-pocket" compensation or charity, respectively. In her 1965 income tax files, Williams indicated a total of $227.76 (about $1,800 in 2018 dollars) in personal payments to several African American musicians: bassist Eustis Guillemet, drummer Granville William "Mickey" Roker (1932–2017), bassist Melbourne R. "Bob" Cranshaw (1932–2016), and a donation to pianist and composer Tadley Ewing Peake "Tadd" Dameron (1917–1965).[52]

It is plausible that Williams enlisted these musicians, and others, as her sidemen for various concert performances in order to afford them steady income and to allow them to continue exercising their musical gifts. But Williams also maintained a long-running correspondence with some musicians, who shared with her their progress in (and frustrations with) the music industry, the details of their daily prayer habits, and their reflections on social unrest. Between 1965 and 1966, Guillemet updated Williams on his decision to leave New York City, in addition to his occasional requests for financial support for music equipment and rent. While staying at a YMCA in Atlantic City, New Jersey, Guillemet informed Williams of the changing social climate: "There might be more marches and sit ins this summer. The whites live on one side[,] the colored on the other. Most of the youngsters are participating in either marches or sit ins. So say some extra prayers that God will show His justice and graces in bettering conditions of both people if it be His Holy Will and salvation of the Souls involved." On his regular Catholic practices, he wrote, "I went to New York and sat with the Blessed Sacrament and a day later I got myself together. I guess I was away too long. The Sacrament isn't exposed too often here and there aren't too many Catholics, active that is. But like you said[,] pray and keep your mind on the music. That I will do with all determination because every time I look the other way I start getting in trouble."[53] Through correspondence, Guillemet conveyed to Williams his religious dedication in moments of personal frustration.

Others brought musicians in need of support to Williams's attention. On December 2, 1964, the New York attorney Bernard Stollman petitioned Williams for help "on behalf of the distressed." Stollman wanted the foundation to assist Chris Anderson (1926–2008), a "blind, crippled Negro pianist and composer, whose artistry and courage have won him strong support from fellow musicians and from those fortunate enough to have heard him perform." According to his 2008 *New York Times* obituary, Anderson was born in Chicago "with limited vision and the congenital condition known as brittle bone disease," becoming completely blind by age twenty due to cataracts. After playing steadily in Chicago, he played with the likes of Charlie Parker and Dinah Washington (1924–1963) when he moved to New York in 1961.[54] Anderson was a mentor to jazz pianist Herbie Hancock (b. 1940), who described him as a "master of harmony and sensitivity." But in 1964, Anderson was not seeking to lean entirely on Bel Canto to support him in any recuperation. He sought membership in the American Federation of Musicians, Local 802, which required an initiation fee of $130 and quarterly dues of $7.50.[55]

On December 3, Williams signed and delivered a check for Chris Anderson in the amount of $50, with the accompanying "Notice of Grant" stipulating that $21 was to cover food costs and $29 was for his rent.[56] On December 8, Irene Phillips sent a letter to Williams to provide an update on Anderson's situation, indicating that the foundation had paid his union dues. At the moment, Anderson was living temporarily with his friend, bassist Bill Lee (b. 1928), who has worked with Duke Ellington, Odetta, Harry Belafonte, and Bob Dylan (one of Lee's children is film director, producer, and writer Shelton Jackson "Spike" Lee, b. 1957). Phillips concluded her letter: "You know, Mary, you are such a DEAR. You have done so many GOOD DEEDS! MAY GOD BLESS YOU!"[57]

Aside from directly contacting the thrift shop, a musician had to forge professional and personal relationships with others who could seek charity on his behalf. Face-to-face requests, phone calls, or written letters represented the methods of interpersonal communication to place oneself in such a charitable network. Having legal advocates make a musician's case for aid ensured that Williams's assistance went to persons with verified need. The nature of financial assistance could depend on the phrasing and reasoning of the request in addition to the requested amount. Williams may have determined the degree of future financial support she provided musicians by the amount of her responses to their initial requests. Having Irene Phillips as a liaison who ensured that Anderson's financial support made it to the intended recipients, and having her report this outcome and any further developments or requests to Williams, reveals that the enactment of singular charitable gestures required diligent recordkeeping that testified to professional accountability. And on the part of "the distressed," entrance into musical worlds of charity inevitably required accountability, partially through others testifying to their true need.

Williams's personal grants and payments to male musicians raise the question of whether the Bel Canto mission was a ministry for jazz *men*. Her donations suggest an inevitable focus on black men (given the male-leaning gender balance of the jazz profession), even though black women in her family were also recipients of her charity. According to a 1965 "Notice of Grant" form, Ada Moore (1926–1991), a Chicago-born singer and Broadway actress, was the recipient of a foundation grant in the amount of $38 ($35 to cover rent, $2 "cash," and $1 for dinner) on November 8, 1965.[58] This form required the "signature of applicant" in addition to Williams's signature.[59] These updated formalities represented recordkeeping transparency, but they also reveal the likelihood that a direct meeting between Williams and persons in need facilitated her charity. Linda Dahl recorded the memory of Delilah Jackson, a "historian of black entertainment" who "wandered into [Williams's] shop one day in 1960, a single black woman pushing a baby carriage."

"Seemed like she knew that I needed things," [Jackson] recalled. "She introduced herself, but didn't say she was a musician, an entertainer, and she asked if I needed anything. I said I didn't have any money and she said, 'I didn't say anything about money, it's for the kid.' She gave me a big bag of clothes for the baby. She was still beautiful then and she was so excited about this shop, it seemed like she had found a new love. She'd put like $5 or $10 in my hand; she felt sorry for me. She was trying to do everything she could for me, this went on for six or seven months."[60]

These relationships that created a charitable community arose out of direct and informal encounters between Williams, some musicians, and curious patrons, as well as professional liaisons.

Williams turned to the Roman Catholic Church in an effort to garner its institutional resources when federal and local financial support appeared impossible to secure. In 1964 Williams began a correspondence with Norman Weyand, a Jesuit priest at Loyola University. Weyand was sympathetic to Williams's concern to attend to musicians battling substance abuse, mentioning her efforts in a book review he wrote of *The Junkie Priest: Father Daniel Egan, S.A.* by John D. Harris. In June, Weyand sent Williams a copy of the review, which addressed drug abuse as an American problem that claimed the lives of talented African American musicians. He wrote, "Religious would do well to include in their prayers and intentions in the Holy Sacrifice people such as Father Egan and Miss Williams and the unfortunate victims whom they are helping with the greatest of self sacrifice."[61] Weyand placed Williams's efforts to aid others alongside those of an established Catholic authority, hoping to bring stature to Williams and attention within the Catholic Church to her efforts.

Following their correspondence, however, the next month Weyand encouraged Williams to discontinue her effort to establish the foundation. Although he commiserated with her interest in realizing her mission, he urged Williams to listen to her other priest friends and reckon with the structural obstacles preventing her thrift shop's success: "As Father Egan, our 'Junkie Priest' discovered, without organized municipal or state backing, effective work among the 'dispossessed' of any type can only be carried on along the lines of Dorothy Day or Baroness de Hueck. And you cannot ^(also) carry on *your important work of music and personal charity* ^(and work) the way those women have done, with their full time labor 4 the unfortunates among God's creatures."[62]

For Weyand, and likely other Catholic friends, Williams could continue her efforts to practice God's will for her without the burden of a failing store and perpetual funding setbacks. Despite her acclaim in the jazz profession, Williams had not attained the religious stature of other prominent Catholic social activist women to garner enough support for her mission beyond reliance on government institutions. Dorothy Day (1897–1980) responded with gratitude when Williams sent a statue and a relic for her farm's chapel as gifts: "Someone said Janet [Burwash] had sent it but I knew it was you, bless you. Your card—the fish—was delightful and is in my missal now so I will be remembering you and praying for your daily. Did you know that after the Angelus [prayer], at every meal, we ask St. Martin [de Porres] to pray for us all. May he pray for you most specially." But even as Day sympathized with Williams in 1968 that "musicians, artists and writers are certainly exploited," earlier she could only support the musician through offers to pray for her and to praise her music.[63] For Weyand and others, Williams's full-time exertions were ideal for her established talents in music. Jazz remained the realm of her unquestioned instrumental charisma.

The irony of Williams never succeeding in raising the profile and resources of her foundation was that the constant care for her immediate family diverted her income, which she could have otherwise put toward the Bel Canto mission. As reflected in her checkbook, Williams's sister, Grace Mickles, and her children were the perpetual recipients of funds for essentials like food, overdue rent, clothing, and bus fare. Williams even paid for Mickles's life insurance policy. Beyond the care of relatives, included in Williams's regular expenses were items essential to her embrace of Catholicism: she wrote checks regularly to Our Lady of Lourdes Church for $20 worth of prayer candles, $4 for a Catholic pamphlet, $5 for prayers from the Mother Mary Missions, $30 for the Franciscan Missionary, a $25 donation to the poor, and a $400 donation to the Catholic Youth Organization. She recorded her donations to other congregations, like the Holy Rosary Church, St. Leo's Church, St. Mary's Catholic Church, and St. Patrick's Church. In addition to substantial but infrequent personal expenses, including $300 gowns for her concerts, $124 to cover recording session costs, and $75 expenses for hair care, the circulation of Williams's personal income for charitable and business purposes siphoned off potential resources for the foundation.[64]

Williams's sizable deposits of her own money into the thrift shop's account, such as personal checks totaling $864, $2,000 in concert revenues, her regular salary of $512.71 for performing at the Hickory House nightclub in New York City, and a bank loan for $2,000, all in 1965 (over $42,000 in total in 2018 dollars), never became enough to offset the store's preexisting rental debt, overdue utility bills, and her perpetual aid to others.[65] These expenses accompanied Williams's support for her mother, by this point ailing from cancer. In part, her immediate charitable generosity and tragic family obligations counteracted the long-term mission she envisioned for a community of musicians.

Conclusion

By 1966, Williams was no longer involved in the daily management of her Bel Canto Thrift Shop. Beyond ongoing fundraising appeals to other prominent Catholics like Dorothy Day, Williams entered into a partnership with Joseph Wells and his wife, Ann, to fund the foundation by changing the store from a thrift shop to a high-end boutique that featured African American designers. This partnership ended acrimoniously in 1968, due to contract arguments over the use of Williams's name to promote events, in addition to rental and maintenance payments.[66] As her friends in Catholic ministry advocated, Williams focused her primary efforts on composing and performing her sacred jazz music. She continued to rely on correspondence with priestly friends through letters and telephone calls, in addition to her monastic retreats in New England and Europe. Father Peter O'Brien and Brother Mario Hancock (1937–2005) entered her life in the mid- to late 1960s, with the former serving as her manager and the latter becoming a reliable confidant.

The well-recounted history of Williams's sacred musical productivity in the 1960s and 1970s establishes her worth in the jazz community as a middle-aged African American jazz woman whose artistic tastes did not quite suit the younger jazz listening audience. Williams served her Catholic community as a high-profile celebrity convert. Her friends in the priesthood worked to ensure that she was well compensated for her musical corpus and that her biography and music mattered to developing narratives of jazz history. However, because of the decisive failure of her efforts in the 1950s and 1960s to establish her foundation and manage her thrift shop, this substantial portion of her daily life and labor has received only passing attention in the public narrative of her career.

The May 27, 1971, edition of *Down Beat* magazine recounted the religious journey in the 1950s that took Williams away from jazz music. The profile noted her instruction in the Catholic faith because of Barry

Ulanov and Father Woods, in addition to the presence of Father Crowley and Dizzy Gillespie in convincing Williams to return to performing and to begin crafting the musical sounds of her newfound Catholicism. According to the article, "A lot of her time then was spent in meditation. From this came a sense of direction. . . . In spite of a busy life full of good works which even gave her a new sense of fulfillment, she also sensed a certain incompleteness."[67] Similar to Herbert Bliss's letter to the IRS in 1960 on her religious journey, the *Down Beat* article rendered her mission efforts in a brief fashion. It lent no weight to the rigor and dedication of a project that appeared futile to almost everyone but Williams herself.

It is unknown whether Williams's foundation efforts would have received more concrete institutional support if she had affiliated religiously with one of the historic African American Protestant denominations. Her celebrity, professed religious convictions, and effort to engage various public audiences may have afforded her favor, visibility, and support among national black middle-class institutions, which were debating the proper course of social action in favor of desegregation, enfranchisement, and increased employment opportunities. And given that the black print press also faithfully documented the range of weekend worship options, sermon topics, and church social events for middle-class African American Protestants, these media outlets might have provided her a larger sympathetic audience for her religious fundraising.

Nevertheless, the social and political activism of prominent Afro-Protestant churches in her Harlem neighborhood did not comport with Williams's pursuit of a contemplative prayer life. These denominations certainly lacked the financial resources for constructing monastic spaces that the Catholic Church's international history and presence afforded. She required these spaces at the level of daily existence. The ideal African American church for Williams—a sacred space that was physically removed from areas fraught with social and political contestation—did not exist in New York City. Because she was opposed to allowing the sounds of social discontent to saturate her prayerful contemplation and the musical ideal she sought to create, Williams journeyed to Catholicism alongside trusted friends in her profession and with the advice of new friends in the priesthood. But her embrace of Catholicism also served to rejuvenate her foundation efforts in the late 1950s and early 1960s, not simply to settle her own soul and revive her creative musical energies.

Williams sought to provide musicians their own contemplative, creative space through her daily labor to manage her thrift shop and seek various fundraising strategies for her foundation. Incidentally, some of the musicians she helped made daily journeys into her Catholic community through Mass attendance, priestly consultations, and correspondence with Williams herself. For Williams, the labor of her thrift shop activity served a purpose distinct from her explicitly Catholic practices and production of sacred jazz: she sought to define her sense of divine calling without dependence on a specific religious home. For many other jazz musicians in need, she served as the financial and communal intermediary between personal (and emotional) destitution and professional stability. She sought to create a new social institution with a new understanding of her divine calling. However, it was for the purpose of reviving jazz creativity to forge "good" and joyful jazz music, not to make new Catholics. In the end, one woman came to embody a religious, social, and cultural institution for marginalized others.

Despite constant financial struggles, Williams asserted, "I've never been hungry one day of my life, but I have had some hard times. The one who came to my aid when I was out of money and sleeping on the floor was Dizzy Gillespie. . . . And during the time [at the Bel Canto Foundation] the priests . . . sent me boxes of stuff. I was just lucky. Maybe praying and reaching God did it; miracles were happening. And since then I've tried to help other people who need it."[68] The luck or blessings from others that Williams received were to be paid forward. This was her daily work in her Bel Canto Foundation effort and through her management of her thrift shop.

As she was ailing from bladder cancer in 1981, Williams received many visits and well-wishing letters from loved ones. Among these was a cross-shaped Hallmark card titled "A Get-Well Prayer." The card's interior read, "Peace and Love from All of Us, Eustis." Surrounding Guillemet's message were the signatures of many musicians associated with the musical revue *Ain't Misbehavin*, named after a 1929 Fats Waller composition and celebrating the jazz culture of the 1920s and 1930s: pianist Hank Jones (1918–2010), trumpeter Virgil Jones (1939–2012), tenor saxophonist and flautist Seldon Powell (1928–1997), bassist Arvell Shaw (1923–2002), baritone saxophonist Frank Haywood Henry (1913–1994), and trombonist Barry Maur.[69] This ultimate communication revealed the success of Williams's labor to create accountability in her profession. At the end of her life, she was able to know that some of the many musicians she aided were alive and performing, that they remained grateful to her, and that some even prayed for her.

9

Virtuoso Ancestors

The 1990 documentary *Mary Lou Williams: Music on My Mind* was filmed by Joanne Burke as she traveled with Williams in her final years and featured the narration of African American singer Roberta Flack (b. ca. 1937/39). While this documentary features commentary by Williams's close friends and associates, including Dizzy Gillespie, Father Peter O'Brien, George Holmes "Buddy" Tate (1913–2001), and Barry Ulanov, Burke's film is driven by Williams's dialogue through interviews, piano playing, and instruction in the history of jazz. A Williams performance from 1980 showcased the artist as she taught her audience about the eras of African American music, consisting of spirituals, ragtime, Kansas City swing, and bop. Williams informed her audience, "All of the music is healing and spiritual music," before playing arrangements of spirituals on piano. The film also provided footage of Williams in her role as guest instructor for jazz band student members at Clark College (which became Clark Atlanta University in 1988). One scene shows Williams at the 1980 Atlanta Jazz Festival as she performs "Gloria" from *Mary Lou's Mass* with two of Clark College's African American women vocalists.

Music on My Mind also captures Williams with O'Brien as she returns to Kansas City, Missouri. They drive on Mary Lou Williams Lane, a road named in her honor. Williams remarks, "Dizzy called me when I was in the hospital. He said, 'Girl, somebody just got killed on your lane!' [*Laughs.*] I said, 'Shut up! What's happening on yours?' [*Laughter.*]" The documentary ends with footage of Williams, ailing from bladder cancer in her hospital bed at the end of 1980, as she listens alertly to a recording of Duke University students rehearsing her wind ensemble composition "The History of Jazz." She provides additional notes on its arrangement to O'Brien from her bed. This scene echoes narratives of Duke Ellington's final days battling cancer, in which he was also in a hospital while relaying notes on unfinished compositions to his son, Mercer. The final

Figure 9.1. *The First Lady of Jazz*, Ella Fitzgerald statue by Vinnie Bagwell. Yonkers, New York, August 13, 2012. (Photo care of Len Holsberg / Alamy Stock Photo. Reprinted with permission.)

scenes show Gillespie and pianist Marian McPartland (1918–2013) performing "Con Alma" and "What's Your Story, Morning Glory," respectively, at Williams's funeral. Vocalist Carmen Lundy (b. 1954) directs the New York Boys Choir in their performance of "Praise the Lord" from *Mary Lou's Mass*. These scenes signal the commitment of musicians and Williams's close associates to keeping her memory alive through subsequent generations' performances of her music.[1]

Music on My Mind now exists alongside many other jazz documentaries that preserve the music performances, conversations, and scenes of travel that mark the lives of popular jazz professionals like Williams. They capture ideal representations of these virtuosos to assert narratives of an individual musician's importance to jazz history, oftentimes proffering narratives of women who were overlooked in critics' initial accounts of jazz as the arena of African American men's talents. Beyond the massive *Jazz* documentary miniseries by Ken Burns, produced in 2000 and broadcast on PBS in 2001, the musicians that this book has chronicled have received documentary treatments in *Cab Calloway: Sketches* (2012); *Duke Ellington: Reminiscing in Tempo* (1991); *Ella Fitzgerald: Something to Live For* (1999); and *Mary Lou Williams: The Lady Who Swings the Band* (2015). These films present musicians in moments where they appear authoritative, contemplative, combative, gregarious, reserved, humorous, and somber. Such documentary work conveys their personalities as family, friends, close associates, and fans experienced them. For her Williams documentary, Burke recalled that she worked closely with O'Brien "to make sure that the film reflected Mary's deepest values." Her task was to curate Williams's perception of her own critical importance to jazz history, which was also mediated by her Catholic priest friend and manager, who was invested in safeguarding her musical legacy.[2] And as films that are accessible through rebroadcast, purchase, and free online viewing, these documentary portraits create televisual monuments that require of fans no physical travel to receive biographical narratives of departed jazz men and women.

In 2014 the Associated Press reported that the Bronx's Woodlawn Cemetery, home to the graves of Duke Ellington, Miles Davis, Lionel Hampton, Illinois Jacquet, and others in a section named "Jazz Corner," was preparing to develop about 2,275 new burial plots to accommodate the demand of many "jazz enthusiasts" to have their remains interred near the musicians they revered. Additionally, the complex contained a newly constructed mausoleum, capable of holding 275 sets of remains for $6,000 per plot, with four additional smaller buildings to be constructed later. Pauline Smith, then seventy-four, an "avid jazz lover" who regularly hosted parties in her home with hired jazz musicians as the entertainment, had purchased her burial plot in 2011. Smith declared, "The music is in the earth and in the air and in the heavens. . . . I love the idea that I could be continuing my love on the other side."[3] This gesture

234 | VIRTUOSO ANCESTORS

of burial near the remains of prominent jazz musicians echoes practices of burial near an individual's ancestors or within more immediate family burial plots.

On May 24, 2014, forty years after Ellington's death, Jazz at Lincoln Center All-Stars musicians gathered at Ellington's grave to celebrate the composer's life. Mercedes Ellington (b. 1939) placed a wreath at her grandfather's grave, marked with two giant crosses as Ellington family headstones. Trombonist Arthur Baron, trumpeter James Zollar, clarinetist Mark Gross, and bassist Jennifer Vincent played Ellington's jazz standard "Mood Indigo" and Billy Strayhorn's "Take the 'A' Train" for a small audience that included photographers and attendees who recorded the performance on their cell phones.[4] Kenny Agosto, the Bronx's leader of the 80th Assembly District, presented Mercedes Ellington with a proclamation recognizing the fortieth anniversary celebration of Duke Ellington. For Ellington family members, and for jazz musicians who worked in the Ellington orchestra or in "Ellingtonian" musical traditions, Woodlawn's Jazz Corner has become a sacred site for marking annually Ellington's physical departure.

This final chapter examines the reverence for departed jazz musicians and the practices of fellow musicians, creative artists, institutions, and the public to celebrate their memory. The jazz community that heralds its prominent members, who are now its ancestors, proclaims the importance of memorializing these musicians, of continuing to perform their music, and of inheriting the improvisational spirit to interpret their works according to the religious and spiritual locations of the reverential performers themselves. African American religious practices of celebrating Duke Ellington, Ella Fitzgerald, and Mary Lou Williams chart the new lives—or afterlives—that these deceased musicians gain from those left to interpret their legacies anew. And among African American celebrants, the creative works of many African American women produce a significant record of religious and spiritual interpretations of jazz virtuosity.

The history of practices to memorialize deceased people of African descent in America prefigures contemporary practices in the jazz community. Institutions have archived these musicians' memorabilia, celebrated their musical legacies, guarded their personal missions, and afforded virtual spaces for jazz fans to reflect on their lives. There are also creative literary practices of communicating spiritually with the two deceased jazz women who are central to this book—Ella Fitzgerald and Mary Lou Williams—including poetic renderings of the religious significance of Fitzgerald. Four performances of Ellington's sacred jazz music reveal theological modifications and interpretations of his musical message that various African American Christian artists have made in their celebration of his affirmation of religious belief. In recent decades, two prominent jazz musicians and composers, Geri Allen (1957–2017) and Wynton Marsalis (b. 1961), have committed to maintaining the traditions of Ellington and Williams in composing sacred works that reflect their own religious beliefs and practices.

Celebrating Black Death

In the twentieth and twenty-first centuries, venerating deceased jazz virtuosos through extensive tribute concerts, ostentatious monuments, and annual celebrations is part of the tradition of African American funerary practices. These ritual traditions affirmed the lives of black women and men in response to the dominant society's disregard for their existence as either wholly expendable or unworthy of recognition as actual human lives. In North America and throughout the broader Atlantic world, the historical emergence of the American nation-state brought with it a variety of shared practices that oriented people around the prospect of human death, encounters with the dead, approaches to treating deceased bodies, and methods of mourning lost loved ones. Who mourned, who was allowed to mourn, how one mourned, where one mourned, and why one mourned mattered immensely as American mourners framed their beliefs and practices in instructive ways, with political and social significance. For enslaved Africans in North America, a portrait of death and mourning included funerary practices that involved sitting up with bodies for wakes, embracing the deceased body, singing and shouting in worship and thankfulness, and decorating the deceased's grave with luminous objects like seashells and with the last objects that they touched. In this framework, no individual became deceased without someone bearing responsibility for the death—either a curse or divine retribution caused the death, and in many West African and diasporic communities of the early colonial period, it was necessary to seek out who or what was responsible for an individual's demise.[5]

For the enslaved Africans in America, death served either as a chance to experience the peace and serenity of a heavenly freedom denied to them on earth, as the opportunity to experience the ironic reversal of the social order (in which there was a reversal of black and white earthly roles), or simply as the promise of relief from earthly hardships in the grave. Death had a theological significance in popular African American Christian thinking as well. Death saturated not only the precarious lives of enslaved Africans but also their ways of narrating the salvation experience of dying, descending into hell, and then proceeding to heavenly glory.[6] White masters who knew that the deceased's body was important to enslaved blacks often engaged in the vicious dismemberment of bodies, the public hanging and/or burning of bodies, and denying bodies proper burials. In the mindsets of many enslaved Africans, these acts prevented the body's spiritual return to its African homeland after physical death.[7]

Because of white surveillance of slave funerals and preaching—if such practices were even permitted at all—it was always a fraught undertaking for enslaved Africans to choose the manner of celebrating one's life and to what degree that celebration could visibly be emotional. Enslaved Africans often felt it important to hold a second funeral for the deceased in order to provide a more celebratory atmosphere; however, this was only possible without the high scrutiny of the white plantation class. Further, if the death occurred during the workday, there was no guarantee that an enslaved person was granted the time to properly bury and mourn a loved one.[8] In light of these harsh realities, to assert that the life of an enslaved African person was worth memorializing, that the body was worth proper treatment, and that others could articulate what that person's humanity meant to them was to assert a humanity for the deceased and for the mourners that the plantation society denied them, because they regarded them as mere commodities or as unthinking and unfeeling tools of manual labor.[9]

The extreme denial of religious rituals and formal recognition of deceased black persons in enslaved societies shaped the emphases on emotional displays of mourning and celebration that free African Americans placed on funerals and practices of memorialization in the Jim Crow era. The history of the funeral industry that emerged within African American communities reveals that they constructed a profession that was ministerial, entrepreneurial, political (at the local and national levels), and scientific (regarding human anatomy). The African American funeral industry standardized practices of taking care of deceased bodies, celebrating their lives with mourning survivors, and seeking justice when instances of racial violence resulted in death.

The "homegoing celebration" became a hallmark of African American life, produced under the circumstance of a segregated funeral industry during Jim Crow. To celebrate and mourn an individual's passing connected local black communities through familiar religious rituals. Such acts could become politically potent in cases of lynchings if, in historian Suzanne Smith's words, funeral directors "had the political instincts to secretly allow a black press photographer to document the atrocity in all its graphic horror." For instance, the decision of Dan Young, a black funeral director, to allow lynched black bodies to be photographed resulted in national press coverage, public memorial services, prayer vigils, and funeral marches in Washington, DC, that sought to compel Congress to pass a federal anti-lynching bill.[10] Mamie Till-Mobley, mother of Emmett Till, along with two Chicago ministers (Bishop Louis Ford and Rev. Isaiah Roberts), were members of the Church of God in Christ (COGIC) denomination who took the steps to vocally support publicizing the murder of her fourteen-year-old son in 1955 as a lynching. This step revealed the risks to the safety and economic security of the denomination's members, many of whom were sharecroppers and day laborers who risked land eviction or violence, that normally kept many COGIC ministers and practitioners from actively mobilizing to tackle civil and social problems. Several COGIC churches were also the settings for prominent civil rights funerals—including Chicago's Roberts Temple Church of God in Christ for Emmett Till's service in 1955, and Harlem's Faith Temple Church of God in Christ for Malcolm X in 1965.[11]

With the rise of African American celebrity culture came the emergence of African American celebrity funerals, born from the black funeral industry that sought to publicize prominent race representatives in the arts like James Reese Europe, Chick Webb, and Mahalia Jackson. Duke Ellington enjoyed a stately funeral celebration at New York City's

Cathedral of St. John the Divine in 1974. This Episcopal church hosted more than twelve thousand attendants, and the service included musical tributes from Ella Fitzgerald, Mary Lou Williams, and other peers in Ellington's profession.[12]

Historian of African American religions Richard Brent Turner has covered New Orleans's "Second Line," jazz funeral processions that have ritual and theological roots in West African Yoruba, African American Protestant, African American Catholic, and Haitian Vodou traditions. Notably, second-line processions of celebrating mourners travel to the grounds of Congo Square within Louis Armstrong Park, a naming that represented emerging African American traditions of dedicating sacred spaces to jazz professionals.[13] Beyond African Americans placing emphases on funerals—particularly celebrity funerals like Ellington's, which garnered live national network coverage—memorializing jazz professionals reveals practices that attest to their meaningful (and lingering) presence years after their passing.

Institutional Legacies

The Duke Ellington and Ruth Ellington collections reside at the Smithsonian's National Museum of American History (NMAH) in Washington, D.C, and the Mary Lou Williams collection is at Rutgers University's Institute of Jazz Studies (IJS) in Newark, New Jersey. Various other university and government archive sites contain materials related to these jazz professionals and many others. These preservation practices signal commitments by a profession and a nation to enshrine the remains of jazz eras, ensembles, and individual men and women deemed the American music form's most noble representatives. Aside from personal documents, the IJS also contains performing attire that musicians wore for concert dates, such as the gowns of Williams and Fitzgerald. When curating showcases of individual musicians for educational events, jazz archives often display deceased musicians' articles of clothing alongside their personal instruments and representative performing microphones and stands, albeit within protected glass display cases to prevent physical handling or theft. Jazz archives are more than repositories for paper ephemera. Akin to the preservation and occasional public displays of

VIRTUOSO ANCESTORS | 239

relics, they often bear an institution's or music collective's appreciation for items that departed jazz artists owned and handled daily.

When not on display, Ellington's Bibles and religious materials reside in the archives of the NMAH. The institutional guidelines for scholars to examine these materials effectively amount to requiring a standard of ritual purity and propriety of the researcher within a space deemed sacred. The NMAH's archival hangars have no Internet or cellular service, no permitted food and drinks, restrictions on which electronic devices are acceptable to record one's archival findings, and minimal verbal communication that reflects the standards of a reading library. Access to photos of Ellington in his Sacred Concert performances, which his sister Ruth both collected and donated, required not only specific handling instructions (the use of plastic gloves) but also direct supervision by archivists. Aside from prohibiting flash photography, which causes archival documents to fade over time, archivists work to ensure that researchers do not mishandle materials, resulting in smudged, creased, or torn pages or photographs. I witnessed one archivist caution another researcher that careless mishandling would result in the removal of the materials that this person was studying. And in the effort to delay deterioration, these low-lit, enclosed hangars afford materials protection from natural sunlight and air. These protective regulations and practices of supervision reveal the preservation of jazz materials to be a mission to guard the belongings of these prominent African American virtuosos to sustain the national memory of their professional work and personal lives.

In contrast to the NMAH's construction of a jazz archive as a silent sacred space, other archives attempt to reflect the liveliness of the departed jazz professionals and their music. Fitzgerald's expansive collection of cookbooks resides at Harvard University's Schlesinger Library. Seldom preparing meals herself, Fitzgerald treated cookbooks more as literature than as instructions for her own cooking. Friends, fans, and authors also gifted cookbooks to her. They provided local or regional books with inscriptions that thanked Fitzgerald after her performances in various cities, gifts that also marked the chronology and geography in which the vocalist provided joy for dedicated audiences during her lifetime. In particular, I can attest that examining Fitzgerald's cookbooks occasions encounters with more than just her annotations on the book pages. Strands of hair, particles of food, cooking oil stains, fingerprints, and strong perfumes wafting from the turn of each cookbook page constitute the particular remnants of materials that mark the deceased jazz vocalist's noteworthy culinary leisure habits. Barbara Haber, food historian and curator of books for Schlesinger Library, has described Fitzgerald's reading habits that fostered memories for the jazz vocalist as she aged and dealt with diabetes:

> Her books reflect a hearty appetite and reveal that she was a lover of soul food and other rich ethnic cuisines. It was clear that she had cooked from her oldest cookbooks, where many recipes had her marginal commentary or little checkmarks she used to register her approval of a dish. Recipes for pork stew, biscuits and gravy, chopped chicken liver, kreplach, and lasagna also had telltale stains to show that a real cook had been at work. But her newer books, acquired after the onset of her illness, were without blemish. . . . Ella Fitzgerald seemed to have read these books in order to bring back memories of bygone meals or vicariously enjoy the taste of new dishes she was not permitted to eat. Evidently, she was reading recipes the way trained musicians read music and hear melodies in their mind's ear.[14]

As another "lively" research space, the IJS includes small listening rooms for playing jazz audio, accessible not only to researchers but also to musicians who want to transcribe songs or memorize specific instrumental solos. Musicians visit the NMAH jazz archives for performance material as well. In preparing her debut album, which was a tribute to Duke Ellington, African American vocalist Candice Hoyes "trolled the Smithsonian's archives for months looking for the perfect songs, many of which hadn't been recorded since the early twentieth century."[15] *On a Turquoise Cloud*, Hoyes's 2015 album, represented the opera and jazz vocalist's work to compose lyrics and vocal improvisations for several wordless Ellington song arrangements. On her archival research trips, Hoyes conveyed a sense of calling to examine Ellington's materials and revive some of his less popular music: "It was an amazing experience to go through boxes at the Smithsonian, touching the yellow paper that the songs were written on. I found stamps, names, hotel phone numbers, addresses of churches scribbled in. That was, to me, the spirit of Ellington telling me there was a lot of life in these songs and I need to bring it out."[16] The album included her performance of staples of Ellington's sacred repertoire, including "Come Sunday," "Heaven," and "Almighty God," the two latter songs suited for Hoyes's mezzo-soprano voice just as they were for Alice Babs. Hoyes concluded her debut album with "Thank You for Everything," a lyrical tribute to Ellington set to the tune of Billy Strayhorn's "Lotus Blossom."

The muted or voluminous sounds of jazz are constantly present in the archival space of the IJS. The archivists welcome and initiate spontaneous conversations about specific jazz professionals that lead to playing audio from their records or live concerts. By fostering communion with musicians' ephemeral remains as well as with their sonic legacies, these practices contribute to the atmosphere of a jazz archive as a celebratory space to engage sacred remains.

Establishing educational institutions like the Duke Ellington School of the Arts in Washington, DC, in 1974, Duke University's Mary Lou Williams Center for Black Culture in 1983, and the Cab Calloway School of the Arts in Wilmington, Delaware, in 1992, and dedicating performing venues like the Ella Fitzgerald Theater in Newport News, Virginia, in 2008 (along 24th Street, which was renamed "Ella Fitzgerald Way") serve as examples of hometown veneration for departed jazz professionals (with Durham as Williams's final home). Annual jazz festivals named to honor prominent musicians mark the lasting contributions of these artists to their professions. Since 1996, New York City's Jazz at Lincoln Center (JALC) has hosted *Essentially Ellington*, an annual festival and competition for high school jazz bands across the United States. For Ellington's centennial celebration in JALC's 1999–2000 season, approximately seven hundred high schools that participated in the *Essentially Ellington* competition received transcriptions of his music.[17] Since 1996, DC's John F. Kennedy Center for the Performing Arts has hosted an annual festival in honor of Williams, founded by pianist Billy Taylor. And since 1997, the city of Newport News and Christopher Newport University have hosted a weeklong Ella Fitzgerald music festival.

Musicologist Kimberly Hannon Teal attended JALC's 2009–2010 Hall of Fame Series performance of Mary Lou Williams's music. Of Williams's lingering presence, Teal noted, "While she could not be there in the flesh, the concert served to canonize her in an almost religious sense, making a new live performance of her work a part of a sainted musician's jazz afterlife." Williams, although physically absent, became one of JALC's "remembered geniuses who loom larger than life above the proceedings" due to the atmosphere that JALC's series programming served to create. Through images, discussions, and performances, the curated celebrations of Williams and other jazz professionals fostered strong perceptions of the departed musician's looming presence:

> Through photographs and documentaries on display in the lobby, pre-concert lectures about the musicians being celebrated, and infusions of biographical details related between musical performances, audiences are constantly reminded of not just the musical sounds of the featured artist but also their histories and personalities. Moreover, by dividing the labor of playing the music of a jazz great between the resident orchestra and multiple guests, no one contemporary musician is allowed to overshadow the person being posthumously featured. In short, JALC is able to capital-ize on the fact that the concerts it presents can never measure up to the ones we can now no longer attend, leaving audiences nostalgic for musi-cians they may have never heard.

JALC's treatment of departed jazz musicians in this manner benefited its larger project of solidifying an institutional reputation as the guardian and representative of an authentic jazz canon, one that symbolizes the cre-ative possibilities of America's democracy and multiculturalism. In death, Williams became "a star of [JALC's] story more so than of her own."[18]

Beyond educational institutions, performance spaces, and jazz fes-tivals, the visible practices of monumentalizing jazz have also included constructions of sculptures of specific musicians. Like religious and governmental figures who have been celebrated in visual art, prominent jazz musicians have had their likenesses immortalized in public spaces. These monuments create occasions for pedestrians and tourists to pause before visages of African American lives that local, national, and inter-national communities have deemed significant. Art historian Kymberly Pinder quotes African American sculptor Richard Hunt (b. 1935) on the social significance of such three-dimensional, representational art: "Public sculpture responds to the dynamics of a community, or of those in it, who have a use for sculpture. It is this aspect of use, of utility, that gives public sculpture its vital and lively place in the public mind."[19]

The Frawley traffic circle, located at Fifth Avenue and 110th Street in New York City's Central Park, was renamed Duke Ellington Circle in 1995 in anticipation of a monument to the composer. In July 1997, sculptor Robert Graham's twenty-five-foot-tall Duke Ellington Memorial was unveiled in the center of the Duke Ellington Circle's shallow amphitheater, presenting Ellington as a guardian marking Harlem's black space and historic past. The *New York Times* described the imposing statue in anticipation of its unveiling: "Standing on each pillar are three nude female figures, nine in all—the Muses, with their arms outstretched, supporting a disk atop which are a bronze piano and an eight-foot-tall standing figure of Ellington."[20]

In October 1996, the city of Yonkers funded a sculpture of Ella Fitzgerald by Vinnie Bagwell, an African American artist specializing in depictions of enslaved Africans and their descendants in the United States. Her Fitzgerald monument, a bronze, life-size (five-foot, ten-inch) statue titled *The First Lady of Jazz*, sits on a granite pedestal in the Trolley Barn Plaza. The statue's pose presents an idealized capture of Fitzgerald as a performer—she is wearing heels and a dress, snapping fingers with her right hand, and her open mouth and outstretched left hand indicate a moment of climactic singing (see figure 9.1).[21]

And because of his Washington, DC, roots, Ellington was immortalized again in March 2012 by Zachary Oxman, an artist who also sculpted commissioned works for US presidents Bill Clinton and Barack Obama. Titled "Encore," Oxman's twenty-five-foot-tall stainless steel and granite sculpture depicts Ellington in front of the Howard Theatre, seated on a large treble clef while enthusiastically playing piano keys that curve upward into the sky on a music staff. In the words of a CBS reporter in DC, Oxman's monument of Ellington surrounded by music creates "a vortex of melodic energy."[22]

In 1993 Fitzgerald established and funded a charity to provide financial support for causes that reflected both her interests and hardships in life. Fitzgerald's official website, a virtual monument showing the images and narrative of the departed vocalist to those who browse its pages, contains information on the Ella Fitzgerald Charitable Foundation. Its mission is "to help the disadvantaged, the at-risk and the needy, whether these conditions have arisen because of financial, medical or other circumstances." Focused on awarding grants to aid "disadvantaged

and at-risk children of all backgrounds," Fitzgerald's foundation donations support "after-school enrichment activities, learning and reading
programs," and college scholarships, as well as "numerous organizations
that provide free or low-cost health and dental care to those who have
no health care coverage, as well as providing funding for organizations
that provide shelter and food for those in need." The foundation also
supports medical research for "diabetes, heart disease, vision/eye problems and childhood illnesses" while promoting music education and
exposure for children and young adults.[23]

Living and deceased musicians have Internet portals for showcasing
iconic portraits and performance photographs of artists as well as information for music consumers to follow their career histories through
tours, music available for purchase, and online videos of interviews and
performances. Estates, foundations, and record companies also manage
Facebook and Twitter accounts to inform followers of important dates in
these musicians' lives and performing careers, in addition to promoting
the release of rare, "previously unreleased," or digitally remastered collections of the musician's recordings and live concerts. Facebook allows
fans of musicians like Fitzgerald to interact with representatives of their
estates and with each other to share their memories of the musician's
live performances they attended, recordings that have informed their
music tastes, and their appreciation of contemporary musicians' tribute
concerts. Fitzgerald's Facebook page, curated and updated by Fitzgerald Estate archivist and foundation executive director Fran Morris Rosman, includes photos of Fitzgerald and other jazz artists, tribute posts
for other departed musicians, links to audio and video performances,
and comment sections for Fitzgerald's nearly two million Facebook followers to interact with each other by posting their appreciation of the
jazz vocalist.

Such virtual spaces for celebration and memorialization also exist
with comment sections for YouTube videos of Fitzgerald's performances.
Global audiences of music fans can discover Fitzgerald's music or testify
to the memorable quality of her live concerts and albums they enjoyed
while she was alive. In 2009 YouTube user cioto84 uploaded the audio
of Fitzgerald's "Cry Me a River," from her 1961 studio album *Clap Hands,
Here Comes Charlie!* The music upload garnered over 18 million views
and more than 115,000 "thumbs up" from viewers by 2019. "Her majesty,

the Queen of jazz herself!!" and "her voice feels like a soft touch on your skin from the softest flower in the spring" ranked among the video's top five comments.[24] With over 10.7 million views and approximately 63,000 "thumbs up" by 2019, the top live performance of Fitzgerald is her version of "Summertime" with the Tee Carson Trio in a 1968 concert broadcast at Berlin's Deutschlandhalle, uploaded to YouTube by user bessjazz in 2010. Notable user comments include "theres a reason why they still play her pieces today like they play mozart and beethoven," "A goddess who once lived on Earth and left her music here," and "Божественная Ella Fitzgerald! Как же я ее люблю! Она такая одна единственная и неповторимая была и остается. Divine Ella Fitzgerald! How I love her! She's the one and only one has been and remains."[25] Virtual sites for memorialization, with their interactive social media interfaces, supplement touristy visits to gravesites, historic performing venues, museum archives, mansions, and childhood residences that serve as the hallowed spaces for the material remnants of these departed jazz professionals. Fans become virtual and physical pilgrims as they consume the music and remember the musicians in different types of public settings.

The year 2017 marked one hundred years since Fitzgerald's birth, and several organizations and performers in the United States and throughout the world marked the occasion with concerts, festivals, albums, and scholarly lectures. On March 6, 2017, Harlem's Schomburg Center for Research in Black Culture began a monthlong series of tribute events to Fitzgerald for the Women's Jazz Festival, subtitled "Ella, Ella: A Centennial Celebration of Mama Jazz!" that year. The March 8 tribute concert, titled "Divine Ella" and organized by harpist Brandee Younger, celebrated Fitzgerald's "influence in both sacred and secular music" with a focus on songs from her religious album *Brighten the Corner*. Featuring vocalist Jean Baylor, vocalist and alto saxophonist Camille Thurman, pianist and composer Courtney Bryan, bassist Dezron Douglas, and drummer Kassa Overall, the concert performances included the gospel song "Just a Closer Walk with Thee," the hymn "God Be with You til We Meet Again," and the jazz standard "How High the Moon."[26]

Fitzgerald's official website and charitable foundation labeled this yearlong collection of celebrations "Ella at 100: The Centennial Celebration" from April 25, 2017, to April 25, 2018.[27] The Apollo Theater hosted "100: The Apollo Celebrates Ella," featuring vocalists Patti Austin (b.

1950), Andra Day (b. 1984), and Lizz Wright (b. 1980), as well as drummer Gregg Field (b. 1956), who toured with Ella Fitzgerald from 1985 through 1986. Austin also toured throughout the United States performing her versions of Fitzgerald standards with ensembles like the Count Basie Orchestra. Violinist Regina Carter (b. 1966) toured her "Simply Ella" concert throughout the United States for the first half of 2017. She also recorded *Ella: Accentuate the Positive*, a collection of tunes Fitzgerald sang from a variety of popular musical genres that included Carter's instrumental interpretation of "Crying in the Chapel." A 2006 MacArthur Foundation fellow, Carter previously composed album dedications to her heritage, including an exploration of her African ancestry with *Reverse Thread* (2010). The exploration of her paternal, Appalachian coal-mining roots in the American South produced *Southern Comfort* (2014), a folk-influenced album that also featured Carter's treatment of the rural Christian conversion tradition of the mourner's bench with the arrangement of the spiritual "I Moaned and I Moaned." For Carter's 2017 Fitzgerald tribute album, her liner notes included a tribute to the "sublime" Fitzgerald, and her acknowledgment notes began with "MOST GRACIOUS PRAISE AND THANKS TO THE CREATOR FOR ENDOWING ME WITH THE SACRED GIFT OF MUSIC."[28] Carter reflected in a press release for the album on what her interviewer characterized as a "daily communion with and lifelong devotion" to Fitzgerald's music: "'Something about her voice made me feel like I had a personal connection,' Carter recalls. 'When she sang, I felt really warm and safe, almost a maternal connection. It just felt like love.' For Carter, the enchantment continued into adulthood . . . 'For years, I would get up and put on an Ella track first thing in the morning. That was the way I needed to start off my day.'"[29]

Festivals and concerts in Argentina, Austria, Canada, Finland, France, Germany, Luxembourg, Sweden, and the United Kingdom demonstrated recognition of the broad and enduring appeal of Fitzgerald's music for vocalists, instrumentalists, jazz scholars, jazz ensembles, and symphony orchestras. The Grammy Museum in Los Angeles presented an exhibit, titled *Ella at 100: Celebrating the Artistry of Ella Fitzgerald*, from April 25 through September 10, 2017, celebrating the first African American to win a Grammy by showcasing Fitzgerald's award statues, well-known wardrobe pieces, performance imagery, rare sheet music and records, and personal telegram correspondences.[30] And with the support of Fitzgerald's charitable foundation and Rutgers University, the IJS presented "cELLAbration!" This free two-day symposium of panels, film, and music on March 24 and 25, 2017, featured Fitzgerald's surviving tour musicians, record producers, close associates, authors, and archivists, as well as performances by young jazz artists in New Jersey.[31]

In addition to posthumous fandom and centennial celebrations, there are African American creative artists who have not only spoken about departed jazz musicians but have also performed direct engagements with those they embrace as artistic ancestors.

Talking to the Ancestors

In 1997, the year after Fitzgerald's death, jazz vocalist Dee Dee Bridgewater (b. 1950) recorded the album *Dear Ella*, which won the Grammy Award for Best Jazz Vocal Album. The album featured several notable jazz musicians, including guitarist Kenny Burrell (b. 1931), vibraphonist Milt Jackson (1923–1999), and drummer Grady Tate (1932–2017). The album also saw the involvement of pianist Lou Levy (1928–2001), who toured and recorded extensively with Fitzgerald, and bassist Ray Brown (1926–2002), Fitzgerald's former husband. The album's final track, "Dear Ella," featured Bridgewater (accompanied by Burrell's electric guitar) singing a poem for the departed vocalist that addressed Fitzgerald directly, promising that "Although she's no longer with us, her spirit will linger on." With Bridgewater's words, it was as if Fitzgerald's physical absence from the music community's lives did not entail her musical or spiritual departure.[32]

Patti Austin released her tribute album, *For Ella*, in 2002. Eleven of the album's twelve tracks were Austin's vocal performances of songs most famously associated with Fitzgerald's career, including her own "A-Tisket, A-Tasket." The penultimate track, "Hearing Ella Sing," contained lyrics by "Cry Me a River" composer Arthur Hamilton (b. ca. 1926) and Patrick Moody Williams (1939–2018). The gerund "Hearing" in the title alone signals the song's assertion of Fitzgerald's enduring vocal presence beyond her physical absence that listeners can still enjoy, because her sound has been preserved through thousands of commercial recordings. But the lyrics to "Hearing Ella Sing" apparently indicate that repeated enjoyment of Fitzgerald's recorded studio albums and concerts also affords regular opportunities for the listener to commune with the departed jazz vocalist. Austin and the orchestra crescendo with the final two stanzas, offering scat vocals as tributes to the "queen of scat" as Austin implores Fitzgerald's fans to continue to make the late Fitzgerald aware of her enduring connection to the living through the valued sounds she created:

> Oh, this ooh-blaa-dee is for my Ella
> Let it flow, let her know.
> Man, we can still hear Ella all around us
> Ella, Ella, we will never let you go!

> Oh, this [scat run] that's for Ella!
> Let it flow, oh, let her know. Oh, you know
> We can, we can still hear Ella all around us
> Come on, come on, come on you gotta let her know
> Oh, Ms. Fitzgerald, we will never let you go!
> Ella! Ella! Oh Ella, we will never let you go![33]

Keeping Fitzgerald's memory alive requires that listeners "let her know" they still enjoy her musical presence, through the continued play of her recordings, performances of her musical repertoire, and (particularly for musicians) the maintenance of her bebop-influenced improvisational style, most notably through scatting. Every opportunity to invoke Fitzgerald's musical presence—to hear Fitzgerald sing—is also an opportunity to convey to her the appreciation of her life.

Poet and University of Pittsburgh English professor Yona Harvey (b. 1974) claims that her larger artistic project, which focuses on African American women's lives and experiences, "explore[s] the visibility and invisibility of Black women, our mental health and self-care, and the evidence of our imaginations in society as manifested in our hair, clothing, speech, parenting, decisions not to parent, and interactions with other women."[34] In a 2012 interview, Harvey recounted a conversation that she had with the poet Yusef Komunyakaa in 1996 in which he advised her to write about Mary Lou Williams: "She composed a lot of songs for herself and for other people, and I think the influence has more to do with the fact that we both had in common religious upbringing, and a breakaway from that upbringing, and a personal search for meaning in art and sacred things in everyday living."[35]

It was with her 2013 book *Hemming the Water* that Harvey revealed how she had embraced Mary Lou Williams as her "anchor."[36] A series of poems in the section "Communion with Mary Lou Williams" captured contemplative conversations Harvey constructed with Williams over the years, calls to the departed jazz artist and responses presented with Williams's own voice and life (italicized to suggest that they were Williams's responses or revelations for Harvey). Harvey expressed to Williams that she clothed herself in her jazz ("your music has tailored a lovely coat"), and the response to this sentiment was a two-line poem, *"I've learned to pray / through my fingertips—*[.]"[37] These lines echoed Williams's notion that she found religious expression through her music, a coat now providing others with warmth, comfort, and protection from life's blustery and torrential elements.

Harvey's poetic approach to communing with Williams involved litanies of salutations that gave the jazz woman many names and titles, representing her multiple identities, commitments, compositions, associations, devotions, and notable life events:

> Dear Composer, Dear Mother, Dear Daughter of the Elusive, Dear Black Coffee, Dear Ambition, Dear Confidence, Dear Zoning, Dear Doubt, Dear Absence, Dear Comeback, Dear Plays Like a Man, Dear Chez Mary Lou, Dear Daring, Dear Rosary in the Palm, Dear Twelve Bars over Dishes Clanking, Dear Muse, Dear Majesty, Dear Live at the Cookery, Dear Sinner in Search of a Saint, Dear Suckled Breast, Dear Ornery, Dear Ornate, Dear Obstacle, Dear Orchid, Dear Ostrich Feather in a Cap, Dear Thrift Store Owner, Dear Shoes from Lucille Armstrong, Dear Mink Bowtie from Ellington, Dear Matron of Music, Dear Holy Spirit, Dear Glory, Dear Daughter of the Imperfect Mother.[38]

These addresses appear as both memory of and invocation to Williams. The address to her as "Black Coffee," the song based on her 1938 composition "What's Your Story, Morning Glory?," represents a naming of Williams that acknowledges her as the rightful author of a popular jazz standard famously "plagiarized" from her musical

work. Harvey even provides recognition of Williams's Catholic commitments as well as her Bel Canto thrift shop ownership. However,
Williams's ancestral voice responds to Harvey's many calls by rebuff-
ing any facile attempt to commune with her through appreciation
of her life and music absent spiritual engagement with the source
responsible for African American music:

> Give me one good reason
>   to fool with you, to roll em & roll em—
> these down-home notes, these
> parts of me, you
>   hip cats, you wannabees, you running men
> & wandering women, you Jesus children.
> Imagine strolling New York streets
>   with stretch-marked sounds
> of bass & trill, the labor
> of music in a childless body
>   sacrificed to the service of
> America's Holy Music & all
> the ancestors with their rattling
>   of bones in the traffic & cursing,
> their voices nudging callused feet
> forward two blocks, two blocks more
>   past all the people trying
> to get right. To get right
> is to get with Memphis & Mississippi.
>   If you wanna boogie
>   with me, you gotta get right
> with the Giver of Blues.[39]

In her poetic contemplation of Williams, Harvey encounters a maternal jazz ancestor, one who dedicated her life to a music profession
and who inhabited "a childless body / sacrificed to the service of /
America's Holy Music" instead of human reproduction. Williams's
response called on Harvey to imagine inhabiting her life in New York
City. The streets were akin to the biblical prophet Ezekiel's Valley
of Dry Bones for the ancestral presences that gave evidence of life

through constant, discontented communication with the jazz woman. These voices propelled Williams along in her mission, beyond engaging those who had not "gotten right" with "the Giver of Blues." Intimacy with the boogie-woogie virtuoso who composed "Roll 'Em" required familiarity with the delta blues tradition that influenced her music, music that Williams declared came from a divine provider and which she was to protect and to offer others for the mending of their troubled souls.

Following these exchanges between a living and a deceased artist, Harvey next entreats the jazz woman as "Reverend Williams—/ what Miles Davis called you / behind your back," seizing here on Davis's dismissive religious title for Williams. Now, Harvey uses it as a suitable address for her to express recognition of her sense of life mission:

> What you wanted was
> a low-down connection.
> Boogie-woogie promise
> of call & response. Music
> joined with spirit like the ball
> & socket of a swinging hip.
>
> You listened to the music slip
> further from muddy water like
> a country man suffering
> in a new bright suit.[40]

The work to produce "music joined with spirit" contested with jazz's divorce from the structural and sonic norms Williams had embraced and performed over her career—norms that she attributed to the music's authentic origins in African American historical experience. With Harvey voicing a poetic recognition of Williams's diagnosis of the sonic and spiritual problem with jazz and society in her era, Williams's two-line response, "*Wooden crosses & rosary beads / Jazz created through suffering,*" marries Catholic devotional materials that speak to Christian narratives of suffering and redemption with the production of spiritually redemptive African American music colored by the history of a sorrowful joy.[41] In contrast to Williams's previous lengthy response, this shorter reply may reflect the jazz matriarch's confirmation of Harvey's understanding of her musical mission.

Recalling in a 2012 interview that her fascination with Williams began following that conversation with Komunyakaa, Harvey added, "I'll probably be writing about her until I die, until I get it right."[42] This potentially lifelong commitment would involve Harvey's further acts of communing with Williams—with continued enjoyment and interpretation of her music may come further appeals to the life, language, and memory of a religious, racial, and artistic ancestor. These acts of communion would likely result in Harvey producing more call-and-response poetic conversations between the living black woman poet and the saintly black woman jazz pianist.

Bearing Witness to the Ancestors

Poet and educator Sascha Feinstein asked fellow poet Sonia Sanchez (b. 1934) to reflect on her poetic engagement with Ella Fitzgerald: "Ella was very much of this earth. She never left this earth. She was given a voice like no other voice; her voice could travel but, as high as it got, it always stayed earthbound. The beauty of it was that it went *inside* the earth, then came up and out, and then came back down." Sanchez's praise of Fitzgerald's vocal ability to surround and penetrate the earth stood in contrast to her appreciation for Sarah Vaughan, whose voice Sanchez claimed was capable of transcending time and space: "But *Sarah* left the universe sometimes. Sarah sang so that you would close your eyes and move out of this world into another world. Sometimes she sounded ancient: She went back—really went back—back to Africa, back to India, back to the Middle East, back to Spain. Ella couldn't do that."[43] Sanchez wrote "A Poem for Ella Fitzgerald" and had performed an a cappella version of it on the Academy of Music concert stage in Philadelphia.

Sanchez rendered Fitzgerald's musical beginnings as akin to fable and apotheosis, the testimony of attending one of her concerts and experiencing her musical anointing. Divine allusions to Christian and Yoruba traditions characterize Sanchez's poetic veneration of the late vocalist, evidencing what Tracey Hucks has identified as a "theological openness" that informs "the lived intersections between African American Yoruba and African American Protestantism" in twentieth-century African American religious history.[44] Sanchez focused on the color yellow as it appears in Fitzgerald's first hit, "A-Tisket, A-Tasket," poetically identifying Fitzgerald with yellow in a way that evokes her association with the orisha Oshun. The song's vocal protagonist and her little yellow basket gave license to Sanchez's descriptions of "high-stepping yellow legs" at Fitzgerald's Apollo premiere, and of Sanchez's experience at a Fitzgerald concert in April marked by the memorable presence of yellow flowers, spring sunlight, and yellow butterflies on a day that "was yellow and silent." These accompanied Oshun's association with flowing fresh water, and Sanchez's poem likens Fitzgerald's voice to the presence of water, waves, and "streams of violins and pianos [that] splashed their welcome."[45]

In the fifth stanza, Sanchez employed Judeo-Christian imagery to celebrate Fitzgerald's scat singing, indicating the singer's glossolalic virtuosity by calling her the "first lady of tongues" with a "voice walking on water" in the fashion of the Christian savior. Like Jeremiah, Fitzgerald, "crossed in prayer" and having become "holy" at that Apollo moment where "she became Ella," unleashes a thousand musical sermons shut up in her bones like the Hebrew prophet's fiery proclamations of the Lord. For Sanchez, Fitzgerald's voice represented at once the monastic purity of "a nun's whisper" and the earthy divulgences of "guitar thickened blues," swinging vocals with the power to pique the interest of those who inhabited tightly wound, "braided spaces" and who were observant of the placid musical propriety of "stained glass" religious sanctuaries.[46]

Aside from "A-Tisket, A-Tasket," Sanchez referenced other songs familiarly associated with Fitzgerald, including "Perdido," "Please Don't Talk about Me When I'm Gone," and "Lady, Be Good." Sanchez likely sang these melodies or written scat portions when performing her poem. In her veneration of Fitzgerald, Sanchez coined the adjective "Ella-tonian" to describe her unique soft voice "like four layers of lace." In this fashion, she imitated the jazz community's neologism "Ellingtonian" when describing sounds or compositional styles reminiscent or in the lineage of Duke Ellington.[47]

At the 2007 musical tribute to Fitzgerald, titled *We Love Ella! A Tribute to the First Lady of Song*, vocalist Natalie Cole (1950–2015) declared to audience laughter and applause, "Ella sang with true joy, and it was all the evidence you needed to know that God was a jazz singer. And a woman."[48] In light of Sanchez's poetic veneration, Cole's remarks before singing "Midnight Sun"—one of Fitzgerald's favorite pieces to perform—point to a community of black women artists who have seen and heard the embodiment of divine joy in Fitzgerald's voice.

In addition to African American poetic encounters with Williams and Fitzgerald, as well as prosaic interpretations of their divine positions and attributes, the sacred musical corpus that resulted from Ellington's own theological engagements has served the reflections of musicians across the theological spectrum of African American Christianity.

Theological Interpretations of the Ancestors

In contemporary forms of African American Christian worship, Ellington's religious compositions have taken on new life in Holiness-Pentecostal, evangelical, and mainline sacred houses of worship, in addition to liberal religious performances beyond these spaces. Musicians have reworked Ellington's lyrics and musical arrangements, and have even added visual and performance elements to recast Ellington as a sacred jazz composer who authorizes others' religious interpretations of his musical messages. Beyond straightforward "classical" replications of the original music, these new performances of Ellington compositions reflect the religious habits and commitments of the performers.

For the *We Love You Madly* tribute to an ailing Duke Ellington in 1973, Ray Charles and Aretha Franklin reimagined Ellington's "Ain't but the One" by setting his lyrics to the basic structure of their song "Spirit in the Dark." The song not only includes an organ, an electric guitar, and a mass gospel choir behind Charles and Franklin, intimately familiar with the idioms of modern gospel music, but also contains a "praise break" showcasing these two musicians' improvisational spirit. This reworking of the song represented Franklin and Charles as they affirmed the theological content of Ellington's lyrics as sufficiently representative of African American Christianity. However, their version uses the pronoun "He" when referring to God, a pronoun that Ellington's theology intentionally avoided. Coupled with their musical arrangement, which supplants Ellington's as a more authentic representation of modern gospel music that is conducive to Pentecostal worship practices, Charles and Franklin translated Ellington's message into the words and sounds most familiar to the black Christian communities with which they were well acquainted. These changes also simply signal generational and religious differences between musicians. Ellington had not been a church-attending religious person, and his Washington, DC, black Baptist and Methodist upbringing in the black middle class exposed him mainly to African American spirituals, not gospel music.[49]

A fundraising benefit produced the album *Goin' Home—A Tribute to Duke Ellington/A Benefit for the Duke Ellington Foundation*, recorded in 1999 to celebrate Ellington's centennial and released in 2001. Among the prominent artists featured on the album were George Duke (1946–2013), Dianne Reeves (b. 1956), Al Jarreau (1940–2017), Jon Hendricks (1921–2017), Nancy Wilson (1937–2018), Christian McBride (b. 1972), and Gregory Hines (1946–2003). The album included a recording of "Come Sunday" that trumpeter and music educator Burgess Gardner arranged with vocal features by Otis Clay (1942–2016) and Delya Chandler. In this recording of "Come Sunday," however, the following lyrics stood in place of the original third and fourth stanzas:

> (*Clay*) I believe, I believe God is now, was then, and always will be
> (*chorus*: always will be)
> (*Chandler*) With God's blessings, we can make it through eternity
> (*chorus*: through eternity)
> (*Clay*) Lord, dear Lord above, God almighty, God of love
> (*Clay and Chandler*) Please look down and see my people through.
> (2x)

> (*Clay*) They're all dressed up this morning, they've been working
> hard all week long, yeah
> Glory, Hallelujah, come Sunday, they can take it to God's throne.
> (*Chandler*) If we keep God in our lives, then I know that
> Sunday can be every day.

> (*Clay*) Come Sunday, they teach us, to do unto others as you would
> have them do unto you.
> That's the Golden Rule, yeah.
> (*Clay and Chandler*) Please look down and see my people through.
> (2x)[50]

These updated lyrics at the turn of the twenty-first century appear to represent a reinterpretation of Ellington's original piece, one that shifts the focus away from simply an appreciation of worshipful black Christian ancestors in the slave era. Instead, they indicate a shift toward a modern sense of God's presence in the everyday, working lives of African American Christians. Sunday is not simply a day of relief from forced toil. Rather, to live every day as Sunday is to carry a sense of God's presence and guidance of the individual's life throughout the work week. And, unlike with Ellington, there is the prospect of an eternal reward for religious devotion (where every day is a Sunday to enjoy God's presence).

The purpose of these revised lyrics is to preach a standard of religious devotion, rather than a musical meditation on divinely guided racial history. And it may not even reflect a religious message about or for just African American Christians—it reflects the approach to living a Christian life that is emblematic of contemporary mainstream American evangelical teachings. Clay, an R&B and soul singer, began his career as a member of a series of gospel groups in the 1950s and 1960s, including the Voices of Hope, the Christian Travelers, the Golden Jubilaires, the Famous Blue Jay Singers, the Holy Wonders, the Pilgrim Harmonizers, the Gospel Songbirds, and the Sensational Nightingales. Clay frequently headlined gospel shows during the final decades of his career.[51] And Chandler, an R&B and jazz singer, went on to release a contemporary gospel album, *Breakthrough*, in 2007.[52] Overall, the lyrical changes that Clay and Chandler sang reflect evangelical and "sanctified" commitments to regular church attendance that would not quite match Ellington's own religious sentiments and habits.

A performance of Ellington's Sacred Concert music at Grace Congregational Church of Harlem, UCC, on June 5, 2016, concluded with the performance of "Praise God and Dance." This finale led into the performance of a praise break, echoing the 1973 reimagining of "Ain't but the One" by Charles and Franklin. Damien Sneed, a choral director who has worked with the Lincoln Center Jazz Orchestra on performances of sacred compositions by Ellington and trumpeter Wynton Marsalis, was the pianist for Grace Congregation's Sunday service, and his YouTube page features a recording of the praise break moment. The Songs of Solomon Inspirational Ensemble, directed by Pastor Chantel Wright of Pneuma Ministries, transitioned from singing "Praise God and Dance," featuring the tap dancing solo of Jared Grimes, to the singing of the "war cry" chant with the continued musical accompaniment and antiphonal solos of the jazz orchestra. During the praise break, the choir alternated between shouts of Ellington's original lyrics ("Dance, dance, dance! / Praise God and dance!") and the "war cry." At the conclusion of the praise break, with continued clapping, dancing, stomping, and shouts of "Hallelujah!" from some choir and audience members, Pastor Wright took her microphone and preached the words of the King James translation of John 4:24, "For God is a Spirit; and they that worship him must worship him in spirit and in truth!" She then instructed the congregants to "clap your sanctified hands in here! Come on and open your mouths and give God a praise!" And like Ellington's original scriptural inspiration for his composition, Wright recites Psalm 150 in the cadence of a chanted sermon. After offering her own shouts of "Hallelujah!" and "He is worthy!," Wright exclaimed, "Oh! I didn't know *He* had planned that! *HOSHA!* I didn't know that was in the plan."

Aside from declaring that it was God who ordained this musical performance, Wright's glossolalic utterance between these last two sentences serves to indicate that this "sanctified" performance of Ellington's sacred music was, indeed, conducive to invoking God's presence in the Holy Spirit for this Sunday celebration. An African American Congregational–United Church of Christ church could utilize Ellington's sacred compositions to host a moment of charismatic praise and worship. This practice testifies not only to the thorough pervasiveness of Holiness-Pentecostal religious expressions across theological and denominational lines but also to the fact that some contemporary black Christians find Ellington's theological presentation of religious praise to comport well with modern exuberant worship practices. The long arc of Ellington's career and posthumous performances of his music chart the path of responses to his work, starting with derision of both jazz culture and the charismatic "jazz religion" by African American mainline Protestants, then a welcome of his sacred music in liberal white mainline congregations, and finally inclusion in sanctified praise and worship within African American mainline Protestant churches.

Legacies of Sacred Compositions

The pianist and composer Geri Allen, who led the Mary Lou Williams Collective music ensemble, was arguably the principal proponent of Williams's life and music in the late twentieth and early twenty-first centuries. She recorded two albums with her trio that celebrated Williams's music: *Zodiac Suite Revisited* in 2006 with the Mary Lou Williams Collective, and *Celebrating Mary Lou Williams (Live at Birdland New York)* in 2011 with drummer Andrew Cyrille, alto saxophonist Oliver Lake, and bassist Reggie Workman. Father Peter O'Brien penned extensive liner notes for both of Allen's tribute albums. The notes for *Celebrating Mary Lou Williams* also contained the recollections of Cyrille, who befriended Williams through her Bel Canto shop. In March 2014, Allen worked with O'Brien and Farah Jasmine Griffin, the Columbia University scholar of African American literature, to create a celebration of Mary Lou Williams at the Harlem Stage Gatehouse that incorporated reinterpretations of her jazz music and spoken word culled from her autobiographical writings and interviews. The production, titled "Geri Allen Celebrates Mary Lou Williams," was directed by actress S. Epatha Merkerson (b. 1952) and featured Allen, bassist Kenny Davis, drummer Kassa Overall, and vocalist Carmen Lundy. The presentation appeared at the John F. Kennedy Center for the Performing Arts under the title "A Conversation with Mary Lou Williams" as part of the center's twenty-first annual Mary Lou Williams Jazz Festival in 2016.[53]

From 1977 until her death in 1981, Williams was an artist-in-residence at Duke University, a sign that, despite her struggles for recognition within her male-dominated profession, she had obtained institutional recognition from academia. She directed a jazz ensemble at Duke and taught a course in which she worked to create a structural outline for the history of jazz. Opportunities for academic recognition for jazz artists, through university fellowships and appointments, and through national grants and awards, have allowed for many jazz artists to thrive in elite institutions and for jazz to become an established black cultural form. Thus, Allen's collaboration with academics to preserve Williams's place in jazz history fit within a lineage of certain forms of black music, like the spirituals, finding an institutional home even if they were no longer financially lucrative in the world of commercial music.

Allen followed in the footsteps of both Ellington and Williams with the creation of her own sacred musical works. She was a recipient of the Guggenheim Fellowship for 2008–2009, and during this period she composed the solo piano album *Flying toward the Sound*, released in 2010. Griffin wrote in the liner notes that Allen "hails from a culture that celebrates flight as a metaphor for freedom." For Allen's sixteen-minute composition titled "GOD's Ancient Sky," Griffin noted that it represents the album's "spiritual centerpiece. Here she imagines flying to places of great spiritual power—the Western Wall of Jerusalem, St. Mary's of Zion in Axum, Ethiopia—and then over the great natural cathedrals: the ocean, the desert, the forest and mountains. The grand gestures of this music are both deeply grounded, yet also in flight, both rooted tree and flute-like branch."[54] Allen provided a musical composition that highlighted sites and themes of religious significance to her—far beyond familiar biblical references, characters, and metaphors, Allen's reflection incorporated post-biblical sites of Christian importance in East African churches, as well as a general sacralization of the entire world as God's creation.

In 2011 Allen recorded *A Child Is Born*, a Christmas album that included liner notes by Rev. Dwight D. Andrews, a multi-instrumentalist, professor of music at Emory, and pastor of First Congregational Church, UCC, of Atlanta. In the acknowledgments of her album liner notes, including first her parents and "our family and our ancestors," Allen extended her gratitude toward "Mary Lou Williams, who continues to have a great impact on my decision to make sacred music as a focus in my life."[55]

Wynton Marsalis, the prominent and controversial jazz trumpeter and composer, represents the most consistent effort to establish and to carry forward Ellington's vision of arranged jazz music, where most of a piece's musical structure is scored, ideally with a big band, while the artist builds in space for improvisation. Marsalis, the director of the Jazz at Lincoln Center Orchestra, is a polarizing figure in the professional and critical jazz community because of his opposition to jazz fusion (particularly, music in the vein of Miles Davis that attempts to combine elements of rock and roll and bop/post-bop jazz). Ironically, a considerable portion of Marsalis's jazz music represents a fusion of different jazz styles and Euro-American classical music. But like Ellington and Williams, Marsalis seeks to preserve elements of African American musical culture. The religious music of his New Orleans roots and of more charismatic African American churches, in general, constitute the cultural repertoire for many of his performances of black sacred culture. In the footsteps of sacred jazz composers like Ellington and Williams, Marsalis composes music that reflects the vocal sounds of gospel music and the spirituals in their arranged university choir versions, and he is also known to use instruments like the trumpet and reeds in his orchestra to imitate the sounds of conventional black chanted or whooped sermons and prayers.

There are several works from Marsalis's music that exemplify his deployment of African American religious musical themes, but two selections reflect the ways that Marsalis worked to capture early twentieth-century African American Christian music and theology. The first example, in particular, demonstrates a strong criticism of Christianization in world history. This critique is present in Marsalis's extended symphony titled *All Rise*, in "Movement VI: Cried, Shouted, Then Sung." The movement features Marsalis's Lincoln Center Jazz Orchestra, the Los Angeles Philharmonic, and the voices of the Morgan State University Choir, a historically black choral ensemble that emphasizes "preserving the heritage of the spiritual, especially in the historic practices of performance" even though the choir's repertoire consists of classical, gospel, and contemporary popular music. From the liner notes: "After the sermon, the choir sings of the arrogant and self-aggrandized viewpoints that always lead to gross inhumanity in the name of God and in the name of Jesus."

With this section, Marsalis's presentation of African American Christianity reflected on the circumstances under which the people became Christian—circumstances that reflect several other colonized or oppressed contexts around the world that became predominantly Christian but disinherited of their material resources, freedoms, or nationhood. At times, the lyrics appear to represent the missionizing voices of those who would colonize or conquer others, offering the Christian religion but ultimately desiring the riches of land, minerals, and bodies. Despite the apparent criticism of Christianity, there is ultimately an ambivalent appreciation of Jesus and the potential for his message of treating others as one wishes to be treated prevailing against the historical realities of so many modern subjects who came to embrace Christianity. And the subsequent movements in *All Rise* contain prayers to God, praise of God, and exhortations to listeners to move from prizing selfish greed to universal fellowship, or, to quote Marsalis's liner notes, "From the I AM of materialistic self-aggrandizement to the great I AM of brotherhood, sharing, and love."[56]

Marsalis's "Abyssinian 200: A Celebration" served as the composer's most recent offering of a sacred concert, and it marked the bicentennial of Harlem's Abyssinian Baptist Church in 2008. This performance featured Marsalis's orchestra, a mass gospel choir, and an interfaith/ecumenical "sermonette" by Abyssinian's pastor, Rev. Calvin O. Butts III (b. 1949). It featured more than two hours of compositions reflecting the liturgical structure or order of service of many middle-class African American Christian worship services in the twentieth century that also revealed the thorough influence of the gospel tradition. Marsalis performed the gospel celebration again in 2013, featuring the vocal talents of the seventy-voice Chorale Le Chateau, a predominantly African American choir directed by Damien Sneed that interprets Renaissance music, jazz, spirituals, gospel, and avant-garde contemporary music. Like Ellington's sacred concerts, Marsalis's celebration toured universities, theaters, and churches in 2013, including Friendship Missionary Baptist Church in Charlotte, North Carolina, Good Shepherd Baptist Church in Augusta, Georgia, and Fountain of Praise Church in Houston, Texas.[57] A 2016 album recording of Marsalis's jazz mass, appropriately titled *The Abyssinian Mass*, resulted from these live performances in 2013.

Conclusion

A quote attributed to Ella Fitzgerald states that when she was performing at the Apollo Theater, she ventured over to the Harlem Opera House between sets and asked Billie Holiday, her vocalist contemporary, for her autograph backstage. Fitzgerald remarked, "I did something then, and I still don't know if it was the right thing to do," likely indicating the potential impropriety of entreating her peer for an inscription that effectively defined herself, the "first lady of song," as subordinate to "Lady Day." In the years and decades following Holiday's death, Fitzgerald endeavored to keep Holiday's musical legacy alive in her own way. She recorded in studio and in live performances Holiday's associated standards "Good Morning Heartache" and "Fine and Mellow." Even "God

Bless the Child" received a studio recording in Fitzgerald's later years with the 1982 album *The Best Is Yet to Come*. She introduced some song performances by urging audiences (particularly the younger members of the crowd) to purchase Holiday's records. In this manner, she participated in the construction of a tradition that jazz vocalists maintained, namely, of keeping singers alive by performing their associated songs, whether the exact arrangements or renditions with unique vocal interpretations and instrumentation.

The deceased jazz professionals who became race representatives maintain lingering presences in the lives of many. Through sacred archives, institution building, dedicated monuments, performing venues, charitable foundations, exhibits, and online communities, jazz fans have constructed significant physical and virtual landscapes to promote the sustained veneration of departed virtuosos. Educational positions extend the charitable spirit of Williams in institutionalizing recognition and performing opportunities for working musicians. Annual festivals and centennial celebrations arrange time according to sacred chronologies of African American lives within jazz communities. These events compel musicians and music patrons alike to mark their calendars in preparation for concert performance dates and festival pilgrimages to celebrate specific figures like Ellington, Fitzgerald, and Williams.

Live tribute performances, dedicated studio albums, poetic reflections, Catholic poetic engagements, and poetic testimonies with Christian and Afro-diasporic religious resonances have represented ways of speaking about *and* to jazz ancestors—practices of music, spoken performance, and the written word to keep them alive by keeping their musical corpuses alive. Embracing and altering the theological messages of sacred works demonstrate practices in African American Christianity of rendering Ellingtonian music conducive to modern praise and worship. And there are African American musicians and composers who have emerged as spiritual heirs to the tradition of rendering religious beliefs and practices rooted in narratives of race history musically legible through jazz. The afterlives of African American jazz ancestors rest in the hands, voices, and minds of those who have committed to sustained celebrations of a music tradition that encompasses religious beliefs, practices, and sacred histories of a people.

Conclusion

Black Artistry and Religious Culture

This book has explored the work of African American jazz musicians as racial and religious representatives in the twentieth century, tracing how jazz artists' emergence as a new kind of representative helped to locate religious authority for African Americans outside of traditional Afro-Protestant institutions. Cab Calloway, Duke Ellington, Ella Fitzgerald, and Mary Lou Williams have captured ways that professional jazz musicians made manifest their religious representations, reflections, and practices for public consumption and private contemplation. In turn, these beliefs and practices reflected and influenced African American religious culture in the twentieth century and in these musicians' afterlives. With vinyl records and ephemeral documents as their archives of sacred contemplation, Duke Ellington and Mary Lou Williams produced public religious music and private religious reflections that also placed a spotlight on racialized religious discourses. The careers of Cab Calloway and Ella Fitzgerald tested the compatibility of nonreligious African American professional occupations with the objectives of progressive racial activism that African American clergy and religious institutions promulgated. All four jazz professionals provide examples of the religious aspects of race representation through their unique performances of religious and racial identities for public consumption, whether crafted intentionally or the result of social and cultural constructs.

The historical study of African American religions recognizes that black religious women and men with Holiness-Pentecostal or rural Baptist roots and affiliations contributed a distinct southern black religious culture to early twentieth-century African American religious practices. This modern religious culture's hallmarks during the Great Migration era included the emergence of gospel music, makeshift storefront religious spaces, charismatic religious practices, and mass-market sermons on race records and over radio broadcasts. However, middle-class black Protestants across the American South and North also made durable contributions that enhance discussions of African American religion. This book has offered a novel concept of Afro-Protestantism that describes the distinct and identifiable contribution to African American culture by middle-class black subjects who were religious artists in this same period and beyond. As exemplified in the lives and works examined in this book, the jazz profession in the twentieth century became fertile soil for the cultivation of artistic religious expressions in popular culture. And these cultural expressions of religious belief, belonging, and practice shed a new light on a dimension of Afro-Protestantism that constituted a consequential artistic movement.

Afro-Protestantism, when viewed as an artistic movement in the long twentieth century, included a robust, oppositional, and self-consciously racialized articulation and practice of scriptural interpretation through cultural production, or "preaching" in various forms. Religious race professionals were the Afro-Protestant representatives who preached an oppositional expression of being, including an explicit challenge to preexisting forms of Protestant Christianity, even as they were often simultaneously in dialogue with representatives and adherents in white denominations. Black men and women's Protestantism—in its etymological sensibility as religious "protest"—is also evident in their self-authorized creation of institutions if they were unable to achieve authority within preexisting ones. To preach their social, cultural, political, and theological goals, they built churches, para-church associations, denominations, schools, and print press outlets. While they preached, however, African American Protestants, or the black Protestant mainline, or the black Protestant middle class also employed artistic expressions in their quest for long-term institutional space and power. The vocalists and instrumentalists who preached through the artistry of the jazz profession amplified Afro-Protestantism as a cultural and artistic presence in history—their voices and legacies call religion scholars to both novel and conventional archives to respond to the fundamentally artistic dimensions of religious thought and expression. With these preaching jazz professionals, Afro-Protestantism also resonates as a mode of performance and vocalization to hear and interpret in the public actors it influences—when African Americans, past or present, evoke preacherly traditions, sacred race histories, or ritual antiphonies in rhetoric, poetry, and music. In popular culture, Afro-Protestantism comes to symbolize a religious orientation toward embodying African American history and black subjectivity.

Afro-Protestantism as an alternative conception of Protestantism was relatively nascent when jazz emerged as a new cultural arena in the twentieth century. As the jazz profession reveals, Afro-Protestantism in the first half of the twentieth century had significant artistic influence among African Americans in the modern world. Much like evangelicalism, Holiness-Pentecostalism, New Thought metaphysics, alternative religio-racial communities during the Great Migration, or Prosperity/Word of Faith, Afro-Protestantism produced black women and men who became popular public representatives with expressive cultural forms. In turn, they produced authoritative expressions of race and religion on record, stage, film, radio, in the black print press, and in national archives. In the twentieth century, this multimedia religious presence saturated African American culture and had the potential to impact African Americans across traditional religious denominations, even if they converted to or affiliated with alternative religious traditions.

As we have seen, the religious leadership and practice of Duke Ellington in white liberal Protestantism and Mary Lou Williams in Roman Catholicism attest to these interdenominational and interracial possibilities. Afro-Protestant cultural production played no small role in Williams's creation of African American sacred jazz for the Roman Catholic Church. Viewed through the lens of artistry, Afro-Protestantism greatly impacted popular mass culture, the ostensibly nonreligious public arena of African American life and entertainment. With Cab Calloway and Ella Fitzgerald, we have seen that the popular public figures who commodified Afro-Protestant religious expressions represented varying degrees of (ir)reverence for religious mores, practices, and pious representatives. And the legacies of artistic professionals, in addition to the cultures of celebrating jazz ancestors, extend the influence of Afro-Protestant artistic expressions upon (African) American popular culture into the twenty-first century.

Recent scholarship in African American religious history acknowledges that there was never a "Black Church" that existed as a race institution analogous to "the (Roman Catholic) Church." The closest possibility for the existence of a large, unified Protestant denomination came with the efforts to unite the various black Methodist denominations in the early twentieth century. However, such a creation still would not have been comparable to Roman Catholicism because of the presence of black Baptists (in greater numbers than the collective of black Methodists), Holiness-Pentecostals, and black congregations within white Protestant and Catholic denominations.[1] Nor was there a single black Protestant denomination that championed something scholars can identify as a "black liberal Protestant" tradition in the twentieth century, although academic schools of thought exposed African American ministers with higher education to the movements of biblical criticism, comparative religious studies, and the Social Gospel, which, in turn, impacted their conversations in black religious newspapers, affected their denominational seminary training, and altered their missions to working-class black migrants.

In the early twentieth century, these intellectual, social, and theological presences manifested not only in some black Protestant pulpits, but also within the cultural production of lay African Americans who emerged from black Protestant churches and social life, as this book's subjects exemplify. Fixating on a concept of black churches as constituting a consistent institutional tradition of theology, ritual, and sociopolitical action often leads to questions of their waxing and waning presence as authorities and representatives of black America. Rather, what this book's centering of jazz professionals has offered is the recasting of Afro-Protestant women and men as the inheritors and innovators of highly visible and audible forms of religious expression and practice for public audiences. This work demonstrates more than just jazz artists' authority as religious and race representatives. It also illuminates the vitality of Afro-Protestantism in modern American history through influential representatives and religious innovators in various professions, not simply clerical ones.

Uncovering the ways in which jazz professionals leveraged their celebrity into a type of religious authority situated beyond institutional church life allows us to reconfigure Afro-Protestantism according to artistry that shaped understandings of theology, religious practice, and public engagement. By adopting a view of Afro-Protestantism as artistry in the history of African American culture, we are able to avoid framing it as a hegemonic religious institution and conceive of it in relative terms, as *one* strand of theological articulation, religious practice, and mode of public engagement alongside other significant religious movements in African American life. To augment the concept of a black Protestantism that is defined by identifiable institutional locations, particularly denominations and church congregations, with the concept of Afro-Protestantism as both a historical movement and an expressive culture, allows us to recognize traditional black Protestant religious spaces as acutely sensitive to change. Such changes occurred in response to the debates that emerged as the result of the influx of black migrants and the varieties of recreational and leisure culture available to younger generations of African Americans that threatened to shift their social lives away from church time and space. For the black Baptist and Methodist churches that existed before, during, and after the migrations of new black populations and their successive generations, theological changes did not represent the waning of institutional religious presence, but the emerging presences of other cultural movements within African American religions that proponents and opponents viewed as competing or complementary innovations. Such developments included the introduction of the varieties of American metaphysical theology in sermons and songs, liturgical modifications that adjusted worship services to anticipate (or accommodate musically) charismatic "Holy Spirit" possession presences through shouting and dancing, and musical changes such as a shift from arranged spirituals to gospel styles. Expressive popular music emerged as another alternative cultural development laden with expressive religious possibilities. Its proponents in jazz viewed it as another viable arena for African American religious expression—the music would either compete with Afro-Protestant authorities, or, as it turned out, complement and reconfigure conventional African American religious life.

Although Afro-Protestantism was culturally ubiquitous, it shared a public religious arena with alternative religio-racial expressions of belief and representations of racial identity. This view of Afro-Protestantism allows us to acknowledge the consequential cultural presence and legacy of black Protestant religious subjects and their cultural work beyond the building, maintenance, and regulation of church life. At the same time, this concept of Afro-Protestantism allows us to recognize the ultimately

insecure position of black Protestant institutional power and authority for quotidian African American existence in the long twentieth century. In the lives of jazz professionals, artistic expression reveals African
American practices of reciting, improvising on, and even drowning out
conventional religious thought and practice.

* * *

African American gospel singer Jennifer Holliday received a Grammy
Award in 1985 for her recording of Duke Ellington's "Come Sunday."
Known for her LGBT rights advocacy and HIV/AIDS awareness fundraising, Holliday became the subject of political controversy when she
agreed to perform for the "Welcome Concert for the People" during the
presidential inauguration of Donald Trump in January 2017 because
the Republican Party and presidential ticket represented opposition
to progressive stances on civil rights and civil liberties. In a letter she
addressed "To My Beloved LGBT Community," Holliday informed her
fans that she had canceled her plans to perform during the Trump inauguration. She wrote, "The LGBT Community was mostly responsible for
birthing my career and I am deeply indebted to you. . . . You have loved
me faithfully and unconditionally and for so many years you provided
me with work even though my star had long since faded."[2]

In response to the inauguration controversy, Holliday appeared on
the daytime talk show *The View* to perform her rendition of what co-
host Whoopi Goldberg described as "Duke Ellington's civil rights–era
classic." The backdrop to Holliday's performance of "Come Sunday" was
a large screen that showcased several black-and-white photographs, a
presentation that appeared to curate the singer's reverence for historical
and modern social movements. As Holliday sang, viewers beheld images
of a civil rights march for integration, equal rights, housing, and an end
to racial bias. Contemporary pictures captured an African American
child with the American flag covering his face, young Muslim American women of color waving the American flag, and marchers carrying
the Mexican flag. Protest photographs included visuals of two women
holding a "Pride over Prejudice" sign, marchers carrying a "Black Lives
Matter" banner, marchers carrying a "Stop the War on Muslims" banner,
and Standing Rock Sioux marchers carrying a "Defend the Sacred" banner in protest of the controversial Dakota Access oil pipeline feared to

endanger sacred indigenous sites. Images containing additional protest statements included a Muslim woman of color holding an American flag with a sign above her, reading, "I am a Muslim and ISIS does not represent me nor does it represent Islam"; an image of Orthodox Jewish rabbis; an iconic portrait of Trayvon Martin held by a marcher; an adolescent protestor holding a poster with "Peace" written on it; a young Muslim woman of color holding a "We Denounce Hate Crime" sign; and a portrait of four young American girls, appearing to be of Latin American, African American, East Asian, and South Asian descent.[3]

"Come Sunday," Ellington's lyrical tribute to the spirituals that became a staple of his ecumenical Sacred Concerts, sounds in Holliday's rendition like a prayer to God pleading to "see my people through" their struggles for justice. For *The View*'s audience, this Christian gospel singer's musical and visual presentation shifted the song away from originally signaling a mid-twentieth-century "Protestant-Catholic-Jew" ecumenism in its presentation in churches, cathedrals, and synagogues. For Holliday, the song came to represent a national, interreligious meditation on social justice advocacy. With "Come Sunday," the audience witnessed the advocacy of American Muslims, Indigenous American communities, Mexican immigrants, Orthodox Jews, and opposition to hate crimes through the selection of accompanying photographs—rather than through any explicit images of Christianity or articulation by Christian clerical representatives, beyond the voice of the Christian singer. Through this African American music professional, Ellington's religiously and racially significant Afro-Protestant song now lent the authority of African American history to Holliday's own authoritative performance of interreligious, interracial, social, and political solidarity for viewing audiences. Nearly eight decades after Lionel Hampton had chastised swing bands for performing spirituals, Jennifer Holliday signaled her position as a race representative by employing Duke Ellington's religious tribute to spirituals.

For African Americans in the jazz century, public religious expression always entailed race representation, and both forms of representation and expression were markers of broader trends and possibilities for religious belief, practice, and articulation in these years. Engaging the public and private archives of African American jazz musicians has revealed complex individual and communal religious identities, expressions, and practices. These complexities, in turn, have allowed us to view African American women and men in their efforts both to define precisely their religious roles and affiliations and to articulate belief in their personal and professional lives. These swing virtuosos represented African American lives in syncopation: at times, they accented what religious and cultural conventions emphasized; at other times, they accented what these conventions downplayed. The unique spiritual expressions of other famous jazz artists, including John Coltrane, Albert Ayler, Sun Ra, and Alice Coltrane Turiyasangitananda, have deep roots in African American cultural and religious history. If we lift voices across generations, classes, regions, and emerging professions, we will be able to note that black religious women and men's professional labor and artistic production have expressed directly, or revealed indirectly, the contested nature of African American institutional forms, individual commitments, and collective identities.

ACKNOWLEDGMENTS

An undergraduate Dartmouth course, "History of Jazz," taught by saxophonist and composer Fred Haas in the fall quarter of 2005, first made me realize that I could think seriously about jazz, race, and religion. It was also during my undergraduate years that several people were responsible for encouraging me to pursue doctoral studies. The most critical academic mentorship came from Clarence E. Hardy III, who supervised my undergraduate honors thesis at Dartmouth. Susan Ackerman, Nancy K. Frankenberry, and A. Kevin Reinhart also encouraged me to find my academic voice during my undergraduate years through their courses. Richard A. Wright supervised the Mellon Mays Undergraduate Fellowship, a program critical to my completion of undergraduate and graduate studies. I never imagined that I would return to Dartmouth as the Thurgood Marshall Dissertation Fellow, soon thereafter to become a colleague with several of my former professors.

The welcoming community of scholars at Dartmouth has made this book possible. In African and African American studies, this includes the invaluable mentoring and writing feedback of Robert M. Baum, Michael A. Chaney, Keith L. Walker, Ayo A. Coly, Trica Keaton, and Jesse Weaver Shipley. In the religion department, this includes the encouragement and mentoring of Susan Ackerman, Zahra Ayubi, Randall Balmer, Robert M. Baum, Ehud Z. Benor, Susannah Heschel, Christopher MacEvitt, Reiko Ohnuma, Gil Raz, A. Kevin Reinhart, and Devin Singh. Bob, Jesse, Randy, and Trica have each provided memorable advice and preparation for the academic profession, and Trica made my connection with Mary Lou Williams documentarian Joanna Burke possible. Laura McTighe, who was a member of Dartmouth's Society of Fellows before joining the religion faculty at Florida State University, sat next to me on a panel at the American Academy of Religion's 2014 annual meeting as we both presented papers, with mine representing my initial study of the Bel Canto Foundation. Laura and Zahra have been wonderful and hospitable colleagues and friends ever since we met. Michelle R. Warren has provided me academic wisdom as I have witnessed her mentor emerging generations of Mellon Mays fellows. Manish Mishra, director of professional education at the Dartmouth Institute for Health Policy and Clinical Practice, has provided me several opportunities to share my research with Dartmouth undergraduates whose medical studies he believes must incorporate the perspectives of the arts and humanities. Department and program administrators, including Kirsten Giebutowski, Lisa Meehan, Meredyth D. Morley, and Marcia Welsh, have graciously helped me to navigate my years at Dartmouth.

Beyond encouraging me to apply to Princeton University's religion program, R. Marie Griffith provided invaluable advice about pursuing the advanced study and research of religion in the Americas through her courses and mentorship. The past and present faculty of Princeton's Religion in the Americas program made the rigorous task of engaging in academic research an amazing experience. I can never thank Wallace D. Best and Judith L. Weisenfeld enough for preparing me to contribute to African American religious history through coursework, examinations, assistant course instruction, and research opportunities. Judith Weisenfeld's critical engagement with my research was an indispensable gift that matured my thinking and writing. The interpretive concerns I bring to the jazz music and prose in this work are shaped by the rich and intensive studies of Harlem Renaissance artists under Wallace Best's instruction. I would not be teaching American religious history without the instruction of Kathryn Gin Lum, who also helped me approach academic writing in the field. Jessica Delgado enhanced the comprehensive scope of my study of early American religious history, and I greatly appreciate her critical eye for finding the argumentative threads in my research. I have been inspired by Seth Perry's scholarship and his advice for beginning a tenure-track faculty position. Albert J. Raboteau provided wisdom about this profession and the study of African American religion over the years in which I've had the opportunity to engage him (when I'm not studying and teaching his scholarship). The Princeton faculty who trained me in African American studies all "demonstrate excellence" (to echo Eddie Glaude's charge) for their graduate students to model. I am exceedingly grateful for the approaches to African American studies that I learned and now carry forward thanks to Tera W.

Hunter, Eddie S. Glaude Jr., Joshua Guild, and Imani Perry. Additionally, I appreciate conversations with Kinohi Nishikawa that have helped me engage studies of humor in African American cultural history. I am fortunate to have friends and colleagues studying religion in the Americas who have modeled kindness, care, and rigor in their professional and personal lives. I appreciate the standards that April C. Armstrong, Rachel B. Gross, Ryan P. Harper, Rachel Mcbride Lindsey, Caleb J. D. Maskell, and James Young set to approach and navigate the academic profession. I would not have gotten through graduate school without Beth Stroud and Leslie Ribovich, my comrades in coursework, exam study, teaching, and dissertation writing. I have had more probing, challenging, and lighthearted conversations with Andrew Walker-Cornetta and Kelsey Moss over the years than I can remember. I have enjoyed years of deep study, meaningful conversation, and good food with Alda Balthrop-Lewis, Kijan Bloomfield, Eden Consenstein, Clifton Granby, Alyssa J. Maldonado-Estrada, Takashi Miura, Rebecca M. Rosen, and William J. Schultz. I have appreciated the wisdom, encouragement, and advice of academic colleagues and leaders in the field, including Courtney Bryan, Kwami Coleman, Matthew J. Cressler, Jamil W. Drake, Gillian Frank, Derek S. Hicks, Elizabeth L. Jemison, Sylvester A. Johnson, Kathryn Lofton, Rhon S. Manigault-Bryant, Lerone A. Martin, Albert G. Miller, Daniel Rivers, Josef Sorett, Michael J. Thate, and Alexis S. Wells-Oghoghomeh.

Several people have provided help in shaping this book from its initial form. I thank Princeton University Library Services, including Wayne Bivens-Tatum, Colleen Burlingham, and Deborah T. Paparone, for helping me to acquire primary sources and church periodicals on microfilm. Wendy Shay and Joe Hursey, archivists for the Smithsonian Institution's National Museum of American History, helped me to navigate the collections of Duke and Ruth Ellington. At Rutgers University's Institute of Jazz Studies, I received crucial archival assistance from Joe Peterson, Tad Hershorn, and Elizabeth Surles in navigating Mary Lou Williams's massive business archive. Richard Wood, archivist for Fountain Street Church in Grand Rapids, Michigan, provided me recordings of the Duke Ellington Orchestra and Ella Fitzgerald concerts at the church. Erik Tweed helped me locate an article that Mary Lou Williams wrote for *Sepia* magazine. I appreciate Christopher J. Wells for alerting me to his scholarship in jazz studies on Ella Fitzgerald. I thank the Estate of Mercer K. Ellington and the Mary Lou Williams Foundation for allowing me to share this archival research with the public.

I have also benefited with formal responses to chapter drafts from Beth Stroud, Clifton Granby, and Kijan Bloomfield. I am grateful for additional extensive chapter feedback from Aaron Rock-Singer and Hillary Kaell. For feedback on research and concepts that eventually materialized in this project, I thank Yolanda Pierce for inviting me to present research in Princeton Theological Seminary's history colloquium in 2013 as well as Curtis J. Evans and Emily D. Crews for selecting me as one of the 2016 African Religions in the Americas workshop participants. I also thank Judith Weisenfeld for her role as respondent to my conference paper containing excerpts from chapter 8 at the 2014 annual meeting of the American Academy of Religion.

I am grateful to the Fund (now Forum) for Theological Education, the Social Science Research Council-Mellon Mays Graduate Initiatives Program, Princeton University's Center for (now Department of) African American Studies, and Princeton University's Department of Religion for providing consequential research and conference travel funding for my research. I also appreciate Jenny W. Legath and Robert Wuthnow of Princeton's Center for the Study of Religion for selecting me as one of the 2014–2015 Religion and Culture workshop participants. A fellowship year at Dartmouth allowed me the funds and time to reshape and expand this research project. Generous funding from the Walter and Constance Burke Research Initiation Award Program at Dartmouth made it possible to finalize this book. The 2019–2020 cohort of the Young Scholars in American Religion program, convened by the Center for the Study of Religion and American Culture at Indiana University, has been a meaningful and encouraging academic community thanks to our faculty mentors, James Bennett and Laura S. Levitt. Jennifer Hammer, Alexia Traganas, and Rosalie Morales Kearns, my editors at New York University Press, provided extraordinary guidance to see this book project through.

As a percussionist in various symphonic and marching bands during my public school years, I express appreciation for the music instructors in my educational journey. Rehman Ali Sheikh, Eric Shieh, and Christopher G. Symeonides are the college friends who have humored me and cheered on my academic journey for nearly two decades. During my graduate education, I had humorous daily conversations with at least one of my siblings, Tamia D. Booker, Taeryn L. Booker, and Valin J. Booker. My parents, Taryn M. Gaynor and Vaughn A. Booker Sr., were in the first generation of their families to complete undergraduate degrees and then set the standard for my generation by also completing graduate education. In elementary school, my mother took me to a jazz concert by her sorority sister, vocalist Sherry Wilson-Butler, and she arranged a phone interview for me with Wilson-Butler as I worked on a class project. In my extended family, my uncle Donn L. Booker Sr., my cousin Hasker Booker, and my great-aunt Geraldine Gary have encouraged my pursuit of higher education for as long as I can remember.

Leatch Booker Jr., Joyce Ann Booker, Clarence Gary Jr., and Ida Ruth Newton are the departed grandparents whom I was able to know. By giving me *Ellington at Newport* in elementary school, Clarence Gary Jr. sparked my fascination with the composer and his orchestra. My maternal grandmother, Ida Ruth Newton, not only sparked my love of jazz music by arguing with me over the vocal merits of Sarah Vaughan and Gloria Lynne versus those of Ella Fitzgerald, but she was the funniest and most irreverent person I have ever met. Hattie Booker, Clarence Gary Sr., and George Marshall are the great-grandparents whose lives overlapped with mine briefly. This book and my academic profession serve to honor the lives and work of the sharecroppers, janitors, maids, homemakers, service members, steel workers, hustlers, secretaries, lawyers, and teachers who comprise this "Royal Ancestry."

MUSIC APPENDIX

The following list includes online recordings of the music compositions selected for analysis in this book, where the copyright holders and managing music distributors have made them officially available. These and other official YouTube uploads are provided by Smithsonian Folkways Recordings, Sony Music Entertainment, Universal Music Group, Warner Music Group, and subsidiary distributors, including The Orchard Enterprises and Ingrooves Music Group. The recordings are listed in order of appearance in each book chapter. All links to YouTube were accurate and available at the time of writing.

CHAPTER 2. "GET HAPPY, ALL YOU SINNERS"
Cab Calloway and His Orchestra, "Harlem Camp Meeting," provided to
    YouTube by Sony Music Entertainment, www.youtube.com/watch?v=
    RSzrJckHuyg.
Cab Calloway and His Orchestra, "Is That Religion?," provided to YouTube by In-
    grooves, www.youtube.com/watch?v=pdM-IpcJQ7M.
Cab Calloway and His Orchestra, "Miss Hallelujah Brown," provided to YouTube by
    Sony Music Entertainment, www.youtube.com/watch?v=2biD10z_vEM.
Cab Calloway and His Orchestra, "A Strictly Cullud Affair," provided to YouTube by
    Ingrooves, www.youtube.com/watch?v=mIX8jU7U2Rk.
Cab Calloway and His Orchestra, "Yaller," provided to YouTube by Ingrooves, www.
    youtube.com/watch?v=jFCW71BJDlY.

CHAPTER 3. "TEARS OF JOY"
Ella Fitzgerald, "I Can't Give You Anything but Love (Live at the Newport Jazz Festi-
    val, 1957)," provided to YouTube by Universal Music Group, www.youtube.com/
    watch?v=94Hhu56EnAQ.
Ella Fitzgerald, "You've Got a Friend," provided to YouTube by Universal Music Group,
    www.youtube.com/watch?v=_OWYLMcuEnI.
Ella Fitzgerald, "Crying in the Chapel," provided to YouTube by Universal Music
    Group, www.youtube.com/watch?v=CzWKDaxJZ3U.
Ella Fitzgerald, "When the Hands of the Clock Pray at Midnight," provided to YouTube
    by Universal Music Group, www.youtube.com/watch?v=Oz61-rv_-UM.

Ella Fitzgerald, *Brighten the Corner*, album playlist provided to YouTube by Universal Music Group, www.youtube.com/playlist?list=OLAK5uy_mRZmGCVooiHN_PsRQ3wdWydsJ8yL47pVE.

Ella Fitzgerald, "Hallelujah I Love Him So," provided to YouTube by Universal Music Group, www.youtube.com/watch?v=SV3JAYcSqQQ.

Ella Fitzgerald, "I Can't Stop Loving You," provided to YouTube by The Orchard Enterprises, www.youtube.com/watch?v=mioz-Yxvguo.

Ella Fitzgerald, "'Tain't Nobody's Bizness if I Do," provided to YouTube by Universal Music Group, www.youtube.com/watch?v=nrhp4OwIKYQ.

CHAPTER 4. "ROYAL ANCESTRY"

Duke Ellington and His Orchestra, "Apes and Peacocks (The Queen's Suite)," provided to YouTube by Universal Music Group, www.youtube.com/watch?v=9nY4q_VtoiU.

Duke Ellington and His Orchestra, "Menelik, the Lion of Judah," provided to YouTube by The Orchard Enterprises, www.youtube.com/watch?v=cZdk9g3_jss.

Mercer Ellington and the Duke Ellington Orchestra, with the Polish National Philharmonic, "Three Black Kings," provided to YouTube by CDBaby, www.youtube.com/watch?v=TdGGH5K7n6g.

Duke Ellington and His Orchestra, "Ko-Ko," provided to YouTube by Universal Music Group, www.youtube.com/watch?v=BQxtrM41lws.

Duke Ellington and His Orchestra, "Carabae Joe / Congo Square," provided to YouTube by Sony Music Entertainment, www.youtube.com/watch?v=dCT4Kuy1f_g.

Duke Ellington and His Orchestra, "I Like the Sunrise (from *Liberian Suite*)," provided to YouTube by Sony Music Entertainment, www.youtube.com/watch?v=6BS4mibBPKM.

CHAPTER 6. "IS GOD A THREE-LETTER WORD FOR LOVE?"

Duke Ellington and His Orchestra, "In the Beginning, God," provided to YouTube by Sony Music Entertainment, www.youtube.com/watch?v=v13Avj8qA1A.

Duke Ellington, "Poetic Commentary—A (for New World A-Comin')," provided to YouTube by Universal Music Group, www.youtube.com/watch?v=MrpLLGwzllU.

Duke Ellington and His Orchestra, and the Cincinnati Symphony Orchestra, "New World A-Comin'," provided to YouTube by Universal Music Group, www.youtube.com/watch?v=ZQQgMviEnmo.

Duke Ellington and His Orchestra, "Will You Be There? / Ain't but the One," provided to YouTube by Sony Music Entertainment, www.youtube.com/watch?v=V-CPxTweRQU.

Duke Ellington and His Orchestra, "Supreme Being," provided to YouTube by Universal Music Group, www.youtube.com/watch?v=lLkUR9npkbc.

Duke Ellington and His Orchestra, "The Lord's Prayer," provided to YouTube by Sony Music Entertainment, www.youtube.com/watch?v=3WJxkJgPCko.
Duke Ellington and His Orchestra, "Tell Me It's the Truth," provided to YouTube by Sony Music Entertainment, www.youtube.com/watch?v=tereNBMeVQw.
Duke Ellington and His Orchestra, "Something 'bout Believing," provided to YouTube by Universal Music Group, www.youtube.com/watch?v=tHoneGCYz_o.
Duke Ellington and His Orchestra, "Heaven," provided to YouTube by Universal Music Group, www.youtube.com/watch?v=QM1x6U2jok4.
Duke Ellington and His Orchestra, "Almighty God," provided to YouTube by Universal Music Group, www.youtube.com/watch?v=-WUJIpAQaaw.
Duke Ellington and His Orchestra, *The River*, provided to YouTube by Warner Music Group, www.youtube.com/watch?v=OfF5jGobsF4.

CHAPTER 8. ACCOUNTING FOR THE VULNERABLE
Mary Lou Williams, *Mary Lou Williams Presents Black Christ of the Andes*, playlist provided to YouTube by Smithsonian Folkways Recordings, www.youtube.com/playlist?list=OLAK5uy_khOT9r8yLSyC_SRcOtsdEvv8TywzRgHEk.

CHAPTER 9. VIRTUOSO ANCESTORS
Candice Hoyes, *On a Turquoise Cloud*, playlist provided to YouTube by CD Baby, Inc., www.youtube.com/playlist?list=OLAK5uy_nsIdMwg4940T3XLcG-bRcAH7444ctRMJ8.
Regina Carter, *Ella: Accentuate the Positive*, playlist provided to YouTube by Sony Music Entertainment, www.youtube.com/playlist?list=OLAK5uy_nbMCmQPEUvryk2Db5OB8i400Dgi846Dek.
Dee Dee Bridgewater, *Dear Ella*, playlist provided to YouTube by Universal Music Group, www.youtube.com/playlist?list=OLAK5uy_kDKKGdf8hAI2gfrEIAlCXgqxrlMIOEKQg.
Patti Austin, *For Ella*, playlist provided to YouTube by Universal Music Group, www.youtube.com/playlist?list=OLAK5uy_lDR5L3hCPaxLEgJXKEluqQSIzOI7iVE_c.
Aretha Franklin and Ray Charles, "Ain't but the One," provided to YouTube by Warner Music Group, www.youtube.com/watch?v=sA1zZ31rK9w.
Goin' Home—A Tribute to Duke Ellington/A Benefit for the Duke Ellington Foundation, playlist provided to YouTube by Universal Music Group, www.youtube.com/playlist?list=OLAK5uy_mnKY6OXhmJWeZx9dIMA3YcfHMVt486QQ8.
Geri Allen, *Flying toward the Sound*, playlist provided to YouTube by The Orchard Enterprises, www.youtube.com/playlist?list=OLAK5uy_lpo3XX4NAJE6GmiWSDBqQ2afBFUpZDGgg.
Geri Allen, *A Child Is Born*, playlist provided to YouTube by The Orchard Enterprises, www.youtube.com/playlist?list=OLAK5uy_nMR2NBJDUIZ00yI5LTVJUTvsCoEqJAI8U.

Wynton Marsalis, Jazz at Lincoln Center Orchestra, Damien Sneed, and Chorale Le Chateau, *The Abyssinian Mass*, playlist provided to YouTube by The Orchard Enterprises, www.youtube.com/playlist?list=OLAK5uy _lZGYIuFSogx34MaopN2ISNRP6Tg726Dew.

CONCLUSION

Jennifer Holliday, "Come Sunday," provided to YouTube by Universal Music Group, www.youtube.com/watch?v=qmpw_YY51J8.

NOTES

INTRODUCTION

1 Douglass Hall, "Lionel Hampton Strong on Christian Science," *Baltimore Afro-American*, February 19, 1944, 7.

2 See Mack, *Representing the Race*, 4–5, 20.

3 See Summers, *Manliness and Its Discontents*, 6–7.

4 Hornsby-Gutting, *Black Manhood and Community Building*, 58.

5 Weisenfeld, *Hollywood Be Thy Name*, 16.

6 Taylor, *Black Churches of Brooklyn*, 88.

7 Martin, *Preaching on Wax*, 49–53.

8 See Ogren, *Jazz Revolution*. See also Hornsby-Gutting's discussion of the "Boy Problem" for North Carolina's black race leaders in *Black Manhood and Community Building*.

9 See Von Eschen, *Satchmo Blows Up the World*.

10 Schenbeck, *Racial Uplift and American Music*, 113.

11 Schenbeck, *Racial Uplift and American Music*, 117–18.

12 Schenbeck, *Racial Uplift and American Music*, 145.

13 Schenbeck, *Racial Uplift and American Music*, 145.

14 Schenbeck, *Racial Uplift and American Music*, 131.

15 Ellington, *Music Is My Mistress*, 95–97; and Anderson, *Deep River*, 164.

16 Weisenfeld, "'Truths That Liberate the Soul,'" 225–28, 243.

17 Weisenfeld, "'Truths That Liberate the Soul,'" 234.

18 Weisenfeld, *Hollywood Be Thy Name*, 43–44.

19 Weisenfeld, "'Truths That Liberate the Soul,'" 230–31.

20 See Weisenfeld, "'The Secret at the Root,'" 39, 41. For further analysis of African American religious themes in the plays of Stephens, Basshe, the Heywards, and Connelly, as well as other white playwrights, see Prentiss, *Staging Faith*, 28–32.

21 Weisenfeld, "'The Secret at the Root,'" 42.

22 See Weisenfeld, *Hollywood Be Thy Name*, 132–36.

23 See Higginbotham, *Righteous Discontent*, 195–97. For further critical examination of the strategies of African American uplift theory, see Gaines, *Uplifting the Race*.

24 Dennis C. Dickerson examined the *Star of Zion* in the context of black Methodist deliberations over uniting as a single denomination in the early decades of the twentieth century in his article "Black Ecumenism." For African American historians' engagement with the *Star of Zion* turn-of-the-century writers, see studies

of Sarah Dudley Pettey in Gilmore, *Gender and Jim Crow*; and Lundeen, "Sarah Dudley Pettey." See African American historians' use of *Star of Zion* discussions of controversies over women's ordination to the ministry in the AMEZ denomination in Jones, *All Bound Up Together*; and for deliberations over concepts of black manhood in Hornsby-Gutting, *Black Manhood and Community Building*.

25 Harlos, "Jazz Autobiography," 149.
26 "About Bryant Rollins," BryantRollins.com, 2012, accessed May 26, 2016, www.bryantrollins.com/About.html.
27 Harlos, "Jazz Autobiography," 137.
28 Farrington, "Narrating the Jazz Life," 375–77.
29 It is likely that Calloway viewed the autobiography as an opportunity to justify his career choices, particularly since his comedic choices included African American stereotypes that had a more racist history in minstrelsy as an entertainment form.
30 Kainer, "Vocal Racial Crossover," 184.
31 Douglas Martin, "Ruth Ellington Boatwright, 88, the Sister of Duke Ellington," *New York Times*, March 11, 2004, accessed October 31, 2014, www.nytimes.com/2004/03/11/arts/ruth-ellington-boatwright-88-the-sister-of-duke-ellington.html.
32 Cressler, *Authentically Black and Truly Catholic*, 15.
33 Cressler, *Authentically Black and Truly Catholic*, 190.
34 Mary Lou Williams, "Has the Black American Musician Lost His Creativeness and Heritage in Jazz?," pp. 1, 4, Mary Lou Williams Collection, Institute of Jazz Studies, Series 5: Personal Papers, ca. 1970–1971, Box 2, Folder 25.
35 Holmes and Thomson, *Jazz Greats*, 36.

CHAPTER 1. "JAZZING RELIGION"

1 E. Elliott Rawlins, "Keeping Fit: The Intoxication of Jazz," *New York Amsterdam News*, April 11, 1923, 12.
2 E. Elliott Rawlins, "Keeping Fit: Jazz—A Drug," *New York Amsterdam News*, April 1, 1925, 16.
3 Historian of African American religions Craig R. Prentiss notes this direct competition in the 1920s through surveys quantifying growing black attendance at theaters. See Prentiss, *Staging Faith*, 12–13.
4 J. S. Williams, "Ministerial Misfits," *Africo-American Presbyterian*, September 27, 1928, 1.
5 W. W. Evans, "Dr. W. E. B. Dubois and the New Negro Church. A Review," *Star of Zion*, August 18, 1921, 1.
6 William J. Walls, "Mr. DuBois Dabbles in Methodism," *Star of Zion*, June 1, 1922, 4.
7 Walls, "Mr. DuBois Dabbles in Methodism."
8 William J. Walls, "Disrespect to Dr. DuBois Justly Rebuked by Bishops," *Star of Zion*, July 6, 1922, 4.
9 "Booker T. Washington's Life Held Up as Model for Tuskegee Students in Annual Founder's Day Exercises," *New York Age*, April 9, 1927, 3.

10 "The Short Circuit of Denunciation," *Star of Zion*, October 31, 1920, 4.

11 William J. Walls, "The Fight Looming on Dancing," *Star of Zion*, March 20, 1924, 4. Walls followed this edition the next week with "The Dancing War," in which he provided additional condemnation of modern dancing from Catholic bishops in the United States and Canada, medical professionals, commercial recreation authorities, Anglican clergy, and the press of the Disciples of Christ. See Walls, "The Dancing War," *Star of Zion*, March 27, 1924, 4.

12 "Comments by The Age Editors on Sayings of Other Editors," *New York Age*, April 5, 1924, 4.

13 William J. Walls, "Beg Your Pardon, The Age Errs," *Star of Zion*, April 24, 1924, 4.

14 "The Church and Recreation," *New York Age*, May 10, 1924, 4.

15 Lester A. Walton, "Harlem Church Fights Jazz with Play—Negro Production of 'Merchant of Venice' Packs Building," *New York World*, June 15, 1930, page unknown; located in the Alexander Gumby Collection of Negroiana, reel 11, vol. 47, Rare Book and Manuscript Library, Columbia University. On socially progressive middle-class black church involvement with the "Little Theatre" movement in 1920s New York City, see Prentiss, *Staging Faith*, 28.

16 William J. Walls, "The Negro Church and the Stage," *Star of Zion*, May 24, 1923, 4.

17 See Ruth R. Dennis, "'Thousands Losing Faith in Church,' Says Woman Evangelist," *Pittsburgh Courier*, June 25, 1927, 8; and Dennis, "Babies 'Too Young to Pray' Can 'Shake That Thing', Says Writer," *Pittsburgh Courier*, July 30, 1927, 2.

18 Ruth R. Dennis, "'Holy Ghost Preaching' Often Styled as 'Gravy,'" *New York Age*, March 14, 1925, 4.

19 Dennis, "'Holy Ghost Preaching,'" 4.

20 W. H. Davenport, "'Whangdoodleism' Must Go," *Star of Zion*, June 19, 1924, 4. See also "Whangdoodleism," *Star of Zion*, September 6, 1934, 4.

21 See "On Being Deeply Religious," *Star of Zion*, July 29, 1937, 4.

22 "Jazzing Religion," *Philadelphia Tribune*, September 11, 1930, 9.

23 McCrary wrote, "I do not believe, however, in jazz music or blues singing in worship services of the church! Even if the jazz be played on the pipe organ, or the blues sung with religious words. I think music should be played where it belongs. I like it there." Henry T. McCrary, "Much Evangelism Today Seen Akin to Theatrical, Minstrel Show Type," *Philadelphia Tribune*, April 26, 1934, 5.

24 McCrary, "Much Evangelism Today," 5.

25 McCrary, "Much Evangelism Today," 20.

26 S. A. Haynes, "Jazz Evangelist Barred by Camden Clergy: Sensational, Racketeering, Soul Savers Are Banned by Jersey Ministers Alliance," *Philadelphia Tribune*, July 26, 1934, 9.

27 "AME Bishop Raps Daddy Grace and Jazz Evangelism," *Baltimore Afro-American*, May 26, 1934, 11.

28 "'Joint Jumps' as Grace Moves In: His House of Prayer Rocks Like Savoy," *New York Amsterdam News*, June 18, 1938, 16.

29 Carter G. Woodson, "Jazz Demoralizing, Creators Should Be Ashamed—Woodson," *Philadelphia Tribune*, October 12, 1933, 5.

30 For a study of jazz musicians' seemingly effortless improvisational ability as the result of arduous, repetitive study and practice, see Monson, *Freedom Sounds*, 295.

31 James G. Bland, "The People's Forum—Need for Better Music, April 15, 1922," *Half-Century Magazine*, May–June 1922, 21.

32 Thomas Walker Wallace, "Bits of Comment," *Star of Zion*, January 21, 1926, 7.

33 "American Jazz Not African," *Star of Zion*, September 23, 1926, 4. The article noted that Ballanta "was educated as a musician from the Freetown branch of Durham University and has directed his energies toward the study of the music of Africa's black people. But for the intervention of England his ancestors would have been brought to America and he would have been born a slave."

34 "If the Shoe Fits—Wanted—A Jazz Religion," *New York Amsterdam News*, May 9, 1928, 16.

35 "Bishop Walls on Jazz," *Star of Zion*, February 28, 1929, 5. William H. Ferris echoed this sentiment: "This race of ours is out on a wild spree, believing that all that it needs is autos and jazz and that it can live without God." See Ferris, "Negro Should Produce Saints and Scholars," *Star of Zion*, January 17, 1929, 1.

36 Quoted in "Bishop Walls on Jazz," 5.

37 D. J. Gilmer, "Week by Week: 'Swing,'" *Star of Zion*, January 12, 1939, 1, 8.

38 Kelly Miller, "Where Is the Negro Heaven," *Star of Zion*, July 14, 1938, 5.

39 "Our Sensitive Negro Ministry," *Star of Zion*, August 4, 1927, 1, 5.

40 "CBS to Present 'The National Negro Hour,'" *Star of Zion*, January 6, 1938, 1, 5.

41 T. J. Jefferson, "Can the Preacher Be Saved?," *Star of Zion*, October 9, 1930, 8.

CHAPTER 2. "GET HAPPY, ALL YOU SINNERS"

1 Author's transcription. From Cab Calloway and His Orchestra, "Harlem Camp Meeting," in *The Chronological Cab Calloway*, vol. 1.

2 Simmons, "Whooping," 865.

3 See Raboteau, *A Fire in the Bones*, 141–44.

4 For a Freudian analysis of Calloway's ability to help audiences "let go of their cares" during the Great Depression, see Garrett, "Humor of Jazz," 59–60.

5 R. Vincent Ottley, "Radio Personalities," *New York Amsterdam News*, July 27, 1932, 7.

6 See Prentiss, *Staging Faith*, 43.

7 Wesley, "Religious Attitudes of Negro Youth," 387.

8 Calloway biographer Alyn Shipton is unable to confirm Cabell Calloway Jr.'s employment as an attorney, deeming it "family legend" and finding him listed as working in real estate in the US census of Baltimore in 1900. Shipton, *Hi-De-Ho*, 237.

9 Calloway and Rollins, *Of Minnie the Moocher and Me*, 11–12.

10 Calloway and Rollins, *Of Minnie the Moocher and Me*, 13–14.

11 Calloway and Rollins, *Of Minnie the Moocher and Me*, 21–22, 24–25, 32.

12 Calloway and Rollins, *Of Minnie the Moocher and Me*, 14.

13 Charles Belfoure, "Pride Flows Forth from Historic Past," *Baltimore Sun*, August 26, 2001, accessed January 15, 2015, http://articles.baltimoresun.com/2001-08-26/business/0108250547_1_wilson-park-neighborhood-association-mcdaniel.

14 Calloway and Rollins, *Of Minnie the Moocher and Me*, 29.

15 Calloway and Rollins, *Of Minnie the Moocher and Me*, 29–30.

16 Calloway and Rollins, *Of Minnie the Moocher and Me*, 7, 30–31.

17 See Hornsby-Gutting, *Black Manhood and Community Building*, 53–54.

18 Calloway and Rollins, *Of Minnie the Moocher and Me*, 18, 26.

19 "Downingtown Industrial and Agricultural School Collection—Background Note," Charles L. Blockson African American Collection, Temple University Libraries, accessed January 12, 2015, http://library.temple.edu/scrc/downingtown-industrial-and.

20 Summers, *Manliness and Its Discontents*, 8.

21 Calloway and Rollins, *Of Minnie the Moocher and Me*, 27–28.

22 Calloway and Rollins, *Of Minnie the Moocher and Me*, 25.

23 Calloway and Rollins, *Of Minnie the Moocher and Me*, 35, 36, 40.

24 Calloway described the "straight jazz" style of Johnny Jones's Arabian Ten Orchestra, one of the bands in which he performed, as "a Baltimore version of New Orleans dixieland [*sic*] with a heavy two-four rhythm, pounding bass drum, banjo, piano, and jumping, syncopated cornets, and trumpets." Calloway and Rollins, *Of Minnie the Moocher and Me*, 38.

25 Calloway and Rollins, *Of Minnie the Moocher and Me*, 40.

26 Calloway and Rollins, *Of Minnie the Moocher and Me*, 32.

27 Calloway and Rollins, *Of Minnie the Moocher and Me*, 38–40.

28 Calloway and Rollins, *Of Minnie the Moocher and Me*, 31.

29 Calloway and Rollins, *Of Minnie the Moocher and Me*, 12.

30 Calloway and Rollins, *Of Minnie the Moocher and Me*, 15.

31 Calloway and Rollins, *Of Minnie the Moocher and Me*, 31.

32 Calloway and Rollins, *Of Minnie the Moocher and Me*, 46.

33 Calloway and Rollins, *Of Minnie the Moocher and Me*, 46–47.

34 Summers, *Manliness and Its Discontents*, 7, 14, 152, 156.

35 Summers, *Manliness and Its Discontents*, 152.

36 Calloway and Rollins, *Of Minnie the Moocher and Me*, 46–49.

37 Calloway and Rollins, *Of Minnie the Moocher and Me*, 51–54, 57. Crane reopened as Herzl Junior College during the Great Depression, and the school was renamed Malcolm X College in 1969. "Malcolm X College Archives," Black Metropolis Research Consortium Survey, University of Chicago, accessed May 26, 2016, http://bmrcsurvey.uchicago.edu/collections/2373-1.

38 Floyd J. Calvin, "Cab Calloway's Rise to Fame Was Sensational: Youngest Orchestra Leader in Country; Only 23 Years Old," *Pittsburgh Courier*, January 31, 1931, A8.

39 Reed, *Holy Profane,* 77–78.

40 Martin, *Preaching on Wax,* 93.

41 See "Going Backstage with the Scribe," *Chicago Defender,* April 4, 1931, 5; and Floyd G. Snelson Jr., "Duke Continues to Lead in Big *Courier* Contest; Others Gain," *Pittsburgh Courier,* September 26, 1931, 11.

42 Author's transcription. From Cab Calloway and His Orchestra, "Is That Religion?," in *The Chronological Cab Calloway,* vol. 1.

43 Author has discussed Ellington's version of "Is That Religion" more extensively in Booker, "'An Authentic Record of My Race.'"

44 Shipton, *Hi-De-Ho,* 44.

45 Cab Calloway, Fred J. Coots, and Benny Davis, "Miss Hallelujah Brown," Frances G. Spencer Collection of American Popular Sheet Music, Baylor University, accessed May 26, 2016, http://contentdm.baylor.edu/cdm/ref/collection/fa-spnc/id/14665. Coots was famous for helping to compose the song "Santa Claus Is Coming to Town" in 1934.

46 Author's transcription. From Cab Calloway and His Orchestra, "Miss Hallelujah Brown," in *The Chronological Cab Calloway,* vol. 1.

47 *Snow-White,* animated film, directed by Dave Fleischer.

48 Calloway and Rollins, *Of Minnie the Moocher and Me,* 12.

49 See Cohen, *Duke Ellington's America.*

50 "Yeh! Cab Calloway Goes to Church," *Philadelphia Tribune,* November 10, 1932, 11.

51 See Oliver, *Songsters and Saints,* 134–39.

52 See "Calloway Balks Whiteface Role: Hi-Di-Hi-Di-Ho Man and His Band Refuse Stunt for Movie Publicity," *New York Amsterdam News,* February 1, 1936, 13.

53 Knight, *Disintegrating the Musical,* 72.

54 Knight, *Disintegrating the Musical,* 73.

55 Author's transcription. From *The Singing Kid,* film, directed by William Keighley. Printed with permission from Warner Bros. Entertainment Inc.

56 Knight, *Disintegrating the Musical,* 73.

57 Knight, *Disintegrating the Musical,* 77–81.

58 Author's transcription. From Cab Calloway and His Orchestra, "A Strictly Cullud Affair," in *The Chronological Cab Calloway,* vol. 1.

59 Calloway and Rollins, *Of Minnie the Moocher and Me,* 41–42. The author assumes Calloway's actual pronunciation of the pejorative "nigger" to have been the colloquial "nigga" pronunciation that African Americans have used.

60 Calloway and Rollins, *Of Minnie the Moocher and Me,* 44–45.

61 Calloway and Rollins, *Of Minnie the Moocher and Me,* 42. Calloway's "hot walking" at Baltimore's Pimlico Race Course was the practice of leading and grooming horses as exercise or to cool them down following their races. See Shipton, *Hi-De-Ho,* 5.

62 Author's transcription. From Cab Calloway and His Orchestra, "Yaller," in *The Chronological Cab Calloway,* vol. 1.

63 Calloway and Rollins, *Of Minnie the Moocher and Me,* 42.

64 Calloway and Rollins, *Of Minnie the Moocher and Me*, 200; and "Zulme Nuffie Calloway, August 24, 1915—October 13, 2008," obituary, Chandler Funeral Homes and Crematory, accessed May 27, 2016, http://hosting-1611.tributes.com/show/ Zulme-Nuffie-Calloway-84342264.

65 Calloway and Rollins, *Of Minnie the Moocher and Me*, 201.

66 According to her online obituary, Nuffie Calloway "held various board positions and was on many committees such as the Abbott House in Ardsley, New York, the Council for Social Services, Adoption Services of Westchester, the YWCA of White Plains, and she was president of the Marymount Mothers Club in Tarrytown, NY. She was also a member of the Northeasterns, the Links and the Continentials and was a member of the Urban League where she devoted her time to the needs of children." "Zulme Nuffie Calloway," obituary.

67 Calloway and Rollins, *Of Minnie the Moocher and Me*, 202–3.

68 See DeVeaux, *Birth of Bebop*, 243.

69 Cab Calloway, "Cab Thinks There's Too Much Talk of 'The Negro's Place,'" *Philadelphia Tribune*, November 5, 1949, 15.

70 "Pulpit and Pew," *Negro Digest* 4, no. 6 (April 1946): 18.

CHAPTER 3. "TEARS OF JOY"

1 Edward Kennedy Ellington and Billy Strayhorn, "Portrait of Ella Fitzgerald, Third Movement: 'Beyond Category,'" Ella Fitzgerald with Duke Ellington and His Orchestra, *Ella Fitzgerald Sings the Duke Ellington Song Book*.

2 Gourse, *Louis' Children*, 260.

3 Nat Hentoff, "Is Ella a Great Jazz Singer? Hentoff says 'No,'" *Negro Digest* 11, no. 11 (September 1962): 26.

4 Nicholson, *Ella Fitzgerald*, 4–7.

5 Nina Bernstein, "Ward of the State; The Gap in Ella Fitzgerald's Life," *New York Times*, June 23, 1996, accessed January 21, 2016, www.nytimes.com/1996/06/23/ weekinreview/ward-of-the-state-the-gap-in-ella-fitzgerald-s-life.html; Russ Immarigeon, "The 'Ungovernable' Ella Fitzgerald," *The Prison Public Memory Project*, October 29, 2014, accessed January 21, 2016, www.prisonpublicmemory. org/blog/2014/the-ungovernable-ella-fitzgerald; and Nicholson, *Ella Fitzgerald*, 13–16.

6 Nicholson, *Ella Fitzgerald*, 14–23.

7 "Ella Fitzgerald Always Did Want to Be One of Those 'Swing' Vocalists," *Atlanta Daily World*, June 28, 1937, 2.

8 See Al Monroe, "Ella Fitzgerald Rejects Offers to Marry: First Lady of Swing Too Busy Working," *Chicago Defender*, July 15, 1939, 20.

9 Lillian Johnson, "Ella Fitzgerald Hasn't Let Success Spoil Her: Swing Music's Biggest Star Hasn't a Boy Friend; Likes Men Short and Hats Dizzy," *Baltimore Afro-American*, October 9, 1937, 5. For Fitzgerald's appreciation of Webb's paternal guidance, see Lillian Johnson, "Ella Fitzgerald's Hardest Job Was to Get Folks to Listen! And Now She's the Queen of Swing," *Baltimore Afro-American*, October 9, 1937, 10.

10 Johnson, "Ella Fitzgerald Hasn't Let Success Spoil Her," 5.

11 "'Benny Should Be Congratulated for His Courage'—Jimmy Dorsey," *Down Beat*, October 15, 1939, accessed January 21, 2016, www.downbeat.com/default. asp?sect=stories&subsect=story_detail&sid=129.

12 "'My Buddy' Is Sung by Ella at Services," *New York Amsterdam News*, July 1, 1939, 2.

13 "It's Really Ella," *Baltimore Afro-American*, September 27, 1941, 13.

14 "Wanna Sing with a Band? Ella Fitzgerald Opens Clinic to Help Ambitious Girl Chirps," *Baltimore Afro-American*, March 15, 1947, 6.

15 "Former Hoofer: Show Folk to Support Rev. Bailey," *Pittsburgh Courier*, October 8, 1949, 19.

16 *Ride 'Em Cowboy*, film, directed by Arthur Lubin.

17 E. B. Rea, "Uncompromisingly Yours . . . What Price Glory in Filmdom?," *Baltimore Afro-American*, April 4, 1942, 13.

18 For a description of Fitzgerald's initial financial success with Granz as her manager, see Hershorn, *Norman Granz*, 223–24.

19 Hershorn, *Norman Granz*, 212–14.

20 Hershorn, *Norman Granz*, 227.

21 Louie Robinson, "First Lady of Jazz," *Ebony*, November 1961, 131–39.

22 Monson, *Freedom Sounds*, 157.

23 Advertisement for "Scottsboro Defense Ball," *New Masses*, February 25, 1936, 30; and Fritts and Vail, *Ella Fitzgerald*, 8.

24 "Ella Fitzgerald Suggest Union of Charity Agencies," *Norfolk Journal and Guide*, May 17, 1947, A17; and "Theatre Authority to Back Ella Fitzgerald," *Chicago Defender*, June 7, 1947, 19.

25 "Fitzgerald Heads Chi. Mixed Bill," *Philadelphia Tribune*, March 9, 1948, 12.

26 See Nicholson, *Ella Fitzgerald*, 148.

27 See L'Heureux, "Illinois Jacquet," 6.

28 See L'Heureux, "Illinois Jacquet," 7; and Gillespie and Fraser, *To Be . . . or Not . . . to Bop*, 407–8. For Granz's reflections on Fitzgerald's appeal, see Hershorn, *Norman Granz*, 244.

29 Paul J. MacArthur, "One for All," *Houston Press*, November 18, 1999, accessed January 10, 2016, www.houstonpress.com/music/one-for-all-6566230.

30 L'Heureux, "Illinois Jacquet," 7–8. For Granz's work to have the charges dropped, see MacArthur, "One for All."

31 Monson, *Freedom Sounds*, 156–58.

32 Jesse H. Walker, "Theatricals," *New York Amsterdam News*, May 18, 1963, 15.

33 See "Rally for Freedom: Ella Fitzgerald Sparks Crescendo Benefit Tues.," *Los Angeles Sentinel*, June 13, 1963, A14; and "Ella Fitzgerald's Hollywood Benefit Aids SCLC," *Jet*, July 4, 1963, 62.

34 See "Ella Fitzgerald Cited for Civil Rights Efforts," *Atlanta Daily World*, July 7, 1963, 2; and "Ella Fitzgerald Benefit Nets $5,000 For SCLC," *Jet*, July 11, 1963, 62.

35 "ASCAP Presents the Billy Taylor Interviews: Ella Fitzgerald," New York Public Library, sound recording, date unknown.

36 Author's transcription. From Fitzgerald, "It's Up to Me and You."
37 Ella Fitzgerald and the Tee Carson Trio, *Ella Fitzgerald: Live at Chautauqua*, vol. 2. The album lists "He Had a Dream" as the title for "It's Up to Me and You."
38 See "Ella to Donate $$ From Disk to King," *Billboard*, June 15, 1968, 3; and "Ella's Tribute to the Late Dr. King," *New York Amsterdam News*, August 17, 1968, 15.
39 See "AKAs Initiate Ella; She's Feted on 'Ella's Night,'" *Jet*, December 19, 1968, 56.
40 Hentoff, "Is Ella a Great Jazz Singer?," 24, 26.
41 Hentoff, "Is Ella a Great Jazz Singer?," 24–25.
42 Hentoff, "Is Ella a Great Jazz Singer?," 25–26.
43 Kainer, "Vocal Racial Crossover," 175.
44 Kainer, "Vocal Racial Crossover," 181.
45 Kainer, "Vocal Racial Crossover," 208.
46 See Wells, "'Go Harlem!,'" 178, 181–82.
47 Kainer, "Vocal Racial Crossover," 209.
48 Kainer, "Vocal Racial Crossover," 233. On critics' privileging of the instrumental over the vocal, as it relates to Fitzgerald's early years with Chick Webb, see Wells, "'Go Harlem!,'" 208.
49 Wells, "'Go Harlem!,'" 215.
50 Kainer, "Vocal Racial Crossover," 222–24.
51 See Kainer, "Vocal Racial Crossover," 240–41; and Cartwright, "Quotation and Reference in Jazz Performance," 190–95.
52 Kainer, "Vocal Racial Crossover," 242. For an example of one critic's claim that Fitzgerald fails to embody or perform any genuine emotion other than earnest, innocent happiness, see Stephen Holden, "A Voice That Always Brings a Happy Ending," *New York Times*, April 25, 1993, accessed January 13, 2016, www.nytimes.com/1993/04/25/arts/pop-view-a-voice-that-always-brings-a-happy-ending.html?pagewanted=all.
53 Kainer, "Vocal Racial Crossover," 248–49.
54 See Ella Fitzgerald, "I Can't Give You Anything but Love," in Fitzgerald, Holiday, and McRae, *At Newport*.
55 See Kainer, "Vocal Racial Crossover," 247–48.
56 See Nicholson, *Ella Fitzgerald*, 45.
57 See "Rabid Fan Leaps Stage and Socks Ella Fitzgerald," *Atlanta Daily World*, July 17, 1957, 1; "Assailant Climbs on NJ Stage," *Baltimore Afro-American*, July 20, 1957, 1; and "Send Attacker of Ella to Mental Hospital," *New York Amsterdam News*, July 20, 1957, 3.
58 Nicholson, *Ella Fitzgerald*, 67–70.
59 See Ella Fitzgerald, "Stompin' at the Savoy (Live at the Shrine Auditorium)," in *Ella Fitzgerald at the Opera House*.
60 Bivins, *Spirits Rejoice!*, 256, 259.

61 "ASCAP Presents the Billy Taylor Interviews: Ella Fitzgerald."

62 Bobbie Wygant, interview with Ella Fitzgerald, *NBC 5*, date unknown, accessed January 21, 2016, http://bobbiewygant.blogspot.com/2011/08/classic-interview-ella-fitzgerald.html.

63 Not to be confused with African American singer, pianist, and composer Ray Charles (1930–2004), the Ray Charles Singers group was the creation of white American singer and songwriter Ray Charles, born Charles Raymond Offenberg (1918–2015).

64 Ella Fitzgerald with the Ray Charles Singers, "Crying in the Chapel."

65 Ella Fitzgerald with the Ray Charles Singers, "When the Hands of the Clock Pray at Midnight."

66 Nicholson, *Ella Fitzgerald*, 127, 141.

67 Jack Smith, "Ella's Not Content and Doesn't Believe She's 'The Greatest,'" *Washington Post, Times Herald*, December 27, 1966, B10.

68 Fitzgerald, *Brighten the Corner*.

69 Ella Fitzgerald, "Hallelujah I Love Him So," in *Rhythm Is My Business*.

70 These and other Fitzgerald recordings included multiple compositions by Duke Ellington and Billy Strayhorn, in addition to Maceo Pinkard's "Sweet Georgia Brown," Dizzy Gillespie's "Night in Tunisia," Gillespie and Luciano "Chano" Pozo González's "Manteca," Thomas Wright "Fats" Waller's "Ain't Misbehavin'" and "Honeysuckle Rose," and Mary Lou Williams's "What's Your Story, Morning Glory?"

71 Ella Fitzgerald with the Fraser McPherson Big Band and the Tee Carson Trio, "I Can't Stop Loving You," in *Live from The Cave Supper Club*.

72 Ella Fitzgerald with the Tommy Flanagan Trio, "'Tain't Nobody's Bizness if I Do," in *Ella Fitzgerald at the Montreux Jazz Festival 1975*.

CHAPTER 4. "ROYAL ANCESTRY"

1 Ellington, *Music Is My Mistress*, 12–15.

2 For a study of Egyptocentrism in Afrocentric thought, see Moses, *Afrotopia*, 6, 23–24.

3 Tucker, "Renaissance Education of Duke Ellington," 117–18.

4 Gray, "Introduction [1]," xxviii–xxix.

5 Ellington, *Music Is My Mistress*, 17.

6 George, *Sweet Man*, 187–88.

7 See Evans, *Burden of Black Religion*, 111–13.

8 Hucks, *Yoruba Traditions*, 17.

9 Prentiss, *Staging Faith*, 147.

10 Hucks, *Yoruba Traditions*, 17.

11 Duke Ellington, "Black, Brown and Beige" script, undated, Ruth Ellington Collection, Series 6: Lyrics, Scripts and Notes, 1939–1986, Box 7, Folder 5.

12 Tucker, "Renaissance Education of Duke Ellington," 112.

13 Cohen, *Duke Ellington's America*, 338–39, 449; Ellington, *Music Is My Mistress*, 113; Hudson, "Duke Ellington's Literary Sources," 23.

14 See Maffly-Kipp, *Setting Down the Sacred Past*, 35–36, 223–24.
15 Franceschina, *Duke Ellington's Music for the Theatre*, 167; Peress, "My Life with 'Black, Brown, and Beige,'" 153.
16 Webb, *Black Man*, 3–4.
17 See Hill, *Marcus Garvey and Universal Negro Improvement Association Papers*, vol. 3, 419 fn. 1.
18 Weisenfeld, *New World A-Coming*, 17.
19 Webb, *Black Man*, 5.
20 Webb, *Black Man*, 33.
21 Webb, *Black Man*, 5–6.
22 Webb, *Black Man*, 7.
23 Webb, *Black Man*, 10–11.
24 Webb, *Black Man*, 8.
25 Webb, *Black Man*, 10–11.
26 Webb, *Black Man*, 35.
27 Webb, *Black Man*, 12–13.
28 Webb, *Black Man*, 35–36.
29 Webb, *Black Man*, 37.
30 Webb, *Black Man*, 38.
31 Cashmore, "'Get Up, Stand Up,'" 424; Chang and Chen, *Reggae Routes*, 242; and Sundquist, *Strangers in the Land*, 124.
32 See James Morris Webb, "Moses Was Rescued by a Negro Woman," in *Goodbye, Babylon—Sermons*.
33 Harris, "St. Paul AME Church," 792.
34 Richardson, *Plays and Pageants*, xlv-xlvi; and Mills, *Church as the Surrogate Family*, 5–7.
35 Richardson, *Plays and Pageants*, 350–51.
36 Richardson, *Plays and Pageants*, 356.
37 Richardson, *Plays and Pageants*, 358.
38 Richardson, *Plays and Pageants*, 345.
39 Parker, *Children of the Sun*, 8–9.
40 Parker, *Children of the Sun*, 20.
41 Prentiss, *Staging Faith*, 112, 149–51.
42 George Wells Parker, "Questions and Answers in Negro History," *Star of Zion*, August 20, 1925, 5.
43 George Wells Parker, "Questions and Answers in Negro History," *Star of Zion*, April 2, 1925, 5.
44 George Wells Parker, "Questions and Answers in Negro History," *Star of Zion*, September 24, 1925, 5.
45 George Wells Parker, "Questions and Answers in Negro History," *Star of Zion*, June 4, 1925, 5.
46 George Wells Parker, "Questions and Answers in Negro History," *Star of Zion*, October 15, 1925, 5.

47 George Wells Parker, "Questions and Answers in Negro History," *Star of Zion*, October 22, 1925, 5.

48 Parker, "Questions and Answers in Negro History," October 22, 1925, 5.

49 "'Because He Lives': A Drama of the Resurrection," *National Baptist Voice*, March 22, 1924, 10.

50 Weisenfeld, "'Truths That Liberate the Soul,'" 238–39.

51 Hucks, *Yoruba Traditions*, 44.

52 R. Alexander Carroll, "Letter to the Editor, 'Jesus Was Not White,'" *Star of Zion*, February 20, 1930, 5.

53 Ellington, "Black, Brown and Beige" script.

54 Blyden, *Christianity, Islam and the Negro Race*, 135.

55 Blyden, *Christianity, Islam and the Negro Race*, 133–34.

56 Drusilla Dunjee Houston, "Does Leadership Understand the Real Nature of the Negro," *Africo-American Presbyterian*, July 30, 1930, 1.

57 Houston, "Does Leadership Understand," 3.

58 "Monotheism of Egyptian Origin," *Star of Zion*, March 1, 1934, 4.

59 Huggins and Jackson, *Introduction to African Civilizations*, 91–92, 206. Jackson republished this book in 1969 with Negro Universities Press.

60 Huggins and Jackson, *Introduction to African Civilizations*, 56–57.

61 Huggins and Jackson, *Introduction to African Civilizations*, 59–60.

62 Hucks, *Yoruba Traditions*, 45.

63 Ellington, "Black, Brown and Beige" script.

64 Ellington, "Black, Brown and Beige" script.

65 Leonard Feather and Maurice Peress, liner notes, Louie Bellson and His All-Star Orchestra, *Duke Ellington: Black, Brown and Beige*. Harvey Cohen provides Ellington's manuscript sketch of this poetic section: "Came Sunday. With all the whites inside / The church, their less fortunate brothers / Emerged from everywhere to congregate / Beneath a tree. Huddled there, they passed / The Word of God around in whispers . . . / When the whites inside lifted voices / In joyous song . . . / The blacks outside would hum along, / Adding their own touches . . . weaving melodic, / Harmonic, rhythmic patterns. / Thus the spiritual was born. / Highly emotional worshipping of God / In SONG." Cohen, *Duke Ellington's America*, 217.

66 Ellington, "Black, Brown and Beige" script.

67 Author's transcription. From Duke Ellington and His Orchestra, "Part IV (a.k.a. Come Sunday)," *Duke Ellington, Black, Brown and Beige—Featuring Mahalia Jackson*. "Come Sunday" lyrics © 1963 Sony/ATV Music Publishing LLC in the USA, copyright renewed. This arrangement © 2019 Sony/ATV Music Publishing LLC in the USA. All Rights on behalf of Sony/ATV Music Publishing LLC administered by Sony/ATV Music Publishing LLC, 424 Church Street, Suite 1200, Nashville, TN 37219. Rights for the world outside the USA controlled by Tempo Music, Inc. c/o Music Sales Corporation. International copyright secured. All rights reserved. Reprinted by permission of Hal Leonard LLC.

68 See Matthew 6:25–34, and Luke 12:22–34.

69 Anderson, *Deep River*, 225.

70 Edward Kennedy Ellington, "Ko-Ko," in *The Duke Ellington Carnegie Hall Concerts: January 1943*.

71 Edward Kennedy Ellington and Billy Strayhorn, "Congo Square," in *A Drum Is a Woman*. "Congo Square" lyrics © 1957 Sony/ATV Music Publishing LLC and Tempo Music, Inc., copyright renewed. This arrangement © 1957 Sony/ATV Music Publishing LLC and Tempo Music, Inc. All Rights on behalf of Sony/ATV Music Publishing LLC administered by Sony/ATV Music Publishing LLC, 424 Church Street, Suite 1200, Nashville, TN 37219. International copyright secured. All rights reserved. Reprinted by permission of Hal Leonard LLC.

72 For a discussion of Ellington's more erotic lyrics for Madam Zajj's Congo Square scene in his manuscript drafts, see Wriggle, "'The Mother of All Albums,'" 285–86.

73 Although "Dance No. 3" from *The Liberian Suite* features William "Cat" Anderson's high-pitched trumpet solo, the composition's style is mainly reminiscent of the tango, a South American dance of African and European origins.

74 Duke Ellington and His Orchestra, "The Liberian Suite: I Like the Sunrise," in *Ellington Uptown*.

CHAPTER 5. GOD'S MESSENGER BOY

1 Cohen, *Duke Ellington's America*, 477.

2 "Temple Emanuel Newsletter, December 1966," Ruth Ellington Collection, Series 5: Performances and Programs, 1963–1989, Box 5, Folder 4 (Duke Ellington's Festival of Religion and the Arts, 1966).

3 Duke Ellington and His Orchestra, and the Fountain Street Choir, *Duke Ellington at Fountain Street, April 17, 1966*.

4 See "'New Religion' Clergymen Call for Action," *Miami News*, February 1, 1968; Elizabeth Coffey, "On Church 'Revolution' Religious Leaders Pessimistic," *Hartford Courant*, February 1, 1968; "Jazz Artists' Message Older Than Gothic," *Milwaukee Sentinel*, February 3, 1968; and "The New Religion," *Times Union*, February 24, 1968.

5 "A Statement from Duke Ellington," Ruth Ellington Collection, Series 5, Box 5, Folder 4.

6 Ellington, "Civilization," in *Music Is My Mistress*, 259.

7 *North Avenue Presbyterian Church Presents a Festival of Religion and the Arts, May 25–June 9*, p. 19, Ruth Ellington Collection, Series 5, Box 5, Folder 4.

8 "Jazz Goes to Fifth Avenue Church," *Christianity Today* 10, no. 8 (January 21, 1966): 43.

9 Bryant M. Kirkland, letter, November 19, 1965, Ruth Ellington Collection, Series 5, Box 5, Folder 2 (Duke Ellington's Concerts of Sacred Music material, 1965–1968).

10 "'New Spirit' Moves Lutheran Synod to Self Examination on Race Issues," *Milwaukee Sentinel*, May 11, 1968.

11 *North Avenue Presbyterian Church Presents*, p. 19.

12 Untitled draft, p. 2, carbon copy, Ruth Ellington Collection, Series 6, Box 7, Folder 9 (Miscellaneous Notes, 1974).
13 Ellington listed Bishop Horace W. B. Donegan, Canon Edward West, Rev. Harold Weicker, Rev. Jack Yaryan, Dean C. Julian Bartlett, Pastor John Gensel, Fr. Norman O'Connor, Dr. Sandford Shapiro, Rev. Henry Jesse Jr., Fr. Egan of Ireland, Frank A. Salisbury of the Christian Scientist Church in Tucson, Rev. Nicholas Freund, Rev. E. Franklin Jackson, Rev. Jerry Moore, actor and choreographer Geoffrey Holder, and Rev. Canon John S. Yaryan as ministers who had encouraged him in particular. See "A Statement from Duke Ellington," Ruth Ellington Collection, Series 5, Box 5, Folder 4.
14 "Sheraton-Ritz, Minneapolis, MN—Coventry Cathedral (All Have Sinned & Come Short of the Glory of God)," Duke Ellington Collection, Archives Center, National Museum of American History, Series 5: Personal Correspondence and Notes, 1941–1974, Box 6, Folder 1 (Notes, undated).
15 Miller, *Christian Encounters*, back cover.
16 See Miller, *Christian Encounters*, 9–10.
17 Miller, *Christian Encounters*, 73–75.
18 Among Ellington's major "tone poems," Miller cites *A Tone Parallel to Harlem, Liberian Suite, Black and Tan Fantasy*, and *Black, Brown, and Beige*. Miller, *Christian Encounters*, 77–78.
19 Miller, *Christian Encounters*, 79–80.
20 Miller, *Christian Encounters*, 100.
21 See Miller, *Christian Encounters*, 106–7.
22 "No Duke Soul in Colored Churches," Associated Negro Press, February 7, 1966.
23 See Cohen, *Duke Ellington's America*, 477–79; and Kenneth Dole, "Pastor Explains Opposition to Jazz Music in Liturgy," *Washington Post, Times Herald*, January 7, 1967, E17.
24 For some reflections on Ellington's sexual practices by himself and others, see Nicholson, *Reminiscing in Tempo*, 366–71.
25 The concert is listed as "Duke Ellington: Piano and Intermittent Talk" for ORTF Studios in Paris, France, on July 2, 1970, in Timner, *Ellingtonia*, 431.
26 See David Hajdu, "A Jazz of Their Own," *Vanity Fair*, May 1999, 196.
27 See James Gavin, "Homophobia in Jazz," *JazzTimes*, December 2001, accessed October 28, 2014, http://jazztimes.com/articles/20073-homophobia-in-jazz.
28 Mathews, *Doctrine and Race*, 109–10.
29 Simeon Booker, "Duke's Hometown Minister," *Jet*, December 22, 1966, 46.
30 "Bangor House Motor Hotel, Bangor, ME," Duke Ellington Collection, Series 14: Religious Material, 1928–1974, Box 2, Folder 1.
31 "First AME Zion Church, Brooklyn, NY Presents Duke Ellington in a Concert of Sacred Music, March 10, 1966," Ruth Ellington Collection, Series 5, Box 5, Folder 2.
32 Gilbert Caldwell to Duke Ellington, telegram, March 18, 1966, Ruth Ellington Collection, Series 5, Box 5, Folder 2.

33 "Union Methodist Presents a Concert of Sacred Music by Duke Ellington, Friday evening, July 22, 1966, Boston, Massachusetts," Ruth Ellington Collection, Series 5, Box 5, Folder 2. As of 2017, Gilbert Caldwell is a retired United Methodist minister who has been active in African American and LGBT civil rights, having participated in the Massachusetts unit of Martin Luther King Jr.'s Southern Christian Leadership Conference, and having cofounded the Black Methodists for Church Renewal and United Methodists of Color for an Inclusive Church. See http://um-insight.net/blogs/gilbert-h-caldwell and www.rmnblog.org/gilbert_caldwell/.

34 Alma C. Hawkins to Duke Ellington, December 20, 1966, Ruth Ellington Collection, Series 5, Box 5, Folder 2. The Interdenominational Church Ushers Association of Washington, DC, was also a member of another African American religious organization, the National United Church Ushers Association of America, founded in 1919.

35 "Sacred Ellington," *Norfolk Journal and Guide*, February 10, 1968.

36 "Centennial Emphasis as Duke Ellington Is Honored—Tougaloo Recognition in Carnegie Hall Program," *Christian* (St. Louis, MO), May 19, 1968.

37 "Sacred Concert Slated June 30 at Boyle Stadium," *Stamford Advocate*, May 31, 1968.

38 "The Cathedral of St. John the Divine—by Invitation of the Bishop of New York, Duke Ellington and His Orchestra Present a Sacred Concert, Friday, January 19, 1968," Ruth Ellington Collection, Series 5, Box 5, Folder 2.

39 Eve Lynn, "Duke Ellington in Concert at Enon Bapt. Church," *Philadelphia Tribune*, February 6, 1968.

40 "Duke Ellington in First Bronx Concert," *New York Amsterdam News*, February 17, 1968; and Rudy Johnson, "A Religious Happening—Duke Ellington's Sacred Concert," *Newark Evening News*, February 19, 1968, 8.

41 "Ellington Approaches Sacred Ideals," *Chicago Daily Defender*, November 7, 1968.

42 Ellington, *Music Is My Mistress*, 281–82.

43 W. Fontaine Jones, "Fifth Avenue Presbyterian Church—Diagrammatic and Longitudinal Sections," Ruth Ellington Collection, Series 5, Box 5, Folder 2.

44 Don DeMicheal, "Duke Scores with Sacred Music in Grace Cathedral," *Down Beat*, November 4, 1965, 13, 34.

CHAPTER 6. "IS GOD A THREE-LETTER WORD FOR LOVE?"

1 "The Detroit Hilton, Detroit, MI," Duke Ellington Collection, Series 5, Box 6, Folder 1.

2 Long, "Passage and Prayer," 279–82.

3 Ellington, *Music Is My Mistress*, 260.

4 "First AME Zion Church, Brooklyn, NY Presents Duke Ellington in a Concert of Sacred Music, March 10, 1966," Ruth Ellington Collection, Series 5, Box 5, Folder 2.

5 See untitled draft, p. 2, carbon copy, Ruth Ellington Collection, Series 6, Box 7, Folder 9.

6 Edward Kennedy Ellington, "In the Beginning God," in *Duke Ellington's Concert of Sacred Music.* "In the Beginning God" lyrics © 1966 Sony/ATV Music Publishing LLC in the USA, copyright renewed. This arrangement © 2019 Sony/ATV Music Publishing LLC in the USA. All Rights on behalf of Sony/ATV Music Publishing LLC administered by Sony/ATV Music Publishing LLC, 424 Church Street, Suite 1200, Nashville, TN 37219. Rights for the world outside the USA controlled by Tempo Music, Inc. c/o Music Sales Corporation. International copyright secured. All rights reserved. Reprinted by permission of Hal Leonard LLC.

7 "In the beginning, God," *Star of Zion*, August 13, 1925, 4.

8 See Steed, *Duke Ellington*, 145.

9 Wimbush, *White Men's Magic*, 17–19.

10 Perry, *Bible Culture and Authority*, 6.

11 Rough copy, p. 2, Ruth Ellington Collection, Series 5, Box 5, Folder 4.

12 "The Baltimore Hilton, Baltimore, MD," Duke Ellington Collection, Series 5, Box 6, Folder 1.

13 "A Statement from Duke Ellington," Ruth Ellington Collection, Series 5, Box 5, Folder 4.

14 Duke Ellington Collection, Series 14, Box 1: Religious Literature. Biographical information on Ida Joseph Atwood is from "Directory of Ministers: Licentiates—Mediums—Healers, N.S.A.C.," in *The Summit of Spiritual Understanding* 55, no. 583 (February 1973): 18.

15 "Obituary—Raymond Walter Johnson," *Seattle Times*, October 17–21, 2010, accessed October 10, 2014, www.legacy.com/obituaries/seattletimes/obituary.aspx?pid=146007696; and "The End Time, Antichrists, Bible Prophecies—Last Days Bible Introduction," accessed October 10, 2014, www.lastdaysbible.org/Introduction.html.

16 *Destined for Greatness*, 12–14, in Duke Ellington Collection, Series 14, Box 2, Folder 2.

17 *Destined for Greatness*, 22.

18 "Jacksonville Hilton, Jacksonville, FL," Duke Ellington Collection, Series 5, Box 6, Folder 1. In quotations of handwritten material, I am using parentheses preceded by a caret (^) for words that the writer inserted above the line.

19 "Downtowner/Rowntowner Motor Inns, location unknown," Duke Ellington Collection, Series 5, Box 6, Folder 1.

20 "Hotel Washington, Washington, DC," Duke Ellington Collection, Series 5, Box 6, Folder 1.

21 Edward Kennedy Ellington, "Poetic Commentary A," in *Orchestral Works*, Duke Ellington with Erich Kunzel and the Cincinnati Symphony Orchestra.

22 Best, *Langston's Salvation*, 11.

23 Best, *Langston's Salvation*, 238.

24 "Ramada Inn Roadside Hotel, San Antonio, TX," Duke Ellington Collection, Series 5, Box 6, Folder 1.

25 "Ramada Inn Roadside Hotel, Greensboro, NC," and "The Baltimore Hilton, Baltimore, MD," Duke Ellington Collection, Series 5, Box 6, Folder 1.

26 "Ilikai Wakiki, Honolulu, HI," Duke Ellington Collection, Series 5, Box 6, Folder 1.

27 Cohen, *Duke Ellington's America*, 395.

28 Cohen, *Duke Ellington's America*, 393.

29 Edward Kennedy Ellington, *Duke Ellington's My People*.

30 See "*My People* by Duke Ellington: Ain't but the One (p. 5)," Duke Ellington Collection, Series 5, Box 8, Folder 12 (Handwritten Notes, etc., Queenie Pie).

31 Edward Kennedy Ellington, "Supreme Being," in *Second Sacred Concert*. "Supreme Being" lyrics © 1968 Sony/ATV Music Publishing LLC in the USA, copyright renewed. This arrangement © 2019 Sony/ATV Music Publishing LLC in the USA. All rights on behalf of Sony/ATV Music Publishing LLC administered by Sony/ATV Music Publishing LLC, 424 Church Street, Suite 1200, Nashville, TN 37219. Rights for the world outside the USA controlled by Tempo Music, Inc. c/o Music Sales Corporation. International copyright secured. All rights reserved. Reprinted by permission of Hal Leonard LLC.

32 Cohen, *Duke Ellington's America*, 448.

33 See Hill, "Sacred Concerts," 76. In some Sacred Concert dates, Jon Hendricks (1921–2017) is the vocalist for "Ain't but the One."

34 This appears to also be the case on the *Duke Ellington at Fountain Street, April 17, 1966* recording.

35 "The Shamrock Hilton, Houston, TX," Duke Ellington Collection, Series 5, Box 6, Folder 1.

36 "Jazz Goes to Fifth Avenue Church," *Christianity Today* 10, no. 8 (January 21, 1966): 42.

37 Russ Wilson, "Jazz and a Cathedral: Ellington to Compose Holy Music," *Oakland Tribune*, August 27, 1965.

38 "The Detroit Hilton, Detroit, MI," Duke Ellington Collection, Series 5, Box 6, Folder 1.

39 "Holiday Inn of Fort Wayne, Fort Wayne, IN," Duke Ellington Collection, Series 5, Box 6, Folder 1.

40 Rough copy, p. 1, Ruth Ellington Collection, Series 5, Box 5, Folder 4.

41 Rough copy, p. 2, Ruth Ellington Collection, Series 5, Box 5, Folder 4.

42 Ellington, "Something 'bout Believing," in *Second Sacred Concert*. "Something 'bout Believing" lyrics © 1968 Sony/ATV Music Publishing LLC in the USA, copyright renewed. This arrangement © 2019 Sony/ATV Music Publishing LLC in the USA. All Rights on behalf of Sony/ATV Music Publishing LLC administered by Sony/ATV Music Publishing LLC, 424 Church Street, Suite 1200, Nashville, TN 37219. Rights for the world outside the USA controlled by Tempo Music, Inc. c/o Music Sales Corporation. International copyright secured. All rights reserved. Reprinted by permission of Hal Leonard LLC. The song's vocalists included the AME Mother Zion Church Choir, Central Connecticut State

College Singers, Choir of St. Hilda's School, Choir of St. Hugh's School, and the Frank Parker Singers.

43 "Something 'bout Believing" Christmas card, Ruth Ellington Collection, Series 3: Personal Papers and Correspondence, 1958–1991, Box 2, Folder 2 (Copies of Christmas cards; various guest lists; n.d., and Christmas card list, 1968).

44 Edward Kennedy Ellington, "Ain't Nobody Nowhere Nothin' without God," in *Duke Ellington's Third Sacred Concert.* "Ain't Nobody Nowhere Nothin' without God" lyrics © 1974 Sony/ATV Music Publishing LLC in the USA, copyright renewed. This arrangement © 2019 Sony/ATV Music Publishing LLC in the USA. All rights on behalf of Sony/ATV Music Publishing LLC administered by Sony/ATV Music Publishing LLC, 424 Church Street, Suite 1200, Nashville, TN 37219. Rights for the world outside the USA controlled by Tempo Music, Inc. c/o Music Sales Corporation. International copyright secured. All rights reserved. Reprinted by permission of Hal Leonard LLC.

45 Duke Ellington Collection, Series 14, Box 2, Folder 1.

46 Ruth Ellington Collection, Series 6, Box 7, Folder 6.

47 Ellington, "Heaven," in *Second Sacred Concert.* "Heaven" lyrics © 1968 Sony/ATV Music Publishing LLC in the USA, copyright renewed. This arrangement © 2019 Sony/ATV Music Publishing LLC in the USA. All rights on behalf of Sony/ATV Music Publishing LLC administered by Sony/ATV Music Publishing LLC, 424 Church Street, Suite 1200, Nashville, TN 37219. Rights for the world outside the USA controlled by Tempo Music, Inc. c/o Music Sales Corporation. International copyright secured. All rights reserved. Reprinted by permission of Hal Leonard LLC.

48 Ellington, "Almighty God," in *Second Sacred Concert.* "Almighty God" lyrics © 1968 Sony/ATV Music Publishing LLC in the USA, copyright renewed. This arrangement © 2019 Sony/ATV Music Publishing LLC in the USA. All rights on behalf of Sony/ATV Music Publishing LLC administered by Sony/ATV Music Publishing LLC, 424 Church Street, Suite 1200, Nashville, TN 37219. Rights for the world outside the USA controlled by Tempo Music, Inc. c/o Music Sales Corporation. International copyright secured. All rights reserved. Reprinted by permission of Hal Leonard LLC.

49 The concert is listed as "Praise God and Dance" for Sverige Radio at the Gustav Vasa Kyrkan in Stockholm, Sweden, on November 6, 1969, date of telecast unknown, in Timner, *Ellingtonia,* 408.

50 Duke Ellington Collection, Series 5, Box 5, Folder 1.

51 "Seasons Greetings," Christmas card (inside), Ruth Ellington Collection, Series 3, Box 2, Folder 2.

52 See "The Edgewater, Madison, WI," Duke Ellington Collection, Series 5, Box 6, Folder 1.

53 McElroy, *Quiet Thoughts,* 28, 31, Duke Ellington Collection, Series 14, Box 1.

54 Addison, *Living Sacrifice,* 23–26, in Duke Ellington Collection, Series 14, Box 2, Folder 4.

55 Addison, *Living Sacrifice*, 12–13.
56 Addison, *Living Sacrifice*, 30.
57 Addison, *Living Sacrifice*, 30–32.
58 *Forward Day by Day: A Manual of Daily Bible Readings (Whitsun and Trinity 1969)* (Cincinnati, OH: Forward Movement, 1969), 18, in Duke Ellington Collection, Series 14, Box 2, Folder 3.
59 *Forward Day by Day*, 19.
60 *Forward Day by Day*, 62.
61 *Forward Day by Day*, 72.
62 "Duke Ellington, Roscoe Gill, Jr., and The Duke Ellington Orchestra Present Sacred Concert Number Three at St. Augustine Presbyterian Church, December 23, 1973," Ruth Ellington Collection, Series 5, Box 5, Folder 2. "Is God a Three-Letter Word for Love?" lyrics © 1974 Sony/ATV Music Publishing LLC in the USA, copyright renewed. This arrangement © 2019 Sony/ATV Music Publishing LLC in the USA. All rights on behalf of Sony/ATV Music Publishing LLC administered by Sony/ATV Music Publishing LLC, 424 Church Street, Suite 1200, Nashville, TN 37219. Rights for the world outside the USA controlled by Tempo Music, Inc. c/o Music Sales Corporation. International copyright secured. All rights reserved. Reprinted by permission of Hal Leonard LLC.
63 "Beverly Wilshire Hotel, Beverly Hills, CA," and "The Ambassador Hotels, location unknown," Duke Ellington Collection, Series 5, Box 6, Folder 1.
64 Gerald Pocock to Duke Ellington, November 28, 1973. A birthday card to Ellington from Pocock read "Happy Fête, Bonne Birthday, with GOD/LOVE today *and* always, Your Pray-Er," Gerry." Duke Ellington Collection, Series 5, Box 5, Folder 1.
65 Ellington, "The Majesty of God," in *Duke Ellington's Third Sacred Concert*. "The Majesty of God" lyrics © 1974 Sony/ATV Music Publishing LLC in the USA, copyright renewed. This arrangement © 2019 Sony/ATV Music Publishing LLC in the USA. All rights on behalf of Sony/ATV Music Publishing LLC administered by Sony/ATV Music Publishing LLC, 424 Church Street, Suite 1200, Nashville, TN 37219. Rights for the world outside the USA controlled by Tempo Music, Inc. c/o Music Sales Corporation. International copyright secured. All rights reserved. Reprinted by permission of Hal Leonard LLC.

CHAPTER 7. JAZZ COMMUNION

1 Mary Lou Williams, "What I Learned from God about Jazz," *Sepia*, April 1958, 57.
2 Smithsonian Institution Interviews with Jazz Musicians: Williams, Mary Lou, Institute of Jazz Studies, Rutgers University, Jazz Oral History Project 117.5.5, Transcript, 144.
3 See Whitney Balliett, "Profiles: Out Here Again," *New Yorker*, May 2, 1964, 67.
4 Kernodle, *Soul on Soul*, 167–77.
5 Williams, "What I Learned from God about Jazz," 60.
6 Jazz Oral History Project, 146.

7 Laurence Jackson to Mary Lou Williams, May 6, 1952, p. 2, and Laurence Jackson to Mary Lou Williams, April 21, 1952, p. 1, Mary Lou Williams Collection, Institute of Jazz Studies, Series 3: Personal Correspondence, Subseries 3C: Correspondence with Musicians, Notables & Students, ca. 1926, 1942, 1947–1949, 1951–1953, 1955–1959, 1961–1981, Box 14, Folder 27 (Jackson, Laurence "Baby," Harts Island, New York, 1950–1964, 1972, undated).

8 Jazz Oral History Project, 146.

9 Kernodle, *Soul on Soul*, 169.

10 Gérard Pochonet to Mary Lou Williams, November 23, 1955, p. 2, Mary Lou Williams Collection, Series 3, Subseries 3C, Box 15, Folder 13 (Gérard "David" Pochonet, France, 1955).

11 "God's Music," pp. 1–2, Mary Lou Williams Collection, Series 5: Personal Papers, Box 1, Folder 11 (Spiral-bound "Stenobloc Helical" notebook, undated).

12 See Jazz Oral History Project, 157–58.

13 Kernodle, *Soul on Soul*, 186–87.

14 Mary Lou Williams to Barry Ulanov, February 17, 1957, Mary Lou Williams Collection, Series 3, Subseries 3C, Box 16, Folder 8 (Correspondence to Barry Ulanov from Mary Lou Williams, 1957).

15 Dahl, *Morning Glory*, 256, 259.

16 Sorett, *Spirit in the Dark*, 85–86.

17 Cressler, *Authentically Black and Truly Catholic*, 2.

18 Cressler, *Authentically Black and Truly Catholic*, 61.

19 Jazz Oral History Project, 146.

20 "Release," Mary Lou Williams Collection, Series 4: Business Papers, Subseries 4L: Bel Canto, ca. 1950–1971, 1977, undated, Box 47, Folder 6 (Benefit Activities [Concert, Rummage Sale, etc.]).

21 Untitled fundraising letter, Mary Lou Williams Collection, Series 4, Subseries 4L, Box 47, Folder 6.

22 Untitled fundraising letter.

23 Untitled fundraising letter.

24 "For Immediate Release," Mary Lou Williams Collection, Series 4, Subseries 4L, Box 47, Folder 6.

25 "Bel Canto Foundation," Mary Lou Williams Collection, Series 4, Subseries 4L, Box 47, Folder 6.

26 Jesse H. Walker, "Theatricals," *New York Amsterdam News*, September 20, 1958, 15.

27 Walker, "Theatricals."

28 Walker, "Theatricals."

29 Untitled fundraising letter.

30 "Why Creative Has Disappeared," p. 1, Mary Lou Williams Collection, Series 5, Box 7, Folder "Why Creative Has Disappeared" + Misc. Writings. The clause in parentheses represents an addition to the document.

31 Williams to Ulanov, February 17, 1957, p. 1.

32 Jazz Oral History Project, 123–25.
33 "All Musicians Are in Need of God," p. 2, Mary Lou Williams Collection, Series 5, Box 2, Folder 20.
34 "Why Creative Has Disappeared," p. 6.
35 Jazz Oral History Project, 142.
36 Mary Lou Williams, "Whatever Happened to Mary Lou Williams?," *New York Amsterdam News*, November 27, 1965, 31.
37 "Why Creative Has Disappeared," pp. 1, 3.
38 Williams, "Whatever Happened to Mary Lou Williams?," 31.
39 Williams, "Whatever Happened to Mary Lou Williams?," 31.
40 "Why Creative Has Disappeared," p. 6.
41 "Why Creative Has Disappeared," p. 7.
42 Griffin, *Harlem Nocturne*, 139–40.
43 Mary Lou Williams to Herbert J. Bliss, October 5, 1958, pp. 1–2, Mary Lou Williams Collection, Series 4, Subseries 4I: Legal Affairs, 1941–1980, undated, Box 41, Folder 2 (Bliss, Herbert J., 1958).
44 Koehler, *Sanctity's Mother Tongue*, 7.
45 Williams to Bliss, October 5, 1958, p. 2.
46 See Monson, *Freedom Sounds*.
47 Holmes and Thomson, *Jazz Greats*, 40.
48 Holmes and Thomson, *Jazz Greats*, 41.

CHAPTER 8. ACCOUNTING FOR THE VULNERABLE
1 Dahl, *Morning Glory*, 245; and Kernodle, *Soul on Soul*, 177.
2 Jazz Oral History Project, 156.
3 See Balliett, "Profiles: Out Here Again," 78–80.
4 Jazz Oral History Project, 160.
5 Dahl, *Morning Glory*, 294.
6 Dahl, *Morning Glory*, 265.
7 Dahl, *Morning Glory*, 255.
8 See Mary Lou Williams Collection, Series 3, Subseries 3D: Correspondence with Religious, Box 20, Folder 14 (Sister Martha Morris: Correspondence, 1967).
9 Kernodle, *Soul on Soul*, 190.
10 Herbert J. Bliss to J. F. Worley, November 7, 1960, pp. 1–2, Mary Lou Williams Collection, Series 4, Subseries 4I, Box 41, Folder 3 (Bliss, Herbert J, 1959–1961).
11 Certificate of Incorporation of Bel Canto Foundation, Inc., Pursuant to the Membership Corporation Law, p. 1, Mary Lou Williams Collection, Series 4, Subseries 4L, Box 67, Folder "Bel Canto, Certificate of Incorporation, New York, New York, 1958."
12 "Bel Canto Account—Disbursement and Receipts," Mary Lou Williams Collection, Series 4, Subseries 4L, Box 47, Folder 6.
13 Dave Brubeck to Mary Lou Williams, September 23, 1958, Mary Lou Williams Collection, Series 4, Subseries 4L, Box 47, Folder 6.

14 "Bell Telephone Company—Deposits," Mary Lou Williams Collection, Series 4, Subseries 4L, Box 47, Folder 6.

15 For an account of the ensuing rift between Williams and her heiress friends, see Dahl, *Morning Glory*, 266.

16 Herbert J. Bliss to Mr. Henry Zaccardi, American Federation of Musicians, September 10, 1958, and Henry Zaccardi to Herbert J. Bliss, September 16, 1958, Mary Lou Williams Collection, Series 4, Subseries 4I, Box 41, Folder 2.

17 "Bell Telephone Company—'Loot to Boot' Paid Out," Mary Lou Williams Collection, Series 4, Subseries 4L, Box 47, Folder 6. Williams wrote checks for advertisements in the *New York Times* and the *New York Amsterdam News*, and for poster and banner advertisements. The Carnegie Hall booking cost $1,740.38, while other miscellaneous costs like parking tickets, supplies, and car rental added to her total. Additionally, Williams's bank statement lists the total cost as $3,210.42, $1 less than the accurate total.

18 George A. Hoffman, American Society of Composers, Authors, and Publishers, to Mary Lou Williams, September 12, 1958, Mary Lou Williams Collection, Series 4, Subseries 4L, Box 47, Folder 6.

19 Sammy Davis Jr. to Mary Lou Williams, April 28, 1958, Mary Lou Williams Collection, Series 4, Subseries 4L, Box 47, Folder 6.

20 Howard Sanders to Mary Lou Williams, undated, Mary Lou Williams Collection, Series 4, Subseries 4L, Box 47, Folder 6.

21 "Rummage Sale—at 318 East 29 St" and "Rummage Sale! 310 East 29th Street," Mary Lou Williams Collection, Series 4, Subseries 4L, Box 47, Folder 6.

22 Irene V. Phillips to Mr. Weinberg, November 23, 1959, Mary Lou Williams Collection, Series 4, Subseries 4L, Box 49, Folder 4 (Licenses, Leases, Insurance, State and Local Documents, 1959–1961).

23 "Bel Canto Expenses," Mary Lou Williams Collection, Series 4, Subseries 4L, Box 47, Folder 8 (Bound Notebook, New York, New York, 1959–1960).

24 "Bel Canto Foundation Expenses . . . 1960," pp. 1–2, and "Summary," Mary Lou Williams Collection, Series 4, Subseries 4L, Box 48, Folders 5–8 (Financial Records— Expenditures, Inventory, Transactions, New York, New York, 1958–1971, undated).

25 Mary Lou Williams to Alice Fishelis, March 6, 1961, Mary Lou Williams Collection, Series 4, Subseries 4L, Box 47, Folder 11 (Donation Correspondence—Donor Requests, New York, New York, 1958–1961, undated).

26 "Bel Canto Foundation—University Note Book," Mary Lou Williams Collection, Series 4, Subseries 4L, Box 47, Folder 8.

27 "Bel Canto Foundation—University Note Book"; and Mary Lou Williams Collection, Series 4, Subseries 4L, Box 49, Folder 7 (Receipt book for Bel Canto Membership, 1960).

28 "Form CR-131, 'Annual Report—Charitable Organizations,'" Mary Lou Williams Collection, Series 4, Subseries 4L, Box 49, Folder 4. Because of a miscalculation, Williams reported $100 less than the actual total.

29 Williams calculated this total as $10 less than the actual amount.

30 "Form M-537g, 'Financial Report,'" Mary Lou Williams Collection, Series 4, Subseries 4L, Box 48, Folders 5–8.

31 Mary Lou Williams to City of New York, Department of Finance, Division of Special Taxes, September 17, 1963, Mary Lou Williams Collection, Series 4, Subseries 4L, Box 49, Folder 4; and Kernodle, *Soul on Soul*, 206.

32 Pearl Bailey to Mary Lou Williams, April 25, 1961, Mary Lou Williams Collection, Series 3, Subseries 3C, Box 13, Folder 6 (Pearl Bailey, 1961–1968).

33 Waldo Parrish was previously Adam Clayton Powell Jr.'s "Personal & Confidential Secretary" and had served as the "Administrative Assistant" of "Congressional Committee when he became Chairman of the Committee on Education and Labor of the United States Congress." Waldo E. Parrish to Mary Lou Williams, September 27, 1963, Mary Lou Williams Collection, Series 4, Subseries 4L, Box 47, Folder 1 (Adam Clayton Powell Foundation Correspondence, Various locations, 1959–1964).

34 Waldo E. Parrish, confidential memorandum to Mary Lou Williams, November 13, 1963, p. 1, Mary Lou Williams Collection, Series 4, Subseries 4L, Box 47, Folder 1.

35 Parrish, confidential memorandum to Williams, November 13, 1963, pp. 2–4.

36 Author's conversation with Peter O'Brien, March 14, 2014; and Gérard Pochonet, liner notes, Mary Lou Williams, *Mary Lou Williams Presents Black Christ of the Andes.*

37 On another page of Williams's income tax accounting, Guillemet received another $18 in cash donations, and he may have also received an additional $60 in cash that year (although the way she recorded this amount makes it unclear). Mary Lou Williams Collection, Series 4, Box 62, Folder "Taxes–Federal Income Taxes, 1965," pp. 1–3.

38 Waldo E. Parrish to Herbert J. Bliss, February 12, 1964, pp. 1–2, Mary Lou Williams Collection, Series 4, Subseries 4L, Box 47, Folder 1.

39 Parrish to Bliss, February 12, 1964, pp. 2–3.

40 Parrish to Bliss, February 12, 1964, pp. 2–4.

41 Waldo E. Parrish to Herbert J. Bliss, March 26, 1964, pp. 1–2, Mary Lou Williams Collection, Series 4, Subseries 4L, Box 47, Folder 1.

42 Herbert J. Bliss to Waldo E. Parrish, March 31, 1964, and Herbert J. Bliss to Henry R. Williams, April 22, 1964, Mary Lou Williams Collection, Series 4, Subseries 4I, Box 41, Folder 2.

43 Mary Lou Williams Collection, Series 4, Subseries 4L, Box 47, Folder 1.

44 Kernodle, *Soul on Soul*, 246.

45 See Amy Lee, "Jazz Philanthropist Calls Up Heritage," *Christian Science Monitor*, December 31, 1963, 2.

46 Balliett, "Profiles: Out Here Again," 82.

47 "State of New York—Department of Correction: Application for Employment," Mary Lou Williams Collection, Series 4, Subseries 4L, Box 48, Folder 3 (Employment Applications—Thrift Shop; New York, New York 1965–1966).

48 Jerry Hemphill, employment application letter to Mary Lou Williams, September 10, 1965, Mary Lou Williams Collection, Series 4, Subseries 4L, Box 48, Folder 3.

49 Mary Lou Williams Collection, Series 3, Subseries 3D, Box 20, Folder 6 (Rev. Thomas W. Jackson, Pennsylvania Bureau of Correction, 1964–1966, 1970), and Folder 11 (Rev. Andrew P. Marinak, United States Penitentiary, 1966–1967).

50 Andrew Cyrille later became an avant-garde drummer for jazz pianist Cecil Taylor, a musician whose style represented a comical foil for Mary Lou Williams in her normative articulation of jazz as music.

51 Checkbooks and balance registers, 1962–1964, Mary Lou Williams Collection, Series 4, Subseries 4M: Banking, Box 50.

52 "Mary Lou Williams (Income Tax)," p. 1, Mary Lou Williams Collection, Series 4, Box 62, Folder "Taxes–Federal Income Taxes, 1965."

53 See Eustis Guillemet to Mary Lou Williams, February 5, 1965, Eustis Guillemet to Mary Lou Williams, May 30, 1966, and Eustis Guillemet to Mary Lou Williams, June 22, 1966, Mary Lou Williams Collection, Series 3, Subseries 3B: Correspondence with Friends, ca. 1925–1952, 1958–1981, Box 8, Folder 11 (Eustis Guillemet, 1965–1973, undated).

54 Nate Chinen, "Chris Anderson, 81, Influential Jazz Pianist, Is Dead," New York Times, February 9, 2008, accessed April 8, 2014, www.nytimes.com/2008/02/09/arts/music/09anderson.html.

55 Bernard Stollman to Mary Lou Williams, December 2, 1964, Mary Lou Williams Collection, Series 4, Subseries 4L, Box 48, Folder 10 (Grants and Donations to Musicians/Organizations, New York, New York, 1959–1965, undated).

56 "Bel Canto Foundation for the Rehabilitation of Musicians, Notice of Grant—Chris Anderson, December 3, 1964," and Mary Lou Williams, Chemical Bank New York Trust Company, check 102, December 3, 1964, Mary Lou Williams Collection, Series 4, Subseries 4L, Box 48, Folder 10.

57 Irene Phillips to Mary Lou Williams, December 8, 1964, Mary Lou Williams Collection, Series 4, Subseries 4L, Box 48, Folder 10.

58 "Ada Moore Is Dead; Singer and Actress, 64," New York Times, January 11, 1991, accessed April 8, 2014, www.nytimes.com/1991/01/11/obituaries/ada-moore-is-dead-singer-and-actress-64.html.

59 "Bel Canto Foundation for the Rehabilitation of Musicians, Notice of Grant—Ada Moore, Musician, November 8, 1965," Mary Lou Williams Collection, Series 4, Subseries 4L, Box 48, Folder 10.

60 Dahl, Morning Glory, 267.

61 Norman Weyand, SJ, "The Junkie Priest—Review for Religious, June 20, 1964," pp. 1–2, Mary Lou Williams Collection, Series 3, Subseries 3D, Box 21, Folder 11 (Norman Weyand, SJ, Loyola University, 1964–1968).

62 Norman Weyand to Mary Lou Williams, July 15, 1964, p. 1, Mary Lou Williams Collection, Series 3, Subseries 3D, Box 21, Folder 11.

63 Dorothy Day to Mary Lou Williams, November 16, 1965, and Dorothy Day to Mary Lou Williams, March 23, 1968, p. 2, Mary Lou Williams Collection, Series 3,

Subseries 3C, Box 14, Folder 2 (Dorothy Day, 1968, n.d.). For more on Williams's interactions with notable radical Catholics, see Dahl, *Morning Glory*, 277.

64 Checkbooks and balance registers, 1962–1964.

65 "Taxes–Federal Income Taxes, 1965," p. 3.

66 Dahl, *Morning Glory*, 294.

67 Lewis K. McMillan Jr., "Mary Lou Williams: First Lady of Jazz," *Down Beat*, May 27, 1971, 16.

68 Holmes and Thomson, *Jazz Greats*, 42.

69 "A Get-Well Prayer," Mary Lou Williams Collection, Series 3, Subseries 3B, Box 8, Folder 12 (Eustis Guillemet—Greeting Cards, 1980–1981).

CHAPTER 9. VIRTUOSO ANCESTORS

1 *Mary Lou Williams: Music on My Mind*, documentary, directed by Joanne Burke. DVD copy provided to author by Joanne Burke.

2 Author's conversation with Joanne Burke, May 10, 2017.

3 Rachelle Blidner, "Jazz Fans Seek Ways to Spend Eternity with Greats," Associated Press, July 10, 2014, accessed January 4, 2017, http://bigstory.ap.org/article/jazz-fans-seek-ways-spend-eternity-greats.

4 For Mercedes Ellington's 1939 birth year, see Clem Richardson, "Mercedes Ellington, Granddaughter of Jazz Legend Duke, Keeps in Step at 70," *New York Daily News*, June 7, 2009, accessed June 12, 2017, www.nydailynews.com/new-york/brooklyn/mercedes-ellington-granddaughter-jazz-legend-duke-step-70-article-1.375770. Various sources list Ellington's birth year as 1949.

5 See Sobel, *World They Made Together*; and Thompson, *Flash of the Spirit*.

6 See Baldwin, "'A Home in Dat Rock'"; and Gin, "'Heavenization' of Earth."

7 See Sobel, *World They Made Together*; and Isenberg and Burstein, *Mortal Remains*.

8 See Baldwin, "'A Home in Dat Rock'"; and Roediger, "And Die in Dixie."

9 Young, *Rituals of Resistance*.

10 Smith, *To Serve the Living*, 8–10. See also Holloway, *Passed On*.

11 White, *Rise to Respectability*, 117–20, 125–26.

12 See Cohen, *Duke Ellington's America*; Kernodle, *Soul on Soul*; and Steed, *Duke Ellington*.

13 Turner, *Jazz Religion*, 89, 95–96.

14 Haber, *From Hardtack to Home Fries*, 210.

15 Leah Donnella, "Candice Hoyes Sings Blackness, Womanhood and History on Her Debut Jazz Album," NPR.org, May 23, 2016, accessed April 26, 2017, www.npr.org/sections/codeswitch/2016/05/23/473814916/candice-hoyes-sings-blackness-womanhood-and-history-on-her-new-jazz-album.

16 Kory Cook, "From Opera to Jazz: Candice Hoyes's 'On a Turquoise Cloud,'" KTRU 91.7, Trinity University, May 1, 2015, accessed April 26, 2017, https://krtu.trinity.edu/news/opera-jazz-candice-hoyes%E2%80%99s-%E2%80%9C-turquoise-cloud%E2%80%9D.

17 Teal, "Posthumously Live," 403.

18 Teal, "Posthumously Live," 407–8.

19 Pinder, *Painting the Gospel*, 14.

20 Rick Lyman, "After an 18-Year Campaign, an Ellington Memorial Rises," *New York Times*, July 1, 1997, accessed February 17, 2017, www.nytimes.com/1997/07/01/arts/after-an-18-year-campaign-an-ellington-memorial-rises.html.

21 "In Tribute to Ella Fitzgerald, and Yonkers," *New York Times*, October 20, 1996, accessed February 17, 2017, www.nytimes.com/1996/10/20/nyregion/in-tribute-to-ella-fitzgerald-and-yonkers.html.

22 Maggie Fazeli Fard, "Duke Ellington Statue Installed in Northwest DC," *Washington Post*, March 29, 2012, accessed February 17, 2017, www.washingtonpost.com/blogs/the-buzz/post/duke-ellington-statue-installed-in-northwest-dc/2012/03/29/gIQAf5J1iS_blog.html?utm_term=.e00b8c295437; and "A 10,000-Pound Statue of DC Native Duke Ellington Has Found Its Way Home," *CBS DC*, March 29, 2012, accessed February 17, 2017, http://washington.cbslocal.com/2012/03/29/a-10000-pound-statue-of-d-c-native-duke-ellington-has-found-its-way-home/.

23 "The Foundation," Ella Fitzgerald Official Site, accessed March 31, 2019, www.ellafitzgerald.com/foundation.

24 "Ella Fitzgerald—Cry Me a River," uploaded by cioto84, March 12, 2009, accessed March 31, 2019, www.youtube.com/watch?v=2Gn9A-kdsRo.

25 "Ella Fitzgerald—Summertime (1968)," uploaded by bessjazz, June 20, 2010, accessed March 31, 2019, www.youtube.com/watch?v=u2bigf337aU.

26 See "Schomburg Center Announces 2017 Annual Women's Jazz Festival, 'Ella, Ella: A Centennial Celebration of Mama Jazz!,'" New York Public Library, February 21, 2017, accessed April 27, 2017, www.nypl.org/press/press-release/february-21-2017/schomburg-center-announces-its-2017-annual-womens-jazz-festival.

27 "Ella Fitzgerald's Centennial Year Commemorated with a Global Ella 100 Celebration," Ella Fitzgerald Official Site, March 13, 2017, accessed March 31, 2019, www.ellafitzgerald.com/news/ella-fitzgeralds-centennial-year-commemorated-global-ella-100-celebration.

28 Regina Carter, liner notes to *Ella: Accentuate the Positive*.

29 "Virtuoso Violinist Regina Carter Digs Deep into the Ella Fitzgerald Catalogue on 'Ella: Accentuate the Positive,'" DL Media Music, March 22, 2017, accessed April 10, 2017, http://dlmediamusic.com/2017/03/11782/.

30 See "Ella at 100: Celebrating the Artistry of Ella Fitzgerald," Grammy Museum at L.A. Live, 2017, accessed March 27, 2017, www.grammymuseum.org/exhibits/current-exhibits/ellafitzgerald.

31 See Tad Hershorn, "Celebrate Ella's 100th Birthday Anniversary," Rutgers University, Newark, March 2, 2017, accessed March 28, 2017, www.newark.rutgers.edu/news/celebrate-ella-fitzgeralds-100th-birthday-anniversary; and "CELLAbration," Institute of Jazz Studies, Rutgers University Libraries, 2017, accessed March 28, 2017, www.libraries.rutgers.edu/jazz/cellabration.

32 Dee Dee Bridgewater, "Dear Ella," in *Dear Ella*, Dee Dee Bridgewater and Kenny Burrell.

33 Hamilton and Williams, "Hearing Ella Sing."

34 "Artist Statement," YonaHarvey.com, accessed January 9, 2017, http://yonaharvey.com/bio/artist-statement/.

35 Michael Alessi, "A Conversation with Yona Harvey," *Barely South Review*, January 2013, 48.

36 "First Book Questionnaire: Yona Harvey," *Volta*, December 7, 2012, accessed January 9, 2017, www.thevolta.org/fridayfeature-fbq-yharvey.html.

37 Harvey, "Communion with Mary Lou Williams," 42.

38 Harvey, "Communion with Mary Lou Williams," 42–43.

39 Harvey, "Communion with Mary Lou Williams," 43–44.

40 Harvey, "Communion with Mary Lou Williams," 44.

41 Harvey, "Communion with Mary Lou Williams," 45.

42 "First Book Questionnaire: Yona Harvey."

43 Sanchez, "Cante Jondo," 364–65.

44 Hucks, *Yoruba Traditions*, 18.

45 Sanchez, "Cante Jondo," 346–48.

46 Sanchez, "Cante Jondo," 347–48.

47 Sanchez, "Cante Jondo," 347–49.

48 *We Love Ella!*

49 See *We Love You Madly*, television special.

50 Duke Ellington and His Orchestra, "Come Sunday," in *Goin' Home*.

51 "Otis Clay," Blind Pig—Artists, accessed February 16, 2017, www.blindpigrecords.com/index.cfm?section=artists&artistid=17.

52 Shon McPeace, "Heaven Sent," *Arkansas Democrat-Gazette Online*, May 16, 2007, accessed February 16, 2017, www.arkansasonline.com/news/2007/may/16/heaven-sent/.

53 "21st Annual Mary Lou Williams Jazz Festival," Kennedy Center, 2016, accessed March 31, 2019, www.kennedy-center.org/calendar/event/MQWIL.

54 Farah Jasmine Griffin, liner notes to *Flying toward the Sound*, Geri Allen.

55 Geri Allen, liner notes to *A Child Is Born*.

56 Wynton Marsalis, liner notes to *All Rise*.

57 "News—Abyssinian: A Gospel Celebration US Tour Dates," WyntonMarsalis.org, August 22, 2013, accessed February 16, 2017, http://wyntonmarsalis.org/news/entry/abyssinian-a-gospel-celebration-u.s.-tour-dates.

CONCLUSION

1 See Savage, "Biblical and Historical Imperatives."

2 Neal Broverman, "Jennifer Holliday Cancels Trump Performance, Apologizes to LGBTs," *Advocate*, January 14, 2017, accessed February 6, 2017, www.advocate.com/politics/2017/1/14/jennifer-holliday-cancels-trump-performance-apologizes-lgbts.

3 "Jennifer Holliday Performs 'Come Sunday,'" *The View*, January 17, 2017, accessed February 6, 2017, www.youtube.com/watch?v=RorADUMGFHI.

BIBLIOGRAPHY

ARTICLES, BOOKS, AND DISSERTATIONS

Addison, James Thayer. *The Living Sacrifice: Thoughts on the Liturgy of the Holy Communion.* 6th ed. Cincinnati, OH: Forward Movement Publications, n.d.

Anderson, Paul Allen. *Deep River: Music and Memory in Harlem Renaissance Thought.* Durham, NC: Duke University Press, 2001.

Baldwin, Lewis. "'A Home in Dat Rock': Afro-American Folk Sources and Slave Visions of Heaven and Hell." *Journal of Religious Thought* 41, no. 1 (1984): 38–57.

Best, Wallace D. *Langston's Salvation: American Religion and the Bard of Harlem.* New York: New York University Press, 2017.

Bivins, Jason C. *Spirits Rejoice! Jazz and American Religion.* New York: Oxford University Press, 2015.

Blyden, Edward Wilmot. *Christianity, Islam and the Negro Race.* London: W. B. Whittingham, 1888.

Booker, Vaughn. "'An Authentic Record of My Race': Exploring the Popular Narratives of African American Religion in the Music of Duke Ellington." *Religion and American Culture: A Journal of Interpretation* 25, no. 1 (2015): 1–36.

Calloway, Cab, and Bryant Rollins. *Of Minnie the Moocher and Me.* New York: Thomas Y. Crowell, 1976.

Cartwright, Katharine. "Quotation and Reference in Jazz Performance: Ella Fitzgerald's 'St. Louis Blues,' 1957–79." PhD diss., City University of New York, 1998.

Cashmore, E. Ellis. "'Get Up, Stand Up': The Rastafarian Movement." In *Disciplines of Faith: Studies in Religion, Politics and Patriarchy,* edited by Jim Obelkevich, Lyndal Roper, and Raphael Samuel. London: Routledge, 1987.

Chang, Kevin O'Brien, and Wayne Chen. *Reggae Routes: The Story of Jamaican Music.* Philadelphia: Temple University Press, 1998.

Cohen, Harvey G. *Duke Ellington's America.* Chicago: University of Chicago Press, 2010.

Cressler, Matthew J. *Authentically Black and Truly Catholic: The Rise of Black Catholicism in the Great Migration.* New York: New York University Press, 2017.

Dahl, Linda. *Morning Glory: A Biography of Mary Lou Williams.* New York: Pantheon, 1999.

Destined for Greatness. Seattle, WA: Life Messengers, n.d.

DeVeaux, Scott. *The Birth of Bebop: A Social and Musical History.* Berkeley: University of California Press, 1997.

Dickerson, Dennis C. "Black Ecumenism: Efforts to Establish a United Methodist Episcopal Church, 1918–1932." *Church History* 52, no. 4 (December 1983): 479–91.

Ellington, Edward Kennedy. *Music Is My Mistress.* New York: Da Capo, 1973.

Evans, Curtis J. *The Burden of Black Religion.* New York: Oxford University Press, 2008.

Farrington, Holly E. "Narrating the Jazz Life: Three Approaches to Jazz Autobiography." *Popular Music and Society* 29, no. 3 (July 2006): 375–86.

Franceschina, John. *Duke Ellington's Music for the Theatre.* Jefferson, NC: McFarland,
2001.

Fritts, Ron, and Ken Vail. *Ella Fitzgerald: The Chick Webb Years and Beyond, 1935–1948.*
Lanham, MD: Scarecrow, 2003.

Gaines, Kevin K. *Uplifting the Race: Black Leadership, Politics, and Culture in the Twentieth Century.* Chapel Hill: University of North Carolina Press, 1996.

Garrett, Charles Hiroshi. "The Humor of Jazz." In *Jazz/Not Jazz: The Music and Its
Boundaries,* edited by David Ake, Charles Hiroshi Garrett, and Daniel Goldmark.
Berkeley: University of California Press, 2012.

George, Don. *Sweet Man: The Real Duke Ellington.* New York: G. P. Putnam's Sons, 1981.

Gillespie, John Birks, and Wilmot Alfred Fraser. *To Be . . . or Not . . . to Bop.* Minneapolis: University of Minnesota Press, 2009.

Gilmore, Glenda Elizabeth. *Gender and Jim Crow: Women and the Politics of White
Supremacy in North Carolina, 1896–1920.* Chapel Hill: University of North Carolina
Press, 1996.

Gin, Kathryn. "The 'Heavenization' of Earth: African American Visions and Uses of
the Afterlife, 1863–1901." *Slavery and Abolition* 31, no. 2 (June 2010): 207–31.

Gourse, Leslie. *Louis' Children: American Jazz Singers.* Updated ed. New York: Cooper
Square Press, 2001/1984.

Gray, Christine R. "Introduction [1]." In *Plays and Pageants from the Life of the Negro,*
edited by Willis Richardson. Jackson: University Press of Mississippi, 1993.

Griffin, Farah Jasmine. *Harlem Nocturne: Women Artists and Progressive Politics during
World War II.* New York: Basic Civitas, 2013.

Haber, Barbara. *From Hardtack to Home Fries: An Uncommon History of American
Cooks and Meals.* New York: Free Press, 2002.

Harlos, Christopher. "Jazz Autobiography: Theory, Practice, Politics." In *Representing
Jazz,* edited by Krin Gabbard. Durham, NC: Duke University Press, 1995.

Harris, Theodore H. H. "St. Paul AME Church." In *The Encyclopedia of Northern
Kentucky,* edited by Paul A. Tenkotte and James C. Claypool. Lexington: University
Press of Kentucky, 2009.

Harvey, Yona. "Communion with Mary Lou Williams." In *Hemming the Water.* New
York: Four Way Books, 2013. Reprinted with the permission of The Permissions
Company, LLC on behalf of Four Way Books, www.fourwaybooks.com.

Hershorn, Tad. *Norman Granz: The Man Who Used Jazz for Justice.* Berkeley: University of California Press, 2011.

Higginbotham, Evelyn Brooks. *Righteous Discontent: The Women's Movement in the
Black Baptist Church, 1880–1920.* Cambridge, MA: Harvard University Press, 1993.

Hill, Robert A., ed. *The Marcus Garvey and Universal Negro Improvement Association Papers*. Vol. 3, *September 1920–August 1921*. Berkeley: University of California Press, 1984.

Hill, Wilbert Weldon. "The Sacred Concerts of Edward Kennedy 'Duke' Ellington." PhD diss., Catholic University of America, 1995.

Holloway, Karla F. C. *Passed On: African American Mourning Stories*. Durham, NC: Duke University Press, 2002.

Holmes, Lowell D., and John W. Thomson. *Jazz Greats: Getting Better with Age*. New York: Holmes and Meier, 1986.

Hornsby-Gutting, Angela. *Black Manhood and Community Building in North Carolina, 1900–1930*. Gainesville: University Press of Florida, 2009.

Hucks, Tracey E. *Yoruba Traditions and African American Religious Nationalism*. Albuquerque: University of New Mexico Press, 2012.

Hudson, Theodore R. "Duke Ellington's Literary Sources." *American Music* 9, no. 1 (Spring 1991): 20–42.

Huggins, Willis N., and John G. Jackson. *An Introduction to African Civilizations, with Main Currents in Ethiopian History*. New York: Avon House, 1937.

Isenberg, Nancy, and Andrew Burstein, eds. *Mortal Remains: Death in Early America*. Philadelphia: University of Pennsylvania Press, 2003.

Jones, Martha S. *All Bound Up Together: The Woman Question in African American Public Culture, 1830–1900*. Chapel Hill: University of North Carolina Press, 2007.

Kainer, Eden E. "Vocal Racial Crossover in the Song Performance of Three Iconic American Vocalists: Sophie Tucker (1884–1966), Elsie Janis (1889–1956) and Ella Fitzgerald (1917–1996)." PhD diss., University of Wisconsin–Madison, 2008.

Kernodle, Tammy L. *Soul on Soul: The Life and Music of Mary Lou Williams*. Boston: Northeastern University Press, 2004.

Knight, Arthur. *Disintegrating the Musical: Black Performance and American Musical Film*. Durham, NC: Duke University Press, 2002.

Koehler, M. Cecilia. *Sanctity's Mother Tongue: An Examination on Silence and Use of the Gift of Speech*. Techny, IL: Mission Press, SVD, 1952.

L'Heureux, Aimee. "Illinois Jacquet: Integrating Houston Jazz Audiences . . . Lands Ella Fitzgerald and Dizzy Gillespie in Jail." *Houston History* 8, no. 1 (Fall 2010): 6–8.

Long, Charles H. "Passage and Prayer: The Origin of Religion in the Atlantic World." In *The Collected Writings of Charles H. Long: Ellipsis*. New York: Bloomsbury Academic, 2018.

Lundeen, Elizabeth A. "Sarah Dudley Pettey: 'A New Age Woman' and the Politics of Race, Class, and Gender in North Carolina, 1869–1906." In *North Carolina Women: Their Lives and Times*, vol. 1, edited by Michele Gillespie and Sally McMillen. Athens: University of Georgia Press, 2014.

Mack, Kenneth W. *Representing the Race: The Creation of the Civil Rights Lawyer*. Cambridge, MA: Harvard University Press, 2012.

Maffly-Kipp, Laurie. *Setting Down the Sacred Past: African American Race Histories*. Cambridge, MA: Belknap Press of Harvard University Press, 2010.

Martin, Lerone A. *Preaching on Wax: The Phonograph and the Shaping of Modern African American Religion*. New York: New York University Press, 2014.

Mathews, Mary Beth Swetnam. *Doctrine and Race: African American Evangelicals and Fundamentalism between the Wars*. Tuscaloosa: University of Alabama Press, 2017.

McElroy, Paul S. *Quiet Thoughts*. Mount Vernon, NY: Peter Pauper, 1964.

Miller, William Robert. *The Christian Encounters the World of Pop Music and Jazz*. St. Louis, MO: Concordia Publishing House, 1965.

Mills, Robbie Edwards. *The Church as the Surrogate Family*. Bloomington: WestBow, 2011.

Monson, Ingrid. *Freedom Sounds: Civil Rights Call Out to Jazz and Africa*. New York: Oxford University Press, 2007.

Moses, Wilson Jeremiah. *Afrotopia: The Roots of African American Popular History*. Cambridge, UK: Cambridge University Press, 1998.

Nicholson, Stuart. *Ella Fitzgerald: A Biography of the First Lady of Jazz*. New York: Routledge, 2004.

———. *Reminiscing in Tempo: A Portrait of Duke Ellington*. Boston: Northeastern University Press, 1999.

Ogren, Kathy J. *The Jazz Revolution: Twenties America and the Meaning of Jazz*. New York: Oxford University Press, 1989.

Oliver, Paul. *Songsters and Saints: Vocal Traditions on Race Records*. New York: Cambridge University Press, 1984.

Parker, George Wells. *The Children of the Sun*. Omaha: Hamitic League of the World, 1918.

Peress, Maurice. "My Life with 'Black, Brown, and Beige.'" *Black Music Research Journal* 13, no. 2 (Autumn 1993): 147–60.

Perry, Seth. *Bible Culture and Authority in the Early United States*. Princeton, NJ: Princeton University Press, 2018.

Pinder, Kymberly N. *Painting the Gospel: Black Public Art and Religion in Chicago*. Urbana: University of Illinois Press, 2016.

Prentiss, Craig R. *Staging Faith: Religion and African American Theater from the Harlem Renaissance to World War II*. New York: New York University Press, 2014.

Raboteau, Albert J. *A Fire in the Bones: Reflections on African-American Religious History*. Boston: Beacon, 1995.

Reed, Teresa L. *The Holy Profane: Religion in Black Popular Music*. Lexington: University Press of Kentucky, 2003.

Richardson, Willis, ed. *Plays and Pageants from the Life of the Negro*. Jackson: University Press of Mississippi, 1993.

Roediger, David R. "And Die in Dixie: Funerals, Death, and Heaven in the Slave Community, 1700–1865." *Massachusetts Review* 22, no. 1 (Spring 1981): 163–83.

Sanchez, Sonia. "Cante Jondo." In *Ask Me Now: Conversations on Jazz and Literature*, edited by Sascha Feinstein. Bloomington: Indiana University Press, 2007.

Savage, Barbara D. "Biblical and Historical Imperatives: Toward a History of Ideas about the Political Role of Black Churches." In *African Americans and the Bible:*

Sacred Texts and Social Textures, edited by Vincent L. Wimbush, 367–88. New York: Continuum, 2000.

Schenbeck, Lawrence. *Racial Uplift and American Music, 1878–1943*. Jackson: University Press of Mississippi, 2012.

Shipton, Alyn. *Hi-De-Ho: The Life of Cab Calloway*. New York: Oxford University Press, 2010.

Simmons, Martha. "Whooping: The Musicality of African American Preaching Past and Present." In *Preaching with Sacred Fire: An Anthology of African American Sermons, 1750 to the Present*, edited by Martha Simmons and Frank A. Thomas. New York: Norton, 2010.

Smith, Suzanne E. *To Serve the Living: Funeral Directors and the African American Way of Death*. Cambridge, MA: Belknap Press of Harvard University Press, 2010.

Sobel, Mechal. *The World They Made Together: Black and White Values in Eighteenth-Century Virginia*. Princeton, NJ: Princeton University Press, 1989.

Sorett, Josef. *Spirit in the Dark: A Religious History of Racial Aesthetics*. New York: Oxford University Press, 2016.

Steed, Janna Tull. *Duke Ellington: A Spiritual Biography*. New York: Crossroad, 1999.

Summers, Martin. *Manliness and Its Discontents: The Black Middle Class and the Transformation of Masculinity, 1900–1930*. Chapel Hill: University of North Carolina Press, 2004.

Sundquist, Eric J. *Strangers in the Land: Blacks, Jews, Post-Holocaust America*. Cambridge, MA: Harvard University Press, 2005.

Taylor, Clarence. *The Black Churches of Brooklyn*. New York: Columbia University Press, 1994.

Teal, Kimberly Hannon. "Posthumously Live: Canon Formation at Jazz at Lincoln Center through the Case of Mary Lou Williams." *American Music* 32, no. 4 (Winter 2014): 400–422.

Thompson, Robert Farris. *Flash of the Spirit: African and Afro-American Art and Philosophy*. New York: Random House, 1983.

Timner, W. E. *Ellingtonia: The Recorded Music of Duke Ellington and His Sidemen*. 5th ed. Lanham, MD: Scarecrow, 2007.

Tucker, Mark, ed. *The Duke Ellington Reader*. New York: Oxford University Press, 1993.

———. "The Renaissance Education of Duke Ellington." In *Black Music in the Harlem Renaissance*, edited by Samuel A. Floyd Jr. Westport, CT: Greenwood, 1990.

Turner, Richard Brent. *Jazz Religion, the Second Line, and Black New Orleans*. Bloomington: Indiana University Press, 2009.

Von Eschen, Penny M. *Satchmo Blows Up the World: Jazz Ambassadors Play the Cold War*. Cambridge, MA: Harvard University Press, 2004.

Webb, James Morris. *The Black Man, the Father of Civilization, Proven by Biblical History*. Seattle, WA: Acme Press, 1910.

Weisenfeld, Judith. *Hollywood Be Thy Name: African American Religion in American Film, 1929–1949*. Berkeley: University of California Press, 2007.

————. *New World A-Coming: Black Religion and Racial Identity during the Great Migration.* New York: New York University Press, 2016.

————. "'The Secret at the Root': Performing African American Religious Modernity in Hall Johnson's *Run, Little Chillun.*" *Religion and American Culture: A Journal of Interpretation* 21, no. 1 (Winter 2011): 39–80.

————. "'Truths That Liberate the Soul': Eva Jessye and the Politics of Religious Performance." In *Women and Religion in the African Diaspora: Knowledge, Power, and Performance,* edited by R. Marie Griffith and Barbara Dianne Savage, 222–44. Baltimore: Johns Hopkins University Press, 2006.

Wells, Christopher J. "'Go Harlem!' Chick Webb and His Dancing Audience during the Great Depression." PhD diss., University of North Carolina at Chapel Hill, 2014.

Wesley, Charles H. "The Religious Attitudes of Negro Youth—A Preliminary Study of Opinion in an Urban and a Rural Community." *Journal of Negro History* 21, no. 4 (October 1936): 376–93.

White, Calvin, Jr. *The Rise to Respectability: Race, Religion, and the Church of God in Christ.* Fayetteville: University of Arkansas Press, 2012.

Wimbush, Vincent L. *White Men's Magic: Scripturalization as Slavery.* New York: Oxford University Press, 2012.

Wriggle, John. "'The Mother of All Albums': Revisiting Ellington's *A Drum Is a Woman.*" In *Duke Ellington Studies,* edited by John Howland. New York: Cambridge University Press, 2017.

Young, Jason R. *Rituals of Resistance: African Atlantic Religion in Kongo and the Lowcountry South in the Era of Slavery.* Baton Rouge: Louisiana State University Press, 2007.

ARCHIVAL COLLECTIONS

ASCAP sponsored radio interviews with musicians and composers. New York Public Library.

Ellington, Duke. Collection. National Museum of American History, Smithsonian Institution.

Ellington, Ruth. Collection. National Museum of American History, Smithsonian Institution.

Gumby, Alexander. Collection of Negroiana. Rare Book and Manuscript Library, Columbia University.

Spencer, Frances G. Collection of American Popular Sheet Music. Baylor University.

Williams, Mary Lou. Collection. Institute of Jazz Studies, Rutgers University.

PERIODICALS

Africo-American Presbyterian
Arkansas Democrat-Gazette Online
Associated Negro Press
Associated Press
Atlanta Daily World

Baltimore Afro-American
Barely South Review
Chicago Defender / Chicago Daily Defender
Christian (St. Louis, MO)
Christianity Today
Christian Science Monitor
Down Beat
Ebony
Half-Century Magazine
Hartford Courant
Houston Press
JazzTimes
Jet
Los Angeles Sentinel
Miami News
Milwaukee Sentinel
National Baptist Voice
Negro Digest
Newark Evening News
New Masses
New York Age
New York Amsterdam News
New York Daily News
New Yorker
New York Times
Norfolk Journal and Guide
Oakland Tribune
Philadelphia Tribune
Pittsburgh Courier
Sepia
Stamford Advocate
Star of Zion
Summit of Spiritual Understanding
Times Union
Washington Post
Washington Post, Times Herald
Vanity Fair

AUDIO

Allen, Geri. *A Child Is Born.* © 2011 by Motéma, MTM-69. Compact disc.
———. *Flying toward the Sound.* © 2010 by Motéma, MTM-37. Compact disc.
Bellson, Louie, and His All-Star Orchestra. *Duke Ellington: Black, Brown and Beige.* © 1994 by Jazz Heritage Inc., 513633L. Compact disc.

Bridgewater, Dee Dee. "Dear Ella." *Dear Ella*. Dee Dee Bridgewater and Kenny Burrell. © 1997 by Verve Records, 314 537 896–2. Compact disc.

Calloway, Cab, and His Orchestra. *The Chronological Cab Calloway*, vol. 1, *The Early Years, 1930–1934*. © 2001, 1933 by JSP Records, JSP908. Compact disc.

Carter, Regina. *Ella: Accentuate the Positive*. © 2017 by Okeh Records, 88985-40604-2. Compact disc.

Ellington, Duke, and His Orchestra. "Come Sunday." *Goin' Home—A Tribute to Duke Ellington/A Benefit for the Duke Ellington Foundation*. Otis Clay and Delya Chandler. © 2000 by Platinum, 3767. Compact disc.

———. *A Drum Is a Woman*. © 1957 by Columbia Records, COL 471320 2. Compact disc.

———. *Duke Ellington, Black, Brown and Beige—Featuring Mahalia Jackson*. © 1999, 1958 by Columbia Records, EJC55430. Compact disc.

———. *The Duke Ellington Carnegie Hall Concerts: January 1943*. © 1991, 1977 by Prestige Records, 2PCD-34004-2. Compact disc.

———. *Duke Ellington's Concert of Sacred Music*. © 1994, 1966 by RCA Victor, RCA 74321192542. Compact disc.

———. *Duke Ellington's My People*. © 1992, 1963 by Legacy Recordings, AK-52759. Compact disc.

———. *Duke Ellington's Third Sacred Concert, The Majesty of God, as Performed in Westminster Abbey*. © 1975, re-released on *The Duke Ellington Centennial Edition: The Complete RCA Victor Recordings (1927–1973)*. © 1999 by RCA Victor, 09026-63386-2. Compact disc.

———. *Ellington Uptown*. © 2004, 1952 by Legacy Recordings, CK-87066. Compact disc.

———. *Second Sacred Concert*. © 1990, 1968 by Prestige Records, PCD 24045–2. Compact disc.

Ellington, Duke, and the Fountain Street Choir. *Duke Ellington at Fountain Street, April 17, 1966*. Grand Rapids, MI, unpublished recording. Compact disc.

Ellington, Duke, with Erich Kunzel and the Cincinnati Symphony Orchestra. *Orchestral Works*. © 1989, 1970 by MCA Records, Inc., MCAD-42318. Compact disc.

Fitzgerald, Ella. *Brighten the Corner*. © 1990, 1967 by Capitol Records, CDP 7 95151 2. Compact disc.

———. *Ella Fitzgerald at the Opera House*. © 1986, 1958 by Verve Records, 831 269–2. Compact disc.

———. "It's Up to Me and You" and "Brighten the Corner (Where You Are)." © 1968 by Capitol Records, 2212. Vinyl record.

———. *Rhythm Is My Business*. © 1999, 1962 by Verve Records, 314 559 513–2. Compact disc.

Fitzgerald, Ella, Billie Holiday, and Carmen McRae. *At Newport*. © 2000, 1957 by Verve Records, 314 559 809–2. Compact disc.

Fitzgerald, Ella, with the Tee Carson Trio. *Ella Fitzgerald: Live at Chautauqua*. Vol. 2. © 2017 by Dot Time Records, DT 8004, Compact disc.

Fitzgerald, Ella, with Duke Ellington and His Orchestra. *Ella Fitzgerald Sings the Duke Ellington Song Book*. © 1999, 1957 by Verve Records, 314 559 248–2. Compact disc.

Fitzgerald, Ella, with the Fraser McPherson Big Band and the Tee Carson Trio. *Live from the Cave Supper Club, Vancouver BC, Canada, 19 May 1968*. © 1999, 1968 by Jazz Band Compact Classics, EBCD 2144–2. Compact disc.

Fitzgerald, Ella, with the Ray Charles Singers. "Crying in the Chapel" and "When the Hands of the Clock Pray at Midnight." © 1953 by Decca Records, 28762. Shellac record.

Fitzgerald, Ella, with the Tommy Flanagan Trio. *Ella Fitzgerald at the Montreux Jazz Festival 1975*. © 1993, 1975 by Original Jazz Classics, OJCCD-789–2. Compact disc.

Goodbye, Babylon—Sermons. Various artists. © 2003 by Dust-to-Digital, DTD-01. Compact disc.

Hamilton, Arthur, and Patrick Williams. "Hearing Ella Sing." *For Ella*. Patti Austin. © 2002 by Playboy Jazz, PBD-7503–2. Compact disc.

Marsalis, Wynton. *All Rise*. Lincoln Center Jazz Orchestra and the Los Angeles Philharmonic. © 2002 by Sony Classical, S2K-89817. Compact disc.

Williams, Mary Lou. *Mary Lou Williams Presents Black Christ of the Andes*. © 2007, 1964 by Smithsonian Folkways Records & Service Corp., FJ 2843. Compact disc.

FILM AND TELEVISION

Duke Ellington: Piano and Intermittent Talk. Television special. July 2, 1970. Paris, France: ORTF Studios.

Mary Lou Williams: Music on My Mind. Documentary. Directed by Joanne Burke. 1990. New York: Women Make Movies. VHS.

Praise God and Dance. Television special. Filmed November 6, 1969, date of telecast unknown. Stockholm, Sweden: Sverige Radio.

Ride 'Em Cowboy. Film. Directed by Arthur Lubin. 1942. Santa Clarita, CA: Universal Studios Home Entertainment, 2008. DVD.

The Singing Kid. Film. Directed by William Keighley. 1936. Beverly Hills and Burbank, CA: Warner Home Video, 2009. DVD.

Snow-White. Animated film. Directed by Dave Fleischer, with Cab Calloway. 1933. Hollywood, CA: Paramount Pictures. https://archive.org/details/bb_snow_white.

We Love Ella! A Tribute to the First Lady of Song. Directed by David Horn and Shelley Berg. Recorded at the Galen Center at the University of Southern California, April 29, 2007. New York: Verve: Universal Music Distribution, 2007. DVD.

We Love You Madly. Television special. February 11, 1973. Los Angeles, CA: CBS.

INDEX

Abyssinian Baptist Church (Harlem, NY), 151, 191, 261

Acoustics, 156–158

Activism. *See* Jazz artists: political activism

Addison, James Thayer, 179–182

Africa, 13, 16, 42, 110–111, 115–117, *117 fig4.1*, 119, 121, 127–129, 136, 160, 252. *See also* West African music

African American: cultural productivity, 4, 8–9, 16, 21, 66, 71, 113, 145–146, 264–266; entertainers, 12, 67, 74–76, 89, 91–92, 148; folk culture, 9, 136; intellectuals, 13, 16, 26, 28–30, 40, 46, 72–74, 111, 115, 127–128, 194, 266; ministers, 6, 11, 27–28, 33, 46, 75, 123, 140, 152, 153, 266; nonreligious spheres, 3, 8, 10, 13, 16, 26, 31, 33, 42, 81, 102, 104, 152, 154, 263, 265; religious music, 1, 10, 66, 104–105, 107–108, 140, 146, 189, 259–260, 263; talent, 3, 41, 43, 74–75, 86, 89, 193, 225, 233; working class, 6–7, 221, 266; youth, 7, 13, 14, 17, 26, 30–31, 35, 39, 40, 42–46, 48, 51, 53, 122. *See also* Associated Negro Press

African American clergy, 4–7, 11, 13, 26–33, 33–38, 40–46, 53, 55, 57, 61–62, 75, 88, 115, 118, 122–124, 127, 140, 148–149, 151–154, 158, 161, 191, 221, 237, 256–257, 259, 261, 263, 266; ministerial sexual practices, 26, 61–62, 70, 75

African American Congregational-United Church of Christ, 257

African diaspora, 41, 203, 236, 262

African American masculinity, 58, 98, 219; black men, 1, 2, 3, 16, 26, 50, 57, 109, 116, *116 fig.4.1*, 224, 233, 264

African American middle-class, 2, 4–7, 13–7, 12–14, 21, 26–28, 34 40, 45–46, 48, 50–55, 57–58, 62, 74–75, 83, 99, 108, 111, 133, 136, 228, 255, 261, 264; "boy problem," 53

African American race histories. *See* Race histories

African American upper class, 74, 221; academics, 13, 16, 35, 40, 111, 114, 128, 192; professional elite, 75, 140. *See also* African American: intellectuals

African Methodist Episcopal Church (AME), 10, 14, 32, 34, 45, 57, 59, 79, 85–86, *86 fig.3.1*, 105, 109, 147, 149, 152–153, 155; bishops, 30, 38, 111, 118

African Methodist Episcopal Zion Church (AMEZ), 14, 17, 26, 28–29, 35, 41, 45, 80, 123, 124, 127, 163

Agosto, Kenny, 234

Allen, Geri, 235, 258–259

American Federation of Musicians, 210, 223

American South, 6, 36, 38, 42, 48–49, 61, 74, 84, 87, 98, 125, 129, 132, 145, 151, 246, 263–264

Anderson, Chris, 223–224

Anderson, William "Cat," 164

Andrews, Dwight D., 259

Anti-gay discourse, 151

Apollo Theater (Harlem, NY), 80, 245, 253, 261

Arlen, Harold, 67, 99

Armstrong, Louis, 64, 95, 96, 99, 213, 238

Arnett, Benjamin William, 111

Artistic expression as religious expression, 4, 7, 264–265, 268, 270

Artistic performance, 10, 27

Associated Negro Press, 41, 94, 121, 125, 126, 147

Atheism, 126, 143

Austin, Patti, 245–246, 247–248

Authenticity, 15, 99, 107; inauthenticity, 107; musical, 8, 81–82, 87, 96–97, 98–99, 242, 251, 254; racial; 3, 81–82, 98–99, 100, 101, 102, 108, 242; religious, 4, 10, 12, 20, 35

Ayler, Albert, 270

Babs, Alice, 155, *157 fig.5.1*, 177–178, 183, 185, 241

Bagwell, Vinnie, *232 fig.9.1*, 243

Bailey, Bill, 88

Bailey, Mildred, 88, 91, 96–97

Bailey, Pearl, 88, 216

Ballanta, Nicholas George Julius, 41

Baptist Church, 14, 18, 32–34, 36, 38, 45, 53, 109, 122, 139, 147–148, 149, 152, 154–155, 255, 261, 263, 266, 267; Baptist Ministers Conference (BMC), 148; National Baptist Convention, USA (NBC), 17, 45, 122. *See also* Abyssinian Baptist Church (Harlem, NY)

Baron, Arthur, 234

Baroness de Hueck, 210, 225

Basie, William "Count," 213. *See also* Count Basie and his Orchestra

Baylor, Jean, 245

Bebop, 15–16, 98, 100, 188, 198, 248; revolution, 15

Bel Canto Foundation, 19, 205–209, 227–230; and accountability for recipients, 220–227; contrasting visions for, 215–220; fundraising for, 197–198; management of, 208, 209–215, 227;

thrift shop, 205–208, *206 fig. 8.1*, 212–215, 220–222, 223, 225, 226–227, 229, 250

Belafonte, Harry, 93, 223

Berry, Chuck, 97

Bible: and African identity, 111–118, *117 fig. 4.1*, 123, 124, 127; biblical characters, 114, 117, 120, 122–123, 250, 259; biblical criticism, 37, 266; biblical narratives, 37, 111–112, 120–121, 126, 163–164; King James Bible, 35, 162–163, 257

Big band music, 1, 7, 15, 47, 74, 98, 187, 259

Bishop, Jim, 176

Black Church, not a monolithic entity, 19, 265

Black Jesus (television series), 97

Blackness, 9, 99, 100, 110, 114, 121, 123; anti-blackness, 112

Blakey, Art, 214

Bland, James G., 40

Bliss, Herbert J., 202, 209–210, 213, 216–219, 228

Blues, 7, 9, 12, 20, 36, 44, 75, 91, 98–99, 102, 106–107, 157, 218, 250–251, 253

Blyden, Edward Wilmot, 125

Boatwright, Ruth Ellington, 17

Bop/post-bop music, 16, 231, 259

Boyd, Malcolm, 140

Brice, Percy, 222

Bridgers, Aaron, 150

Bridgewater, Dee Dee, 247

Brown, James, 76

Brown, Ray, 247

Brown, Ray, Jr., 90

Brubeck, Dave, 145, 210

Bryan, Courtney, 245

Bryant, Willie, 88

Burke, Joanne, 231, 233

Burleigh, Harry T., 8, 41

Burrell, Kenny, 247

Bussey, John D., 148–149, 151

Butts, Calvin O., III, 261

Cab Calloway and His Orchestra, 47, 60, 63, 67

Caldwell, Gilbert Haven, 153–154

Calloway III, Cabell "Cab": adoption of racial slur, 70–71; and Camay Calloway, 58; conversion of, 65; and film, 51, 64, 67–69; irreverence, 14–16, 49–50, 57, 64–65, 69–72, 76–77; "Is that Religion?," 50, 59–62, 64; legacy, 76; middle-class upbringing, 50–59; racial identity, 69–75; "Harlem Camp Meeting," 47, 49, 50, 65; "Hi-De-Ho," 49, 59, 67; humor of, 14–15, 50, 56, 61–63, 65–67, 71–72, 76; "Miss Hallelujah Brown," 50, 63–64; *Of Minnie the Moocher and Me*, 14, 50; "Save Me Sister," 68–69; voice of Koko the Clown, 64; and Zarita Steptoe, 57; and Zelma Proctor, 57–58

Calloway, Zulme "Nuffie" (MacNeal), 72–74, *73 fig.2.1*

Carnegie Hall, 133, 154, 197, 210–211, 216

Carroll, Richard Alexander, 123–124

Carter, Benny, 94, 106

Carter, Regina, 246

Carver, George Washington, 111

Cenacle Sisters Convent, 208

Chandler, Delya, 255–256

Charles, Ray, 105–106, 147, 254–255, 256

Christ, Jesus, 29, 37, 43–44, 45, 79, 260; identified as black, 113, 116–117, 121–123; Ellington's writings on, 18, 151–152, 162, 167, 171–175, 180–183, 186

Christian, Charlie, 84

Christian Century, 173

Christian Church (Disciples of Christ), 154

Christian Encounters, 144

Christian Science, 2, 144, 165, 220

Christianity, criticism of, 260

Christianity Today, 173

Church of God in Christ (COGIC), 237

Civilization. *See* Race histories: civilization

Classical music, 8, 9, 20, 54, 55, 145, 259, 260

Clay, Otis, 255–256

Colored/Christian Methodist Episcopal Church, 45

Coffin, William Sloane, Jr., 140

Cohen, Harvey, 148–149

Cold War, 7, 155

Cole, Natalie, 253–254

Cole, Nat King, 213

Colemon, Johnnie, 155

Coltrane, John, 270

Congress of Racial Equality (CORE), 93

Cook, Will Marion, 8–10

Coots, J. Fred, 63–64

Cotton Club (New York, NY), 49

Count Basie and his Orchestra, 98, 106, 246

Cranshaw, Melbourne R. "Bob," 222

Crowley, John, 192, 194, 228

Cushite, 119, 120, 125–126

Cyrille, Andrew, 222, 258

Dahl, Linda, 224

Dameron, Tadley Ewing Peake "Tadd," 188, 222

Dance, 6, 64, 72, 80; evils of, 42–44; hall, 5, 30–31, 158; music, 7; religious, 35, 152–153, 154, 185, 256; "Praise God and Dance," 154, 185, 256–257; suit (clothing), 39

Davenport, William H., 35, 151

Davis, Benny, 63–64

Davis, Sammy, Jr., 210–211

Davis, Kenny, 258

Davis, Miles, 188, 207, 233, 251, 259

Day, Andra, 246

Day, Dorothy, 225–226, 227

De Porres, Martin, 20, 217, 226

Decca Records, 83, 89, 95, 103, 104

de Koenigswarter, Kathleen Annie Pannonica, 210

Dennis, Ruth R., 34–35

Desegregation, 77, 81, 85, 89–92, 108, 228

Dett, R. Nathaniel, 8–9, 11

Dixie Jubilee Singers, 10

Dole, Kenneth, 148

Donaldson, Lou, 214

Dorsey, Thomas, 102

Douglas, Dezron, 245

Du Bois, W. E. B., 6, 28–30, 117

Duke, George, 255

Dvořák, Antonín, 8–9

Dylan, Bob, 223

Ebony (magazine), 72, 90

Eckstine, Billy, 97

Ecumenism, 7, 17, 28, 139, 140–146, 152, 154, 155–156, 162, 174, 179, 181–182, 186, 261, 269

Eldridge, Roy, 93

Ellington, Edward Kennedy "Duke": Africa as site of biblical civilizations, 113–114; "Ain't But the One," 170, 172, 254, 256; annotation of religious texts, 179–183; and agnosticism, 143–144, 182; and atheism, 143–144, 175–176, 182; belief in God, 18, 174–183; "Black and Tan Fantasy," 9, 110; changes in tone over time, 158; Christmas cards, 176, 178, 185; "Come Sunday," 113, 124, 130–133, 139–140, 153, 170, 241, 255–256, 268–269; composer, 16, 18, 66, 114, 128, 129, 134, 135, 139–141, 145, 149–150, 151, 161, 165, 168, 170–171, 181, 183–184, 234, 243, 254, 260; defined God as synonymous with love, 159, 161–162, 170, 182–186; early life, 109–110; engagement with formal Christian theology, 179–183; ideas about heaven, 162–163, 171, 176–178, 183, 185; "In the Beginning, God," 149, 154, 162–164, 171, 184; Madam Zajj, 133–134; Music is my Mistress, 15, 110; omission of Holy Spirit in religious writings, 171–172; omission of Jesus Christ in religious writings, 18, 151–152, 162, 167,

171–175, 180–183, 186; pleas for protection of black people, 269; racial pride of, 110–111, 113, 128, 130, 135; religious sound of, 155, 158, 185–186, 253, 254–255, 260; religious writings on hotel stationary, 18, 159–161, 164, 167, 172, 174, 178, 185; sacred concerts as ecumenical project, 144; sacred music of, 17, 18, 140, 144, 146, 148, 152–153, 159, 163, 165, 185, 257, 259; sacred West Africa, 133–136; "seeing God," 159, 161; sexuality, 149–152; terminology for God, 168–171; theology of, 17–18, 136, 140–141, 158, 160–162, 165, 167–168, 172–173, 176, 179, 182, 185, 254, 257; uncategorizable religious beliefs, 18, 160–162; views on Christianity's essential nature, 180–182. See also First Sacred Concert; Sacred Concerts; Sacred space; Strayhorn, Billy

Ellington, Evie, 166, 210

Ellington, Mercedes, 234

Ellington, Mercer, 114, 150–151, 231

El-Shabazz, El-Hajj Malik. See Malcolm X

Emancipation, 110, 125, 128, 130, 132

Emotion, 10–11, 26, 35–38, 40, 45–46, 49, 110, 129–130, 135, 142, 148–149, 187, 193, 196–197, 199, 201, 229, 236–237; over-emotion, 148. See also Fitzgerald, Ella: and emotion

Eucharist, 181

Euro-American music, 1, 259

Europe, James Reese, 237

Eva Jessye Choir, 10

Evans, W. W., 28

Father Divine's Peace Mission, 39

Feather, Leonard, 96, 98

Film, 4, 6, 8–12, 51, 64, 67–69, 74, 76, 88–89, 150, 223, 231, 233, 247; soundtracks, 11; race films, 6, 11, 50, 265

First Humanist Society of New York, 127

First Sacred Concert, 139, 141, 148, 152, 153–154, 156, 162, 168, 171, 172

Fitzgerald, Ella: arrest of jazz musicians in her dressing room, 92–93; "A Tisket, A-Tasket," 88, 247, 253; bebop influence, 15–16, 98, 248; and black womanhood, 82, 101, 108; children's broadcast, 83–84; collection of cookbooks, 239–240; and Count Basie, 98, 106; criticism of her music, 95–102; crossover appeal, 77, 81, 95; did not smoke or drink, 83; early life, 79–80; Ella Fitzgerald Charitable Foundation, 243, 245, 247; and emotion, 78, 81, 85, 87, 94, 96–97, 99, 100–102, 104; "girl singer," 88, 98; and the Iranian Hostage Crisis, 103; irreverence, 107–108; and Joseph Da Silva, 79; and joy, 81, 99, 100–101, 103, 105, 108, 239, 253–254; and Louis Armstrong, 95–96, 99; nicknames of, 82, 89, 248, 253; once believed jazz and religion did not mix, 105; religious beliefs, 103–108; religious delight, 103–104; and scat music, 16, 95–96, 98–99, 101, 248, 253; and Scottsboro Defense Ball, 91; and Virginia Williams, 79–80; whites expound for, 89. *See also* Webb, Chick
Fitzgerald, Temperance "Tempie" Williams, 79
Flack, Roberta, 231
Flanagan, Tommy, 78, 93, 107
Ford, Louis, 237
Four Dusty Travelers, 10
Franklin, Aretha, 102–103, 254, 256; *Amazing Grace*, 102
Funeral services, 64, 85–87, *86 fig. 3.1*, 232, 235–238

Gale, Moe, 83, 85, 89–90
Gardner, Burgess, 255
Gardner, DeVonne, 183
Garner, Erroll, 203, 210
Garvey, Marcus (Garveyites), 25, 111, 115, 118, 136
Gensel, John Garcia, 140

George, Don, 110–111
Gershwin, George 10, 44–45; and Ira Gershwin, 100
Gibson, Don, 106
Gillespie, John Birks "Dizzy," 16, 19, 92–93, 98, 188, 205, 213, 217, 228, 229, 231–232
Gillespie, Lorraine, 189, 192, 194, 207
Gilmer, D. J., 43–44
God: and gender, 167–170, 174–175, 181, 254; pronouns for, 167–171, 181
Golden rule, 42, 255
Goodman, Benny, 84–85, 100, 145
Gordon, George, 215
Gospel music, 12, 18, 20, 36, 102–105, 107–108, 131, 139, 142, 148–149, 155, 157, 170, 172, 245, 254–256, 260
Grace, Charles "Daddy," 38–39
Grammy award, 154, 247, 268; museum, 246–247
Granz, Norman, 89–90, 92–93, 95, 98, 100, 105
Great Migration, 26, 79, 263, 265
Greene, Madeline, 88
Griffin, Farah Jasmine, 201, 258–259
Grimes, Jared, 257
Gross, Mark, 234
Guillemet, Eustis, 217–218, 222–223, 229

Hall, Arsenio, 76
Hallelujah (film), 10
Hall Johnson Choir, 9, 11, 69
Hamilton, Arthur, 247
Hammond, John, 98, 104, 194
Hampton, Lionel, 1–2, 7, 233, 269
Hancock, Herbie, 223, 227
Hancock, Mario, 19, 205, 227
Hart, Lorenz, 99
Harvey, Yona, 248–252
Hawkins, Alma C., 154
Hawkins, John R., 118
Hayes, Roland, 41
Hayes, William P., 32
Henderson, Fletcher, 84

Henderson, Luther, Jr., 114
Hendricks, Jon, 255
Hendrix, Jimi, 97
Henry, Frank Haywood, 230
Henry, Georgiana, 92–93
Hentoff, Nat, 78, 96–97, 141
Hines, Gregory, 255
Hinton, Milton John "Milt," 97, 222
HIV/AIDS, 268
Hodges, Johnny, 177–178
Holder, Geoffrey, 154
Holiday, Billie, 15, 96–97, 107, 261
Holiness-Pentecostal religion, 18, 26, 33, 34, 36, 61, 149, 254, 257, 263, 265–266
Holliday, Jennifer, 268–269
Holy Ghost, 34–35, 171, 193
Holy Spirit, 18, 48, 168, 172, 181, 249, 257, 267
Horne, Lena, 213
Houston, Drusilla Dunjee, 125–127
Hoyes, Candice, 240–241
Huggins, Willis N., 127
Hughes, Langston, 76, 168
Hymns, 55, 105, 149, 165, 245

Immigrants, 79, 269
Indigenous Americans, 8, 35, 259
Institute of Jazz Studies (Rutgers University), 17, 238, 240–241, 247
Integration, 7, 67, 70, 75, 81, 84–86, 90, 92–94, 105, 108, 139, 143, 145–146, 185, 268; nighttime integration, 70–71
Internal Revenue Service (IRS), 19, 216, 228
International Church Ushers Association, 154
Irreverence/irreverent, 13–16, 49–51, 57, 64–65, 69, 71–72, 76–77, 107–108
Irving Bunton Singers, 170
Islam, 181, 269

Jackson, Delilah, 224
Jackson, E. Franklin, 149

Jackson, John G., 127–128
Jackson, Laurence "Baby," 190–191
Jackson, Mahalia, 105, 131, 139, 146, 237
Jackson, Milt, 247
Jackson, Thomas, 221
Jacquet, Jean-Baptiste Illinois, 92–93, 233
Jarreau, Al, 255
Jazz artists; academic recognition, 16, 238–241, 258–259; autobiographies, 14–15, 50–51, 54, 62, 69, 72, 110, 141, 155, 258; combos, 7; cross-racial appeal, 66, 81, 95, 104–105, 108; civil rights, 3, 13, 77, 82, 85, 91–93; political activism, 108, 133, 200–201, 203, 228, 263; professionals, 2–4, 13, 20–21, 85, 87, 91, 196–197, 204, 208, 233, 238–239, 241–242, 245, 262, 263–264, 266; require unique working environment, 199. See also Virtuoso veneration
Jazz at Lincoln Center (JALC), 241–242
Jazz at the Philharmonic (JATP), 89, 92, 98
Jazz music: archetype, 112; ancestors, 234, 250, 252–257, 262, 265; criticisms of, 2, 28, 40, 89; as intoxicant, 25, 27; as means to reconstitute community, 195–199; and public opinion, 2–3; pure jazz, 98; as spiritual gift, 146, 190, 193, 195, 201, 203–204, 209, 218, 222, 246; tempo, 1, 25, 61, 95–96, 100–101, 104, 148, 158, 163, 185; as tool of false prophets, 36, 38; white consumption of, 9, 11, 13–14, 45–46, 49, 65–67, 72, 81, 97, 100, 104, 139–140, 142–147, 153, 155, 158, 161, 265–266. See also Race histories
Jazz religion, 26, 42, 257; band revivalism, 36; evangelists, 36–38, 143; as "good sounds," 193–194, 203, 204, 229; jazzing religion, 33–39. See also Sacred Concerts; Sacred space: Ellington's Sacred Concerts played in
Jessye, Eva, 9–10, 11, 122–123
Jet Magazine, 72, 95, 151

Jethro (biblical figure), 117, 127
Judaism (Jewish), 60, 114, 116–117, 127, 139, 144, 161, 163, 181, 182, 193, 269
Jim Crow, 13, 46, 50, 66, 130–131, 200, 237
John Alldis Choir, 185
John F. Kennedy Center for the Performing Arts, 241, 258
Johnson, Francis Hall, 10–12
Johnson, James "Osie," 222
Johnson, John H., 72
Johnson, Lillian, 83–85
Johnson, Ray W., 166
Johnson, Vera, 166
Jolson, Al, 67–69
Jones, Hank, 229
Jones, Quincy, 106
Jones, Virgil, 229
Jordan, Louis, 76
The Junkie Priest: Father Daniel Egan, S.A. (Harris), 225

Kennedy, John F., 20, 93
King, Carole, 102
King, Jr. Martin Luther, 93–95, 114, 142, 145, 154; Martin Luther King Foundation, 94–95
Kirkland, Bryant M., 141–142
Komunyakaa, Yusef, 248, 252

Lake, Oliver, 258
Lee, Bill, 223
Lee, Peggy, 96
Leisure culture, 5–6, 12, 14, 28, 40, 42–43, 55–58, 89, 99, 154, 240, 267
Levy, Lou, 97, 214, 247
Lewis, John, 92, 189
Lexi Allen and the Playmakers, 76
LGBT rights, 268
Lincoln Center Jazz Orchestra, 234, 241, 256, 259–260
Linton, Charles, 80–81
Locke, Alain, 72, 112
Los Angeles Philharmonic, 260

Lundy, Carmen, 232, 258
Lutheran/Lutheranism, 17, 140, 142–144
Lynching/anti-lynching, 30, 237

Macabee, Ruth, 54–55
Malcolm X (El-Hajj Malik El-Shabazz), 237
Manhood/masculinity, 54, 58, 98, 105, 134, 167, 170–171, 181, 219
Markham, Pigmeat, 88
Marrow, Queen Esther, 142, 157, 172
Marsalis, Wynton, 235, 256–261
Marshall, Thurgood, 72
Maur, Barry, 230
McBride, Christian, 255
McCoo, Edward J., 118–119
McCrary, Henry T., 36–38
McPhail, Jimmy, 157, 170–172
McRae, Carmen, 93
Mehegan, John, 197
Mencken, H. L., 44
Merkerson, S. Epatha, 258
Methodist Episcopal Church, 29, 30, 32, 66
Micheaux, Oscar, 11–12
Mickles, Grace, 213, 226
Migrant, 5–7, 36, 79, 266, 267, 269
Miller, Annette, 79
Miller, Kelly, 44, 120–121
Miller, May, 120
Miller, William Robert, 144–147
Mills, Irving, 66
Mims, Edwin, 30
Ministers Interdenominational Alliance, 38
Minstrelsy, 8, 12, 38, 44, 67, 72
Miriam (biblical figure), 37, 120–121
Monroe, Marilyn, 90
Moody, Dwight L., 35
Moore, Ada, 224
Morgan, Lee, 214
Morgan State University (Morgan State College), 51, 260
Morgen, Joe, 150
Morris, George E., 38

Moses (biblical figure), 111, 117, *117 fig. 4.1*, 118, 120, 127, 163

Musicals, 6, 9

Music criticism, 4, 97, 99–103, 148–149. *See also* Jazz music: criticisms of

Musso, Vido, 100

Mutual Benefit Society, 52

Myers, Henry, 71

Myth of Ham, 116–118; Hamitic League of the World, 121

National Association for the Advancement of Colored People (NAACP), 72, 74, 92, 93

Nation of Islam, 200, 202

Neiburg, Allen J., 70

New Negro, 75, 112, 125

New Thought, 155, 165

Nostalgia, 76–77, 242

O'Brien, Peter, 206, 217, 227, 231, 233, 258

O'Connor, Norman James, 143

O'Day, Anita, 197

O'Neal, Frederick, 93

O'Rourke, E. M., 80

Odetta, 223

Old time religion, 50, 65, 66, 68

Omega Psi Phi, 154

Opera, 6, 10, 54, 74, 240

Oshun, 253

Ottley, Vincent L. "Roi," 50, 168

Our Lady of Lourdes Church (New York, NY), 192, 205, 226

Overall, Kassa, 245, 258

Pan-Africanism, 16, 115, 125, 127, 136

Parish, Mitchell, 60–61

Parker, Charlie, 19, 97, 102, 188–189, 205, 223

Parker, George Wells, 119–122

Parrish, Waldo E., 216–219

Peters, Brock, 162–163

Phillips, Irene, 212–213, 223–224

Philipson, Davis, 30

Piety, 8, 31, 41, 64, 125, 126, 128, 132–133, 165, 265

Pinkard, Maceo, 60, 70

Pneuma Ministries, 256

Pochonet, Gérard "Dave," 191, 217

Pocock, Gerald, 165, 178, 184

Police abuse and violence, 92–93, 142, 145

Porgy and Bess, 10, 74, 95

Porter, Cole, 100

Potter, Charles Francis, 126–127

Powell, Earl Rudolph "Bud", 188, 198–199, 203

Powell, Jr., Adam Clayton Powell, 191, 219; Adam Clayton Powell Foundation, 216, 219

Powell, Seldon, 230

Powell, Sr. Adam Clayton Powell, 151

Preacher, 11–12, 26, 28, 32–36, 38, 45–46, 48–49, 60–62, 66, 75–76, 105, 107, 160, 190, 265; preacherly traditions, 265; preaching, 26, 33–35, 38, 40, 46, 48, 51, 62, 69, 88, 202, 236, 264

Presbyterianism/Presbyterians, 56, 120, 141, 143, 144, 155–156, 165, 183

Primitivism, 8, 35, 101, 119, 133–135; de-primitivization, 128

Procope, Russell, 177

Prohibition, 25, 51

Prosperity/Word of Faith movements, 265

Race film. *See* Film: race films

Race histories: Sacred Concert Series (*see* Sacred Concerts); civilization, 5, 16, 32, 42, 109–111, 113–116, 118–119, 121, 125, 127–128, 145; Egypt, 16, 110, 113, 116–121, 125–127; Ethiopia, 109–110, 113–114, 117–120, 121–123, 125–127, 135–136; King Solomon, 114, 116–117, *117 fig. 4.1*, 120–121; post-biblical Christianity, 259. *See also* Religious race professionals

Race records, 8, 16, 62, 118, 264

Race representatives, 1–4, 5–7, 13, 16–17, 21, 25–27, 30–31, 45–46, 50, 54, 58, 65–67,

71–72, 74, 77, 81–82, 85, 87–89, 95, 108, 110, 133, 140, 153, 237, 262, 263, 266, 269–270

Racial essentialism, 8–9, 19, 54, 55, 67, 101, 112–113, 145, 259, 260

Radio, 6, 8, 9, 10, 34, 45–46, 49–50, 62–63, 76, 122, 203, 214, 264, 265

Ragtime, 12, 38, 231

Ralph Carmichael Choir, 105

Rawlins, E. Elliott, 25–26

Ray Charles Singers, 103–104

Redemption, 181, 251

Reeves, Dianne, 255

Reisner, Christian F., 66

Religio-racial communities, 115, 265, 267

Religious authority, 3, 6, 10, 20, 21, 27, 31, 115, 140, 141, 161, 163–164, 191, 193, 207–208, 221, 225, 263–268, 269

Religious essentialism, 124–128, 130, 132–133

Religious expression, 2, 3–4, 7–8, 12–13, 16–18, 21, 50, 102, 249, 265, 267, 269; artistic, 264; audible and visible, 266; ecstatic/charismatic, 26, 27, 33, 36–37, 47–48, 65, 133, 257, 259–260, 263, 267; sexualized, 10

Religious practice, 3–4, 17–18, 21, 49, 66, 76, 107, 204, 234, 263–264, 266–267

Religious race professionals, 13–14, 26–27, 30, 46, 77, 149, 154, 264

Religious revivals, 28, 35, 40, 47, 48, 67, 151

Roberts, Isaiah, 237

Robeson, Paul, 10, 11

Robinson, Jackie, 93

Robinson, John W., 32

Robinson, Louie, 90

Robinson, Sugar Ray, 88

Rodgers, Richard, 99

Roker, Granville William "Mickey," 222

Rollins, Bryant, 15

Roman Catholicism, 2, 20, 31–32, 92, 140, 143, 144, 155, 161, 165, 178, 182, 184, 238, 262, 265–266, 269; Black Catholicism, 19–20; National Office for Black Catholics, 20; Vatican II, 19. See also Williams, Mary Lou: and Catholicism

Rosman, Fran Morris, 244

Rubenstein, Richard, 140

Rural churches, 5, 6, 34, 48, 158, 246, 263

Sabbath (Christian), 49, 57, 62

Sacred Concerts, 18, 139–142, 146–149, 151, 155, 158, 159–161, 164–165, 168, 170, 173, 178–179, 261, 269; played in sacred spaces. See also First Sacred Concert; Sacred space: Ellington's Sacred Concerts played in; Second Sacred Concert; Third Sacred Concert

Sacred jazz, 17, 19, 208, 227, 229, 235, 254, 260, 265

Sacred space: African American, 5, 33, 85, 87, 161, 254, 263–264, 267; archives, 239–241; critiques of jazz being played in, 147–148, 152; Ellington's Sacred Concerts played in, 155–158, 162; environment for jazz professionals, 199, 228–229, 238; virtual, 235, 244–245; white, 17–18, 140, 143–144, 158, 161, 186

Sanchez, Sonia, 252–253

Scarborough, W. S., 117

Scat, 16, 47–48, 49, 51, 96, 98–99, 101, 106, 248, 253

Schomburg Center for Research in Black Culture, 245

Schwab, Charles M., 71

Scott, Hazel, 189, 191, 219

Second Sacred Concert, 141–142, 152–153, 154–155, 157 fig. 5.1, 165–166, 171, 174–175, 177

Seme, Pixley Ka Isaka, 115

Semple, Jesse, 76

Sermon, 11, 16, 26, 40, 43, 45, 48–49, 56, 60–63, 68–69, 106, 118, 124, 173, 228, 253, 257, 260–261, 263, 267; scat sermon, 47–48

Settle, Glenn T., 45

Shankar, Ravi, 143
Shaw, Arvell, 230
Shaw, Wini, 68
Shepherd, Berisford "Shep," 222
Sinatra, Frank, 90, 96
Slavery (enslaved people), 12, 16, 49, 110–111, 116, 119–120, 124–125, 128–132, 133, 135, 160, 201, 235–236, 243, 256; Middle Passage, 160; religious death rituals, 236–237
Smiley, Rickey, 76
Smith, Bessie, 91, 107
Smithsonian Institution's National Museum of American History (NMAH), 17, 238–240
Social Gospel, 180, 266
"Sorrow songs," 110, 201
Soul, human, 19, 20, 30, 31, 36, 37, 40–41, 67, 128, 11, 160, 176, 177, 178, 190, 192, 201, 204, 222, 229, 251; measure of black vocal ability, 102–103, 147, 148, 157; music, 93, 102
Southern Christian Leadership Council (SCLC), 81, 93
Speaks, Ruben L., 152–153
Spirituals, 1–2, 8–12, 20–21, 30, 39, 40–42, 55, 61, 66–68, 102, 105, 110, 115, 122–123, 124, 129, 130, 132, 139, 145, 149, 152, 155, 170, 231, 246, 255, 258, 260, 261, 267, 269
The Star of Zion (weekly), 14, 26, 28–32, 35, 42, 46, 121–123, 126, 151
Stollman, Bernard, 223
Storefront churches, 157–158, 263
Stowe, Harriet Beecher, 111
Strayhorn, Billy, 106, 114, 149–151, 168, 234, 241
Substance abuse, 19, 25, 192, 197–199, 210, 213, 225
Suffering, 20, 41, 52, 79, 110, 130–132, 167, 173, 179, 181, 183, 191, 196, 203, 210, 251
Sullivan, Ed, 88
Sunday school, 31, 51, 53, 55–56, 79, 122, 173

Sun Ra, 270
Swing (music), 40, 43–44, 47, 69, 78, 81, 85, 96, 163, 231, 253, 269, 270; culture, 46; era, 15, 39, 98; and religion, 68; spirituals, 1–2
Sy Oliver and His Orchestra, 103

Tate, George Holmes "Buddy," 231
Tate, Grady, 247
Taylor, Billy, 94, 102, 214, 241
Teagarden, Jack, 96
Theology, 3, 6, 10, 34, 37, 46, 50, 107, 112, 115–116, 118, 120, 123, 133, 136, 139–141, 144, 236, 238, 252, 254–257, 260, 262, 266–267; lay engagement with, 18; theologian, 126. See also Ellington, Edward Kennedy "Duke": theology of
Third Sacred Concert, 144, 176, 183–185
Thurman, Camille, 245
Till, Emmett, 237
Till-Mobley, Mamie, 237
Tougaloo College Choir, 154
Tucker, Earl "Snake Hips," 39
Tucker, George, 222
Tunney, Thomas, 80
Turiyasangitananda, Alice Coltrane, 270
Turner, Henry McNeal, 118
Tuskegee Institute, 30, 53

Ulanov, Barry, 192–194, 198, 228, 231
Unitarianism, 173
Unitarian Universalism, 126, 139, 144, 165
United Church of Christ, 154, 257
United Service Organization (USO)
Urban North, 32, 36
Urbanization, 5

Vaudeville, 33, 36, 55, 64
Vaughan, Sarah, 93, 252
Verve Records, 95, 106
Vice, 7, 28–33, 92–93, 151
Vincent, Jennifer, 234

Virtuoso veneration: documentaries, 231–233, 242; educational institutions, 241–242; funerary practices, 235–238; geographical markers, 233, 235, 242–243, 245, 262; institutional legacies, 238–241; jazz festivals, 6, 231, 241–242, 245–246, 258, 262; musical tributes, 238, 253, 254; online, 233, 244–245, 262; poetry, 248–253, 265; sculpture, 232 *fig. 9.1*, 242–243, 269; tribute albums, 240–241, 246, 247–248, 255, 258; tribute concerts, 235, 244–245, 262. *See also* Institute of Jazz Studies (Rutgers University); Smithsonian Institution's National Museum of American History

Vodou, 238

Walls, William J., 29–33, 42, 44–45
Walton, Lester A., 32–33
Warwick, Dionne, 97
Washington, Booker T., 30, 117
Washington, Dinah, 223
Watkins, Toney, 139, 142, 155, *157 fig. 5.1*, 176
Webb, Chick, 39, 81, 82–84, 89, 91, 97–98, 100, 237; death of, 85–87, *86 fig. 3.1*
Webb, James Morris, 113, 115–118, *117 fig. 4.1*
Webb, Sallye, 85–86, *86 fig. 3.1*
Wells, Ann, 227
Wells, Joseph, 216, 227
West African music, 12, 16, 113, 119, 133–135, 150, 236, 238; drumming, 133, 135
Weyand, Norman, 225–226
White, Harry, 47
White, Josh, 88
White, Walter, 74
White Protestant Christianity, 29–32, 46, 66, 105, 126, 130, 142–144, 146–147, 153–155, 158, 161, 264, 266; mainline liberal Protestantism, 17–18, 139–140, 155, 257, 265

Wholesomeness, 7, 46, 90
Williams, Henry R., 219
Williams, Joe, 93
Williams, Mary Lou: and accountability, 189–190, 197, 204, 208, 211–214, 217, 220–221, 224, 230; asceticism of, 19, 192, 199, 209; *Black Christ of the Andes*, 20, 217–218; on black spiritual gifts, 193; called Reverend Williams, 207, 251; and Catholicism, 195–199, 202–204, 207–208, 209, 225–226, 22–228, 229; Cecilia Publishing Company, 219; charisma of, 226; charitable vision, 197–198, 210–211, 215–216, 220, 227; commitment to helping jazz musicians, 188, 208, 211–212, 221; "Communion with Mary Lou Williams," 249; conversion to Catholicism, 189–195, 204, 208; good sounds, 193–194, 203–204; happy music, 200–201; helping those with substance abuse struggles, 19, 192, 197, 199, 225; hosted struggling musicians in own apartment, 19, 188, 192, 202, 205–207, 209, 212; institutionalization of care, 204, 211–212; and internal peace, 20, 194, 198, 203–204, 209; Mary Lou Williams Collective, 258; Mary Lou Williams Jazz Festival, 258; Mary Records, 217, 219; and masculine legal professionalism, 218–220; philanthropy a reflection of faith, 201; and professional jazz world, 189, 202, 207, 263; rehabilitation of musicians, 204–205, 215–217, 220; religious intensity of, 19, 188, 209; and sacred jazz, 17, 19, 208, 227, 229, 260, 265; and social change, 199–200, chapter 8; viewed music as spiritual gift, 19, 190, 193, 194, 195–196, 201, 202, 203–204, 209, 218, 222; visions, 18–19. *See also* Bel Canto Foundation; Bliss, Herbert
Williams, Patrick Moody, 247
Wilson, Flip, 76

Wilson, Gerald, 106
Wilson, Harry O'Neill, 52
Wilson, Jackie, 93
Wilson, Llewelyn, 55
Wilson, Nancy, 255
Woodlawn Cemetery "Jazz Corner" (Bronx, NY), 233–234
Woods, Anthony S., 192, 193, 202, 217, 228
Woodson, Carter G., 12, 39–40, 112
Workman, Reggie, 258

World's Parliament of Religions (1893), 111
Wright, Chantel, 256–257
Wright, Lizz, 246
Wygant, Bobbie, 103

Yoruba, 238, 252
Young, Dan, 237

Zipporah (biblical figure), 117, 120–121, 127
Zollar, James, 234

ABOUT THE AUTHOR

Vaughn A. Booker is Assistant Professor in the Department of Religion and the Program in African and African American Studies at Dartmouth College.